BLACK SEXUAL ECONOMIES

The New Black Studies Series

Edited by Darlene Clark Hine and Dwight A. McBride

A list of books in the series appears at the end of this book.

BLACK SEXUAL ECONOMIES

RACE AND SEX IN A
CULTURE OF CAPITAL

EDITED BY
Adrienne D. Davis and the BSE Collective

**UNIVERSITY OF
ILLINOIS PRESS**
Urbana, Chicago, and Springfield

Chapter 1 has been previously published and is used by permission.
Adrienne D. Davis, "'Don't Let Nobody Bother Yo' Principle': The Sexual
Economy of American Slavery," in *Sister Circle: Black Women and Work*,
edited by Sharon Harley and the Black Women and Work Collective (New
Brunswick, NJ: Rutgers University Press, 2002), 103–27.
The poem cited in chapter 15 is by P. M. Trotter, "Blurred Lines of
Invisibility: Queering Black Girlhood, Femininity, and Masculinities,"
presented at the "Hip Hop and Punk Feminisms" conference, University of
Illinois at Urbana-Champaign, December 5, 2013. Used by permission.

Library of Congress Cataloging-in-Publication Data

Names: Davis, Adrienne D., 1965– editor.
Title: Black sexual economies : race and sex in a culture of capital / edited
    by Adrienne Davis and the BSE Collective.
Description: Urbana : University of Illinois Press, [2019] | Series: The new
    black studies series | Includes bibliographical references and index.
Identifiers: LCCN 2019005365 (print) |ISBN 9780252042645 (cloth : alk.
    paper) |ISBN 9780252084485 (pbk. : alk. paper) | ISBN 9780252051494
    (ebook)
Subjects: LCSH: African Americans—Sexual behavior. | African
    Americans—Social conditions. | Sex—United States. | Blacks—Sexual
    behavior. | Blacks—Social conditions. | Sex. | Ethnicity.
Classification: LCC E185.86 .B5358 2019 (print) | LCC E185.86 (ebook) | DDC
    305.896/07—dc23
LC record available at https://lccn.loc.gov/2019005365
LC ebook record available at https://lccn.loc.gov/2019980985

Contents

Acknowledgments   ix

Black Sexual Economies: An Introduction   1
   The BSE Collective

Part I. Sexual Labor and Race Play

1 "Don't Let Nobody Bother Yo' Principle": The Sexual Economy
   of American Slavery   15
   Adrienne D. Davis

2 Black Stud, White Desire: Black Masculinity
   in Cuckold Pornography and Sex Work   39
   Mireille Miller-Young and Xavier Livermon

3 "Hannah Elias Talks Freely": Interracial Sex and Black Female
   Subjectivity in Turn-of-the-Century New York City   59
   Cheryl D. Hicks

4 Playin' Race: Race Play, Black Women, and BDSM   73
   Ariane Cruz

Part II. Sexual Economies of Sexual Publics

5   No Bodily Rights Worth Protecting: Transnational Circulations
    of Black Hypersexuality in Brazil   89
    Erica Lorraine Williams

6   "Will the Real Men Stand Up?": Regulating Gender and Policing
    Sexuality through Black Common Sense   108
    Marlon M. Bailey and Matt Richardson

7   "Happy at Last": Carving the White "Closet" Past,
    Creating an "Out" Future   124
    Jeffrey Q. McCune Jr.

Part III. The Drag of Cultural Dissemblance

8   Gospel Drag: Intimate Labor and the Blues Stage   139
    Shana L. Redmond

9   Branded Beautiful: Brand Rihanna Meets Brand Barbados   151
    Lia T. Bascomb

10 Framing the Video Vixen: Intraracial Readings
    of Unruly Desire   166
    Felice Blake

Part IV. Beyond Black Social Life as Death: The Erotics of Black Lives

11 In the Life: Queering Violence in the Stories
    of G. Winston James   187
    Darius Bost

12 The Dramedy in Queer of Color: *Noah's Arc* and the Seriously
    "Trashy" Pleasure of Critique   200
    Pier Dominguez

13 Cheryl Clarke's Clit Agency, or, An Erotic Reading
    of *Living as a Lesbian*   216
    David B. Green Jr.

Part V. Imagine: Pedagogy, Black Feminist Arts,
              and Creative Methodologies

14 On Being a Black Sexual Intellectual:
    Thoughts on Caribbean Sexual Politics and Freedom   237
    Angelique V. Nixon

15 The Book of Joy: A Creative Archive of Young Queer
    Black Women's Pleasures   250
        Anya M. Wallace and Jillian Hernandez

16 The Mist and the Rain: A Trickster Tale   260
        L. H. Stallings

    References   263

    Contributors   281

    Index   287

Acknowledgments

The Black Sexual Economies (BSE) Collective is grateful for the extraordinary support we received from numerous agencies, divisions, campuses, mentors, artists, and activists in the process of establishing the collective and bringing this collection to fruition. Our collective began as a working group of eight scholars from seven US research universities working in the fields of law; African American and African diaspora studies; English; women's, gender, and sexuality studies; film and media studies; history; American studies; and the performing arts. The goal of the Black Sexual Economies Collective was to be an incubator for the crafting of new paradigms for thinking about race, gender, sexuality, and class and the use of innovative interdisciplinary methodologies. This collection of essays, *Black Sexual Economies: Race and Sex in a Culture of Capital*, which emerges from the BSE scholarly research project workshops and a larger community of scholars with whom we have collaborated, demonstrates the power of boundary-transgressing research exchanges to spotlight cutting-edge thinking at the forefront of black sexualities studies.

It was Adrienne D. Davis, William M. Van Cleve Professor of Law and vice provost at Washington University School of Law in St. Louis, a leading black feminist legal scholar, who laid the foundation both for the emergence of our research collaboration and for the theoretical architecture we have constructed around her concept of black sexual economy. Her intellectual rigor is matched by her creative vision of possibility, her indefatigable leadership, and her infinite generosity. In St. Louis she fed bellies, intellect, and creativity. We remain in awe of her talent and commitment to scholarship and to black feminist praxis. Adrienne, we thank you for your pioneering thinking and visionary support. We are simply the backup singers, the Davisetts.

We wish to thank Marion Crain, the Wiley B. Rutledge Professor of Law and past director of the Center for the Interdisciplinary Study of Work and Social Capital at Washington University School of Law, for awarding us the grant to create the BSE Collective and meet regularly on the WU campus for four years (2010–13). The center was also instrumental in organizing and hosting our 2013 international conference, "Black Sexual Economies: Transforming Black Sexualities Research." We thank the superlative administrative staff of Washington University School of Law, especially Gail Boker and Shelly Henderson Ford, for making the workshop and conference a success.

We offer thanks and appreciation to Cathy Cohen, Jennifer DeVere Brody, E. Patrick Johnson, Dwight McBride, Rinaldo Walcott, Darieck Scott, and Tricia Rose, senior scholars who generously anointed our conference with black scholar magic and provided invaluable engagement and feedback on our papers, which were the foundation for the essays in this book. We also thank all the participants of the conference who do not appear in the book but were crucial in shaping it and are crucially shaping the field of black sexualities studies, including Aliyya Abdur-Rahman, Juan Battle, Nicola Beisel, Bonnie Bright, Darrias Carter, Alix Chapman, Tabitha Chester, Cecilio Cooper, Shea Dunham, Erica Edwards, Jordache Ellapen, Asha French, Kai Green, LaNita Gregory Campbell, Henry Hamilton, Jillian Hernandez, Amanda Hobson, Kwame Holmes, Zakiyya Iman Jackson, Jennifer Jones, Sara Clarke Kaplan, Rosamond S. King, Jennifer Leath, Jared Leighton, Shannon Miller, Marlon Moore, Amber Jamilla Musser, Jennifer Nash, Ianna Owen, Emily Alyssa Owens, Alison Reed, Quincey James Rinehart, Jasmine Salters, Tanya Saunders, Sami Schalk, Kai Small, Christopher Smith, Sarah Smith, Ciann Wilson, and Tsione Wolde-Michael. We are grateful for your intellectual innovations and community.

We wish to thank Jean-Paul Rocchi and our colleagues at the Collegium for African American Research (CAAR) for the international venue in which we first presented our collective ideas, the historic 2011 conference, "Black States of Desire: Dispossession, Circulation, Transformation," at the University of Paris Diderot–Paris 7. The support, enthusiasm, and critical engagement of our European colleagues specializing in black cultural studies were amazingly generative and truly appreciated.

A number of students supported the creation of this book, working as research assistants and editors, and we would like to thank Rony Eduardo Castellanos, Ursula Chan, Kimberly Coffman, Rogelia Mata, and Teddy Pozo for their superlative work on the manuscript. Allison Pierce and Jordan Victorian, thank you for your indispensable research, editing, and indexing labor, and we are grateful to Megan Spencer for her gorgeous cover art for this book. The University of California, Santa Barbara, Academic Senate kindly provided support for research assistance, editing, and publishing subvention. We count ourselves lucky to have worked with Dawn Durante and her team at the University of Illinois Press. Thank you, Dawn, for your support of our vision for this collection and your steady hand in navigating the process.

Finally, we thank our scholarly networks and universities for championing not only black intellectual production but also the process of its formation. Creating the conditions that enable the development of critical analyses, mentorship opportunities, and intellectual collaborations has been vital for our individual success and productivity. This support in turn enabled us to create a critical discourse and opportunities for black emerging and senior scholars in various fields to engage and learn from one another, continuing the black radical tradition by way of powerfully and unapologetically inserting sex and sexuality into the discussion. We continue to work to develop black public and intellectual spaces informed by radical and queer and black epistemologies and practices, as well as methodologies that center, give voice to, and work in coalition with black sexual minorities and gender-nonconforming people. We endeavor to continue this work and to support future generations of emerging scholars doing this risky yet necessary scholarship, and we hope that more universities and funding agencies will invest in the future of black scholarship.

BLACK SEXUAL ECONOMIES

Black Sexual Economies

An Introduction

The BSE Collective

In 2009 Adrienne Davis (project director and co-convener) and Mireille Miller-Young (co-convener) initiated the Black Sexual Economies Collective at the Washington University School of Law at the Center for the Interdisciplinary Study of Work and Social Capital in St. Louis. The Black Sexual Economies Project became a working group comprised of eight scholars: Mireille Miller-Young, Adrienne Davis, Marlon Bailey, Matt Richardson, Jeffrey McCune, Felice Blake, Xavier Livermon, and L. H. Stallings. These scholars, from seven U.S. research universities, worked in the fields of law; English; African diaspora studies; feminist, gender, and sexuality studies; film and media studies; history; American studies; and the performing arts. The goal of the critical race feminist project became quite simply to stimulate cross-disciplinary dialogue that would influence the development of theory and research in black sexuality studies in ways that would not have occurred absent the opportunity for such an interdisciplinary forum. The project also worked to clarify black sexuality studies as a field that could push beyond topics centered on race and family, normative models of gender, and the binaries of heterosexuality and homosexuality, as well as exceed the disciplinary boundaries established by biological and psychological sciences. Because black sexualities studies is not a discipline but rather an intellectual focus that relies upon interdisciplinary and transdisciplinary approaches, the research cluster also benefited from the institutional space created by Davis and Miller-Young.

Black feminist praxis has historically placed value on collaborative work and collectives, and this project was no different. Early on, many of the participants confided in each other about the difficulties of doing work on black sexuality in isolation and in the face of tremendous critique that such work might do more harm than good to black political projects and knowledge production efforts carried out by the field of black studies. In the process, we all learned that the potential of such a cluster, as well as the excitement about working with others in these areas, signaled both a necessity for collaborative and interdisciplinary work and a support system for junior scholars doing "controversial" work on black bodies, communities, and cultures often not supported in black studies or sexuality studies at various institutions across the nation. In a sense, these concerns were very much a continuation of what had been noted some years before at the "Black Nations / Queer Nations" conference in 1995, the "Black Queer Studies in the Millennium" conference in 2000, and the "Race, Sex, and Power: New Movements in Black and Latina/o Sexualities" conference in 2008. These three conferences centered on the concerted effort to write and develop policy on sexuality and to study and teach sexuality and its intersections with race, class, gender, and nation. The Black Sexual Economies Collective's strength, however, would be that its approach and methodology would be very much shaped by director Adrienne Davis's theory: the "sexual economy of slavery." The Black Sexual Economies Project became a fruitful exploration and experiment that resulted in a successful three-year model of how to initiate public scholarship around black sexualities. Designed as a four-year working group, the project's goal resulted in individuals' freedom to craft innovative paradigms for thinking about race, gender, and sexuality through open dialogue and papers, which eventually culminated in a public conference in 2013.

It is not a new claim to state that black sexualities have been constructed as a site of sexual panic and pathology in US culture. Viewed as a threat to normative ideas about sexuality, the family, and the nation, black sexualities are intimately linked to and regulated by political and socioeconomic discourses and institutions. As a legal scholar Adrienne Davis has shown that slavery provided the foundation for modern black sexual political economies, hence our adoption of the name Black Sexual Economies. Davis's work has made explicit the links between markets, labor structure, and sexual exploitation and the false dichotomy between notions of public and private relations. Slavery rendered black sexuality irrevocably deviant and at the same time produced economies of desire and flesh that made black sexual deviance desirable, accessible, and even profitable. In light of the historical and continuing forces of commodification, exploitation, and appropriation of black sexuality and black bodies, black people have struggled to represent, recuperate, and reimagine their own sexualities and sexual politics. Thus, the collective and this volume consider the inevitable and enduring link between capitalism and market and imagination and culture in its theories of black sexualities in ways that traditional scholarship on sexuality and race have refused or sublimated for the work of politics.

Though the study of sexuality continues to be marginalized in the field of black studies, research and scholarship on black sexualities continue to be noted as important and needed interventions for the field, as well as for how the construction of blackness and the white history of sexuality are engaged by other fields. In the last decade alone, black sexuality studies have been essential to reconceptualizing ideologies about genders and sexualities. Whereas previous studies of black sexuality at the end of the twentieth century were centered on issues such as trauma and pain, contemporary examinations have taken up those factors as well as asked what other elements might be useful to studies of black sexuality. Though not a department, discipline, or institutionally supported field, black sexuality studies' most important contribution to twenty-first-century fields of study can be seen in how it challenges its scholars to undo and innovate formations of knowledge in numerous traditional disciplines, fields, or departments. For to study black sexuality in all its rich nuanced and complicated existence, scholars must rethink questions of genealogy, locate undiscovered archives, excavate lost texts and narratives, and become versed in numerous methodologies that exceed biological constructions of gender and sexual orientation. Perhaps one of the notable attributes of black sexuality studies not being a department or discipline is that interest in the area has meant an expansion of thinking, which has spread outside and away from historically white institutions to historically black colleges and universities, with institutions such as Spelman University and Bowie State offering courses specifically centered on black sexuality.[1]

In the *Chronicle of Higher Education: Chronicle Review*, Stacy Patton's "Who's Afraid of Black Sexuality" demonstrates why black sexuality studies may be important to how we consider the future of black life, racism, and antiblackness.[2] In Patton's examination of how black studies has left the research and scholarship of black sexuality to other fields such as queer studies, she turns to Marlon M. Bailey and Mireille Miller-Young, two of the scholars contributing to this volume, as changing and challenging these old restrictions within the field of black studies. Citing the hunger for more novel and fearless work by undergraduate and graduate students, as well as the need for better culturally informed social and health policies about sexuality for African Americans, Patton's inquiry signals that the study of sexuality remains central to projects of decolonization, liberation, wellbeing, and radical knowledge production.

The study of black sexuality has changed traditional disciplines and evolved black studies. Tremendously aided by queer of color critique, studies on black sexuality have been the source of radical and necessary interventions within feminism, queer theory, Afro-pessimism, social justice, and public health studies. In

3

simply examining the citational practices of scholars examining black sexualities, you can find a vibrant exchange and appreciation of other scholars of color. Black sexualities is just as influenced by the work of José Muñoz, Juana Rodriguez, Deb Vargas, Martin Manalasan, Amy Sueyoshi, Chandan Reddy, Gayatri Gopinath, and Grace Hong as it as by the likes of Cathy Cohen, E. Patrick Johnson, Cheryl Clarke, Dwight McBride, Sharon Holland, Robert Reid-Pharr, Evelyn Hammonds, and Roderick Ferguson. Additionally, the ways in which theories of diaspora and transnationalism are discussed have also shifted based on attention to eroticism and sexuality. In addition, the examinations of black sexualities outside of the United States have been phenomenal. Diasporic and Pan-Africanist scholarship by Dagmouwi Woubshet, Jafari Sinclair Allen, Omisoke Natasha Tinsley, Erica Williams, Greg Thomas, Angelique Nixon, Vanessa Agard-Jones, Nadia Ellis, Xavier Limon, and Aisha Finch joins the work of Rinaldo Walcott, Kamala Kempadoo, and M. Jacqui Alexander.

The study of black sexualities has also transformed the way gender is theorized in black studies and other fields. C. Riley Snorton, Matt Richardson, and Kai Green have combined queer of color critique and black feminist traditions to serve up the foundations of black transgender studies. Marlon Moore, Mingon Moore, Matt Richardson, Kara Keeling, and L. H. Stallings have filled in a void about black lesbian and bisexual women's life and culture. C. Riley Snorton, Jeffrey McCune, and Kevin Mumford have asked us to rethink black masculinities and sexuality. These are advancements that were previously disregarded or rendered irrelevant in black politics. Questions of nation and race have shifted, and so too have concerns of family. Marlon Bailey's work on queer counterpublics like ballroom culture and Mingon Moore's work on lesbian families intervene in traditional scholarship about black families with their assessment of new kinship structures that seek to triumph over racial, gendered, and class oppression.

In regard to new black feminist theories and sexuality, contemporary research moves beyond the work and ideologies presented by black feminists during the sex wars of the 1980s and 1990s. Whereas Audre Lorde, Alice Walker, and bell hooks were the popular and monolithic voices centered on sexual representation, trauma, and pain, black feminist approaches to eroticism and sexuality have now been shaped by voices such as M. Jacqui Alexander, Jennifer Nash, Ariane Cruz, Treva Lindsay, Nicole Fleetwood, Erica Edwards, Lisa Thompson, and Joan Morgan. Theories, cultures, and policies concerned with race, sexual labor, and gender have been reconsidered by scholars such as Erica Williams, Mireille Miller-Young, Cynthia Blair, LaShawan Harris, Cheryl Hicks, and Emily Owens.

Whereas Hortense Spillers was once one of the trailblazing voices of psychoanalysis and race, black sexuality scholars have been doing interesting work to follow in her path. Daerick Scott's work on black masculinity and abjection, alongside Amber Musser's work on psychoanalysis and BDSM and Michelle A. Stephens's examination of black male performance and psychoanalysis, exceeds Kathryn Bond Stockton's work on bottoms, shame, and queerness. Other radical investigations have happened outside of queries into twentieth- and twenty-first-century sexuality. For example, the Queering Slavery Working Group, organized by Vanessa Holden and Jessica Marie Johnson, has altered approaches to researching eighteenth- and nineteenth-century politics and sexuality, agency, and subjectivity. According to the group's website, it "was formed to discuss issues related to reading, researching, and writing histories of intimacy, sex, and sexuality during the period of Atlantic slavery. Guided by the question, 'What would it mean to Queer Slavery?' the group seeks out queer encounters in slavery's archive."[3] Two of the group's participants, Christina Sharpe and Aliyyah Abdur-Rhaman, have already produced some of the most sophisticated and innovate theories around black bodies, building upon theories developed in Hortense Spillers's "Mama's Baby, Papa's Maybe" and Saidiya Hartman's *Scenes of Subjection*. At the "Black Sexuality" conference held at George Washington University in 2016, Jennifer Nash noted that at the same time there has been a turn to Afro-pessimism and death, there has also been a rising interest in black sexuality and eroticism. This is certainly the case for several essays in this collection, as well as the conference proceedings that led to the collection.

The "Black Sexual Economies: Conference on Transforming Black Sexualities Research," held in 2013 at Washington University, allowed conference participants and attendees to see that there are a number of up-and-coming scholars who are not afraid of black sexuality or the study of it. That conference served as the impetus for this collection. The conference consisted of plenary sessions featuring the work of the Black Sexual Economies Collective research scholars in conversation with some of the scholars whose work has provided the foundation for the current trajectory of black sexuality studies: E. Patrick Johnson, Cathy Cohen, Rinaldo Walcott, Jennifer Brody, Tricia Rose, and Darieck Scott (in the unexpected absence of Dwight McBride). The format allowed these senior scholars to provide constructive criticism to emerging scholars and provided an example of collaborative engagement. Notably, the foundational work of other important senior scholars not in attendance was also engaged and recognized. Scholarship by Robert Reid-Phar, Roderick Ferguson, Audre Lorde, Barbara Christian, Dwight McBride, Greg Thomas, and Wahneema Lubiano shaped many of the ideas presented in the plenary and panel sessions.

In addition to these senior scholars and the Black Sexual Economies Collective, scholars such as Erica Williams, Erica Edwards, Aliyyah Abdur-Rahman, Sara Clarke Kaplan, Cheryl Hicks, Amber Jamilla Musser, Rosamond S. King, Marlon Moore, Jennifer Nash, Shana Redmond, Angelique Nixon, Ariane Cruz,

Kwame Homes, Juan Battle, and Zakiyyah Iman Jackson were only a few of the people who delivered papers that showcased the original and ground-breaking work being done on black sexualities in the early twenty-first century. The paper panels, as well as breakout workshop groups, focused on pedagogy, social justice, administration, and research, and they were carried out by a mix of graduate students, junior scholars, and senior scholars who exchanged ideas about research, pedagogy, and administration for both university and community institutions. The success of the conference was one of the reasons we believed a collection in the spirit of the conference should be developed. Though we could not publish papers by everyone at the conference, this edited collection contains a small representative sample of the great energy and ideas presented that weekend. Black sexuality studies continue to transform even at the time of this text's publication, and we hope that this collection will be seen as relevant to such change.

Despite the dynamic ways that black people attempt to define and negotiate their gender and sexual identities, practices, and communities, there has been a paucity of scholarship examining black sexual economies. While research on black sexuality has interrogated the powerful traumas, silences, and invisibilities that influence sexuality within the black community, black sexualities scholarship still has work to do to untangle the complex mechanisms of dominance and subordination, as well as forms of productivity and expression, as they are attached to political and socioeconomic forces, cultural productions, and our own academic lenses.

This collection provides new conceptual frameworks by which to evaluate and analyze black sexualities and sexual cultures, and it maintains a commitment to radically interdisciplinary approaches. To this end, this project seeks to craft innovative paradigms for thinking about race, gender, and sexuality in tandem. If most studies of race and sexuality have emphasized injury, trauma, and representation, then this project emphasizes other, underattended factors in the analysis of black sexual cultures, including pleasure, regulation, labor, consumption, and production. It takes an interdisciplinary approach that combines a focus on law and legal regulation with analyses of identity politics; networks of sexual exchange; social policy; and literature, media, and cultural performances. This book presents a collection of essays that illuminate how the forces of commodification, exploitation, and appropriation that render black sexualities both desirable and deviant also provide the spaces, networks, and relationships that have allowed black people to revise, recuperate, and rearticulate their sexual identities, erotic capital, and gender and sexual expressions and relations.

The essays in this collection are by scholars who employ methodologies from performance and feminist ethnographies, oral history, archival research, discourse and textual analysis, cultural criticism, ethnomusicology, and film theory. Building on black feminist, queer, and critical race studies, one of the aims of the texts is to develop linkages between methodologies in biomedical and behavioral sciences and humanistic approaches. Finally, and of no less importance, this project engages the subject of sex and culture from a place of deep commitment to communities, as well as to understanding the intersections of race, class, gender, sexuality, and social policy.

The collection focuses on five themes, and these are woven together by the major theme of the collection, black sexual economies, and how these economies manifest throughout black life, history, and culture and in ways that overlap and converge throughout the essays. "Sexual Labor and Race Play," the first theme in the collection, asks readers to think about the economies of black sexual labor and the eroticism of playing with race so as to dismantle notions of a fixed binary division of public and private when it comes to black sexual histories and communities. Beginning with the originating essay, "'Don't Let Nobody Bother Yo' Principle': The Sexual Economy of American Slavery," Adrienne Davis politicizes work and then explores how black women's reproductive capacity and sexuality toward white pleasure and profit are situated as the early foundations of US capitalism, naming it sexual economy. Other essays in this part move readers forward and throughout time to think about the consequences of sexual economies, specifically when interracial sex is involved.

The remaining essays in this part explore what that sexual economy has produced, specifically representing deviant and defiant cultures, communities, and performances. Because black sexuality has been so thoroughly sutured to concepts of deviance, we are interested in how black people make use of marginality, particularly through the framework of sexuality. The essays in this part illuminate how defiance is a key aspect of negotiating black deviance and an essential process or site at which black subjectivities are formed, negotiated, and used as resources for survival and resistance under tremendous structural oppression. Thus, Mireille Miller-Young and Xavier Livermon's chapter, "Black Stud, White Desire: Black Masculinity in Cuckold Pornography and Sex Work," investigates the sexual economy of subcultural, amateur pornography in which black men are figured as BBC (big black cock) studs central to the fetishistic fantasies of white couples. Highlighting the multiple and mobile desires, relations, and labors evident in "cuckolding socialities," their chapter looks at pornography as a market for black men's sex work and as a space of discipline and containment, as well as of queer possibility. Cheryl D. Hicks's chapter, "'Hannah Elias Talks Freely': Interracial Sex and Black Female Subjectivity in Turn-of-the-Century New York City" addresses the case of Hannah Elias, who labored in New York's interracial sex trade and became the mistress of one of her white customers, John R. Platt. Ariane Cruz's "Playin' Race: Race Play, Black Women, and BDSM" examines the BDSM practice of race play. Focusing on the sexual performances of black women, Cruz reveals performances of domination and submission in BDSM as inventive modes for and of black women's pleasure, power, and agency. Together these essays showcase how defiance allows black subjects to mobilize deviance in new ways and to create cultural or aesthetic forms, communities, and performances of self that communicate the complexities of this site of subjecthood.

The second themed part, "Sexual Economies of Sexual Publics," traces contemporary markets for sexual labor and systems of erotic capital, underlines the ways in which many authors in this collection are interested in the political economies of black sexuality as presented by Adrienne Davis's early work, and examines how both economic markets and political orders conceive of, cultivate, shape, and regulate black sexuality. In tracing these systems of sexual value, economy, and trade, scholars are also interested in what black subjects *do* to employ their sexual labor and mobilize it within such networks of capital. Erica Lorraine Williams's "No Bodily Rights Worth Protecting: Transnational Circulations of Black Hypersexuality in Brazil" directs readers to attend to the transnational circulation of notions of black hypersexuality in Brazil and beyond. It focuses on three sites of analysis that explore how cross-cultural perceptions of sexual difference are produced and perpetuated in the tourism industry. In this final theme, these essays and others within the part return to how questions of subjectivity and agentive innovation become important for black subjects under the weight of racialized and sexualized oppression. In Marlon Bailey and Matt Richardson's essay, "'Will the Real Men Stand Up?': Regulating Gender and Policing Sexuality through Black Common Sense," questions African American gender common sense as demonstrated in dominant institutions of the black megachurch and historically black colleges and universities impact our understanding of trans or nonconforming masculinities. Additionally, Jeffrey McCune's "'Happy at Last': Carving the White 'Closet' Past, Creating an 'Out' Future" confronts the public/private binary in his examination of race and outness. He interrogates how white homonormative narratives perform tyrannous acts that distort understandings of queerness for people of color. With this understanding, the scholars of this collection ask how knowledge of sex and race converge and what this convergence means for black people's navigations of gender, class, and space.

Essays under the third theme, "The Drag of Cultural Dissemblance," elide questions of silence and policing to understand and animate the poles of respectability and deviance undergirding early black feminist scholarship on sexuality. The essays in this part rethink objects of study to complicate questions of agency, subjectivity, and objecthood in black women's popular culture. Consequently, Shana L. Redmond's "Gospel Drag: Intimate Labor and the Blues Stage" exposes the queer labor connection between gospel and blues through fashion and a focus on Gertrude Ma Rainey's costumes designed by Nettie Dorsey, the wife of gospel music composer Thomas Dorsey. Redmond exposes the close proximities that exist within the costumes sewn by Mrs. Dorsey and worn by Rainey, namely, the relationship between pious respectability and working-class nonheteronormativity, laboring femininity and sonorous vocalities. Redmond documents Dorsey's dressmaking as a sonic production capable of facilitating the growth of new industries and challenging the normative practices within the early twentieth-century black public sphere.

Lia Bascomb's "Branded Beautiful: Brand Rihanna Meets Brand Barbados" examines the relationship between individual pop celebrity, the promotion of a national identity, and the use of sexuality while branding each. Using Robyn "Rihanna" Fenty's August 2011 LOUD tour concert in Barbados, "Branded Beautiful" argues that the events surrounding the show shed light on the differences between the construction of a national brand name and the construction of a celebrity empire; that such divergences highlight the insecurities of nation-states seeking to make a name for themselves within a global market; and that despite the distinctions it is quite hard for a nation-state to divorce celebrity focused attention from an ideal national image.

Next, in what is both nostalgia and critical reflection, Felice Blake's "Framing the Video Vixen: Intraracial Readings of Unruly Desire" returns us to the late 1990s era video vixen to rethink black hypersexuality before the twenty-first century. In line with black feminist politics centered on dissemblance offered by the likes of Tricia Rose and Tracey Whitey Sharpey, Blake's essay on Karrine Steffan's *Confessions of a Video Vixen* serves as a fitting bookend to the late 1990s hip-hop wars. In her essay, Blake proposes that hypersexuality continues to be an affective site of politics ranging from progressive, queer, or fearful panics that imagine sexual labor as solely a source of disrespectability. Blake offers a critique of respectability while still suggesting that black hypersexuality needs to be overcome.

The essays under the fourth theme, "Beyond Black Social Life as Death: The Erotics of Black Lives," rethink sexual politics and gender panics through genealogies of blackness/race presented in queer literature and culture. Within this concept we learn that popular representations of black sexual or gender deviance are often articulated in ways specific to the racialization of blackness under capitalism. In many ways, these essays also think through Afro-pessimism's considerations of black social life as death alongside considerations of the erotic to get beyond the grammar of suffering. In "The Erotics of Death: Queering Violence in the Stories of G. Winston James," Darius Bost explores how the distinct sexual economy of queer sex publics shapes black queer subjectivity. Focusing on how the illicit economies of the street and the illicit sexual labor of black same-sex-desiring men overlap in queer sex publics, sometimes posing a threat to black men engaging in such "risky" sexual activity, this chapter argues that black queer subjectivity emerges precisely within these spatiotemporal entanglements of death and desire through close readings of two short stories by Jamaican American gay author G. Winston James.

Alternately, Pier Dominguez's "The Dramedy in Queer of Color: *Noah's Arc* and the Seriously 'Trashy' Pleasure of Critique" turns to ideologies of "trashy" to focus on *Noah's Arc* (2005–6), a dramedy featuring four gay men of color that aired for two seasons on the gay cable channel Logo. Refusing eulogistic narratives of tragic black masculinity, it argues that *Noah's Arc* works within the popular cultural genre of the dramedy to engage with—while also contradicting and disrupting—new normativities of race, sexuality, and their intersections. First, it contextualizes the anxieties around black heteronormative middle-class normativity and outlines some of the ways in which these anxieties have been negotiated through black televisuality. Then it provides an interpretation of *Noah's Arc* from a queer of color perspective to understand its problematic framing of race, sexuality, and their intersections as mostly an intraracial problem of gay black masculinities and femininities.

Additionally, David Green Jr.'s essay, "Cheryl Clarke's Clit Agency, Or, An Erotic Reading of *Living as a Lesbian*" provides a critical reading of Cheryl Clarke's second volume of poetry, *Living as a Lesbian*. Situating this text within the larger context of black women's poetry, Green argues that its erotic aesthetic works to critique the historic erasure of the black lesbian body in the discourse of African American life as it simultaneously pushes toward and away from theories of sexuality that limit and thus reduce black women's linguistic economies to metaphors of sexual desire.

Finally, the last theme of the collection, "Imagine: Pedagogy, Black Feminist Arts, and Creative Methodologies," provides a moment for readers to rethink the scholarly or disciplinary methodologies that shape black sexuality studies and sexual economies. It underscores why pleasure might also be essential to methodologies for research and teaching on black sexualities, as well as black sexuality itself. Whereas other parts showcase interdisciplinary rigor in black sexuality, the chapters in this part demonstrate how black sexuality studies relies upon a different order and economy of knowledge from artistic aesthetics, community activism, and imaginative mobility between community, academic, and art/performance spaces or institutes.

Lest we forget that communities throughout the African diaspora continue to work toward sexual decolonization in ways that highlight the tensions and conflicts of a public/private binary embedded in sexual economies, Angelique Nixon's "On Being a Black Sexual Intellectual: Thoughts on Caribbean Sexual Politics and Freedom" allows us to understand what is at stake for persons of color in the Caribbean by researching what has been articulated as a private concern:

"sexuality." The black sexual intellectual blurs the boundaries between public and private binaries, and in articulating the conflicts between making sex public and thus research on sexuality accessible, Nixon reminds readers of the importance of embodiment and activism for African diasporic communities where the end goal is sexual decolonization.

In moving away from the Caribbean, "The Book of Joy: A Creative Archive of Young Queer Black Women's Pleasures" by Anya Wallace and Jillian Hernandez takes reader to the United States in their creative examination of the link between pleasure, joy, and social justice. In the curatorial statement about the women's work, subtitled "(re)Collecting Pleasure with Young Black Women and Girls in the Vibrator Project," the organizers provide insight into the action research, design, and methodology of this study, in which each participant constructs and examines her personal sexual narrative. Their piece notes that, as action research, the Vibrator Project chronicles a collective learning experience of young black women and girls ages fourteen through twenty-one. By way of dialogue with the study participants, Wallace and Hernandez investigate the sexual narratives in participants' art and analyze their perceptions of hypersexuality, unplanned pregnancy, and significant life choices influenced by racialized class disparities. The last creative piece, "The Mist and the Rain: A Trickster Tale" (an excerpt), is a short tale composed by L. H. Stallings in which the author deploys African American folklore as a methodology for delivering accessible sex-positive education about masturbation.

In the end, this book presents a collaboration aimed to reveal the lives, everyday negotiations, and cultural or aesthetic interventions of black gender and sexual minorities, as well as the systems and beliefs that structure the range of possibility that exists for all black sexualities under capitalism. The creative negotiations and forms of agency evinced by black sexual subjects and enacted through networks and flows of sexual economy, however, remind us that race and sex present opportunities for dynamic ways of knowing and living. This collection opens up new ways of thinking about contemporary and historical taboo, outlaw, deviant, and subversive embodiments and practices by black people as they live and move within black sexual economies.

Notes

1. Erica Williams, "Women's Studies and Sexuality Studies at HBCUs: The Audre Lorde Project at Spelman College," in "W/G/S Studies, Women's Studies and Sexuality Studies in Conversation," forum, *Feminist Studies* 39, no. 2 (October 2013): 520–25.

2. "Who's Afraid of Black Sexuality?," *Chronicle of Higher Education* 59, no. 15 (December 7, 2012).

3. See https://qswg.wordpress.com/about/.

PART I

Sexual Labor and Race Play

CHAPTER 1

"Don't Let Nobody Bother Yo' Principle"

The Sexual Economy of American Slavery

Adrienne D. Davis

> Many . . . young women are afraid to speak, let alone write. When
> I witness their fear, their silences, I know no woman has written
> enough.
>
> —bell hooks, *Remembered Rapture*

Personal Statement

I was an Afro-American studies major in college. Yes, *Afro*-American studies, so you can imagine this was the 1980s. Not the hard-edged black studies of the 1970s or the gentle chicness of African American or Africana studies in the 1990s. Afro-American. Language situates us in time and politics.

The two events that remain most impressed upon my mind from college occurred in the course of pursuing my major. I was a student of black feminist theorist bell hooks, Gloria Watkins, who taught courses in literature, specializing in fiction by black women. For Gloria, as we called the woman, and her classes, into which we crowded, the rigorous study of literature yielded the greatest gift of all: mastery of language, the fundamental Western tool of self-articulation and representation. The students of all races who "took Gloria" learned how, through language, one acquires a voice, thus demanding recognition by others. Through these linguistic eruptions into existence, people achieve subjectivity, agency, humanity. Her courses, unable to contain the student excitement over the possibilities that language suggested for our agency, spilled over into her office.

There, she encouraged black undergraduate women to use the study of literature to reclaim our sexuality, our lives, to realize that in a world structured to deny our humanity, we had choices, options. Through language, we could represent, and thus reclaim, our intimate selves.

This conversation, which continued over the course of two years, was punctuated by a moment when Toni Morrison came to campus to speak. After *Sula* and *The Bluest Eye*, before *Beloved* and *Paradise*, she talked about the paucity of language to describe the horror of American slavery. What language can we use to represent human bondage, to describe the conversion of humans into property, to capture the experience of being possessed or, even more grimly perhaps, of *possessing* another? The emptiness of language to describe the process of enslavement mirrors the void of slavery in the nation's memory.

Yet slavery, like our sexuality, lies continually at the periphery of our consciousness; eluding representation, it hovers over us. It disrupts our lives with unpredictable eruptions. Mimicking the American conspiracy of silence around slavery, black women often avoid speaking of sex and intimacy. But in slavery's repression, black women continually create images, representations, which we then either embody in flat unidimensional cartoons of "respectable good girls" or reject, thereby risking sanction by our sisters. Without language, both slavery and black women's sexuality remain unspeakable—repressed, yet ever present.

Comprehending and filling the linguistic vacuums around slavery and black women's sexuality are directly linked to the purpose of this essay: representing black women's work. What I now realize, as a scholar and a woman with her own sexual battlegrounds to conquer, is how the unspeakability of slavery contains the seeds of the unspeakability, for black women, of our own sexuality. As I expound in this essay, the economy of American slavery systematically expropriated black women's sexuality and reproductive capacity for white pleasure and profit. As their descendants, we continue to suffer from the silence. The failure of language to document and archive the sexual abuse of reproductive exploitation of enslaved women is the origin of the absence of language to articulate for contemporary black women sexual identities that are empowering, fulfilling, and joyous.

In much of my professional adult life, through my research and my writing, I have tried to restore and engage that voice, to offer myself and other black women a voice sketched through history and law. My essay in this volume tries to combine and, to an extent, reconcile those two defining moments from a decade ago in my life when Toni Morrison and bell hooks urged me and other black women students to see that understanding both history and ourselves lay in mastering language and its mysteries. Without a vocabulary to describe slavery, contemporary black women have been without a voice to describe and confront the history of sexual and reproductive expropriation and exploitation that slavery entailed.

In my essay, I propose to label slavery as a "sexual economy," hoping that this may give us the tools we need to excavate black women's history, document our exploitation, and archive our resistance. We can use this vocabulary to understand our collective sexual histories and then confront our choices, realizing that each of us makes different ones.

Toni Morrison and bell hooks were right: without language, we can't represent; without representation, we can't imagine; without imagination, we can't comprehend; without comprehension, we can't move forward.

Beyond the backbreaking, soul-savaging labor that all enslaved people performed, American slavery extracted from black women another form of "work" that remains almost inarticulable in its horror: reproducing the slave workforce through giving birth and serving as forced sexual labor to countless men of all races. The political economy of slavery systematically expropriated black women's sexuality and reproductive capacity for white pleasure and profit. Yet what discourse has confronted and accused this national horror? What documents record its effects on enslaved women? In the face of this unspeakable work, chroniclers of American history have all but erased its existence. This essay attempts to initiate the beginnings of just such a conversation by naming the world of these legal conflicts a "sexual economy."

Voice and vocabulary are vitally important in antiracist and antisexist politics. Vocabulary is much more than grammatical choice, as represented in debates as diverse as the validity of Ebonics and whether "sex worker" or "prostitute" is the better word. Word choices represent political views of the world, especially when describing the topic of this book: work. We may need new terms, such as "sexual economy," to capture that history and reality and begin a discourse of national confrontation and, ultimately, of personal reconciliation.

This essay examines two cases in which enslaved black women's sexuality was at the heart of the dispute. It starts with an 1806 Virginia case in which two enslaved women used slavery's rules of reproduction and race to argue that they were not legally black and hence should be set free. The second case, an 1859 Mississippi case, involved the rape of an enslaved girl. I use these cases to investigate some of the primary legal doctrines that enabled elite white men to extract forced sexual and reproductive labor from enslaved women. Taken together, these cases and rules reveal how law and markets of the antebellum South seized enslaved women's intimate lives, converting private relations of sex and reproduction into political and economic relations. This interplay of sex and markets leads me to name this world a sexual political economy.

The idea of a "sexual economy of slavery" may seem odd on first impression. We divide our economic relationships in the workplace from our intimate, family interactions. We view these relations as taking place in two segregated spheres:

the market and our intimate lives. It is in this latter space that we feel enabled to make our decisions, conduct our lives, love our own families. We may experience dissonances when sex and economics are juxtaposed. In addition, many of us imagine slavery as an institution of racial hierarchies, not gender hierarchies. But the cases and rules I will examine expose a different relationship between sex and markets for enslaved black women. In the process, they expose the brutal gender subordination that slavery entailed.

One quick caveat: slavery varied from region to region and slaveholder to slaveholder. It also evolved and mutated during its 250-odd years. I use two cases from two significantly different regions and periods (Virginia in 1806 and Mississippi in 1859). I do not mean to suggest that these cases are representative of slavery. However, I use them because individually and taken together they raise intriguing questions about the central and distinctive role that black women's sexuality and reproductive capacity played in the southern political economy.[1]

A Life of Labor: Production and Reproduction

When we think of enslavement, we think of labor. Canonical studies of enslaved women have shown that they labored no less than enslaved men. As activist-scholar Angela Davis put it, "As slaves, compulsory labor overshadowed every other aspect of women's existence. It would seem, therefore, that the starting point for any exploration of Black women's lives under slavery would be an appraisal of their role as workers."[2] Historian Jacqueline Jones discovered that "in the 1850s at least 90 percent of all female slaves over sixteen years of age labored more than 261 days per year, eleven to thirteen hours each day."[3]

But the labor that slavery compelled of enslaved women was distinct from the way others worked in two ways. First, unlike white women, enslaved women performed the same work as men while also doing the domestic work typically reserved for women, free and enslaved. In the middle of the nineteenth century, seven-eighths of enslaved people, regardless of sex, were field workers.[4] In 1800, when the Santee Canal was built in North Carolina, enslaved women constituted 50 percent of the construction crew.[5] Deborah Gray White notes: "It appears that [enslaved women] did a variety of heavy and dirty labor, work which was also done by men. In 1853, Frederick Olmsted saw South Carolina slaves of both sexes carting manure on their heads to the cotton fields where they spread it with their hands between the ridges in which cotton was planted. In Fayetteville, North Carolina, he noticed that women not only hoed and shoveled but they also cut down trees and drew wood."[6] Thus, enslaved women performed much of the same productive labor done by men who shared their race and status as slaves.[7] Jones notes that while the form of *extracting* their labor differed from that of a free labor system, the content of what enslaved men did could be analogized at some level to the work that all men did on farms, including in New England and on smaller southern farms.[8] This was not so for enslaved women, whose labor differed markedly from that performed by white women.

In colonial American society, privileged white women rarely worked in the fields. Occasionally, white female indentured servants were forced to work in the fields as punishment for misdeeds, but this was not a common practice. In the eyes of colonial white Americans, only debased and degraded members of the female sex labored in the fields. And any white woman forced by circumstances to work in the fields was regarded as unworthy of the title "woman."[9] Historians caution us not to overstate the point: there was gender differentiation in enslaved men's and women's labor.[10] Still, enslaved women did not perform gender-segregated labor nearly to the same extent that white women did.[11]

Performance by enslaved women of conventionally male work distinguished their labor from that of black men, white women, and white men. Enslaved men and free whites of both sexes worked in accord with gender roles. In fact, when enslaved men were assigned "women's work," it was often for the specific purpose of humiliation or discipline.[12] And historians Nell Painter and Chris Tomlins reinforce the intriguing point that for those white women who did work in the fields, the reality of their daily lives departed from the rhetoric of white femininity.[13] The existence of this disjuncture in the lives of many working white women stemmed from the cultural and radicalized importance of rigid gender roles: "While white women's field labor challenged gender roles, African women's field labor *confirmed* racial roles. Enslaved African women's substitution for white women field workers (occurring far earlier than the late 17th / early 18th century 'transition to slavery' would suggest) then increased opportunities for white women's participation in household formation, stabilizing white culture with an approximation of 'good wife' domesticity."[14] Within a society that enforced strict adherence to sex roles, only enslaved women were compelled to labor consistently across gender boundaries. This aspect of their physical work is one of the distinguishing features of their experience.

But slavery's political economy forced enslaved women to labor in a second way that was not required of any other group. As the remainder of this essay shows, enslaved women, and only enslaved women, were forced to perform sexual and reproductive labor to satisfy the economic, political, and personal interests of white men of the elite class. Even more so than crossing gender boundaries in physical labor, this second distinguishing feature of their experience under slavery foregrounds their gender and demonstrates how embedded their sexuality was in slavery's economic markets.

In an 1806 case, *Hudgins v. Wrights*, two enslaved women, Hannah and her unnamed daughter, sued for their freedom.[15] They alleged the wrongful enslavement of the woman who was, respectively, their mother and grandmother, Butterwood Nan. Let me consider in some detail the arguments of both Hannah and her daughter (the plaintiffs) and the man claiming to be their master (the defendant). Ultimately, Hannah's and her daughter's freedom turned on how the law decided to characterize Butterwood Nan's reproduction.

The defendant, who claimed ownership of Hannah and her daughter, did so based on a fundamental rule of slavery: *partus sequitur ventrem*, Latin for "the child follows the mother." Under this law, adopted in every enslaving state, children inherited their status as enslaved or free from their mothers. This rule dictated that enslaved women gave birth to enslaved children and free women gave birth to free children. Accordingly, the slaveholder argued that because the ancestral matriarch, Butterwood Nan, had been enslaved, her daughter Hannah had inherited her enslaved status and subsequently passed it on to her own daughter, akin almost to tainted blood.

As early as 1662 Virginia adopted the rule that enslaved black women gave birth to enslaved children.[16] By the time of the founding of our democratic nation, all of the enslaving states dictated that enslaved black women gave birth to enslaved children, regardless of the father's status or race. As one judge said, "The father of a slave is unknown to our law."[17] This is a striking conclusion, given the general patriarchal and patrilineal nature of antebellum Anglo-American law. But it is not a surprising one, given the direction of the political economy and wealth holding. Historians agree that "land and slaves became the two great vehicles through which slaveholders realized their ambitions of fortune.... The usefulness of land increased in proportion to the availability of black slaves."[18] Peter Kolchin documents the need for growing numbers of forced laborers as early as the colonial period: "Cultivating [tobacco and rice], however, required labor; in an environment where land was plentiful and people few, the amount of tobacco or rice one could grow depended on the number of laborers one could command."[19] Of course, the United States was not alone in basing its economy on black slave labor. It did distinguish itself, however, in how it met the ongoing need to replenish its workforce.

Other New World slave systems continued to kidnap Africans through the international slave trade to meet their labor needs. Varying combinations of higher ratios of men to women, low fertility rates, and extreme mortality rates meant that natural reproduction did not sustain the enslaved populations of Latin America and the Caribbean. The demography of these slave societies stood in stark contrast to the US slave system. One "unquestionable—indeed unique—mark of slavery in the Southern states was the natural increase of the slave population. In all other slave societies of the New World, the slave population failed to reproduce itself and was sustained or increased only by constant injections of new slaves from Africa."[20] This had striking demographic effects. "Jamaica, Cuba, and

Haiti each imported many more slaves than the whole of the North American mainland. Yet, in stark contrast, by 1825 the southern states of the United States had the largest slave population of any country in the New World, amounting to well over one-third of the total."[21] Thus, the rule that children's status followed their mothers' was a foundational one for our economy. It converted enslaved women's reproductive capacity into market capital to serve economic interests. In the United States, it was enslaved women who reproduced the workforce.

Thus, childbearing by enslaved women created economic value independent of the physical, productive labor they performed. Southern legal rules harnessed black reproductive capacity for market purposes, extracting from it the profits one might expect from a factory or livestock. According to historian James Oakes, "The distinguishing function of slaves in the South's market economy was to serve not only as a labor supply but also as capital assets."[22] Law and markets operated synthetically in converting black reproductive capacity into capital creation. Slaveholders used the same logic of reproductive profits to get courts to void sales of enslaved women who couldn't bear children.[23] Functionally, reproductive relations were market relations of incredible economic significance. In its centrality to the political economy, enslaved women's reproduction was arguably the most valuable labor performed in the entire economy.

Thus, when the slaveholder in *Hudgins* invoked the rule that a child inherits its status from its mother, he was drawing on a foundational cultural assumption. Slaveholders owned all of the offspring of women they enslaved. The legal rule had immense economic and political significance for antebellum culture. Not only did slaves constitute the overwhelming proportion of the southern labor force, but this rule meant that it was a workforce that reproduced itself. Enslaved women gave birth to enslaved children and did so in a system that set considerable economic importance on this fact.

One of the nation's earliest and most prominent leaders, President Thomas Jefferson, personally proclaimed the unique, dual value of an enslaved workforce. Jefferson, who enslaved more than 144 people, said, "I consider a woman who brings a child every two years as more profitable than the best man on the farm; what she produces is an addition to capital." The value of short-term productive labor, such as that provided by the male slaves or by the female slaves when viewed as mere field hands, "disappeared in mere consumption."[24] In keeping with this, Jefferson instructed his plantation manager to monitor the overseers and ensure that they were encouraging female slave reproduction, the source of his wealth. Repeated references to enslaved females' fertility in advertisements and negotiations for sales indicate that Jefferson was not alone in his sentiments.[25]

The secretary of the treasury and president of the Georgia Cotton Planters Association estimated that a slaveholder's workforce would double every fifteen years through the process of normal reproduction.[26] Slavery scholar Deborah Gray White estimates that 5 to 6 percent of profit came from the increase of slaves due to reproduction.[27] Indeed, many members of the planting aristocracy owed their success to initial large gifts or inheritances of enslaved persons from their families.[28] Gray White notes, "Many farmers made their first investment not in a male slave, but in a young childbearing woman."[29] As one judge stated, "With us, nothing is so usual as to advance children by gifts of slaves. They stand with us, instead of money."[30] Historian Cheryl Ann Cody found that one of the men she studied "acquired slaves, once his estate was well established in the 1790s, primarily to give his sons their economic start rather than to expand his own labor force."[31]

Finally, southern judges drew analogies to rules governing livestock. Owners of female animals also got legal possession of their offspring. Should there be any doubt that southern whites grasped this analogy, one South Carolina judge declared that "the young of slaves . . . stand on the same footing as other animals."[32] Meanwhile, a famous observer of the American South, Frederick Olmsted, concluded from his travels that "a slave woman is commonly esteemed least for her working qualities, most for those qualities which give value to a brood mare."[33]

The date of the case, 1806, is significant. The US Constitution provided that no enslaved people could be imported (legally) from abroad after 1808.[34] Yet the expanding economies of the Deep South required larger and larger workforces. In 1806 Old South slave states such as Virginia were poised to take over the (legal) international slave trade with a domestic trade in slaves.[35] With enormous profits from reproduction anticipated, rules determining status became more crucial than ever.[36]

Therefore, the slaveholder in *Hudgins* drew upon the strong cultural expectation that personal economic profit would and should stem from an enslaved woman's childbearing. His lawyers cast his case as a question of "rights of *property*": "Those rules which have been established, are not to be departed from, because *freedom* is in question."[37] In other words, white economic rights trumped black liberty rights.[38]

Against this American backdrop of property rights in people, how could Hannah and her daughter have possibly responded? One would assume that the force of this law and custom would have dictated the outcome of the case: the law would side with the slaveholder, declaring him to be the legal owner of Hannah and her daughter. But as central as these property rights were in the slaveholding South, they were countered by another, equally fundamental tenet of slavery: the rules of race. Hannah and her daughter argued that they could not be enslaved because, by law, they were *legally not black*.

Under Virginia law, only people of African descent could be enslaved.[39] Proving membership in the Native American or white race constituted a legal defense to slavery. Southern law dictated that blacks were presumptively slaves, while whites and Native Americans were presumptively free.[40] Judge Roane stated the law in *Hudgins*: "In the case of a person visibly appearing to be a negro, the presumption is, in this country, that he is a slave, and it is incumbent on him to make out his right to freedom: but in the case of a person visibly appearing to be a white man, or an Indian, the presumption is that he is free, and it is necessary for his adversary to shew that he is a slave."[41] Accordingly, Hannah and her daughter claimed that Butterwood Nan was Native American and therefore illegally enslaved. If Butterwood Nan had been wrongfully enslaved, then as a free woman she could not have transmitted any enslaved status to her daughter Hannah, who, in turn, could not transmit it to her own daughter. In a fascinating instance of valuing white racial privilege over white wealth, the laws of race trumped the law that enslaved the children of female slaves. From within this legal box of race and status, Hannah and her daughter asserted the only legal argument that could win their freedom: their own nonblackness.

The plaintiffs' argument rested on gender as well as racial rules of slavery. Mother and daughter claimed their freedom through Butterwood Nan. To counter this, the slaveholder argued that Nan was, in fact, black and that it was her sexual partner who was Native American. Therefore, the nonblack (and legally free) ancestor was male. The establishment of nonblack ancestry had to be done through the maternal line to a female ancestor to be grounds for a claim of wrongful enslavement. Strikingly, within this deeply patriarchal culture, neither the father's race nor his status was relevant to the legal inquiry.[42] Free black men who took up with enslaved women fathered children who were enslaved by law. Moreover, showing white ancestry through one's father's side—indeed, showing that one's father was white—was no defense to enslavement. As noted before, by American law, the child of an enslaved black mother had no father. An enslaved woman who was black could not alter the status of her children through selecting either a free black or a white sexual partner.

Even more brutally, because the race of the father did not alter the status of an enslaved black woman's child, tens of thousands of white men were able to sexually abuse and coerce individual enslaved women without the risk that the women would bear children whose legal status would be affected in any way by their own. Such a child would not be construed by law as white or free but as black and the father's slave.

Within what we now understand to be an absurd system, the assertions of both the slaveholder and the women he claimed as his property raise fascinating questions. Was Butterwood Nan exempted from the rule by virtue of being Native

American? Had she lived her entire life held illegally as a slave? Were Hannah and her daughter free or enslaved? The arguments of both sides illustrate the centrality of enslaved women's reproduction to the political economy and culture of American slavery.

Let me finally reveal the outcome of the case. Judge Roane decided: "No testimony can be more complete and conclusive than that which exists in this cause to shew that *Hannah* had every appearance of an Indian. That *appearance* . . . will suffice for the claim of her posterity, unless it is opposed by counter-evidence shewing that some *female* ancester [*sic*] of her's [*sic*] was a *negro* slave, or that *she* or some female ancestor, was *lawfully* an Indian slave."[43] The court never described Butterwood Nan's appearance. Most likely she was deceased or had been sold out of the area and away from her family. But because Hannah and her daughter did not look black, they were presumptively free. The burden was on the slaveholder to prove that Butterwood Nan had been legally enslaved. He failed to do so. Hannah and her daughter went free.

Hannah's successful efforts to seek a racial exemption from slavery's status classifications left intact legal assumptions that relegated the overwhelming majority of blacks to enslavement. So is this a case to be celebrated? Condemned? How do we evaluate the efforts of Hannah and her daughter to escape from the grip of *partus sequitur ventrem*? Their lawyer started his argument before the court by saying, "This is not a common case of mere *blacks* suing for their freedom."[44] Looking backward from the twenty-first century, should we blame Hannah for seeking her family's freedom with such arguments? What other argument could she make within a racial logic that drew a legal equivalent between blackness and enslavement? What else could Hannah argue, except that she was not black?

Earlier, this essay identified black women's deployment across the conventional sexual division of labor as one of the things that distinguished their lives from those of other groups. The physical labor of enslaved women differed from white women's work both absolutely and relative to the work done by enslaved men. The case of Hannah and her daughter exposes a second, more brutal way that the economic roles that slavery assigned enslaved women distinguished their labor from other groups. White men and black men (free and enslaved) could father children either free or enslaved, and white women could give birth only to free children.[45] Laws of race and gender merged with *partus sequitur ventrem*'s status classifications to condemn the wombs of enslaved black women. This is a point about race and gender: only black women could give birth to enslaved children, and every black woman who was enslaved and gave birth did so to an enslaved child. In other words, the class that reproduced the workforce was limited to black women.[46] It is this terrorizing aspect of enslaved women's lives that also distinguished their role in the political economy from that of black men, white women, and white men. At labor in the fields and in labor in the birthing bed, the enslaved woman was both a mode of production and a mode of reproduction.

I turn now from reproductive relations to sexual relations. Like reproduction, from a contemporary perspective, many of us tend to think of sexual relationships as intimate, noneconomic relationships. But again like reproduction, enslaved women's sexuality played an essential role in the antebellum political economy. If the rule of *partus sequitur ventrem* reflected the southern investment in enslaved women's reproductive capacity, then the law of rape reveals the interests, economic and political, in their sexuality.

Pleasure, Profit, and Punishment:
Sexual Exploitation of Enslaved Women

In Mississippi in 1859 an enslaved man was accused of raping an unnamed enslaved girl who was under ten years old.[47] Convicted at trial, the defendant, named only as George, appealed to the Mississippi Supreme Court. The lawyer representing him argued: "The crime of rape does not exist in this State between African slaves. Our laws recognize no marital rights as between slaves; their sexual intercourse is left to be regulated by their owners. The regulations of law, as to the white race, on the subject of sexual intercourse, do not and cannot, for obvious reasons, apply to slaves; their intercourse is promiscuous, and the violation of a female slave by a male slave would be a mere assault and battery."[48] Influential legal commentator Thomas Cobb agreed: "The violation of the person of a female slave, carries with it no other punishment than the damages which the master may recover for the trespass upon his property."[49] This meant that an enslaved woman's master could prosecute her rape as a crime against his property, but the state would not prosecute her rape as a crime against her person. The court agreed and overturned George's conviction. Nearly every southern court that ruled on rape and enslaved women followed this ruling.[50] As Carolyn Pitt Jones, a student, succinctly summarized it, within slavery's sexual subtext, the female slave was an extralegal creature who could not use the law to protect herself.[51]

It would be folly to overgeneralize about a society's sexual norms based solely on its laws of rape. But criminal laws of rape define the boundaries of sexual access to bodies, especially women's and children's.[52] And the doctrine in *George v. State* shows how white institutions, including law, created and legitimized black women's sexual vulnerability. The refusal of law to protect enslaved women from rape institutionalized access to their bodies. Their exclusion from rape doctrine enabled their sexuality to be seized for multiple purposes.

First, slaveholders could force the relations they had with enslaved women as their laborers beyond the economic arena and into the sexual one without significant social disruption. Not only productive labor and reproduction could be demanded of enslaved women but also sexual gratification. The refusal of law to recognize sexual crimes against enslaved women enabled masters to compel sex: "Since the white male could rape the black female who did not willingly respond to his demands, passive submission on the part of the enslaved black women cannot be seen as complicity. Those women who did not willingly respond to the sexual overture of masters and overseers were brutalized and punished. Any show of resistance on the part of enslaved females increased the determination of white owners eager to demonstrate their power."[53] Sexual relations were part and parcel of what women were expected to do as members of an enslaved workforce.

Under this theory of law and on a brutal daily basis, enslaved women's sexuality was under the direct control of men in the slaveholding class. But it is important to note that sexual abuse of enslaved women was not limited to white men in slaveholding families. This group comprised only a small percentage of whites in the South. Other men, poorer, nonslaveholding whites and black men, took advantage of enslaved women's sexual vulnerability. Overseers frequently sexually assaulted or coerced enslaved women. In addition, a slaveholder could compel an enslaved woman to have sexual relations with his friends or to "initiate" a son or younger nephew, much as he might hire her out for her productive labor. In the alternative, he might by his silence authorize sexual access for men related to him by blood or economics. In short, law granted masters not only economic and political authority but also sexual authority.

Sadly, there is a need for intraracial as well as interracial critiques of sexual abuse. Recall that the case of *George v. State* involved the rape of a ten-year-old enslaved girl by an enslaved man. This may be one of the reasons the case was ever prosecuted. While certainly many black men of this era respected black women's sexual integrity and rights over their own bodies even in the absence of legal dictates to do so, others did not. Black women's sexual vulnerability was created and legitimized by white institutions of law and social power, but black men as well as white took advantage of it. Intraracial sexual abuse of black women surely has a social meaning and significance different from their abuse by white men. But that should not preclude our investigating what that different meaning is and why some black men and not others took advantage of their sisters.[54]

Second, some white slaveholders embraced the sexual exploitation of enslaved women to defend slavery against abolitionists who charged sexual abuse as one of the evils of slavery. According to Chancellor Harper, a judge,

And can it be doubted that this purity [of the white woman] is caused by, and is a compensation for, the evils resulting from the existence of an enslaved class of more relaxed morals? . . . I do not hesitate to say that the intercourse which takes place with enslaved females is less depraving in its effects than when it is carried on with females of their own caste. . . . [The white man] feels that he is connecting him with one of an inferior and servile caste, and there is something of degradation in the act. The intercourse is generally casual; he does not make her habitually an associate, and is less likely to receive any taint from her habits and manners.[55]

Southern white men openly justified their exploitation of enslaved women as resulting in the better treatment of white women. The same sexual norms that protected (white) female chastity with vigilance and brutality (sometimes directed at the women themselves) construed enslaved women as perpetual "outlets."[56] Elite white women, represented as delicate and often asexual, found their own sexual relations closely guarded and monitored by these same men: "Whereas the lady was deprived of her sexuality, the black woman was defined by hers."[57] Sexual access to enslaved women was central in the creation and maintenance of this repressive ideology of white femininity. Black enslaved women were therefore excluded from, yet essential to, the gender ideology of white masculinity and femininity.

Third, sexual abuse of enslaved women must be understood as an exercise of political power as well as sexual license. Contemporary feminists have demonstrated that rape entails power relations as much as sexual relations. Men rape women not only for personal pleasure but to discipline women into conforming to certain behaviors: to achieve women's submissiveness in personal relationships or adherence to conservative dress codes or to dictate physical activity, that is, where and when women feel safe. Slavery offers a primary and stark example of the power relations embedded in forced sexual relations.

An enslaved woman might be sexually punished for any number of perceived or actual offenses. Forced sex reminded an enslaved woman of her powerlessness in the hands of her master or his agent, the overseer. It functioned to humiliate her and demonstrate that the legal system had given control over her body to the man who enslaved her. Angela Davis offers the following characterization: "Rape was a weapon of domination, a weapon of repression, whose covert goal was to extinguish slave women's will to resist, and in the process, to demoralize their men."[58] Rape under slavery was an extremely powerful tool of disciplining women workers.[59]

In addition, rape helped to maintain racial hierarchy by reminding black women and men of black men's subordinate status to white men. As noted, a hallmark of southern antebellum culture was the protection of female chastity by male family members. An enslaved man who sought to do the same risked his life and that of the woman: "Clearly the master hoped that once the black man was struck by his manifest inability to rescue his women from sexual assaults of the master, he would begin to experience deep-seated doubts about his ability to resist at all."[60] Rape of enslaved women demoralized the entire black community. Law thus endorsed the use of sexual power as a mechanism of labor, racial, and gender control.

Finally, in addition to serving antebellum interests of pleasure and politics, enslaved women's sexuality was a source of economic profits for those inclined to reap them. Historians have identified an active market in enslaved women for prostitution, called the "fancy trade": "Slaves selected for their grace, beauty and light skins were shipped to the 'fancy-girl markets' of New Orleans and other cities. At a time when prime field hands sold for $1,600, a 'fancy girl' brought $5,000. Some ended up in bordellos, but the majority became the mistresses of wealthy planters, gamblers, or businessmen."[61] Sex might be extracted from any enslaved woman or girl. However, an enslaved woman sold primarily for sex commanded a higher price than other enslaved women.[62] The market assigned economic value directly related to sexual attractiveness. The seller reaped as extra profit the market's valuation of the women's sexuality, whether in skin color, hair, or whatever the buyer happened to personally value as erotic. As Brenda Stevenson incisively puts it, "What, after all, could be more valuable than a woman of 'white' complexion who could be bought as one's private 'sex slave'?"[63] To accommodate these buyers and ensure that they were getting what they expected, fancy-girl traders might allow the buyer to "inspect" his proposed purchase alone. At this juncture, sexual abuse and economic profits brutally collided.

The appearance of enslaved women as explicit sexual commodities in markets illuminates yet another way in which the South profited from enslaved women's sexuality. The fancy trade offers perhaps the most vivid image of how enslaved women's sexual relations were integrally tied to market relations in the antebellum political economy. Many historians now acknowledge that white men used enslaved women for sexual gratification. But with the above analysis I have tried to point out the nuances of their sexual labor. At the southern antebellum juncture of sex and markets, enslaved women were sexually exploited for a variety of purposes: pleasure, politics, punishment, and profit. In addition, as I have described earlier, slavery replenished its workforce through black women. This convergence of sexual and reproductive relations with market and political relations is what leads me to name slavery a sexual political economy.

A Sexual Economy

A political economy is characterized in some part by how wealth is defined, who owns it, and who creates it. In their descriptions of expected profits, ways to maximize yield, and transmissions of wealth between generations, elite members of antebellum society characterized enslaved women's reproductive capacity in the language of capital assets. Judges, cabinet members, and at least one president declared the economic value of enslaved women's childbearing capacity. This reproduction was integral to the plantation economy, which required a steady flow of cheap, largely unskilled labor. Hence black reproduction yielded economic profits, creating value for the slaveholding class. Enslaved black women gave birth to white wealth.

A political economy is also characterized by the interests it prioritizes and how those are served. White men established enslaved women as sexual outlets, forcing them to perform sexual labor. In the process, their sexuality could be exploited to reinforce gender conventions among elite whites and to defend slavery against northern charges. In addition, enslaved women could be sexually terrorized in order to coerce economic work or quell political resistance. Their exploitation could also be used to discipline enslaved men. Finally, as the fancy trade illustrates, economic profits were to be made in slavery's sexual markets. Pleasure, punishment, politics, and profit: once laws of rape authorized elite white male legal and economic control over enslaved women's sexuality, it could be manipulated to serve any number of interests.

Taken together, *Hudgins v. Wrights* and *George v. State* show how law extracted and markets expected dual labor from enslaved women. Like enslaved men, they were coerced into performing grueling physical productive labor. But they were also compelled to do sexual and reproductive labor required of no other group. This suggests the need for attention to gender to fully understand the economics and effects of US enslavement. Economists of slavery have characterized the political economy of slavery as a system in which blacks transferred millions of dollars of uncompensated labor to white slaveholders: "[Slavery] directly enriched those who bought, sold, transported, financed, bred, leased, and managed slaves in agriculture. But it was also important in other sectors, including mining, transportation, manufacturing, and public works—roads, dams, canals, levees, railroads, clearing land—and so on."[64] Wealth was transferred not only from blacks to whites, as scholars have noted, but also from black women to white men. Hence the economics of slavery were gendered as well as racialized.

In addition, the economic impact of its sexual exploitation distinguishes the antebellum South from other enslaving systems. Other slave societies entailed sexual and reproductive exploitation.[65] Indeed, some cultures enslaved primarily women (and children). In this sense, these societies were more gendered than US slavery, with its relatively equal sex ratios. But what I have tried to show in this essay is the extent to which enslaved women's sexual and reproductive labor was an integral and critical part of the economic and political viability of the South. One measure of slavery is how central or peripheral it is to the immediate economic functioning of the society. People might be enslaved to serve primarily as servants, political officials, soldiers, wives, or concubines.[66] Enslavement in the United States stands in stark contrast to all of these. David Brion Davis elaborates the relationship of slavery to the US market economy: "No slave system in history was quite like that of the West Indies and the Southern states of America. Marked off from the free population by racial and cultural differences, for the most part deprived of the hope of manumission, the Negro slave also found his life regimented in a highly organized system that was geared to maximize production for a market economy."[67] Enslaved women both labored in and reproduced this workforce. I have also shown how their sexual exploitation was inextricably tied not only to economic viability but also to maintaining and defending the social order, ranging from pleasure to punishment to politics. In sum, slavery's legal and cultural institutions systematically made enslaved women's reproductive and sexual capacity available to serve any number of political and economic interests of elite white men. For all these reasons, I name the antebellum South a sexual political economy. Rules of race, rape, gender, and *partus sequitur ventrem* formed the legal core of slavery's sexual economy.

What, then, do we gain from viewing slavery as a sexual economy? I would suggest three things. One purpose in labeling the antebellum South a sexual economy is to draw attention to the extent to which slavery drew distinctions on the basis of sex as well as race. It was a gendered and sexualized as well as a racial institution. Or, in the language of subordination, a language that may more aptly characterize slavery's brutal hierarchies, American slavery, while obviously racially supremacist, was also fundamentally a system of gender supremacy. Designating it as a sexual economy draws attention to its axes of both male power and racial power, thereby shedding light on the lives and exploitation of both enslaved women and enslaved men.

Viewing slavery through the sexual economy lens also suggests insights about the very nature of gender itself. "Masculine" and "feminine" mean different things in different races, classes, and ethnicities. Sexual roles and norms evolve over time and across cultural boundaries. Enslaved women offer an early, dramatic example of the political, cultural, economic, and violent forces that can shape gender. Angela Davis offers an excellent description of the manipulation of enslaved women's gender: "Expediency governed the slaveholders' posture toward female slaves: when it was profitable to exploit them as if they were men, they were regarded, in effect, as genderless, but when they could be exploited, punished and repressed in ways suited only for women, they were locked into their exclusively female roles."[68] Jacqueline Jones concurs: "The master took a more crudely opportunistic approach toward the labor of slave women, revealing the interaction (and at times conflict) between notions of women qua 'equal' black workers and women qua unequal reproducers."[69] Against the feminine delicacy and chastity ascribed to most white women in this society, enslaved women were clearly gendered differently. They were gendered as masculine when performing conventionally male work or suffering the same brutal physical discipline as enslaved men. But an enslaved woman might have her sexuality or childbearing capacity seized for pleasure, profit, or punishment at any moment, suffering rape or giving birth to white wealth. She was male when convenient and horrifically female when needed. In this sense, she was "gendered to the ground," as legal feminist theorist Catharine MacKinnon would say.[70] Comprehending gender as brutally malleable may uncover deeply buried historical facts.

Finally, seeing slavery in this way challenges the way we divide the intimate from the economic. For enslaved women, sexual and reproductive relations were economic and market relations.[71] While enslaved women's family lives and personal relationships offered some solace from the daily brutality of slavery, white men could invade this sphere at will, abusing women sexually or reproductively. Excellent work by historians Darlene Clark Hine and Nell Painter invites our attention to the ongoing sociological and psychological effects of slavery's sexual economy. Clark Hine makes the powerful argument that all of these manipulations and abuses of sexuality were primary factors in shaping cultures of resistance in southern black women. Dissemblance, flight northward, and, most tragically, violence targeted at their own bodies were tactics black women employed.[72] And Painter argues that because sexual abuse of enslaved women was woven into the fabric of southern households and families, its cultural, sociological, and psychological effects reached far beyond enslaved females or even the larger enslaved and black communities.[73]

In the black community too often we still view sexuality as something to be kept private and not spoken about. Black women's magazines are filled with stories of the trauma and loss of self-esteem this repression causes. Perhaps understanding black women's sexual history as something under public control for so long can help us to see the inherently political nature of our sexuality.[74] For black women to reclaim our sexuality, our intimate selves, from all of the people and forces who would seek to expropriate it, regulate it, define it, and confine it, we must first become comfortable speaking about it. The language of the sexual economy may help in this process.

To summarize, enslaved black women shared the world of productive labor with white men, black men, and white women but also inhabited a separate world of compelled sexual and reproductive labor. By understanding American slavery as a sexual economy in which black women's reproduction and sexuality were appropriated for any number of white economic and political interests, we can see more clearly how slavery was a deeply gendered and sexualized institution in which there was a constant interplay between black sexuality and white economic profits. Such an understanding collapses the distinctions we draw between sex and work, families and markets, also showing how this distinction was itself largely under male control. It also enables us to see more clearly the institutions, including law, that slavery erected, institutions that systematically made enslaved women's reproductive and sexual capacity available for sale and consumption.

Afterword: Reclaiming Ourselves

> Grandma Baby said people look down on her because she had eight children with different men. Colored people and white people both look down on her for that. Slaves not supposed to have pleasurable feelings on their own; their bodies not supposed to be like that, but they have to have as many children as they can to please whoever owned them. Still, they were not supposed to have pleasure deep down. She said for me not to listen to that. That I should always listen to my body and love it.
>
> —Toni Morrison, *Beloved*

Beyond the brutal exploitation and abuse of the slave economy, black women have reclaimed productive work as something that can be fulfilling and affirming. But much of the labor that slavery extracted from women in the enslaved workforce was sexual and reproductive. Toni Morrison's Pulitzer Prize–winning novel, *Beloved*, is a story about a black woman who is thoroughly brutalized and haunted by the sexual economy of slavery described above. Morrison poetically renders her character's exhausting struggle to reclaim herself and her family from the terror of her past.

Have we today fully reclaimed our own intimate lives from that horror? What are the ongoing effects of slavery's systemic expropriation of black women's reproduction and sexuality for market and political purposes? How does the sexual economy of slavery continue to affect the policing of black women's sexuality? From current national debates about welfare reform to local debates within the black community about sexual aggression by black men against black women, our intimate lives cannot be tidily defined as and confined to a private space. This essay has used cases and legal doctrine that document and record the real lives and experiences of black women who were enslaved not only for academic insight but to enable us to combat the effects of sexual economies, past and present.

Notes

The title of this essay comes from Minnie Folkes, a former Virginia slave. Her full statement was, "Don't let nobody bother yo' principle, 'cause dat wuz all yo' had" (Blassingame, *The Slave Community*, 163).

1. On the specificity of slavery, see Parish, *Slavery*, 3–6, 97–112.

2. Davis, *Women, Race, and Class*, 5. Leslie Schwalm's study of enslaved women on South Carolina rice plantations also reinforces this point. See *A Hard Fight for We*, 19–46.

3. Jones, *Labor of Love*, 18.

4. Davis, *Women, Race, and Class*, 5.

5. Ibid., 10.

6. White, "Female Slaves," 56, 59.

7. See also Stevenson, *Life in Black and White*, 159, 187–92; Schwalm, *A Hard Fight for We*, 19–23; Shammas, "Black Women's Work," 5–6.

8. Jones, *Labor of Love*, 12. Brenda Stevenson notes that this was not the case in many African tribes (*Life in Black and White*, 171). (Under the sexual division of labor in many African tribes, men did not perform agricultural labor, which was considered women's work.)

9. hooks, *Ain't I a Woman*, 22.

10. For instance, Deborah Gray White warns: "It would be a mistake to say that there was no differentiation of field labor on southern farms and plantations. . . . Yet the exceptions to the rule were so numerous as to make a mockery of it" ("Female Slaves," 59–60, emphasis added). In addition, "pregnant women, and sometimes women breastfeeding infants, were usually given less physically demanding work" (ibid., 60, footnote omitted). See also Berlin, *Many Thousands Gone*, 56, 135, 168 (describing the evolution of sexual division of labor); Stevenson, *Life in Black and White*, 192–93.

11. See hooks, *Ain't I a Woman*, 22–23. Ira Berlin notes, "Only rarely—for the very young and the very old—did household labor occupy slave women on a full-time basis" (*Many Thousands Gone*, 270–71, 311–12, quote on 271). See also Genovese, *Roll Jordan, Roll*, 495; and Schwalm, *A Hard Fight for We*, 19–28.

12. See, for example, Kolcbin, *American Slavery*, 121–22 (describing one slaveholder who used this tactic).

13. Painter, "Soul Murder and Slavery," 125, 142; and Tomlins, "Why Wait for Industrialism?," 5.

14. See Tomlins, "Why Wait for Industrialism?," 32.

15. Hudgins v. Wrights, II Va. (1 Hen. and M.) 134 (1806).

16. Act XII, 2 Laws of Virginia 170 (Hening 1823) (enacted 1662). For further discussion of this rule in Virginia, see Getman, "Note," 115, 130–32; Higginbotham and Kopytoff, "Racial Purity," 1967, 1970–75; hooks, *Ain't I a Woman*, 39–44; Moore, "Slave Law," 171, 184–91 (intriguing early discussion about definitions of enslavement).

17. Frazier v. Spear, 5 Ky. (2 Bibb) 385, 386 (1811).

18. Oakes, *The Ruling Race*, 73.

19. Kolchin, *American Slavery*, 6–7.

20. Parish, *Slavery*, 23. "The North American mainland was one of the smallest importers of slaves from Africa, and yet became the home of the largest slave population in the Western hemisphere" (ibid., 112, see also 16). See also Raboteau, *Slave Religion*, 91. Slavery in the United States was not static, however, and at times failed to reproduce by natural increase. See, for example, Berlin, *Many Thousands Gone*, 149 (through most of the eighteenth century, the slave population in the low country did not naturally reproduce); and Parish, *Slavery*, 16 ("the first generation of slaves did not even reproduce their own population, let alone produce a natural increase").

21. Parish, *Slavery*, 12, footnote omitted.

22. Oakes, *The Ruling Race*, 26.

23. Margaret Burnham discusses such cases in her excellent article on the legal treatment of enslaved families, "An Impossible Marriage," 187, 198–99.

24. Thomas Jefferson to Joel Yancy, January 17, 1819, reprinted in *Thomas Jefferson's Farm Book*, 42, 43.

25. Stevenson, *Life in Black and White*, 245.

26. Gutman, *The Black Family*, 76.

27. White, *Ar'n't I a Woman?*, 177n22. She describes the economics in excellent detail on pages 67–70.

28. In 1818 one southerner wrote: "For a young man, just commencing life the best stock, in which he can invest Capital, is, I think, negro Stock . . . ; negroes will yield a much larger income than any Bank dividend" (Oakes, *The Ruling Race*, 73, quoted in Owens, *This Species of Property*, 16). Similarly, an uncle advised his young nephew: "Get as many young negro women as you can. Get as many cows as you can. . . . It is the greatest country for an increase that I have ever saw in my life. I have been hear [*sic*] six years and I have had fifteen negro children born and last year three more young negro women commenced breeding which added seven born last year and five of them is living and doing well" (Oakes, *The Ruling Race*, 74, quoting Alva Fitzpatrick to Phillips Fitzpatrick, August 20, 1849, Fitzpatrick Papers, University of North Carolina, Chapel Hill).

29. Gray White, *Ar'n't I a Woman?*, 67–70.

30. Jones v. Mason, 22 Va. (1 Rand.) 577, n. l (August 1827) (*J. Carr, concurring*).

31. Cody, "Naming," 242.

32. M'Vaughters v. Elder, 4 S.C.L. (2 Brev.) 307, 314 (1809). See also Parish, *Slavery*, 80 (describing a South Carolina planter who registered the births of enslaved children and of colts, naming the horses' sires but not the slaves' fathers).

33. Gray White, *Ar'n't I a Woman?*, 177n22, quoting *DeBow's Review* 30 (1857): 74, which is quoting Frederick Olmsted, *The Cotton Kingdom*, ed. David Freeman Hawke (Indianapolis: Bobbs-Merrill, 1971), 12, 72.

34. U.S. Constitution, art. I, § 9, d. I.

35. See, for example, Meier and Rudwick, *From Plantation to Ghetto*, 40–41 (describing the role of the United States in ongoing illegal trade). On the slave trade generally, see Curtin,

The Atlantic Slave Trade; Klein, *The Middle Passage*; Engerman and Inikori, *The Atlantic Slave Trade*. On the domestic slave trade, see, for example, Stevenson, *Life in Black and White*, 175–76; Johnson, *Soul by Soul*; Tadman, *Speculators and Slaves*; see also Parish, *Slavery*, 56–57 (summarizing the debate over the extent and effects of the domestic slave trade).

36. The scope, design, and profitability of breeding enslaved females remain deeply contested among historians. See Parish, *Slavery*, 63n33; Sutch, "The Breeding of Slaves"; Lowe and Campbell, "The Slave Breeding Hypothesis."

37. Hudgins v. Wrights, 11 Va. (1 Hen. and M.), 136 (emphasis in original).

38. The *Hudgins* ruling suggests a different outcome when the contest is between white economic versus white liberty interests. See *Hudgins*, 140–41. For further discussion of this point, see Davis, "Identity Notes Part One," 695, 702–7.

39. Native Americans could be enslaved in Virginia only during a certain period of time, and whites could not be enslaved at all.

40. In an earlier essay, I joined other commentators in arguing that the decision in the case exemplifies the role of law in shaping the existence and meaning of racial categories such as black, white, and Native American in the US law that protected those who were not black from being enslaved. One of the judges, for instance, said, "The distinguishing characteristics of the different species of the human race are so visibly marked, that those species may be readily discriminated from each other by mere inspection only" (*Hudgins*, 141). The essay calls this assignment of race based on visual appearance a "scopic" determination of race, which it contrasts with assignments based on ancestry or genealogy. While many slave laws protected white economic interests, I argue that *Hudgins's* scopic rule of racial classification identified a second legally protected interest, the white liberty interest. Not surprisingly, under such a rule, the definition of "black" itself became a matter of legal contestation. See, for example, Davis, "Identity Notes Part One," 702–11; Gross, "Litigating Whiteness," 109; and Higginbotham and Kopytoff, "Racial Purity," 1975–88.

41. *Hudgins*, 141 (emphasis in original).

42. See *Frazier*.

43. *Hudgins*, 142 (emphasis in original).

44. Ibid., 135 (emphasis in original).

45. At various points, white women, too, suffered regulations not unlike those suffered by enslaved black women. At times, white women giving birth to children deemed to be black could be sold into indentured servitude, and their children could be indentured. If an indentured white woman had a child, her own period of indenture could be extended (the child would be indentured until he or she was an adult, as well). In one extreme iteration, in 1664 Maryland enslaved white women who married enslaved men for the lifetime of the husband and also enslaved any children. This law was repealed due to fear of its abuse by white masters seeking to extend white female servants' period of service. See, for example, Johnston, *Race Relations*, 172–79; Morris, *Southern Slavery*, 23; Hodes, *White Women, Black Men*, 24–25.

46. Darlene Clark Hine concurs: "Slave women were expected to serve a dual function in this system and therefore suffered a dual oppression. They constituted an important and necessary part of the work force and they were, through their child-bearing function, the

one group most responsible for the size and indeed the maintenance of the slave labor pool" ("Female Slave Resistance," 27, 34).

47. State v. George, 37 Miss. 316 (1859).

48. Ibid., 317.

49. Cobb, *An Inquiry*, § 107.

50. See, for example, Higginbotham and Kopytoff, "Racial Purity"; and Morris, *Southern Slavery*, 304–7.

51. Carolyn Pitt Jones, "Litigating Reparations for African-American Female Victims of Coerced/Uninformed Sterilization and Coerced/Uninformed Norplant Implantation," 1999, 41 (memorandum written for class, on file with the author).

52. "Serious prohibitions of rape strengthen the bargaining power of the weaker sexual player by making the stronger obtain consent from the weaker rather than force the sexual transaction. The various possible incarnations of rape—stranger rape, statutory rape, marital rape, acquaintance rape, and rape by abuse of familial or professional authority—mark the boundaries of one person forcibly claiming access to another's body without their consent and accordingly are central in setting the terms of such consent. . . . The law governing forcible rape also reflects the core beliefs of a society about the role of sexual access" (Hirshman and Larson, *Hard Bargains*, 6).

53. hooks, *Ain't I a Woman*, 25–26.

54. Brenda Stevenson, for instance, describes a variety of factors that may have led some enslaved men to sexually objectify enslaved women. See *Life in Black and White*, 242–43.

55. Genovese, *Roll, Jordan, Roll*, 420, quoting Harper, *Cotton Is King*, 44–45, 61. See also Painter, "Soul Murder and Slavery," 142 (describing the complex reasoning of apologists defending the sexual norms of slavery).

56. Darlene Clark Hine notes: "Another major aspect of black women under slavery took the form of the white master's consciously constructed view of black female sexuality. This construct, which was designed to justify his own sexual passion toward her, also blamed the female slave for the sexual exploitation she experienced at the hands of her master" ("Female Slave Resistance," 28).

57. Fishburn, *Women in Popular Culture*, 10–11.

58. Davis, *Women, Race, and Class*, 23–24.

59. Enslaved men may have been sexually victimized for similar purposes; this topic is underexplored in the literature. For discussion, see Painter, "Soul Murder and Slavery," 137–38; Stevenson, *Life in Black and White*, 181, 195–96. Judith Kelleher Schafer discusses the sexual torture of an enslaved boy in "Sexual Cruelty to Slaves," 1313. In *Beloved*, Toni Morrison alludes to sexual abuse of black men on the chain gang (107–8).

60. Davis, "Reflections," 111, 124; see also Stevenson, *Life in Black and White*, 240.

61. Sterling, *We Are Your Sisters*, 27. Deborah Gray White notes that the cities of New Orleans, Charleston, St. Louis, and Lexington seem to have been the centers of the trade (*Ar'n't I a Woman?*, 37). One trader insisted on separating a mother and daughter, speculating that when the daughter was a few years older, "there were men enough in New Orleans who would give five thousand dollars for such an extra handsome, fancy piece as Emily would be"

(ibid., 38, quoting Northrup, "Twelve Years a Slave," 268). See also Bancroft, *Slave Trading*, 57, 102, 131, 328–30, in reprint; Stevenson, *Life in Black and White*, 180–81, 239.

62. "Only 'fancy' women commanded higher prices than skilled male slaves.... Joe Bruin of the Alexandria firm of Bruin and Hill placed Emily Russell, a beautiful mulatto whom he planned to sell as a prostitute in New Orleans, on the market for $1800. Bruin and Hill realized the profit that could be garnered from the 'fancy girl' market and often purchased females in Virginia and Maryland for that purpose" (Stevenson, *Life in Black and White*, 180). This item appeared in a southern newspaper: "A slave woman is advertised to be sold in St. Louis who is so surpassingly beautiful that $5,000 has already been offered for her, at private sale, and refused" (Bancroft, *Slave Trading*, 329, see also 329–33). See also Stampp, *The Peculiar Institution*, 259.

63. Stevenson, *Life in Black and White*, 180.

64. America, *Paying the Social Debt*, 6.

65. Patterson, *Slavery and Social Death*, 50, 229, 230, 261.

66. See, for example, Kolchin, *American Slavery*, 4. The sexual labor of enslaved women in the United States differed from sexual exploitation in other societies. The South was practically alone among slave systems in denying and prohibiting any legal recognition of women who built sexual families with their masters. See, for example, Patterson, *Slavery and Social Death*, 231–32, 260–61.

67. Davis, *The Problem of Slavery*, 60.

68. Davis, *Women, Race, and Class*, 6.

69. Jones, *Labor of Love*, 12.

70. MacKinnon, *Feminism Unmodified*, 173; MacKinnon, *Toward a Feminist Theory*, 183, 198.

71. "When the profitability of slaves as capital became that great, as it did very early on, the market economy came to intrude deeply into the most intimate of human relationships" (Oakes, *The Ruling Race*, 26).

72. "Rape and the threat of rape influenced the development of a culture of dissemblance among southern black women" in the late nineteenth and early twentieth centuries (Hine, "Rape and the Inner Lives," 37). She continues, "Black women as a rule developed a politics of silence, and adhered to a cult of secrecy, a culture of dissemblance, to protect the sanctity of the inner aspects of their lives" (ibid., 41). She also makes the case that "the most common, and certainly the most compelling, motive for running, fleeing, or migrating was a desire to retain or claim some control of their own sexual beings and the children they bore" (ibid., 40–41). In addition, Hine argues that enslaved women understood their own sexual economic value and used that to resist slavery: "When they resisted sexual exploitation through such means as sexual abstention, abortion, and infanticide, they were, at the same time, rejecting their vital economic function as breeders.... The female slave, through her sexual resistance, attacked the very assumptions upon which the slave order was constructed and maintained. Resistance to sexual exploitation therefore had major political and economic implications" (Hine, "Female Slave Resistance," 34). See also Stevenson, *Life in Black and White*, 245–46.

73. In two path-breaking essays, Painter argues that historians have failed to approach sexual abuse in the context of interracial households as families and enslaved women as workers and hence have missed critical psychological effects that spanned all of southern society. See Painter, "Of *Lily*," 93; and Painter, "Soul Murder and Slavery," 126–28.

74. Darlene Clark Hine puts it powerfully: "The fundamental tensions between black women and the rest of the society—especially white men, white women, and to a lesser extent, black men—involved a multifaceted struggle to determine who would control black women's productive and reproductive capacities and their sexuality. At stake for black women caught up in this ever evolving, constantly shifting, but relentless war was the acquisition of personal autonomy and economic liberation" ("Rape and the Inner Lives," 41).

CHAPTER 2

Black Stud, White Desire

Black Masculinity in Cuckold Pornography and Sex Work

Mireille Miller-Young and Xavier Livermon

> I am informed that the sexual power[s] of negroes . . . are the cause of
> the favor with which they are viewed by some white women of strong
> sexual passions in America and by many prostitutes. At one time there
> was a special house in New York City to which white women resorted
> for these "buck lovers"; the women came heavily veiled and would
> inspect the penises of the men before making the selection.
>
> —Havelock Ellis, *Studies in the Psychology of Sex, Volume III*

In March 2008 *Vogue* magazine glowingly announced that LeBron James would
become only the third man—and the first black man—to appear on its cover. The
choice of James seemed odd, given that *Vogue* is a high fashion women's magazine
that has rarely featured black women as either models or celebrities on its covers.
However, James's spread was part of *Vogue*'s Shape issue, which highlights the
"best bodies," pairing high fashion models in a variety of poses with prominent
American athletes. In the cover image, shot by photographer Annie Liebowitz,
James appears in standard nondescript athleticwear that, save for stripes at the
arms, is black. His tennis shoes, save for some white coloring, are also black.
In his left arm James holds the supermodel Gisele Bündchen, who is wearing a
loose-fitting, bias-cut, strapless dress, while his right arm is free, allowing him to
dribble a basketball. The five-foot, eleven-inch Bündchen appears small next to
James. A wind machine blows back her hair, revealing her large, buoyant smile.
James, whose blackness blends almost seamlessly with his black attire, is shown

Figure 2.1: The April 2008 *US Vogue* cover of LeBron James and Gisele Bündchen was featured in "The Top 5 Most Controversial Vogue Covers Ever Published" by the Fashion Spot.

frozen, openmouthed, middribble, as if captured in the midst of a primal scream. Upon closer examination, the photograph becomes increasingly ambiguous: Is Bündchen playfully struggling against James's clutches, or is she happily surrendering to his embrace?

The *Vogue* cover image produced a swift reaction among media and cultural commentators, many of whom criticized the image for perpetuating racist stereotypes.[1] According to *Slate* writer Wesley Morris, however, the image also attracted attention for its erotic charge. Morris writes that Bündchen "is now recognizable as the girlfriend of American sports' golden boy [Tom Brady, quarterback of the New England Patriots]. Somebody at that magazine knew what he or she was doing. The picture's visual inspiration might be *King Kong* [1933], but the narrative corollary is D. W. Griffith's *Birth of a Nation* [1915]. Men, lock up your ladies! Here comes LeBron!" While other commentators criticized the *Vogue* image for blatant racism, Morris saw the connections with *King Kong* and *Birth of a Nation* as subtexts that a reader must strain to decipher: James is "triumphant," not "mad" or "simian"; Bündchen appears "exhilarated," not "terrified." Morris opines, "I was struck less by the stereotypes at play than by its *erotic value: It's a hot image,* and what's sexy about it is more a matter of celebrity than race."[2] Thus, for Morris, the celebrity of these two figures in some ways removes race from the image, and the image's erotic value as "hot" somehow occurs in spite of, not because of, the racial difference between the two well-known media figures. We would like to suggest that no such separation exists in determining the erotic value of this and other images that structure interracial sex in the contemporary United States. The eroticism of the image occurs precisely because of the racial and bodily differences between Bündchen and James and the dynamics of interracial infidelity—or "cuckolding"—the image invokes. LeBron James's *Vogue* cover thus embodies a form of erotic value that cannot be separated from historical and material realities.

In particular, James conforms strongly to the *Mandingo archetype*: dark, large, sexually available, and, through his hold on Bündchen, desirous of interracial sex with white women. This archetype developed as a specific reaction to shifts in the American sociopolity occasioned by the demise of slavery and served as an excuse for white supremacist violence. As Martha Hodes argues, "Only after the Civil War would whites' ideas about the dangers of black male sexuality merge with their fears of political and economic independence for African-American men to produce a deadly combination."[3] Hodes points to the ways in which portraying black men as sexual brutes excused white supremacist violence and buttressed white heteropatriarchy with the express purpose of curtailing black (male) political and economic competition.[4] Legal scholar Marques P. Richeson writes that there exists in American society a *Mandingo theory*, an ideology of "the purported sexual prowess of black men." According to Richeson, "Rumors of black male sexual prowess continue to simultaneously stimulate and intimidate the imaginations of white America."[5] Contemporary manifestations of this ideology abound, emerging most publicly in the arena of competitive sports, where black men's bodies literally become desired consumer commodities.[6] As Dwight McBride argues in *Why I Hate Abercrombie & Fitch,* the purported sexual prowess of black men overdetermines the roles that black male bodies can play and the acceptable manner in which they may be desired or desirable.[7] In a similar way, black men who commoditize their sexualities in pornography and the sex industry put the hypersexual figure of the buck or Mandingo to work.

This chapter focuses on how the eroticized Mandingo archetype invoked in James's *Vogue* cover is specifically articulated in the "cuckold" genre of pornographic film and video and in the swinger communities that both produce and consume these texts. Through a series of case studies focusing on the fantasies and narratives of white women and black men, we examine how the particular sexual economies of the Mandingo play out in a variety of spaces that we term *cuckolding sociality.* Most commentary on the Mandingo as an archetypical character tend to center on white male heteropatriarchal fantasies. It is, of course, from the viewpoint of the white male—in the realms of both political economy and psychoanalysis—that the dangerous black buck stereotype emerges. According to this commentary, the Mandingo stereotype emerges through the interplay of desire and disgust both as an expression of the real fear and envy that white men have toward black male sexuality and in order to cover white men's own interracial desires for and sexual subjugation of black women.[8] However, little has been said about what forms of desire might be produced within the Mandingo archetype by black men, by white women, or by white men for black men. In other words, what productive possibilities and queer potential emerge for all actors in the triad within the fantasy space of the Mandingo archetype?

The concept of *cuckolding sociality* offers a way to think about the mobile desires at play in racial fetishism and how, by enacting a neomiscegenation drama, sexual relations across racial borders allow for a multiplicity of pleasures for prohibited, dangerous sex. By mobile desires we mean to describe the shifting meaning of cuckolding scenes, depending on the perspective of each of the members of the triad. A playful script in which white men, white women, and black men can write their illicit desires, cuckolding sociality also demands the sexual labor of black men. It underscores how the representation of black male hypersexuality requires sexual labor, even when, as is the case with some Mandingo swingers, they are not paid for their sex performances.

Current manifestations of the Mandingo in sexual economies open up spaces for distinct desires to be explicitly enacted. These enacted desires expose shifts in contemporary erotic social relations and show how the political economies of sexual knowledge and exchange across racial lines, which Adrienne Davis addresses in her work on sexual economies during slavery, are being updated and revised in today's technologically enhanced and socially networked sexual cultures.[9] We illuminate our claims through an examination of racial cuckolding and cuckolding sociality with respect to pornography, sex work, and sex parties and swinging cultures. For the purposes of this preliminary examination we eschew the use of interview data; however, we anticipate that additional work will contain an ethnographic component. That pornography may be one of the few places where our most privately held societal views about race are most revealed makes this inquiry possible.

The Mandingo in Cuckold Pornography

Pornography offers a generative site to explore the representation and potential enactments of racial fantasy. It is a genre of the body, an economy of visible flesh, designed for the specific purpose of titillation and arousal. And it is a genre that makes visible the proof of the Mandingo's threat, in that pornog-raphy actually allows the viewer to *see* the black male penis in explicit detail disallowed by other forms of media. Pornography has historically drawn on racial fetishism to construct its fantasies.[10] An obsessive sexualization of racial difference was embedded in the emergence of the visual technologies, like photography and film, that were essential to the development and circulation of modern pornography.[11] Like the unabashedly hypersexual Jezebel, which determines many codes of representation in black female pornography, the Mandingo archetype has been the overriding frame for representing black men's sexualities in pornography, a powerful mechanism for the eroticization of inter-racial, black-white sex. This pornography demands that black men perform a typically assertive, sometimes brutish, sexuality, because the Mandingo figure defines black masculinity as such.

Cuckold pornography, a subgenre of pornographic media, eroticizes the sexual powerlessness, and sometimes humiliation, of the (usually) white hus-band or head of household. Although the fantasy of a wife cheating on her husband with the plumber or pizza delivery man has been circulating at least since the stag film era of the 1920s through the 1960s, cuckold pornography began to develop as a distinct genre in the early 2000s, joined by a range of other fetishes that became unique categories for adult entertainment products based on the kinds of bodies and relationships featured. What marks cuckold pornography as distinct from the rather common story of the cheating wife or girlfriend is the participation of the husband in the sexual performance. Cuckolded husbands do not catch the wife in the sex act with another man and then replace him by taking back ownership of their wives, as seen in numerous pornographic films. Instead, husbands are present all along—sometimes eager and sometimes forced to watch their wives have sex with one or more men. The genre is growing in popularity.[12]

In cuckold pornography that is specifically about racial dynamics, the cuck-oldress, sometimes called the Hot Wife, performs sex with a man of another race who is not her husband. The genre is overwhelmingly composed of white couples and black men, known as bulls or BBCs (Big Black Cocks) within the subculture of producers and consumers of the product. Erotic tension is produced in the fantasy of the black man's extreme sexual prowess and the threat that he will dis-place the white husband. In racial cuckold pornography like *I Can't Believe You Sucked a Negro* (JM Productions, 2008), it is white male desire that constitutes the scene.[13] The DVD cover for *I Can't Believe You Sucked a Negro* reads: "Have you ever imagined yourself happily married? It's time to wake up, loser. Negroes are claiming white women and a wedding band is not going to stop them from fucking your beloved wife's head. So pull out your tiny limp cock and prepare for your grim future." Though the cover addresses white men as the imagined "you" of the DVD's audience, it depicts a fantasy of white masculinity undermined or displaced, or even shamed and abused. This fantasy demands a particular kind of labor on the part of black men as they are called upon to perform the role of a Mandingo who uses his sexual prowess to seduce white women and undermine white men.

While racial cuckold pornography has become a profitable subgenre for professional production companies in the adult film industry, its commercial success only reflects a fraction of the interest and activity around the phenomenon. Producers and fans of amateur pornographic media, including members of the swinger subculture devoted to racial cuckold, use online media networks to create, share, and sometimes sell hardcore images of sex in real-life racial cuckold scenarios. Not just consumers, these amateur porn practitioners create independent images alongside, but often in competition with, the established commercial pornography industry.

Adult videos produced by amateurs often take place in their own bedrooms rather than on a film set. Ranging from around two minutes to over one hour, these roughly made videos are produced under low-budget conditions. The videos often have poor lighting and sound quality, little editing, and limited camerawork, conditioned by the placement of a digital camcorder on a tripod or by the husband's jerky movements as he circles the bed where his wife and a black man engage in intercourse. Unlike in much commercial cuckolding pornography, this grassroots media emerging from swinging subcultures usually lacks scenes of black men shaming the white male husbands of their sexual partners. Instead, husbands are presented as much more active in facilitating their wives' enjoyment, making sure they are safe and comfortable. Further, the relationship between the husbands and black men are often cordial, collaborative, or familiar.

One such video, *Cherry's 1st Interracial*, follows a script common in amateur cuckold pornography and in cuckolding sociality.[14] The video begins with cuckold husband "Bob" positioning the camcorder on a tripod in the corner of their cramped bedroom. "Cherry," his wife, is already performing fellatio while Bob complains that "it's kind of close quarters here." Soon the Black Lover—we never learn his name—disrobes Cherry, pushes her back on the bed, opens her legs, and begins to perform cunnilingus.[15] Cherry writhes and screams as Bob takes the camcorder off the tripod to move in closer for the shot. He later replaces the camera on the tripod to join the sex. He fingers his wife while she performs oral sex on the black man. Bob moves in and out of the action to take photos or adjust the camcorder, but he remains attentive to his wife. "Honey, are you OK?" he nervously asks as the black man starts to penetrate her. She doesn't answer him, as she is whispering to the black man looming over her. Soon she begins to yell, "Fuck me! Yes! Oh God! Holy shit!" The Black Lover of this video—an attractive, tall, muscular, dark-skinned, and bald man in his thirties—easily moves Cherry's body into different positions as he sets into an aggressive, ungentle penetrative style. Participants in the subculture often term this athletic fashion of fucking "hard pounding," and it is part of the cuckolding sexual performance of most Black Lovers, or, as they are often called in the amateur video and by white swinger couples, BBCs.

In this video Bob seems both aroused by and worried about what is happening between his wife and the BBC. He appears at various moments circling the bed or touching his wife, naked and erect. He strokes his penis as he watches the scene from each angle and smiles as he caresses his wife's breasts and stomach. But when Cherry seems to be in pain as the lover attempts to penetrate her anus, Bob asks him to stop, and the BBC complies. Although the pairing of Cherry and the BBC is made possible by Bob's displacement as Cherry's proper mate, Bob takes a clear role in permitting and directing Cherry's infidelity. Bob's pleasure in this displacement is depicted at the end of the sex, when the BBC discusses how his penis is as thick as his wrist. Bob looks down at his own increasingly flaccid penis and, shaking his head, says, "Wow." This and other scenes demonstrate how Bob desires the BBC. At 25:30 Bob lies alongside his wife as she is penetrated and asks the BBC, "You got a steel pipe in that thing or what?"

In *Married Couple Invite a Black Guy Over for Sex* Cherry and Bob reprise their roles as cuckold and cuckoldress, revealing how the social world created in interracial cuckolding opens up a range of possibilities for desire. In this video, Bob takes an active role in the sex, even enthusiastically performing oral sex and a "hand job" on the BBC. While another cuckolded husband in amateur pornography may guide the BBC's penis into his wife's vagina or come into contact with the black male body in some way as he videotapes or facilitates the sex, Bob centers his own desire for the black man's sex in this video by constantly touching the BBC. Bob also represents his own pleasure by placing his own body at the center of the camera's frame. What is striking about this particular video is the representation of bisexuality for both men and how the cuckold's voyeurism gives way to a more honest fetishization and objectification of the black man's body. This video testifies to the range of possibilities explored through cuckolding sociality, including the queering of white conjugality and the emergence of explicit interracial desire and interracial sex between white and black men. Such explicit interracial desire between men does the work of queering both normative white and black masculinities and disturbing one of the foundational tenets of white supremacy, the matrimonial bond between white men and white women.

There are several ritualistic aspects in these videos, but one of the most significant is the husband's fetishization of the black man's ejaculate. In *Bull Breeds Cuckold Cleans* and many similar videos, there is a close-up shot of the ejaculate as it seeps out of the wife's splayed, ravaged genitals.[16] In this representational trope, the husband either volunteers or is directed by the wife to do "cleanup," that is, to ingest the BBC's ejaculate as it drips out of the cuckoldress's genitals. Some in the racial cuckolding community explain cleaning up as a way to ensure that the contagion of the black man's semen does not impregnate the white wife. Because it provides access to black men's bodily fluids, cleaning up may also provide a way for the purportedly heterosexual husband to erotically engage the black man without having to touch him. It shows how much the white husband desires access to the black man's body but displaces this desire because of prohibitions against homoeroticism between black and white purportedly heterosexual men. Acting as a conduit of white male desires for racial purity and/or for the black man's body, the white female body allows this interaction to take place without it being deemed "gay." Cleaning up is also about roleplay, as the husband performs the submissive role to the wife's dominant, acting as a servant of sorts, made to clean up the evidence of her pleasure and his own diminished/derided manhood. The submissive man serves his "Domina" by doing an act deemed pleasurable by her and framed as demeaning to him, masochistically displaying his powerlessness and displacement in the social theater of cuckolding sociality. In this racialized drama, then, black men's ejaculate takes on a particular fetishistic symbolism. It is a tangible substance seen to represent ideas about black invasion and the degeneration of white racial purity, ideas that are enacted in this form of sexual play.

Sometimes the BBC's ejaculate is not cleaned up by the masochistic husband but left inside the Hot Wife's vagina to symbolize the exciting threat of her becoming pregnant. "Breeding" media, a subgenre of this fetish, specifically focuses on the idea of the BBC delivering his "seed" to a "Breeding Wife."[17] Referencing the Mandingo's labor in the system of controlled reproduction common during slavery, these videos portray a *neomiscegenation drama*.[18] What is distinctive in this new version of the miscegenation drama is that this imagined threat of contamination is turned into erotic or economic value for each of the actors. For white men and white women, the possibility of pregnancy creates erotic charge and sexual excitement. Furthermore, unlike under slavery, the black men who perform this labor do so freely. In the following sections, we explore how the neomiscegenation drama of cuckold pornography is renegotiated in spaces of cuckolding sociality: on "Hot Wife" blogs by white women and by black male escorts who either identify with or disavow the label "Mandingo."

"Black Cock Only": Mandingo Fantasy and Social Media in the "Hot Wife" Blogosphere

In this section we focus on the forms Mandingo and cuckolding fantasies take in the narratives of "Hot Wives" and "Mandingos" as they are distributed online. By analyzing online spaces of expression, desire, and interactivity, we can better understand the nature of cuckolding sociality by examining how each actor in the triad of white husband, white wife, and black lover (cuckold, Hot Wife, and BBC) identifies their role and fetishizes, or projects their desires onto, others. In the interest of space, this chapter focuses on white women's use of social media.

"Hot Wife" blogs like *Hot Wife Allie* offer a space for white women in the swinging subculture to perform and narrate their curiosity about interracial sex. Through blog entries and participation in online forums, Hot Wives express agency and desires that exceed the heteronormative relationship of the marriage contract while simultaneously celebrating their privileged roles as wives in white families. According to the Hot Wives' entries we reviewed, white husbands take care of "most needs," which we imagine to include financial, social, emotional, and perhaps even spiritual or psychic needs for their white wives. Black studs are strictly for physical needs, needs that presumably white husbands cannot fulfill either because they do not possess large enough penises to please their wives or because the wives' desires surpass the husbands' abilities.

In a break from traditional demands for white women to express loyalty to their husbands and their race, these women narrate their potential to have needs and desires exceeding the bounds of normative monogamy and fidelity in marriage. By winning her husband's consent to infidelity, a Hot Wife walks a fine line whereby she must simultaneously reassure her husband of his patriarchal role and sexual value while taking up practices that can be seen to undermine that role and value. Unlike commercial cuckold pornography, in our research we found that amateur Hot Wives do not often verbally abuse or explicitly demean their husbands. Instead, a Hot Wife's form of exhibitionist cuckolding serves her husband's fantasy and invokes his arousal, even as it challenges his perceived status and authority.

Hot Wives provide detailed narratives of their sexual relations with black men in their online narratives. In these stories, Hot Wives portray their encounters with BBCs as shocking in a titillating style similar to that of amateur erotic fan fiction, describing themselves in terms of bisexual identities that negotiate the multiple vectors of power at play in the triad. On a blog entitled *Hot Wife Allie*, a contributor named Sara tells the story of an encounter at a "Mandingo Party," a swingers' party where black men are invited or hired to have sex with mostly white couples:

47

He kept his hand over mine and showed me how he liked it stroked. "You're probably not used to stroking a real big dick like mine." He looked over at Jeff, who was watching. I looked over at Jeff and licked my lips. Sometimes, when I want to be really naughty, I pretend I'm a porn star with the camera rolling. I can do anything when I feel like I'm a porn star. I switched into p.s. mode, and keeping my eyes on my hubby's, I reached forward and brought the guy's dark head to my mouth and outlined my lips with it. It was oozing plenty of pre-cum so it slid around smoothly. Jeff mouthed "slut." My favorite word![19]

In this story, Hot Wife Sara presents herself as at first somewhat sexually innocent. The BBC takes on the role of teacher as he instructs her how to hold and caress his penis, a sex act she presents herself as ignorant of, given its large size. She then discusses the exchange of looks signifying the axis of power in the triad: the BBC looks at her husband, Jeff, who looks back as if to confirm his consent for what is about to happen. She looks at Jeff and signals her desire to him by licking her lips. She then "switches to porn star mode," assertively performing fellatio on the BBC as her husband watches. Jeff then validates Sara's performance by mouthing the word "slut." She affirms that she likes this word, presumably because it gives her license to "flaunt her 'infidelity.'"[20] It also acknowledges that her sexual desires are normatively prohibited and dangerous. In this space, created by this community, illicit economies of sex are in fact permissible, as long as all parties give consent.

Part of this fantasy of illicitness is the framing of consensual nonmarital sexual contact as infidelity. While it may at first seem counterintuitive to frame such sexual activity through this lens, we suggest that it is a necessary part of the Hot Wife persona and of cuckolding sociality in general. Because cuckolding sociality is based on the fantasy of the cuckold—the cheated-on and therefore humiliated husband—Hot Wives are required to frame their extramarital activity within the lens of adultery or infidelity. This also adds a transgressive element to what is essentially a consensual sexual activity. The Hot Wife becomes a "slut," her sexual appetite unable to be satisfied within the confines of white conjugality, its excess only tamed by a BBC. In what might be termed *performative infidelity*, the narratives of Hot Wives argue that all parties in the triad, but particularly white women, take tremendous pleasure in the wife's performance of being a slut. Cuckolding sociality in this instance allows for a controlled destabilization of virtuous white womanhood, one of the foundational pillars of white supremacy.

Essential to Hot Wives' narratives of pleasure is the fetishization of the black male body. Sara and other Hot Wives tend to focus on what they see as the animalistic, aggressive, and forcefully raw qualities of black male sexuality—and the labor it does for them. Hot Wife blogs rarely mention the names, occupations, backgrounds, or personal qualities of the BBCs in their encounters. In blog posts, forums, comments sections of adult video "tube sites," and even the burgeoning genre of cuckold-oriented erotic nonfiction sold on Amazon, Hot Wives describe being ravished by black men, overcome with their size and intense, athletic sexual performance. Hot Wives enjoy marking their bodies in ways that signify their participation in the subculture and their submission to bulls and cuckolds. They share images of custom-made necklaces and ankle bracelets inscribed with the words "Hot Wife" and post pictures of their own bodies with "wife writing" sensationalizing their interracial desires: "Cunt for Big Black Cock" or "Black Cock Only!"[21]

As much as cuckolding sociality is about the trespass of the racial-sexual border, it is also about marking and upholding that border. For white couples in the Hot Wife subculture, pleasure in illicit sex with black men is inextricable from their understanding of their own privilege and power over black men's bodies. What makes cuckolding sociality sustainable for Hot Wife husbands is their understanding of the limits in their triadic relationships, an understanding that is cultivated and performed through husbands' contributions to Hot Wife blogs. Hot Wife husbands explain the rules, whereby the BBC is only there for sex and not for deeper intimacy, which remains the husband's domain. "The wife's sexual pleasure should not be confused with her romantic feelings," one cuckold husband claims. "She is only in love with her husband."[22] Thus interracial encounters, as represented on Hot Wife blogs, buttress white women's erotic capital in the racial hierarchy, invest in black men's sex work remaining primary to their claims for manhood, and ultimately affirm white men's place as the architects of racial-sexual structures.

Cuckolding sociality allows for a range of forbidden desires to be enacted, including queer desires between men and across race and gender, even while it erases the presence and value of black women, who are made outsiders to this triadic dynamic. It is a community practice that is continuously being defined, reworked, and invested in. "Make no mistake though," writes David of *Hot Wife Allie*. "This isn't some kind of small niche within the swinger lifestyle. This kind of interracial action is happening throughout America, in the cities and suburbs. It's a popular fetish, and it's growing."[23] Thus Hot Wife blogs represent a fantasy of a community and lifestyle of cuckolding sociality that is not limited to the realm of pornographic film and video.

The Labor of Mandingo

In 2007 *Details* magazine ran an exposé on the phenomenon of Mandingo parties that garnered a lot of attention from inside and outside the interracial cuckolding community. The article describes journalist Sanjiv Bhattacharya's experiences at a private sex party organized by "Jeff (not his real name)," a forty-year-old "staunch Republican" mortgage broker and self-confessed former bigot from Clearwater, Florida. Brought in to provide the Mandingos is Art Hammer, head of the social network *Florida Mandingos*, webmaster for DarkCavern.com, an interracial swingers' sex website, and a self-identified Mandingo himself.[24] Hammer, an Ivy League–educated former military man in his forties, manages a list of nearly one hundred Mandingos in a company that serves both "upscale interracial swing parties"—described in the article as "Chocolate Parties"—and amateur cuckold porn websites. Describing the requirements to become a Florida Mandingo, Hammer says, "They have to have at least eight inches, and most have a college degree. They have to be able to role-play, and most important of all, they have to be gentlemen."[25] As Hammer describes it, a key skill of the men recruited for his parties is their ability to role-play, that is, to perform the kinds of sexual labor required to fulfill the expectations of his clientele. Aside from their physical endowment, Florida Mandingos must be educated and professional gentlemen. For Hammer, this means that his Mandingos appear nonthreatening to the white couples in the scene. Discretion is key for the upper- and upper-middle-class white couples on the "down low" about their black male fetish: they do not want their friends, neighbors, and colleagues to know what they are up to, and while they want to consume black male sexuality, they do not necessarily want to give up their fantasies about what that sexuality means. "People in this lifestyle are affluent," says Hammer. "I'm talking judges, CEOs, FBI agents, important people—so before they invite a bunch of black men into their homes, they want to know they're safe, they're not going to get robbed, and everyone is discreet. So that's what I provide—a gentleman in the street and a thug in the bedroom."[26] For Hammer, being a Mandingo allows black men to use the preexisting archetype that overdetermines black male sexuality to explore their own interracial desires. In Hammer's estimation, the Mandingo is a disidentificatory performance, one that seeks to work within rather than outside the spaces of racial fetishism.[27]

In highlighting the labor of Mandingo, this *Details* article points to the importance of expanding the category of sex work to include Mandingo swingers, who do not get paid yet perform a form of sexual labor nonetheless. For black male sex workers, including Mandingo swingers, negotiating the tension between perceptions of their embodied threat to whiteness and their own pleasure in taking on the role of Mandingo is critical. Given the lack of research on black male sex workers, especially in the heterosexual marketplace, we are interested in exploring what both casual and professional sex workers have to say about the labor of Mandingo and what it means for their sense of manhood and value as black men.

In light of how reductive, stereotypical, and objectifying the discourse of Mandingo is historically, how do contemporary black men who do the work

of Mandingo "put hypersexuality to work"?[28] In asking this question, we want
to explore how even within the conscripted sexual performance of Mandingo
there is space for black men's agency and pleasure. In demarcating this space,
we do not suggest that the black men themselves overturn violent structures of
representation that overdetermine their sexuality and limit the types of sexual
performances available to them. Rather, what we are interested in is how the
Mandingo archetype as engaged in cuckolding sociality allows a space for black
men to explore their pleasures and desires with the understanding that this desire is always mitigated by history and materiality and thus is framed by white
supremacy. In the Hot Wife blogs discussed above, the excess of Hot Wives'
performative infidelity—which we argue represents a controlled destabilization
of the symbolic power of white womanhood—only materializes through the labor of the black men who participate. Art Hammer suggests that black men who
perform as Mandingo swingers also take pleasure in the fact that their bodies and
performances have the power to defile white womanhood. "The fantasy goes both
ways," Hammer explains. "The women get to fuck our guys while their husbands
watch, and we get to fuck rich white women, really mutt 'em out. It works!"[29] In
this scenario, Hammer contends that the men who appear as Mandingos take
pleasure in the performative labor of defiling white women, in a way reversing
the power dynamic.

There are two possible axes of pleasure around notions of virtuous white womanhood for Mandingo swingers. First, the act of "mutting out" rich white women
challenges the women's claim to virtue by disrupting their raced and classed claims
to sexual purity. Moreover, Mandingo swingers who have sexual experiences
with rich white women gain the embodied knowledge of these women's sexual
similarity to other women, proving that their hierarchal power among women
rests on false claims. Second, in providing these white women with pleasures
that presumably their husbands cannot offer, black men take symbolic ownership of white women's bodies if only ephemerally, embodying a form of power
in relation to white men that reveals the dependency and fragility of white masculine dominance. Through providing their sexual labor, the Mandingos reveal
the instability of white consanguinity and in the process reveal the fissures of the
project of white supremacy.

According to one of Hammer's websites, MandingoMania.com, his Mandingos "specialize in hot, intense, nasty" sex, including "gang bangs," for white
couples.[30] As the words evoke, gang bangs (both straight and gay male) are a
group sex practice that emphasizes the vulnerability of the submissive, often
feminized partner to the demands of a number of more dominant men. Playing the "gang," Mandingos perform the threat of an ominous mob of thuggish
men who aggressively or sometimes violently "bang" married white women in

sight of their husbands. This is just one practice in which black men's brutish sexuality is perceived as a force of contamination of and danger to a pure white womanhood but nonetheless is desired and invited to undermine the very quality of purity, inviolability, and consanguinity that gives meaning to whiteness as a system of power. What we suggest is that cuckolding sociality provides a space for the notion of contamination to be reread not only for its white supremacist heteropatriarchal meanings but for alternative possibilities that ultimately reveal the cracks within those meanings. These fissures include the pleasures in exposing the old myths of the black male rapists as fantasy and revealing a desire by white men for black men's sexual labor.

Damien Decker, a black Swedish escort in his twenties living in New York, describes his experience working with elite white male clients who specifically request him to perform in elaborately designed racial cuckold fantasies:

> They want to see me take a white girl—they want to see normal straight porn. Thug black man, go crazy for white booty, that's me, ravage her. Or they want to see her have sex with me or her pleasuring me. Because she is only with him for money. The husband knows he doesn't really satisfy her. It's like a control device also. People say how can you do that? But at the end of the day, [the clients] are gonna tell me "Run away now, little boy. You are such a pervert, go away and she will stay here with me." I'm like, "Hey, I have a B.A., I speak five languages, I went to boarding school, I play rugby. My relatives work for the United Nations. And my dad is an ex-diplomat." So you know . . . it's kind of like intelligence is not needed for them. I don't have lots of speaking parts.[31]

Decker speaks candidly about the frustrations of enacting a racialized fantasy that black men, regardless of class status or cultural capital, must negotiate. For Decker, a European who does not identify with and indeed pushes back from the figure of the black American thug, these fantasies about black male sexuality reduce black men's sexual labor into its most dehumanized form. Yet Decker attempts to take control of the dehumanizing aspects of his work by reducing it to its transactional components and making clear that he receives a certain amount of pleasure from taking white men's money to perform these sexually prescribed roles. He states:

> I'm for hire, and I don't understand some of these Mandingo guys that they are so willing to be just a walking hard on. They are not paid. I see it like this: "I'm more than just a walking hard on." I feel minimalized by it. I try to exert a bit of control that I have by only doing the things that I like to do. . . . At the end of the day, I try to make sure that the clients know that I'm for hire and not just for fun. That is my control, that he has to give me something or else I won't come.[32]

Decker reconfigures the pleasure principle at work in these transactions. By making it clear that he performs the Mandingo persona for money and not pleasure, Decker attempts to reassert control over an inequitable financial transaction, and one that he notes in the first quote remains defined by the effective control of the white male client. This control by the white client, who fashions the role-play according to his fantasy, also belies a sadomasochistic tendency whereby white women's desire facilitates his ability to homoerotically access the sexuality of black men. Both white women and black men remain in white men's control to possess or cast out, and Decker uses his labor and the boundaries of his professional role as an escort to exact his own measure of control over this relationship. His ability to cancel the performance altogether ultimately controls the play but not the game.

By distancing himself from Mandingos, Decker distinguishes between himself—a paid sex worker—and those who participate in the Mandingo swinger sex parties ostensibly for no financial compensation. We insist that both perform a type of labor that involves deliberate calculations that cannot be divided into pleasure versus profit. Instead, pleasure and profit work together to create the performance, whether that profit is financial or affective. The performance of Mandingo, like all other racialized sexual performances, is heavily imbricated with fantasy and play, which may provide a substantive "compensation" for Mandingos who are not paid financially. Instead, Mandingo swingers may trade on notions of power in ways similar to or at least congruent with the trade of money or other material benefit.

Both black male sex workers and Mandingo swingers, however, participate in a sexual economy built upon notions of black male hypersexuality but in which their labor is feminized and disempowered in relationship to white men. We observe that both employ a form of embodied autonomy or agency that puts to use but also resists the mobile historical meanings of this overburdened eroticism as it is played out in performances with white partners or clients. Finally, both use their performances as sites of labor and pleasure, though in differing ways, that ultimately involve the play of power within these sex acts but also in a broader sense in terms of the stakes of race and sex as currencies of power in society today.

Conclusion

The Mandingo archetype is a historical and material stereotype of black masculine sexuality that permeates contemporary American popular culture. It is therefore unsurprising that elements of the Mandingo fantasy emerge at sites of black masculine sexual performance, including cuckolding pornography and cuckolding sociality. Material functions of white supremacy override the construction and the performance of this type of black masculine sexuality. Yet as Butler reminds us, performance reveals the very constructed nature of the various performative identities enacted.[33] It is within that construction of identity that instability exists. Like E. Patrick Johnson, we understand that racialized performances, in this case enacted in the neomiscegenation drama of (hyper)sexuality, are not mere play and that there are material and, as Frantz Fanon has suggested, psychic consequences to the overriding burden on black men to perform the Mandingo.[34] Yet even as we acknowledge these limitations, we argue that within cuckolding sociality, the roles that each figure—the white man, the white woman, and the black man—is required to play contribute to the simultaneous buttressing and destabilization of white heteropatriarchal supremacy.

The logic of fetishism undergirds much of the relationship between the Mandingo and the white couples who deploy his services, particularly the fetishization of the black men's ejaculate and with it the possibility of racial impurity. Yet we insist that fetishism is not the only relationship that can be read out of the interplay between white couples and black men. In *The Fire Next Time*, James Baldwin argued that the United States could not be free of its racial pathologies until whites were willing to give up being white and in doing so imagine a future that breaks down racial categorizations of being.[35] One productive possibility of cuckolding sociality is that white couples' desire for degeneration and despoliation at the hands of aggressive black men signals a desire for the loss of their white racial identity. In being overcome by black men, white men enact, if only ephemerally, if only in the space of sexual exchange and performance, a loss of control over the sexual choices of white women. If we concede that racial nationalism is built upon the control and manipulation of the sexual choices of the women of that group, particularly its reproductive value, then the fetishization of black men's ejaculate and the threat of black(er) babies may also articulate white desire toward its own demise. Even if we accept that racialized cuckolding sociality further accentuates and hardens racial categories, the ecstasy involved in being overcome by blackness shifts white self-identification significantly. Blackness is not merely something to be possessed or owned; instead, in contemporary manifestations of cuckolding sociality, it becomes something to be *possessed by*. We suggest that the simultaneous desire to possess and be possessed by represents a shift in white self-identification that is also potentially productive and destabilizing.

For the Mandingos themselves, part of the difficulty in finding pleasure in these performances is the tremendous psychic anxiety that must constantly be negotiated, particularly in relationship to performative black masculinity, which is expected to be sexually dominant and in control but must never hold actual control. If white men hold the keys to access of white women's bodies in cuckolding sociality, where is the pleasure for black men? Black escort Damien Decker attempts to manage this anxiety by distinguishing his labor from that of those men who attend the Mandingo parties. We argue that such a distinction, while perhaps of value to Decker's own sense of worth, is not necessarily true of Mandingo swingers. Instead, we suggest, following Art Hammer's description, that Mandingo swingers' pleasure in working within and through the norms of black masculine performance—enjoying the simultaneous feminized position of sexual labor while performing the ultramasculinity required of the Mandingo role—also constitutes labor and payment. This pleasure and labor may be located in the power that is traded between Mandingos and white couples in their performative relationship.

Lastly, by looking at the neomiscegenation drama through the lens of each of the different actors in the triad, we argue that different kinds of pleasures, and thus different kinds of destabilizations, can occur. These are mobile desires whose meanings are unstable, shifting, and contingent. What happens to the sexual foundations of white supremacy when it is clear that white men desire black men? What myths of heteronormativity are destabilized when black men reciprocate that desire? What happens when white women desire transgressive interracial sex outside the bounds and norms of the heteronormative constructs of marriage? What happens when white women use their desires for interracial sex to humiliate their husbands? What if the husbands enjoy their humiliation? What happens when black men enjoy "mutting out" rich white women? What does it mean if these black men are hardly the stereotypes they perform?

The answers to these questions may lie in a reexamination of the Bündchen-James cover with which we began our chapter. While the Mandingo archetype is certainly not new, we argue that the ways in which it is mobilized in interracial sexual communities and industries, including in amateur and professional pornography, social media, escorting, and swingers' parties, provide new opportunities to consider the utility of sexual stereotypes for black people defined by them, as well as for others. The space of homoerotic desire, the interplay of sadomasochism and role-play, the agency and desires of white women, and the agency and desires of black men, all part of the cuckolding sociality nexus, provide space for a reimagination of interracial sex and desire beyond the simple story of violence and sexual expropriation. Looking again at the *Vogue* magazine cover, Tom Brady may be having a good time watching Gisele and LeBron interact, but maybe he's been looking at LeBron all along? Is Gisele Bündchen presenting a fantasy of defiance to strict roles controlling her desires while maintaining her status through her relationship to the figure of Tom Brady? Or is it LeBron who is playing the brute-stud because the role allows him to ultimately make the cover about his work and his pleasure? All of these meanings are possible, as are so many more.

Notes

1. Megan K. Scott, "LeBron James Vogue Cover Criticized for 'Perpetuating Racial Stereotypes,'" *Huffington Post*, April 2, 2008, accessed September 12, 2011, huffingtonpost.com/2008/03/25/lebron-james-vogue-cover-_n_93252.html.

2. Wesley Morris, "Monkey Business, So Is That Vogue Cover Racist or Not," *Slate*, March 31, 2008, accessed September 12, 2011, slate.com/id/2187797/, emphasis ours.

3. Hodes, *White Women, Black Men*, 4.

4. Black activists of the period, most notably Ida B. Wells-Barnett, similarly noted the shift in the representation of black men's sexuality, linking it with economic and political competition between white and black men in the South. See Wells-Barnett, *Southern Horrors*.

5. Richeson, "Sex, Drugs," 104, 209, 105.

6. Writing about the NFL draft, Thomas Oates argues that a history of white supremacy and masculine (hetero)patriarchal competition allows for black men's bodies to be made available for white male sexualized perusal for the purpose of affirming white male supremacy in a society that otherwise proscribes open expressions of same-sex desire ("The Erotic Gaze"). See also duCille, "The Unbearable Darkness"; Hall, *Representation*; Mercer, *Welcome to the Jungle*; Fanon, *Black Skin, White Masks*; McBride, *Why I Hate Abercrombie & Fitch*; Hernton, *Sex and Racism*; Staples, *The Black Family*.

7. McBride, *Why I Hate Abercrombie & Fitch*, 88–131.

8. See, for example, Wells-Barnett, *Southern Horrors*; Hall, *Representation*; and Mercer, *Welcome to the Jungle*.

9. Adrienne D. Davis, "'Don't Let Nobody Bother Yo' Principle': The Sexual Economy of American Slavery," in this volume.

10. See Williams, "Skin Flicks"; Shimizu, *The Hypersexuality of Race*; Fung, "Looking for My Penis"; Nash, *The Black Body in Ecstasy*; and Miller-Young, *A Taste for Brown Sugar*.

11. Miller-Young, *A Taste for Brown Sugar*.

12. According to Ogi Ogas and Sai Gaddam's book *A Billion Wicked Thoughts*, "cuckold porn" is second only to "youth" in heterosexual porn searches online. On cuckolding as a subculture, see Ley, *Insatiable Wives*.

13. We were not able to find mainstream pornographic representations of racial cuckold scenarios with black couples and white men or white couples and black women.

14. *Cherry's 1st Interracial*, YouPorn, August 9, 2008, accessed September 17, 2014, youporn.com/watch/137632/cherrys-1st-interracial/.

15. Though YouPorn offers an option to "tag a pornstar" in videos posted on the site, no black male performers are tagged, and no name is given for the man who sleeps with the cuckoldress anywhere else on the site or in the video.

16. *Bull Breeds Cuckold Cleans*, accessed January 7, 2019, https://xhamster.com/videos/bull-breeds-and-cuckold-cleans-2920509.

17. Breeding themes are common in racial cuckolding community forums, videos, and blogs. An example of the media culture around this theme can be seen in the tumblr blogs BBC-Breeder.tumblr.com. Search categories for breeding themes on Pornhub.com include

"breeding party," "black insemination," "cuckold breeding," "wife bbc creampie," and "interracial breeding."

18. Through the term *neomiscegenation drama* we gesture to how cuckolding sociality reinterprets familiar tropes of racial mixture through this contemporary racialized, sexualized performance.

19. Sara, "Hot Wife Sara: The Mandingo Party," *Hot Wife Allie: The Sexual Adventures of a Very Special Hot Wife and the Blog Musings of Her Very Loving Cuckold Husband*, December 13, 2007, accessed September 17, 2014, hotwivesonline.com/2007/12/13/hot-wife-sara-the-mandingo-party/.

20. David, "What Is a 'Hot Wife'?," *Hot Wife Allie: The Sexual Adventures of a Very Special Hot Wife and the Blog Musings of Her Very Loving Cuckold Husband*, January 16, 2007, accessed September 17, 2014, hotwivesonline.com/hot-wife-and-cuckold-advice/what-is-a-hotwife/.

21. The interracial pornographic website Dark Cavern has a category for Wife Writing, and Wifewriting.com is another pornographic pay site featuring images of amateur performers. Some of these amateur actresses, such as Dee Siren, use the platform of the Hot Wife subculture to launch themselves into professional porn careers. See Coldcoffee.com Productions, Inc., *The Dark Cavern: Interracial Sex at Its Most Hardcore*, 2013, accessed September 17, 2014, darkcavern.com; Dogfart Productions, *Official Wife Writing Site: Amateur Interracial Slut Wives Tagged by Hung Black Cock Studs*, accessed September 17, 2014, wifewriting.com; Dee Siren, MrsSiren.com: Official Site of XXX Star and HOTWIFE Dee Siren, accessed September 17, 2014, mrssiren.com.

22. David, "What Is a 'Hot Wife'?"

23. David, "Details Magazine: Meet the Mandingos," *Hot Wife Allie: The Sexual Adventures of a Very Special Hot Wife and the Blog Musings of Her Very Loving Cuckold Husband*, March 27, 2007, accessed September 17, 2014, hotwivesonline.com/2007/03/27/details-magazine-meet-the-mandingos/.

24. In an interview with VSB.TV, Art Hammer takes on and valorizes the identity of Mandingo, identifying with the strength, virility, and warrior-like quality ascribed to Mandingos in the antebellum South. He argues that while white slaveowners took advantage of enslaved women, plantation wives exploited black men sexually as well. He then contends that modern-day Mandingos "flip the script" and make white women "bend to our needs." Jamal N Tisha, "Hotwife Convention Cuckold Convention Guest Speaker Art Hammer The Original Mandingo Bull," YouTube, May 2, 2014, accessed September 10, 2016, youtube.com/watch?v=dp663x9CDMk.

25. Sanjiv Bhattacharya, "Meet the Mandingos," *Details*, n.d., accessed September 24, 2014, details.com/sex-relationships/sex-and-other-releases/200703/meet-the-mandingos?currentPage=2.

26. Ibid.

27. See Muñoz, *Disidentifications*.

28. See Miller-Young, *A Taste for Brown Sugar*.

29. Ibid.

30. DiCarlo Enterprises, *Mandingo Mania: The Premiere Site for Interracial Porn at Its Hottest*, 2005, accessed September 19, 2014, http://www.mandingomania.com/.

31. Damien Decker, personal interview with the author, March 22, 2010. Decker gave me permission to use his real name. See also Damien Decker, "Diary of a Manhattan Masseur, 2008–2010," accessed September 19, 2014, manhattanmasseur.blogspot.com/?zx =ff8d9430c479963f.

32. Decker, personal interview.

33. Butler, *Gender Trouble*.

34. Johnson, *Appropriating Blackness*; Fanon, *Black Skins, White Masks*.

35. Baldwin, *The Fire Next Time*.

CHAPTER 3

"Hannah Elias Talks Freely"

Interracial Sex and Black Female Subjectivity in Turn-of-the-Century New York City

Cheryl D. Hicks

I was born in Philadelphia. I had a little trouble their [*sic*] before I left. I have given birth in my life to three or four children, and the fathers of these children were not my husbands. I was at one time, I think, sent to jail from here [New York].

—*Platt v. Elias*

This man John R. Platt has been supporting me for 20 years and there was never any fuss about it until this time. I am not worrying[;] I have not done anything wrong and I have nothing to fear.

—"Elias Woman in Jail! Police Smash in Doors with Axes"

The 1905 *San Francisco Call* headline "Hannah Elias Talks Freely" typifies the publicity that turned a New York City extortion case into a national scandal. White businessman John R. Platt claimed that black homeowner Hannah Elias had blackmailed him for over $685,000.[1] He argued that from 1896 to 1903 he deposited large sums of money into her bank accounts: $19,075 in 1896, for example, and $186,409 in 1903.[2] While the charges leveled against Elias alleged criminal activity, the court testimony revealed the contours of a consensual sixteen-year rather than eight-year sexual relationship. Influenced by the court proceedings, the tone of the *Call*'s article implied Elias's culpability by emphasizing her questionable background and her apparently undeserved receipt of riches: "It was an extraordinary tale of sudden elevation from the lowest and most vicious surroundings to a position of affluence, where money was rained upon her and where she had everything that great wealth could provide."[3] Indeed, Elias's vocal self-defense and determination to "talk ... freely," as the two quotes above illustrate, troubled the *Call*'s racial and Victorian sensibilities. Instead of dealing with the fact that a black woman profited from her sexual relationship with a wealthy married white man, the press and court officials used the stock image of the sexually deviant black woman prevalent in popular culture and white society to contend that she threatened Platt with public exposure after he was "induced by" her "to have illicit intercourse."[4] Elias, however, challenged this public narrative by dismissing the age-old assumption that this represented the "case of an old man tricked by an unscrupulous woman."[5] The press, shocked by the fact that Elias "made no attempt to cover the details of her early life," insisting that "she had nothing to conceal and ... that every dollar that Platt gave her had been given voluntarily," recorded and published what it understood to be the sordid details of the affair with disdain.[6] Her unapologetic revelations about her "low life" as a working-class, sometimes poor woman, recidivist, sex worker, entrepreneur, and mistress provide a unique opportunity to explore how one turn-of-the-twentieth-century black woman publicly framed the story of her sexual behavior. Indeed, her testimonies reveal how sexual labor could simultaneously produce erotic and nonerotic pleasure.

What might we learn from the fact that Elias's court defense compelled her to be vocal rather than silent about her consensual interracial sexual relationship? She was not a blues woman whose illicit lyrics provided insight into black urban sexuality.[7] She was not a church member or clubwoman striving to achieve traditional Victorian purity standards or respectability.[8] The extortion charges against her made dissemblance impossible, as she had to talk freely about her relationship with Platt to defend herself.[9] Her public voice, straightforward and uncompromising, provides a glimpse into a black woman's inner life, especially her complicated experience as a sexual being—her sexual subjectivity. Hannah Elias offers a lens through which we can examine black women's "power for sexual choice, autonomy" and "freedom."[10] Her choice to participate in and profit from the sex economy illustrates how she negotiated her material ambitions and erotic desires. Her story connects with the growing black sexual economies' scholarship by focusing on excavating the pleasure rather than simply illustrating the pain in histories of black women's sexuality.[11] Consider, for instance, feminist scholar Jennifer Nash's critical question: "What if pleasure were understood at its broadest as a *good*, fundamentally linked to subjectivity, and experienced in a multiplicity of ways, including those that were not sexual?"[12] This chapter demonstrates how Elias's sexual labor provided her with the opportunity to experience pleasure (sexual and nonsexual) amid myriad challenges in turn-of-the-century New York City; moreover, it showcases how black responses to Elias's sex scandal reveal the range of black thought and activism.

Elias's testimonies, in court and in the press, provide an opportunity to explore one black woman's self-presentation and self-commodification alongside scholars' arguments regarding silences, exploitation, and oppression. Although not representative of all black women, her unique story captures the social and economic challenges that poor and working-class black women faced overall. Unlike Elias, most black sex workers, as Cynthia Blair's scholarship shows, did not always "prosper" from their "sexual labors" and left little evidence of how they understood their participation in the sex economy.[13] Elias's words and case, however, offer a chance to address the thought-provoking questions posed by feminist scholar Kimberly Springer: "What historically have U.S. black women had to say about their own sexuality?" and "What have been the sociopolitical reactions to an articulation of black female sexuality?"[14] Characterized as simultaneously immoral, dangerous, and a pawn in the racialized sex marketplace, Elias either dismissed or manipulated these labels as she defined her own sexual subjectivity. A number of New Yorkers, black as well as white, suspected that Elias was guilty of extorting John R. Platt because she had begun her relationship with Platt as a sex worker and eventually became his mistress. He claimed that she was "a woman of bad character and reputation, and . . . [had], for some years past, been consorting with disreputable characters."[15] Elias, however, denied not only the extortion charges but also Platt's insults. She insisted that she had "not done anything wrong" and that Platt "voluntarily cohabited with" and "maintained" her.[16] In order to prove that Platt had willingly engaged in their relationship and supported her financially rather than being blackmailed into paying her, Elias understood that she needed to reveal the trajectory of their intimate liaisons. She also claimed that she was not only Platt's mistress but also his friend. In doing so, she used her voice to define her own experience by revising the narrative that might define her as a predator or victim and stated plainly the reality of her relationship with Platt.

Elias's "Low Life"

Elias's early life suggests that her materialistic aspirations never quite coincided with those of her occasionally impoverished but respectable family in mid-nineteenth-century Philadelphia. Born in 1865 to Charles and Eliza Elias, she was one of nine children; she and her twin, David, were the family's third set of twins. The press emphasized the racial mixture of her parentage, describing her mother as "mulatto" and her father as of "Indian and negro blood." "From her father, she inherited large black eyes and a clever temperament; from her mother a certain sort of beauty and very light skin."[17] When reporters who hoped to uncover tawdry details of Elias's early life interviewed her neighbors from the old neighborhood, Elias was remembered as a "precocious" girl.[18] As a teenager, she was a "pretty girl with smooth, dark hair" and had "features in which the negro blood appeared, to be sure, but not obtrusive."[19] Much like her parents and siblings, Elias experienced situations in which her fair skin created ambiguity regarding her blackness. In 1880, for example, US census takers noted that the fourteen-year-old Elias was a mulatto when it recorded her at work as a domestic servant but defined her as black when listing her with her own family (she and her family were categorized as mulatto in 1870).[20] In her youth she was known for her beauty and "perfect figure" and reveled in ideas of a better life that included "a love for fine clothes."[21] For instance, Elias reportedly said to her sisters that "times will change, and I won't always be washing dishes."[22] In 1885 her desire to adorn her working-class body with beautiful clothing, or, as one newspaper noted, to "gratify her desire to shine," led to her incarceration in Philadelphia's Moyamensing Prison after she stole a "splendid brocaded frock" from her employer in order to appear well-dressed at her older sister Hattie's wedding.[23] Although the Elias family experienced indigence intermittently, which led to her employment as a domestic, it seemed that rather than pilfering the dress because of abject poverty, Elias sought the attention and pleasure she believed wearing such a garment would bring.

Elias's testimony corroborates many of the mainstream press's opinions regarding her early "low life"; she acknowledged that she had "a little trouble" in Philadelphia.[24] Her life was radically altered upon her release from three months' incarceration. She may have chosen not to return to her family, but the press contended that she found "the door of her father's house shut against her."[25] Alone and poor, Elias may have also decided to use her erotic capital in order to benefit from the fetishization of black women of mixed ancestry in Philadelphia's sex trade. Concerned about her welfare, her twin brother, David, and his friend Frank Satterfield searched for and eventually found her at a "resort for colored women," which their "combined pleadings impelled her to leave."[26] Instead of moving in with her brother, who probably still lived with their family, she moved in with Satterfield, with whom she developed a relationship. She became pregnant, but they were too poor to care for the child, so in 1886 Elias gave birth to a daughter in the Blockley Almshouse.[27] Subsequently, she gave the child to a local couple whose own child had died "a few days before." (Others later alleged that she abandoned the baby.)[28] Nearly a year later she again became pregnant and claimed that Satterfield was the father. He questioned his paternity, and when he thought "matters were getting a little uncomfortable" he moved to New York City.[29] In her eighth month of pregnancy, claiming that he deserted her, Elias followed Satterfield to the city, demanding that he take financial responsibility for the child. After an argument outside his workplace, they were both arrested. Satterfield was granted an adjournment and later presented the court with evidence that Elias was a prostitute by submitting an affidavit from a fellow black porter named Arthur

Gale. Gale stated that he had known Elias for ten years in Philadelphia, that she was a "common woman," and that he met her in the house of a known madam. The charges against Satterfield were dropped, but Elias was incarcerated for thirty days in Blackwell's Island for disorderly conduct.[30] A month later, in 1887, she gave birth to a son in a public institution for New York's destitute black residents, the Colored Home and Hospital.[31] Eventually, she returned to Philadelphia with her son, but he died seven weeks later.[32] At the age of twenty-two, Elias might well have agreed that she had experienced a "low life": she had briefly been in Philadelphia's sex trade; she had been imprisoned in two states; she had given up her first child, and her second child had died less than two months after his birth, because Elias had not received adequate financial or emotional support from the children's father; she was estranged from her family; and she had achieved nothing but poverty. Yet she began to make choices based on her material and financial aspirations as well as her youthful beauty that changed the trajectory of her life. She returned to New York City and may have been a streetwalker before meeting a wealthy married sixty-seven-year-old white retired glass manufacturer, John R. Platt, who sought out the sexual services of women of color. Initially, he was her customer, but ultimately they developed an open-ended relationship. When Platt later charged her with extortion, she downplayed her sexual labor during their relationship and argued that she was his "mistress and friend."[33]

"Mistress and Friend"

By the time Elias and Platt met in 1888, chattel slavery had been illegal in New York State for sixty years, but the legacy of enslavement directly shaped the dynamics of their relationship and influenced the everyday political, economic, and social interactions of black and white New Yorkers. In 1904, at the beginning of the first trial in the case of *Platt v. Elias*, the city was grappling with racial tensions that were inflamed by the ideology of white supremacy, the myth of black inferiority, and the explosive implications of interracial sex.[34] Platt's initial interest in Elias resembled what scholars have defined as the "fancy trade," in which enslaved women chosen for their "grace, beauty, and light skins" were purchased specifically for prostitution as well as concubinage.[35] In fact, Elias remembered that early in their relationship Platt called her "Irene" because he believed she "looked like a girl he kept down South when he went to Florida."[36] According to Elias, she had met Platt on the street in New York's black Tenderloin district, and he told her to meet him at French Madame's, an assignation house. Elias testified that "they stayed there about two hours," and she consented to his inspection of her body, recalling that they did not have sex, but "he asked me to undress and show him my shape and I did so." When he requested that she meet him the next day at "eleven o'clock," she agreed.[37] Their second encounter lasted three hours. He told her she was a "very nice girl," they had "intimate relations," and he gave her $500 "to get some clothes." According to her memory of these meetings, which happened sixteen years earlier, Platt told her that he desired to "keep me for himself."[38] He advised her to move out of her furnished room and live at Pop Miller's business, which she described as an "assignation house" that provided "colored girls for white men"; there Elias and other women also "danced the can-can for the amusement" of Platt, his friends, and other customers.[39]

Hannah Elias's poverty and social isolation compelled her to begin and maintain her relationship with the millionaire Platt. We might even see her position as similar to that of enslaved black women who were forced into being "sexual commodities" by powerful white men.[40] But if we listen to Elias as she "talks freely," it is clear that she made choices different from those of other women, and we must seriously consider what she said about her own experience. Inspecting her body and approving of what he saw, Platt "assigned economic value directly to" Elias's "sexual attractiveness" when he gave her $500 for clothes so that she would continue to meet him.[41] Yet she also consented to the transaction by showing up a second time and having "intimate relations with" Platt.[42] When he suggested that he wanted to "keep" Elias "for himself," a number of factors influenced how she assessed the benefits of being kept. His quasi-bodily possession of Elias not only highlights how he saw her as a sexual commodity that satisfied his racialized desire but also illustrates the fact that, unlike enslaved women, Elias had the ability to either consent to his acting on that desire or refuse his request. Her sexual-economic agreement meant that she successfully used her erotic capital to access pleasure in myriad ways: in the intimacy she experienced in relationships with Platt and other men; the ability to purchase material possessions like jewelry, clothing, and her first home; and the ability to protect herself and her subsequent children from poverty and the indignities of racism.

Elias contended that as their relationship developed, she shifted from being a sex worker to being Platt's mistress. For the first two years, Platt paid $30 a week for her rent at Pop Miller's and gave her between "200" and "1,000" to spend or save. Elias recalled that she would "make the girls in the house presents," "get nice things" for herself, and "put some of it in the savings bank." Elias moved several times after leaving Pop Miller's, and when Platt was in town he visited her "three or four times a week." Her encounters with Platt included kissing, fondling, and "intimate relations." Elias remembered that initially "he never ate dinners there, but light cheese, ham, crackers, and a little lunch" and left before five o'clock. Later he stayed over infrequently.[43] Her accounts suggest that Platt began to see her as more than a sexual commodity and that she found pleasure in his company: "He was very loving to me, and I was very loving with Mr. Platt. . . . We never had any disputes or disagreements."[44] In fact, six months after becoming a widower in 1893, Platt gave Elias his wife's watch and pocketbook. She repeatedly emphasized that she never wanted their relationship exposed, because "Mr. Platt had been very good" to her.[45] "He told me that he always had a warm feeling in his heart for me ... and he would do anything for me; always gave me advice about keeping my-self nice, and a house in a nice, quiet neighborhood."[46] Yet Elias's account of their developing "friendship" also revealed how these intimate sexual acts constituted labor that was consistently compensated in a way that placed her mistress status on a type of continuum of sex work. Platt's behavior never changed, even after his wife's death, as he worked to keep their relationship viable, secret, and isolated from white and black New Yorkers.

Elias did not give up her relationship with Platt after she met a black porter named Matthew Davis, even though they married in 1895. She testified that after her marriage she still "had intimate relations with Mr. Platt" and received money from him with her "husband's full knowledge."[47] This decision might simultane-ously illustrate that Elias did not confuse her relationship with Platt with love, nor did she believe that their arrangement demanded monogamy. Moreover, she distinguished between her sexual labor with Platt and her personal life. She also revealed her experience with domestic violence: "I told Mr. Platt that my husband kicked me in the stomach and beat me, and he broke a plate glass at the vestibule door."[48] Whether or not Davis abused Elias because of her affair, he eventually sought legal counsel to address her infidelity. Davis allegedly filed a case against Platt based on "alienation of affection," and Platt provided Elias with $500 to pay her husband off.[49] In fact, she contended that Platt told her that if she got a divorce, "he would make" her "a present of a house."[50]

After her 1897 divorce, Platt emphasized his desire to make Elias a secluded and kept woman. When she separated from her husband a year earlier, Platt helped her purchase a home (for $13,500) on West 53rd Street, which she ran as a boarding-house. Platt, however, continually told Elias that he was concerned about having to navigate her black neighborhood and that "he wanted" her "to get out of the neighborhood because it was objectionable there on account of so many colored people being in the street."[51] One of Elias's black boarders, Cornelius Williams, remembered an altercation when Platt visited her. As he was leaving the house one evening, Williams opened the door for "an old man" who intended to call on Elias. Williams "got mad at . . . [Platt's] style and talked ugly to him" and then "slammed the door in . . . [Platt's] face." Later, the black man tried to take a good look at Platt and was told erroneously by a servant that Elias's visitor was named Green. (Williams would later believe that Platt was Andrew H. Green.)[52] In 1898 Platt bought Elias another house on West 68th Street for $35,000. A year later she moved to Central Park West to a house that cost $45,000.[53]

The move from the black neighborhood estranged Elias from other black people and seemed to suggest that she herself was not black. In turn-of-the-century New York City, which was affected by surges in immigration from eastern and southern Europe as well as the Spanish-American War and the US attempt to build an empire in Cuba and Puerto Rico, the racial designation of either white (meaning Anglo-Saxon) or black failed to apply to most urban residents.[54] Thus, when Elias's wealthy Central Park West white neighbors believed that she was "either Cuban or an East Indian woman or of some Oriental race" rather than an African American they were attempting to decipher an increasingly confusing matrix of race, ethnicity, and class.[55] Her apparent wealth insulated her from further queries about her racial identity and why Platt, "her counselor," visited her home so regularly.[56] Indeed, Platt's attempt to keep her for himself benefited Elias too. Paying off her husband protected her from domestic violence, and buying her a boardinghouse and financing her move to several white neighborhoods shielded her from poverty. From Platt's perspective, however, her marriage and entrepreneurial presence within the Tenderloin constituted impediments to his having full, uncomplicated access to Elias. Providing her the money to buy homes in her own name protected him from public exposure for almost five years.

The Platt-Elias Scandal

The Platt-Elias affair became public knowledge because of the 1903 murder of eighty-three-year-old Andrew H. Green. Green played a central role in the consolidation of New York and Brooklyn in 1898. He was the executor of Governor Samuel J. Tilden's estate, which resulted in the New York Public Library, and he helped to plan Central Park.[57] There is no evidence that Green, affectionately called the "father of Greater New York," knew Elias or Platt. On November 13 Green encountered Elias's former black lodger, Cornelius Williams, who mistook the older white man for Platt. Williams argued with Green about a woman named Bessie Davis, and when he believed Green summarily dismissed him, Williams responded by fatally shooting the beloved New Yorker.[58] After a neighborhood investigation, the black woman called Bessie Davis was revealed to be Hannah Elias.

For six months, many New Yorkers wondered what connection the "Father of New York" had with a black woman. When Platt's family discovered his affair and strongly encouraged him to take Elias to court in May 1904 for blackmail, investigators realized that Williams had murdered the wrong man. John R. Platt, who had a striking resemblance to Green, was the actual target and consistent visitor to Elias's home. By the time Cornelius Williams was boarding with Elias in 1896 in New York's heavily black Tenderloin district, Elias and Platt had been in an open-ended sexual and financial relationship for eight years. By 1903, when

Green was murdered, Elias had been living in Central Park West for at least four years. One white neighbor explained, "I do not know much about my next door neighbor but until now I always believed her to be perfectly respectable. So far as we know she has always conducted her household in a perfectly orderly manner."[59] Indeed, most white New Yorkers could only imagine a nonblack woman owning four homes and employing a vast array of immigrant servants, "including a French maid, a Chinese cook, an English coachman, and a Japanese butler."[60]

After Platt filed suit against her, Elias knew that in order to keep her money and real estate holdings from being returned to Platt's family she had to speak for and defend herself. First, she absolved herself of Green's death by declaring that she did not know him and that she was "exceedingly sorry that he met so untimely a fate through the fault of another man."[61] Although she had remained silent about their relationship until Platt's filing, she knew that a black woman who had benefited financially from an interracial affair could not claim victim status. As a kept woman for close to twenty years, she would never be seen as respectable. She understood that, rather than scrutinizing the actions of a wealthy married white man who sought the company of and possibly manipulated a much younger vulnerable woman, the public would impose its stereotypes of criminality and promiscuity on her as a black woman. Yet in the first of three trials, Platt was his own worst witness, appearing confused, forgetting key information, and, most importantly, refusing to accuse Elias of being an extortionist. With no convincing evidence against her, Elias was acquitted. After the first trial, she reframed the narrative by stressing that she pitied Platt for being manipulated by his family: "I do not blame the poor man at all. I know that he was forced to bring the suit against me, and that he had no choice left him in the matter of swearing out the warrant for my arrest. . . . I felt very sorry for him while he was on the witness stand." Yet she continued to stress her innocence: "I never did anything wrong in taking the money which he gave me. It is all nonsense to talk of my having blackmailed him, as he plainly showed himself this afternoon when he refused to say that I had extorted any money from him by threats."[62] Elias portrayed herself as a friendly mistress who received extravagant gifts rather than an unscrupulous woman resorting to blackmail. While the criminal case was dismissed, Elias knew that she needed to tell her story in order to prevail, especially when she faced two more civil cases. The nation seemed captured by the scandal, especially African Americans.

Black residents and community leaders through the mainstream and black press publicly stated how they believed Elias's individual predicament had far-ranging implications for the race overall. Some deemed Elias a race traitor whose immoral behavior negatively influenced racial advancement because her case obscured the critical problems of employment and housing discrimination that respectable working-class and poor black New Yorkers faced on a daily basis. The Reverend Charles S. Morris's letter to the editor of the *New York Times* published on June 14, 1904, reinforced the impression that no matter how badly Elias was treated during her arrest and trial, black New Yorkers had more pressing concerns than supporting a woman with supposedly over half a million dollars in at least fourteen different banks. In response to the press's preoccupation with Elias's racial identity, Morris suggested that her immoral actions were more reflective of white rather than black culture. "In view of the fact that this woman is an octoroon—seven-eighths white—in view of her having divorced her colored husband and abandoned her colored child and lived among white people for years, it is hardly just or fair in her hour of exposure and calamity to brand her a 'negress.'" Emphasizing the irrationality of the 1896 *Plessy v. Ferguson* decision's attempt to define race while responding to white New Yorkers' racism, he posed the provocative question: If "blood will tell, which blood tells in her case—the one-eighth or the seven-eighths?" Finally, he dismissed Elias's case by emphasizing, "We have neither sympathy nor money to waste on a woman of this stamp."[63]

Although Elias's wealth compelled the public—black and white—to view the scandal through their own moral lens, it also allowed her to take less seriously the Victorian mores of the day and provided her a level of protection that she failed to attain before entering the sex trade and meeting Platt. She could dismiss Reverend Morris's critique of her actions because her choices provided her with opportunities that respectable but unrelenting poverty could not. While Morris castigated her for multiple infractions, she might have viewed her life quite differently: passing for nonblack, she might argue, was a reasonable response to white people's inability to implement the irrational dictates of racial segregation; divorcing her abusive husband strengthened her financial relationship with Platt; giving up her child meant that someone else could give her a better life. Her wealth provided her with the opportunity to be an entrepreneur as well as a property owner and served as a buffer against the many challenges that Morris argued black New Yorkers faced in turn-of-the-century America.

Even more importantly, as a thirty-nine-year-old black woman who faced difficult decisions with her first two children in her youth, Elias used her wealth to protect her two younger children, who she suggested were fathered by Platt: one was born in October 1902 but died five months later, and another was born in April 1904. When jailed on the extortion charge, Elias exposed the injustice involved: "I left a six weeks old baby at home but she is being well cared for. . . . I have left plenty for the baby and I feel she will be all right."[64] Indeed, Elias could protect and care for her child in ways that had been impossible earlier in her life. Yet Elias seemed to reject reconnecting with her first child, who, with her adoptive father, Travis Hudson, contacted her in order to ask for money. Elias contended that the young woman was not her child, while Hudson responded angrily, "It is no more right for Hannah Elias to pay me something for what I have laid out on the care and education of her daughter. When she gave the child to me seventeen years ago she was poor and friendless. Now that she is rich she ought to remember who took her baby in."[65] Hudson's anger at and Morris's dismissal of Elias, however, captured only a portion of black responses to the scandal.

Instead of avoiding the case, black people's local and national responses also showed how they used the case to protest racial discrimination overall. Despite the criticisms about Elias's passing and sexual behavior, their responses consistently referenced how the stigma of blackness shaped Elias's experiences with the criminal justice system. Unlike Morris, black people believed Elias was a "negress."[66] They belittled white New Yorkers for their inability to identify blackness. A 1904 editorial in the *Colored American* joked, "Shrewd colored people who play under the guise of Cuban, Hawaiian, Spanish, and the like, are giving gullible white people a run for their money."[67] Police officers breaking down Elias's front door with axes for a midnight home arrest and her exorbitant bail alarmed black leaders and residents who saw their protest for Elias consistent with their demands for equitable treatment from the legal system for all black New Yorkers. An editorial in the *Appeal,* published in St. Paul, Minnesota, noted that if Elias had been white, the case would have less attention, and because she did have "an infinitesimal portion of African blood in her composition," she was "languishing in jail in lieu of $30,000 bail."[68] Even Clara Hudson, the wife of the angry Travis Hudson, commented on the case from a fiscal rather than a moral perspective. Hudson's comment in the *Evening Bulletin* berated Platt, not Elias, for reneging on the economic terms of their working relationship, which would have been a concern of working-class and poor blacks with white employers: "So far as Mrs. Elias is concerned the whole trouble now is that she is a black woman and the old man who is troubling her is a white man. He doesn't deserve one penny of the money the black woman has. He thought enough of her to give what he did, and now he wants it back. He is like a good many other white men, and I believe that most people feel he should not get a cent back."[69] These distinct examples regarding the hypocrisy of the *Plessy* decision, the corrupt criminal justice system, and the contested nature of interracial labor agreements indicate how the concerns raised through Elias's case represent the complex ways that black protest might be revealed through the sentiments of everyday people as well as established black leaders. Ultimately, the courts reinforced their sentiment that Elias was innocent. She won all three cases and retained her wealth.

Focusing on how Hannah Elias talked freely about her sexual behavior in turn-of-the-century New York City and the varied black responses to her case reveals different perspectives on the significance of black women's sexuality. Elias was unrepentant about her sexual behavior, and her fight to defend herself against extortion charges forced her to expose her sexual choices. Consistently, she argued that she had "not done anything wrong."[70] Based on her testimonies, Elias understood her sexual labor as an effective alternative path to self-sufficiency and economic advancement. Exploring Elias through the lens of the black sexual economy scholarship allows for a perspective that acknowledges how Elias not only profited financially from her sexual labor but also experienced (sexual and nonsexual) pleasure. She used her relationship with Platt to fulfill her desire for intimacy, sex, security, and the freedom to enjoy her life. The black reactions to Elias's self-presentation varied and reveal the distinctiveness in how black people understood the case's larger political implications. Some African Americans argued that focusing on this sex scandal was a moral liability that obscured the practical everyday concerns of black folk. Other black people contended that this case was important because many of the issues Elias faced, in spite of her wealth, mirrored their own struggles with racial discrimination in the urban North. Engaging Elias's humanity through her sexual subjectivity offers a different way to think about her and other black women's experiences, as historian Kali Gross suggests, with "depression and joy, with desire and love, as well as contempt and rage."[71]

Notes

1. "Hannah Elias Talks Freely," *San Francisco Call*, January 19, 1905.

2. "Platt's Own Story: Why He Gave Hannah Elias Nearly $700,000," *Evening Sun*, June 1, 1904, New York County District Attorney Scrapbooks, Municipal Archives, vol. 231 (October 24, 1903–December 16, 1903) to vol. 237 (July 11, 1904–November 1, 1904), reel 32 (hereafter cited as DA 32).

3. "Hannah Elias Talks Freely."

4. See 101 A.D. 518; 91 N.Y.S. 1079; 1905 N.Y. App. Div. LEXIS 400 (February 1905, decided), 2.

5. "Hannah Elias, Adventuress, Her Life Story," *New York World*, June 2, 1904.

6. "Hannah Elias Talks Freely."

7. Carby, "'It Jus Be's Dat Way Sometime': The Sexual Politics of Black Women's Blues," in DuBois and Ruiz, *Unequal Sisters*.

8. Higginbotham, *Righteous Discontent*, 185–229.

9. Hine, "Rape and the Inner Lives of Black Women in the Middle West."

10. Miller-Young, "Hip-Hop Honeys," 278.

11. See Miller-Young, *A Taste for Brown Sugar*, 16–17; Nash, *The Black Body in Ecstasy*; Chude-Sokei et al., "Race, Pornography, and Desire," 50, 53–54, 60–61.

12. Nash, "Theorizing Pleasure," 514.

13. Blair, *I've Got to Make My Livin'*, 2, 10.

14. Springer, "Policing Black Women's Sexual Expression."

15. Platt v. Elias, 186 N.Y. 374 (1906, vol. 73), page 35, in series J2002-82A, Court of Appeals, cases and briefs on appeal (box 413), New York State Archives, 11A36 Cultural Education Center, Albany, NY.

16. "Hannah Elias Talks Freely," 12; *Platt*, 186 N.Y. 36.

17. "Her Strange Career from the Almshouse to Barbaric Luxury," *Evening Sun*, June 4, 1904, DA 32.

18. "Rich Hannah Elias Once in Poorhouse," *New York World*, Saturday evening, November 21, 1903.

19. "Her Strange Career."

20. See 1880 U.S. Census, Philadelphia, Pennsylvania, Hannah Elias, Mulatto, page 5, Enumeration District No. 122, June 2, 1880, Ancestry.com, https://search.ancestry.com/cgi-bin/ sse.dll?indiv=1&dbid=6742&h=305738&tid=&pid=&usePUB=true&_phsrc=tgp3&_phstart =successSource; 1880 U.S. Census, Philadelphia, Pennsylvania, Hannah Elias, Black, page 22, Enumeration District No. 130, June 1880 (all family members noted with a "B" for Black), Ancestry.com, https://search.ancestry.com/cgi-bin/sse.dll?indiv=1&dbid=6742&h=297641 &tid=&pid=&usePUB=true&_phsrc=tgp5&_phstart=successSource; 1870 U.S. Census, Philadelphia Ward District 13, Philadelphia, Pennsylvania, pages 91–92, June 21, 1870 (all family members noted with an "M" for Mulatto), Ancestry.com, https://www.ancestry.com/interactive/ 7163/4278573_00460?pid=8806893&backurl=https://search.ancestry.com/cgi-bin/sse.dll ?indiv%3D1%26dbid%3D7163%26h%3D8806893%26tid%3D%26pid%3D%26usePUB%3D true%26_phsrc%3Dtgp7%26_phstart%3DsuccessSource&treeid=&personid=&hintid=&use PUB=true&_phsrc=tgp7&_phstart=successSource&usePUBJs=true.

21. "Rich Hannah Elias."

22. "Her Strange Career."

23. "Rich Hannah Elias"; "Her Strange Career."

24. *Platt*, 186 N.Y. 277.

25. "Rich Hannah Elias."

26. Ibid.

27. Ibid.

28. "Her Strange Career."

29. *Platt*, 186 N.Y. 235.

30. "Rich Hannah Elias."

31. State of New York, City of New York, Birth Return, Frank Elias, October 26, 1887, #504665, New York City Municipal Archives. She named Frank Satterfield as the father and stated that he was a twenty-six-year-old porter who was born in New York.

32. L. H. Elias, December 19, 1887, Philadelphia, Pennsylvania, Death Certificates Index, 1803–1915, City Archives, Philadelphia.

33. *Platt*, 186 N.Y. 36; "Negress Admits Platt Gave Her Thousands," *New York Times*, January 19, 1905.

34. Other scholars have used the case to address issues of race, sex, power, and the law. See Wilks, "Life, Liberty, and the Pursuit of Capital."

35. Adrienne Davis, "'Don't Let Nobody Bother Yo' Principle': The Sexual Economy of American Slavery," in this volume.

36. *Platt*, 186 N.Y. 260.

37. Ibid., 259, 280–81.

38. Ibid., 259, 281.

39. Ibid., 259, 282.

40. Davis in this volume.

41. Ibid.

42. *Platt*, 186 N.Y. 281.

43. Ibid., 274.

44. Ibid., 272.

45. Ibid., 275.

46. Ibid., 274.

47. Ibid., 286.

48. Ibid., 270.

49. Ibid., 211–12.

50. Ibid., 262.

51. Ibid., 11, 264.

52. "The Murderer's Mistake," *New York Times*, June 2, 1904.

53. *Platt*, 186 N.Y. 15–17.

54. See Jacobsen, *Whiteness of a Different Color*.

55. "Jerome to Question Mrs. Elias," New York newspaper, ca. 1903, item 122, no. 21, Hampton University Newsclipping File.

56. *Platt*, 186 N.Y. 275.

57. "Negro Kills Andrew H. Green," *New York Tribune*, November 14, 1903; "Mr. Green, the Good Citizen," *New York Sun*, November 14, 1903.

58. "A. H. Green Murdered," *New York Sun*, November 14, 1903.

59. *New York Tribune*, November 15, 1903.

60. "Public Funeral of Mr. Green," *New York Sun*, November 15, 1903.

61. "Hannah Elias Free; Pities J. R. Platt," *Public Ledger*, June 11, 1904.

62. Ibid.

63. "Race Question in New York: A Negro Pastor's Recital of the Wrongs of His People," *New York Times*, June 14, 1904.

64. "Elias Woman in Jail! Police Smash in Doors with Axes," *New York American*, June 8, 1904, DA 32.

65. "Mrs. Elias Locks Out Her Daughter," *New York World*, November 23, 1903, 2.

66. "Has Letter Accusing Three!," *New York American*, June 10, 1904, DA 32; "Former Counsel Would Tell of Hannah Elias," *New York Times*, June 10, 1904.

67. "The National Association of Women," *Colored American*, July 23, 1904.

68. *Appeal* (St. Paul, MN), June 11, 1904.

69. "Daughter after Mrs. Elias," *Evening Bulletin*, June 5, 1904.

70. "Elias Woman in Jail!"

71. Gross, *Hannah Mary Tabbs*, 5.

CHAPTER 4

Playin' Race

Race Play, Black Women, and BDSM

Ariane Cruz

Alone in the darkness of my quarters my mind is reliving the scene of a few nights ago. I can feel my Mistress's body beneath me. I can feel her voice, raspy and sexual, in my ear. "Fuck, Niggah. That's what I bought you for." With little if any mechanical aid I cum. My orgasm is sudden, and powerful. For a brief second I am exhausted and happy. But in only a moment there is a little voice creeping into the back of my consciousness (You shouldn't be turned on to the word NIGGER).

—Viola Johnson, "Playing with Racial Stereotypes The Love That Dare Not Speak Its Name" (1994)

I have been the meaning of rape
I have been the problem everyone seeks to
eliminate by forced
penetrations with or without the evidence of slime

—June Jordan, *Poem about My Rights* (1989)

The Evidence of Slime

A type of slime itself, slavery and its legacies remain an active marketplace for the production, performance, and representation of black female sexuality.[1] Black feminist scholars have theorized the impact of chattel slavery and the pervasive rape of black female slaves on modern constructions and representations of black women and, in turn, worked to dismantle what Darlene Clark Hine terms the *culture of dissemblance*, the politics of silence shrouding expressions of black female sexuality.[2] While the antebellum legacy of sexual violence on black women is substantive, what we have not effectively considered is how black women deliberately employ the shadows of slavery in the deliverance and/or receiving of sexual pleasure. That is, how the *evidence of slime*—a staining sludge of pain and violence—becomes a type of lubricant to stimulate sexual fantasies, access pleasure, and heighten desire. In this essay I explore how black women facilitate a complex and contradictory negotiation of pain, pleasure, and power in their performances in the fetish realm of race play, a BDSM practice that explicitly uses race to script power exchange and the dynamics of domination and submission.[3] Most commonly an interracial erotic play, it often involves the exchange of racist language, role-playing, and the construction of racist scenes.

I argue that BDSM is a critical site from which to reimagine the formative links between black female sexuality and violence. I am interested in staging the unique theoretical and practical challenges, hinged upon the unspeakable pleasure aroused in racial submission and domination, that race play presents to black women. Eroticizing not just racism but the miscegenation taboo, racial difference, and (hyper)racialization itself, race play is a controversial and contradictory act in BDSM communities and beyond. I examine race play as a particularly problematic yet powerful practice for black women that illuminates the fraught dynamics of racialized pleasure and power via the eroticization of racism and racial sexual alterity.[4] Using textual analysis, archival research, and interviews, I reveal how violence becomes not just a vehicle of pleasure but also a mode of accessing and critiquing power.[5] BDSM—as a set of practices in which violence, pleasure, and power intermingle—becomes a fertile site from which to consider the complexity and diverseness of black women's sexual practice and the mutability of black female sexuality. Informed by a critical genealogy of scholars who study performance as a site of the entangled identities of race, sexuality, and gender, I am interested in not just the ways that race play performance lays bear categories of race, sexuality, and gender as performance but also the many ways that racial performance remains vital to our experience of race—its economies of pleasure and abjection.[6]

BDSM educator, writer, and outspoken race play advocate Mollena Williams, "The Perverted Negress," believes that "the prime motive in a 'Race Play' scene is to underscore and investigate the challenges of racial or cultural differences."[7] Race play typically involves racist language, narratives, and mise-en-scènes. Like other BDSM practices, it relies on the simultaneous observance and violation of sociocultural interdictions. Race play reveals how performances of black/white interracial intimacy in BDSM are scripted by historical narratives of racialized sexual violence and pleasure hinged on the legacies of chattel slavery. The practice eroticizes not only racism but also a vibrantly imagined and enacted racial difference in which the color line is *played* with—blurred, redelineated, and crossed.

Race play is of course not relegated to black and white. Online race play discussion groups, such as "Racial Name Calling, And Racist Fantasies" attest to the all-inclusive spirit of fetish racial play, facetiously advertising, "This group is for all of the Honkies, Niggers, Spics, Gooks, Chinks, Dago Wops, Bogs, Canucks, Flips, Heebs, Hymies, Japs, Krauts, and Polaks, and any other derogatory named group, who have racist sexual fantasies."[8] In this essay, I focus on black/white bodily intimacy as what Sharon Holland calls the "primal scene of racist practice" when she urges us to "rethink the black/white binary and its hold upon exemplary epistemologies."[9] Race play evinces how historically loaded black/interracial sex remains—how, as historian Kevin Mumford notes, interracial sex is always "more than just sex."[10] If, as Mumford argues, black/white interracial sex is always "more than just sex," then BDSM practiced among black/white interracial partners might always be a kind of race play. Mollena Williams's statement, "I do 'race play' whether or not I want to," is resonant here.[11] It articulates the always alreadyness of race play for black women—the fact that we may be involved in race play whether or not we desire to be—while critically expanding, spatially and temporally, race play's ambit.

Drawing from the diverse lived experiences of black women BDSMers, I unveil the ambivalence that underlines the practice to expose, not resolve, the multitude of contradictions operating within race play and its encircling discourse. I marshal these voices to facilitate a resistance to theorizing race play in a manner that further pathologizes both BDSM and black female sexuality. Beyond the binary of black/white, race play is animated by a number of entangled dichotomies such as fantasy/reality and mind/body and policed by a racialized and gendered code of sexual ethics. For renowned black queer female "Leather Mother," Viola Johnson, race play is not only pleasurable but also empowering.[12] Reconciling her own vexed practice decades before Williams and others began speaking and writing publicly about the controversial practice, Johnson asks, "Why is it that we, as Leathermen and women of color, can't accept the possibility that to some of us, Nigger may be empowering?"[13] Johnson vocalizes the tensions between pleasure, power, racism, and the history of enslavement that continue to animate race play and its discourse. She annotates the "depth of American racism" in the libidinal economy that race play so trenchantly marks.[14] Race play means different things and feels differently to those who enact it at diverse times and trajectories in their lives. While this essay reads largely examples of heterosexual race play performance, I argue elsewhere that queerness is essential to the perverse pleasures of race play and that race play brings into relief the queerness of black heterosexual pornographic desire.[15]

Though many in the BDSM community consider race play "on the edge of edgy sex," it remains a popular topic in BDSM social networking websites and is becoming increasingly more prevalent in hardcore pornography.[16] One popular kink social network houses groups like "Black Women Who Love to be Called Names During Race Play" and "Black Cum Whores For White Masters," each of which has well over two thousand members.[17] Like other arenas of BDSM, race play is a consensual experienced practice recommended only for "advanced" players by many established BDSM trainers like Midori, whose race play pedagogy includes reconstructing scenes of antebellum plantation auction blocks in which she plays the white mistress inspecting the black male slave prior to purchasing his body.[18] Midori is a well-known Japanese American sexuality educator, and her enactment of a US chattel slavery scene speaks to the complex racial landscape of doms, submissives, and trainers, as well as the erotic power of the black/white binary. In *playing* race, Midori uses as "her setting the greatest of American interracial sex factories, the antebellum plantation."[19] One professional black dom states that race play is not as commonly requested as other BDSM acts and is often a practice built up to: "Most guys prefer garden variety humiliation and they don't dip their toe into racial humiliation until they can tell me a little bit."[20] While most serious practitioners of BDSM, professional and quotidian, recommend the importance of training, technical skill, and discipline, setting race play apart from "garden variety humiliation" reveals the currency that race brings into already illicit BDSM performances.

At least three fascinating entangled elements emerge in the context of the discussion of race play in BDSM circles, both kink and scholarly: the unstable dichotomies of fantasy/reality and mind/body, and the racialized and gendered codes of sexual ethics that police the practice. First, highlighting the play in race play, many practitioners voice an imagined split between the fantasy play space of BDSM and the "real"-world arena.[21] For example, black dominatrix, the Black Fuhrer, a pioneer in the public race play dialogue, draws attention to the contrast between the "world outside of fetish" and that "inside of fetish."[22] She reminds us of the foundations of BDSM as already a fantastic enactment of taboo sexual fantasies: "You kind of have to understand that you know whatever is being said is probably being played out as somebody's fantasy. It's somebody's fetish. You can't take it literally."[23] Yet while the Black Fuhrer verbally architects race play "inside" the chimerical realm of fantasy—"you know emphasis on the word *play*"—her name moors the practice within a real history of domination while signifying the historical discourse regarding BDSM's (and pornography's) eroticization of Nazism and Fascism.[24] The rhetoric of play obfuscates the physical and psychic labor of the practice. Importing "real"-world racism and racial scripts into the "fantasy" world of fetish reveals just how permeable, although nonetheless vital, the line between fantasy and reality, inside and outside, is.

Central to the concept of fantasy is that of play itself. Somewhat of a misnomer, if play in BDSM contexts is already complex, demanding emotional and physical labor while requiring training and education, race further complicates the dynamics of pleasure and power exchange that play facilitates. Staci Newmahr defines "SM play [a]s the joint boundary transgression of personal boundaries between people, of hegemonic social and ethical boundaries, and often of physical and physiological boundaries."[25] In race play, boundaries of race and racial ethics are transgressed and reified. I would like us to consider that these women are not only playing with race but also demonstrating the *play* of race—how we *play* race and even how race *plays* us. That is, race play allows for the eroticized transgression of racial boundaries, enables a dramatization of race that sheds light on the performativity of race itself, and signals the ways that race, to borrow from black vernacular, *plays* us. A dated African American colloquialism, play is a synonym for sexual action and a term to describe a kind of exploitation, deceit, or delusion. I elicit this sense of play here to signal the multiple ways race, despite its function as a primary disciplining principle of humankind, is riddled with paradoxes. Robert Bernasconi's theory of race as a "border concept" inspires my conceptualization of how race *plays* us and the dynamic conflicts of racialization.[26] Revealing the contradictory and volatile landscape of racial borders, Bernasconi reveals how sexual transgression is historically constitutive of race.[27] He unveils the relationality of race as a concept "whose core lies not at the center but at its edges" while simultaneously enacting the paradox of the sexual border traverse—that "to map the racial borders, the borders must be crossed."[28] In race play, racial boundaries are delineated only to be (inter)crossed. Like the line between fantasy and reality, the racial border is marked by its "selective permeability."[29] Race play illuminates how race *plays* us in multiple ways. Race postures itself as a steadfast, sovereign truth when, on the contrary, it is a contested, dynamic, and fluid site of demarcation—often legible as a classification of purity yet historically engendered only as a result of profound hybridization. It embodies what Holland terms the "lie of difference," masquerading as a fundamental marker of difference and separation while it is actually an emblem of relation and intimacy in that its borders, as race play evinces, are marked by an erotically charged crossing.[30] If race is a practice of "the drawing and redrawing of the racial boundaries," then race play heightens such sketching—setting, pushing, and retracting the physical and psychic borders of the "play territory."[31] In race play, racial boundaries collide with psychosexual and somatic boundaries in an unresolved melodrama animated by racism, eroticism, racial sexual alterity, power, pleasure, and pain.

A slippage between play and labor is at the heart of race play. The elaborate labor of race is inextricable from the multiplex erotic labor of BDSM, both physical and psychic. If the question of race and its labor in commercial BDSM remains undertheorized, black feminist scholars have examined the critical ways that race informs sex work. Siobhan Brooks and Mireille Miller-Young have illuminated the myriad ways that race nuances sexual economies of labor. In her ethnographic study of black and Latina strippers in New York City and the San Francisco Bay Area, Brooks documents how race affects dancers' "racialized erotic capital" to demonstrate how black women navigate a hierarchy of power wherein blackness is devalued to affect hiring practices, digital marketing, pay, safety, environment, and more.[32] Like Brooks, Miller-Young documents the structural and symbolic modalities of black women's sexual labor to reveal their devaluation within pornography, a domain where white women reign as "stars," a term that marks a zenith on pornography's racialized sexual commodity ladder.[33] She documents the complex auxiliary labor demanded of black female performers in the face of this racial hierarchy as they navigate the structural racism of the industry, including wage inequality, segregation of labor, and the more insidious, multifaceted "*work of racial fantasy*."[34] Like black women in the porn industry who strategically "play up race," black women BDSMers engage the drama of race to play with black sexual economies in their erotic labor.[35]

Second, a conception of the body/mind divide often undergirds race play. Mollena Williams's statement, "My vagina isn't really interested in uplifting the race. What pussy wants is fucked up stuff, really dark scenarios to test the boundaries and cut with an exhilarating level of danger," exemplifies this rift between soma and psyche.[36] When race play is conceived of as a somatic act, black women BDSMers are asserting that it is the body that is aroused by racist fantasies rather than the mind. This partitioning facilitates a critical syncretization of race play wherein the entity of the body assumes responsibility for an arousal the mind ostensibly repudiates.

Other black women express not just an intense pleasure from but also an empowering, therapeutic, and restorative quality in race play. Scholars have analyzed the therapeutic power of race play as a practice of negotiating trauma and anxiety.[37] Danielle Lindemann theorizes race play as a technique of racial anxiety that enables the reproduction or subversion of racial hierarchies and problematizes the therapeutic discourse she unveils as integral to professional erotic dominance.[38] Her assessment of the practice differs from that of Margot Weiss, who posits that while race play reflects the white privilege of the BDSM community, it might become a site from which to challenge this racial hegemony.[39] Though Lindemann's either/or posture flattens out the distinctions between these two moments—reproduction and subversion—obfuscating a spectrum of possibilities, it is through this manipulation that racial hierarchies themselves are revealed as performative and unnatural. For some black women, the therapeutic capability of race play may reside in (en)acting this performativity, exercising not only the choice to be dominated—a vital and pleasurable volition—but also the recognition of one's mantle in the construction and performance of the racial regime.[40]

Nevertheless, the antidotal capability and analeptic dynamic of shame and humiliation are fundamentally complicated by race. Lindeman finds that shaming is restorative in revealing the ephemerality of abjection because it "confirms that which the client is *not*—that is 'You are no longer a pig or a dog or whatever'"; however, blackness, as a state that one typically cannot effortlessly slip in and out of, problematizes such apperception.[41] Can one no longer be a nigger in the same way she is no longer a pig, slave, or whore? The endurance of black abjection, the *fact* of blackness, to borrow from Fanon, is such that outside of the dungeon, bedroom, or stage, one not only may still be race playing, as Williams poignantly states, but also may very well remain a nigger. Williams's statement, "[I] can go into the Big Ass Ice Cream Parlor of Racism and have a sample spoon, and leave. I'm not trapped there being force fed the Rocky Road Ice Cream of Oppression until I am sick," reiterates race play's potential temporary suspension of a more ongoing quotidian experience of black abjection, further compromising the possibilities of and for the subversion of racial hierarchies.[42] It also highlights the importance of consent in performing the violent, erotic play of race.

Consent is a vital element of BDSM's artful negotiation of the mercurial fantasy/reality divide facilitating a critical delineation of one "world" (fantasy) from the other (reality). Reflecting the abiding motto of the kink community, SSC (safe sane consensual), and its more recent aphorism, RACK (risk aware consensual kink), numerous scholars have argued the ways that consent operates as a principal feature of BDSM practice.[43] However, the racialized dynamic of consent in BDSM remains undertheorized. Amplifying the complexity of sexual consent itself, race play evidences what Biman Basu calls the "crucial but constrained" nature of consent within BDSM sexuality.[44] Christina Sharpe has also theorized ways that desire and consent serve to encode the history of violent domination, or that which consent veils.[45] While Sharpe questions the possibility of sexual consent for the enslaved—"as much as an enslaved person can be said to participate in nonconsensual sexual acts"—she confronts the fraught site of sexual consent under the institution of chattel slavery and its continuing existence as a conflicted territory for postslavery subjects.[46] Critically modulating the possibility of consent, Sharpe engages with the probability of the enslaved subject's sexual desire, arguing that indeed, as black women who perform race play also express, "sadomasochistic desire might be a place from which to exercise power and to exorcise it through the repetition of particular power relations."[47] The dynamics of domination and submission, particularly when stratified by the processes of racialization, disrupt understandings and enactments of an already complicated

79

sexual consent. Mirroring the complexity of the many binaries that galvanize BDSM, consent is rarely ever a simple yes/no binary.

As pussy personified (i.e., "What pussy wants is fucked up stuff"), Williams realizes a Cartesian-like disassociation to enjoy race play. However, some black women BDSMers I've spoken to are unable to do this. Though she does not get many requests for it, professional femdom Goddess Sonya does not practice race play because she does not experience pleasure from it.[48] Moreover, requests for what she refers to as "nigger play" are not frequent as a black femdom with primarily white submissive male clients. Her statement, "There is nothing really racially charged in calling a white man a honky," attests to race play's grounding in a white heteropatriarchal foundation of American racism and its reliance on a specific (and very familiar) hierarchy of race.[49] It prompts us to consider how race play's erotic current ebbs and flows with the shifting racial and gender dynamics of racial abjection performed. There are different tensions nuanced between dominant's and submissive's involvement in race play. While it is tempting to think that power differentials are strongest when applied to black women doms rather than subs, I encourage a thinking of race play that challenges this notion, as the practice elucidates the experience of a kind of affective agency in (black) abjection. At the same time, however, Sonya's sentiment also suggests the limits of subversion via race play that I previously discussed in the context of race's *playing* of us. If, as expressed by Sonya and others, calling a white man a honky lacks the same "charge" as calling a black woman a nigger, then race play's potentiality for racial subversion is limited, circumscribed by race and gender and disciplined by white heteropatriarchy, seemingly a powerful and stable force both "inside" and "outside" the world of fetish.

Third, and linked to this body/mind chasm, is the contradictory undercurrent of political correctness that informs race play. For example, certain scenarios like black dom / white slave are often deemed more "palatable," "acceptable," and "less racist" than black slave / white master. Such protocol reflects a common but problematic understanding of power and racism as top down, rather than a more fluid exchange dependent upon relationality, resistance, and exchange between master/slave, oppressor/oppressed, and dom/sub. Affirming that power "come[s] from below," BDSM has long challenged conventional understandings of power, revealing how positions that are conventionally imagined as subordinate (like bottom and submissive) enact power, exert control, and deploy influence.[50] Black women who perform race play navigate a conflicted, violent terrain of gender, race, and sexuality, traversing antebellum legacies of black women's sexual violence and the feminist (more largely lesbian feminist-led) debates about BDSM stemming from the late 1970s and early 1980s in which women of color, though marginalized, played a significant part.

Audre Lorde and Tina Portillo, two early voices in the BDSM debate, introduce what's at stake for black women. For Lorde, BDSM reflects and perpetuates social patterns of domination and submission.[51] In contrast, black female BDSM practitioner and writer Tina Portillo (self-identified "S/M dyke of color") relishes playing sub to a white top even in a "plantation slave and master" scene. She embraces and asserts her "sadomasochistic soul," a characteristic that she sees as contradicting her black female identification.[52] Lorde's and Portillo's voices are dated but pertinent, echoing the larger debates surrounding BDSM, pornography, heteropatriarchy, and violence stemming from the so-called feminist sex wars beginning in the late 1970s. During this time there was a vibrant debate concerning BDSM with groups like Samois, a small San Francisco–based collective of lesbian feminist BDSM practitioners, championing the productive potential of BDSM.[53] Formed in the late 1970s, Samois contended that BDSM was not incompatible with being a lesbian or a feminist. Rather, they asserted that BDSM was a productive and pleasurable sexual expression offering a critique of heteropatriarchy and its naturalization of gendered hierarchies of power.[54] Opponents of BDSM, however, did not view it as a way to theorize gendered and sexualized power outside of the rigid binary of male/female relationships and identifications.[55] On the contrary, they avowed that it was entrenched in patriarchy and heterosexism. In particular, BDSM among lesbians stood as a testament to the regime of heterosexuality. Feminist women of color rejected Samois's proclaiming themselves as "an oppressed sexual minority," viewing it as a mockery of the lived realities of minorities like themselves.[56]

Still, many contemporary black women BDSMers question this moral logic while citing the pleasures of playing sub to a white dom. Williams, for example, expresses the double standards marking ethical claims against race play. She disputes the sentiment that it is "OK if the Black person is dominant, but not 'UPLIFTING THE RACE!!!' if she's submissive."[57] Williams articulates race play's shifting erotic capital and the dynamic slippages in its reception and policing. The racial and gender configuration of racial abjection performed and the veering positions of domination and submission further complicate these slippages. However, I read these women's voices not so much as a renouncement or vindication of race play but as a critical assertion of sexual autonomy—a staking agency in and of one's own sexual pleasure.

In a 1982 interview, Michel Foucault, a theorist and practitioner of BDSM, stated, "The idea that S&M is related to a deep violence, that S&M practice is a way of liberating this violence, this aggression, is stupid. We know very well that what all those people are doing is not aggressive; they are inventing new possibilities of pleasure with strange parts of their body—through the eroticization of the body."[58] Reflecting the mind/body split, Foucault acknowledged the somatic potentiality of BDSM in "inventing new possibilities of pleasure"; however, he denied the kind of psychosomatic historical record of BDSM and the possibility **of** "uncovering... S & M tendencies deep within our unconscious."[59] À la Foucault, if BDSM is not about violence (or history) at all but rather about innovating fresh modes of accessing pleasure, then race play cannot be about working out and through a black female (un)consciousness haunted by a history of sexual violence. However, it is evident from attending to the voices of black women who practice BDSM and race play specifically that their pleasure, though certainly vexed, is influenced by the black female's psychic and somatic memory of trauma and the constitutive historical links between black female sexuality and violence, as well as inventing avenues for experiencing pleasure.

If BDSM cannot heal historical trauma and/or enable some kind of actual or symbolic remedy for black women, it might serve as an arena in which to revisit the relationship between pleasure, power, race, and sex and to re*play* scenes of black/white sexual intimacy. This essay unveils the important ways that the sociopolitical and cultural histories engaging black women, sexuality, pleasure, and violence inform black women's performances in BDSM. Mobilizing the voices of black women BDSMers, I have argued that BDSM expands how we conceptualize the entanglement of black female sexuality and violence. In addition to serving as a vehicle of desire and pleasure, violence can become a mode of accessing and contesting power. Animated by the construction of elastic yet enduring boundaries between the binaries of fantasy/reality, inside/outside, mind/body, and black/white, black women BDSMers enact an intricate *play* of race exercising sexual desire, power, and sentience.

Notes

1. Here, the term *black women* refers to African American women for whom the history of chattel slavery in the Americas has produced the sociohistorical conditions that uniquely inform black female subjectivity and sexual politics. I use the term not to essentialize black American womanhood but to gesture to a black women's standpoint influenced by the condition and experience of gendered and racialized abjection, a "common experience of being black women in a society that denigrates women of African descent." In this essay I focus on black women who practice BDSM, a small but nonetheless heterogeneous group of women in the already marginalized larger kink community. See Collins, *Black Feminist Thought*, 22.

2. Hine, "Rape and the Inner Lives of Black Women in the Middle West," 912. For more on black female slave sexual assault and its aftermath, see Carby, *Reconstructing Womanhood*; duCille, "'Othered' Matters"; Brown, "Imaging Lynching"; Harris, "Whiteness as Property."

3. BDSM is an umbrella term that stands in for bondage and discipline (B/D), domination/submission (D/S), and sadism/masochism, or sadomasochism (S/M). For the purposes of this chapter, I interchange S/M, S&M, and/or SM with its more contemporary label, BDSM.

4. I devised the term *racial sexual alterity* to describe the perceived entangled racial and sexual otherness that characterizes the lived experience of black womanhood. Historically, this alterity has been produced (pseudo)scientifically, theoretically, and aesthetically and inscribed corporeally as well as psychically. Racial sexual alterity signifies the ways black womanhood is constituted, though not produced solely, via a dynamic invention of racial and sexual otherness. Hence it does not signify a fixed core. It designates a particular, though neither static nor essential, sociocultural experience of subjectivity, one where sexual categories of difference are always linked to systems of power and social hierarchies. As race play makes lucid, such difference is highly ambivalent, oscillating between not just desire and derision, sameness and otherness, but threat and necessitation.

5. This article borrows from a larger project on black women's performance in race play and its representation in contemporary American pornography. Here, I draw from my own and others' interviews with black women BDSMers, as well as their own online testimonies. See Cruz, *The Color of Kink*.

6. Johnson, *Black Queer Studies*; Johnson, *Appropriating Blackness*; DeFrantz and Gonzalez, *Black Performance Theory*; Scott, *Extravagant Abjection*; Butler, *Bodies That Matter*; and Butler, *Gender Trouble*.

7. Andrea Plaid, "Interview with the Perverted Negress," *Racialicious*, July 10, 2009, accessed September 7, 2010, racialicious.com/2009/07/10/interview-with-the-perverted-negress/.

8. "Racial Name Calling, and Racist Fantasies" group page, accessed June 8, 2012, fetlife .com/groups/8118/about.

9. Holland, *The Erotic Life of Racism*, 26, 29.

10. Mumford, *Interzones*, xi.

11. See Williams, "BDSM and Playing with Race," 70.

12. Johnson has been an active figure of the BDSM community since the mid-1970s. Johnson, *To Love, to Obey, to Serve*, 276.

13. Johnson, "Playing with Racial Stereotypes The Love That Dare Not Speak Its Name," *Leatherweb* (copyright 1994), accessed April 5, 2012, leatherweb.com/raceplayh.htm.

14. McBride, *Why I Hate Abercrombie & Fitch*, 117.

15. Cruz, *The Color of Kink*.

16. Daisy Hernandez, "Playing with Race," *Colorlines: News for Action*, Tuesday, December 21, 2004, accessed June 26, 2011, colorlines.com/archives/2004/12/playing_with_race.html.

17. "Black Women Who Love to Be Called Names during Race Play," Fetlife group page, last accessed December 5, 2018, https://fetlife.com/groups/13670; "Black Cum Whores for White Masters," Fetlife group page, last accessed December 5, 2018, https://fetlife.com/groups/23986.

18. Hernandez, "Playing."

19. Davis, "Bad Girls of Art and Law," 102.

20. Interview with the author, June 19, 2012.

21. Many BDSM scholars have revealed how "fantasy is critical to sadomasochistic interactions." According to Thomas S. Weinberg, fantasy both drafts the particular BDSM scenarios and serves as a scapegoat for the guilt participants may feel enjoying the enactment of taboo sexual fantasies. See Weinberg, "Sadomasochism and the Social Sciences," 33.

22. Black Fuhrer, "White on Black Race Play—My Views," YouTube, October 26, 2009, youtube.com/watch?v=04W8f-xmCEE.

23. Interview with the author.

24. These debates surrounding the historical legacies of violence (and pleasure) in our intimate lives reflect similar tensions as those regarding race play. The scholarship on BDSM's appropriation of Nazism and Fascism is vast; for a sampling, see Reti, "Remember the Fire"; Susan Sontag, "Fascinating Fascism," in Sontag, *Under the Sign of Saturn*, 73–105; Griffin, *Pornography and Silence*; Wayne, "S/M Symbols"; Star, "Swastikas"; and Kantrowitz, "Swastika Toys."

25. Newmahr, *Playing on the Edge*, 163.

26. Bernasconi, "Crossed Lines."

27. Ibid., 216.

28. Ibid., 212, 227.

29. JanMohamed, *The Death-Bound-Subject*, 99.

30. Holland, *The Erotic Life*, 2, 88.

31. Bernasconi, "Crossed Lines," 222; and Bean, *Leathersex*, 131.

32. Brooks, *Unequal Desires*, 7.

33. Miller-Young, *A Taste for Brown Sugar*, 230.

34. Ibid., 9, italics in original.

35. Ibid., 10.

36. Plaid, "Interview."

37. Lindemann, "BDSM as Therapy?," 159.

38. Ibid. See also Lindemann, *Dominatrix*.

39. Weiss, *Techniques of Pleasure*, 210–11.

40. Williams, "BDSM and Playing with Race," 71.

41. Lindemann, "BDSM as Therapy?," 162.

42. Plaid, "Interview."

43. Wiseman, *SM 101*; Newmahr, *Playing*; Cowling and Reynolds, *Making Sense of Sexual Consent*; Barker and Langdridge, *Safe, Sane, and Consensual*; Weiss, *Techniques*; Kleinplatz and Moser, *Sadomasochism*; Beckmann, "'Sexual Rights,'" 195–96; and Hanna, "Sex Is Not a Sport."

44. Basu, *The Commerce of Peoples*, 136.

45. Sharpe, *Monstrous Intimacies*, 4.

46. Sharpe, "The Costs of Re-Membering," 322.

47. Ibid., 327.

48. Interview with the author, November 2, 2011. Goddess Sonya has been working as a professional dominatrix for over ten years. She maintains her own website, goddesssonya .com, specializing in "ethnic kink" and featuring primarily black women.

49. Ibid.

50. Foucault, *History of Sexuality*, 1:94.

51. "Interview with Audre Lorde: Audre Lorde and Susan Leigh Star," in Linden et al., *Against Sadomasochism*, 68.

52. See Portillo, "I Get Real," 51, 49.

53. This debate is far more complex than a binary of for/against BDSM. For the purposes of this chapter, such polarity effectively animates the feminist exchange and demonstrates that BDSM occupied an always already controversial space in the field of women's sexual praxis.

54. For more, see Collins, *Coming to Power*. In 1979 Samois self-published a booklet entitled *What Color Is Your Handkerchief? A Lesbian S/M Sexuality Reader*.

55. For more about the radical feminist opposition of BDSM during this time, see Linden et al., *Against Sadomasochism*.

56. Karen Sims and Rose Mason with Darlene R. Pagano, "Racism and Sadomasochism: A Conversation with Two Black Lesbians," in Linden et al., *Against Sadomasochism*, 101. Additionally, Alice Walker portrays BDSM as a derision of the history of black female enslavement during chattel slavery and a "'fantasy' that still strikes terror in black women's hearts" ("A Letter of the Times, Or Should This Sado-Masochism Be Saved?," in Linden et al., *Against Sadomasochism*, 207).

57. Plaid, "Interview."

58. Foucault, *Ethics*, 165.

59. Ibid.

PART II

Sexual Economies of Sexual Publics

CHAPTER 5

No Bodily Rights Worth Protecting

Transnational Circulations
of Black Hypersexuality in Brazil

Erica Lorraine Williams

This chapter explores the transnational circulation of notions of black hyper-sexuality in Brazil and beyond. It engages in a close reading of a 1983 video clip entitled *Arnold Goes to Carnival in Rio*, using it as a site of analysis to illuminate how cross-cultural perceptions of sexual difference are produced and perpetuated within the tourism industry. My analysis of *Arnold Goes to Carnival in Rio* draws from my extensive ethnographic research on the sexual economies of tourism in Salvador, capital of the state of Bahia in the northeast of Brazil. My book, *Sex Tourism in Bahia: Ambiguous Entanglements*, interrogates notions of gender, race, and sexuality that are constructed within sexualized tourist practices.[1]

This chapter uses the concept of sexual economies as a framework for analysis.[2] Adrienne Davis conceptualizes slavery as a sexual economy due to the ways in which it converted "private relations of sex and reproduction into political and economic relations."[3] Similarly, for anthropologist Ara Wilson, the concept of sexual economies highlights the "intersections between economic systems and social life."[4] While scholarship on race and sexuality has often focused on in-jury, trauma, representation, sexual panics, and pathologies, the interdisciplinary project of black sexual economies shifts the lens to focus on issues of "pleasure, regulation, labor, consumption, and production," as well as "identity politics, sexual exchange, social policy, literature, media, and cultural performances."[5] It is this perspective that I utilize to analyze the representations of black sexualities in the video and also address how black Brazilian women recuperate and reimagine their sexualities within a transnational tourism industry that depends upon their bodies and their emotional and sexual labor. Ultimately, I argue for a *both/and* approach that allows scholars to recognize, name, and critique troubling representations of black sexualities that persist in the contemporary period while also emphasizing the voices, agency, desires, and pleasures of the very people who are being sexualized.

There are two versions of the video that have been published on YouTube since the early 2000s: a five-minute, fifteen-second clip and an extended fifty-six-minute version.[6] Produced by Shep Morgan, *Carnival in Rio* was originally made for the Playboy Channel in 1983. Playboy then licensed the video rights to Elite Home Video in the early 1990s.[7] According to Peter Nicholas's 2005 *Los Angeles Times* article, there was a renewed interest in the video after Arnold Schwarzenegger entered the California governor recall campaign in 2003. There were even attempts to suppress the video so that it would not ruin his chances at the gubernatorial race.[8] In this chapter, I analyze both the short clip and the extended version of the video, paying particular attention to the national and transnational imaginations of black women's sexual accessibility and the racial differences in how Brazilian women are depicted therein. This chapter seeks to address the question, How can transnational feminisms help move us further in our conversations around black sexualities in a global context? While Jafari S. Allen notes that transnational sexuality studies scholarship has been critiqued for silencing and ignoring blackness, Inderpal Grewal and Caren Kaplan warn us that "ignoring transnational formations has left studies of sexualities without the tools to address questions of globalization, race, political economy, immigration, migration, and geopolitics."[9] In analyzing media and cultural performances, this chapter contributes to the growing and important body of work on black sexual economies by moving beyond the US context to provide a transnational, African diasporic case study.

Brazil is an extremely important and timely place to embark upon a conversation about black sexual economies in a transnational context. With the largest economy in Latin America, Brazil is an increasingly important global player. In recent years, Brazil has witnessed the best and the worst of times. The nation experienced unprecedented levels of economic growth, becoming the world's sixth largest economy in 2012, and international recognition as host of the 2014 World Cup and 2016 Summer Olympics. However, Brazil has also suffered a political crisis with the impeachment of its first female president, Dilma Rousseff, in 2016, and an economic recession starting in 2014.[10] Nonetheless, through all of the political and economic changes, racial and socioeconomic inequalities have persisted in Brazil.[11] In the state of Bahia, where people of African descent comprise nearly 80 percent of the population, this inequality has clear racial overtones.

A roadmap for the chapter is as follows. First, I delve into the close reading of the aforementioned video. Then, I historicize the video as fitting into the context of sexualized representations of Brazilian women of African descent that have long been central to the Brazilian tourism industry. I show how the video references Oswaldo Sargentelli's Oba-Oba *mulata* shows, which situated the mulata onstage as an eroticized spectacle for the consumption of white male foreigners. In the second half of the chapter, I include material that illustrates how Afro-Brazilian women have been fighting back to reclaim their sexualities, pleasures, and desires and reject the ways in which their bodies and sexualities have been pathologized. While Brazilian women of African descent are seen as having no bodily rights worth protecting, black Brazilian feminists have been actively speaking back to these representations through various projects and campaigns that they have carried out since 2011. The remainder of this chapter addresses these questions as it provides a compelling case study of transnational sexualities centered around blackness.

What Is Arnold Doing during Carnival in Rio?

Arnold Goes to Carnival in Rio opens with thirty-six-year-old Arnold Schwarzenegger exploring the Cidade Maravilhosa (Marvelous City), a popular nickname for Rio de Janeiro. He says, "Rio, the most beautiful city in the world. . . . It's hard to find more gorgeous mountains, beaches, and women anywhere." Consistent with Brazilian tourism advertisements that have used erotic undertones to market Brazil as a racial-sexual paradise since the 1970s, Schwarzenegger views women as an example of the natural beauty and attractions to be found in Brazil.[12] He expresses his excitement about visiting Rio for Carnival, where "once a year a whole city goes absolutely crazy." Viewers are quickly transported to a scene where they hear the agitated, percussive rhythm of the samba as the camera zooms in for a close-up of an Afro-Brazilian woman's behind. We do not see her face or know her name. We do not know her dreams or aspirations or how she feels with all eyes on her as she skillfully shakes, gyrates, and shimmies to the fast-paced rhythm. All we see is her *bunda* (butt) in a sparkly beaded thong.

Before long, viewers get a front-row seat to the show at the Oba-Oba nightclub, which Schwarzenegger says was his first taste of Carnival. This club was aptly named after the "mulata shows" that Oswaldo Sargentelli, a white Brazilian radio and television personality, created in Rio de Janeiro in the 1960s. Sargentelli's mulata shows positioned *mulatas* (mixed-race Brazilian women) onstage as spectacle and entertainment for elite Brazilians and foreigners alike. As Brazilian anthropologist Suzana Maia notes, Sargentelli's mulatas became "icons of the Brazilian sex tourism industry inside and outside the country."[13] Moreover, these shows contributed to the international marketing of the mulata as the quintessential symbol of exotic Brazilianness and a source of national pride and tourist revenue.[14]

Adriana, a white Brazilian model, facilitated Schwarzenegger's visit to the Oba-Oba nightclub by serving as both his date and his cultural translator. She told him that witnessing the mulata show would help him truly understand the Brazilian "triple threat: the bunda, the mulata, and the samba." This statement paradoxically situates Brazilian women of African descent, who have long been associated with the body, sensuality, and rhythmic expression, as a representation and embodiment of the Brazilian nation. This is ironic, given the extreme marginalization that Brazilian women of African descent face within the nation. As Adriana and Schwarzenegger sit comfortably in their booth and toast each other with their *caipirinhas* (the Brazilian national drink, made from *cachaça* [sugarcane rum], lime, and sugar), viewers see more Afro-Brazilian women dancing onstage. A close-up on a black woman's behind in a thong gyrating slowly serves as the visual background as Schwarzenegger ponders Brazilian culture. He concludes, "To Brazilians, especially men, the mulata is the symbol of everything sexy and erotic. During Carnival, gorgeous mulata bodies begin to move in ways that even a fitness expert like myself can't believe." Interestingly, here it is the bodies of mulatas that have agency rather than the women themselves.

Adriana explains to Schwarzenegger that Brazilians believe that "a central part of the woman is the ass." Schwarzenegger smiles a goofy smile and quips, "I knew I had something in common with the Brazilian man." As they sit at their table watching the performance onstage, Schwarzenegger dramatically uses his fingers to make "googly eyes" at the Afro-Brazilian women dancers. Adriana laughs. In his analysis of this video, journalist, blogger, and Brazilian music aficionado Chris McGowan claimed that Adriana looked "mortified" by Schwarzenegger's obnoxious behavior in the nightclub.[15] However, in my reading, she seemed to be supporting and even encouraging his behavior. Ironically, the white Brazilian woman serves as a cultural broker or intermediary for Schwarzenegger in a context in which black women's bodies are simultaneously the backdrop and the spectacle.

All of a sudden, Schwarzenegger is struck by a moment of self-reflection. He states, "After watching the mulata shake it, I can absolutely understand why Brazil is totally devoted to my favorite body part: the ass, especially during Carnival." At this point, we see an Afro-Brazilian woman dancing samba in slow motion to highlight each and every jiggle of her backside. "I wasn't sure if I was ready to dance the samba," he says, "but like everything else in Brazil, when you let it happen, you get into it *very* quickly." Schwarzenegger emphasizes "very" in a suggestive manner full of sexual innuendo. Soon after, the master of ceremonies invites "Mr. Universe" to the stage.[16] The spotlight is now on him; it is his turn to perform rather than merely ogle and admire. Three brown-skinned Afro-Brazilian women promptly encircle and dance around him. Without a moment's hesitation,

Schwarzenegger grabs one woman's bunda, holding on to it very tightly. The look on her face registers extreme discomfort as she grabs his hands and struggles to pry them off of her behind and move them up to her waist. One by one, he grabs each woman. He grabs one from behind. He kneels down and puts his face near one woman's crotch and then picks her up off the ground. The video quickly moves on, as if Schwarzenegger's entry into the carnal and corporeal pleasures of dancing samba onstage with three beautiful Afro-Brazilian women was the culmination of the nightclub experience. The video then flashes to a chaotic scene where Schwarzenegger is dancing in the middle of Carnival in Rio de Janeiro.

In describing this moment, Peter Nicholas says, "At one point, he grabs a dancer's buttocks; she immediately clasps his wrists and pushes his hands away."[17] Anyone who is remotely familiar with samba would know that it is not a partner dance.[18] There is no touching, grabbing, or lifting involved. However, the fact that Schwarzenegger violated one of the unspoken rules of samba dancing is more than merely a case of a young, single, European man "acting out" in Brazil.[19] Schwarzenegger's behavior in his samba-dancing debut in Rio de Janeiro is telling. It highlights how Afro-Brazilian women's bodies in general—and scantily clad, dancing bodies in particular—are seen as available and accessible. There are no rules governing black women's bodies. They are seen to have no bodily rights worth protecting. As Beverly Guy-Sheftall notes in her classic essay, "The Body Politic: Black Female Sexuality and the 19th Century Euro-American Imagination," "being black and female is characterized by the private being made public."[20] In other words, black women's bodies are "not off-limits, untouchable, or unseeable."[21] Accounting for cross-cultural differences, it is worth pointing out that the samba-dancing Afro-Brazilian women in Brazil do not forfeit their right to bodily autonomy and integrity. In the next section, I continue to analyze the video in more detail, paying close attention to the racial differences in how Brazilian women are sexualized.

Bundas and "Nice Words Like Love"

After the nightclub and Carnival scenes, Schwarzenegger decides that he wants to learn Portuguese. He says he found the perfect teacher in a beautiful Brazilian woman named Beli. While not Afro-Brazilian, her skin color is slightly more brown than Adriana's, his white nightclub companion, which suggests some degree of racial mixture. Beli and Schwarzenegger are sitting at a table in a restaurant. The soft, glowing lighting lends a sensual air to the setting and their conversation. Schwarzenegger says he thinks the Portuguese language is "so romantic" and asks Beli to teach him some "nice words like love." "*Amor*," she says. He tells her that he learned the word *bunda* the day before. She giggles. He then offers to teach her a few words of English. He takes a baby carrot and puts it in his mouth and says, "biting." Why he thinks that is an important word for her to learn in English is unclear. He then puts the same bitten baby carrot in her mouth, sliding it in and out a few times. The camera zooms in to focus on her lips, and the suggestion of fellatio is clear.

In the extended version of the video, we see more of the cross-cultural conversation between Arnold and Beli when they were teaching each other a few key words and phrases in Portuguese and English. After Beli teaches him the word for "love," she teaches him how to say "I love you": "Eu te amo." After he shares with her that he learned the word *bunda*, he comments, "That's good, huh? I like bunda." She cuts a piece of fruit and eats it, moaning softly as she says, "Gostoso" (Tasty). She then teaches him the word *carinho* (affection) as she gently strokes his face and his arms and the word *forte* (strong) as her hands caress his biceps. She teaches him *abraço* (hug) as she hugs him. After teaching her the word "biting" with the carrot, he puts it in her mouth, and she says that the word in Portuguese is *chupar* (to suck). That part is edited out of the shorter version of the film.

After their sexually charged language lesson, the next scene shows Schwarzenegger's head resting comfortably in Beli's lap. She strokes his hair and sings a melodious song in Portuguese. Another scene shows them at a party with all white Brazilians eating *feijoada*, the hearty black bean stew that is the national dish of Brazil. Another scene shows him and Beli at an outdoor restaurant with a white couple. In the extended version of the video, the opening scenes of the Rio de Janeiro landscape include a close-up and pause on the bare breasts of a sun-kissed woman on the beach. Other brief scenes in the extended version include a group of people playing *capoeira* (an Afro-Brazilian martial art), more close-ups on women's glittery bodies at Carnival, and people exercising on the beach. In the capoeira scene, there is only one woman in the group. True to form, Schwarzenegger manages to find a reason to pick up this woman and kiss her on the cheek after she finishes playing capoeira. At the beach, we see him lifting weights and doing pull-ups in the exercise area. Before long, a slim, blond, white Brazilian woman appears and begins smiling at him while he is doing pull-ups. He notices her and lifts her up to the bar so that she can do a few pull-ups too. At one point, Schwarzenegger talks about the atmosphere of the beach at Ipanema, where "you can feel the sexual power" everywhere. Thus, Brazilian sexuality is seen as an essential, supernatural, potent, and contagious presence in Rio de Janeiro.

At the fifty-four-minute mark in the extended video, we hear the frenetic drumbeat of the samba as the camera focuses in on black women's bundas. As Schwarzenegger describes his trip to Rio as "one of the craziest five days I've ever spent," we see black bundas in sequined thongs gyrating and shaking to the beat. Finally, the video ends with another panoramic view of the beautiful Rio de Janeiro landscape and a focus on a slim, attractive, white woman alone at the beach on the rocks. In Chris McGowan's 2003 analysis of the video, he says that although Schwarzenegger "tries to be charming and funny," he "comes across as a clueless gringo on a sex tour."[22] Furthermore, McGowan takes offense at how the video reduces Brazil to "breasts and buttocks" and emphasizes "sex and skin." To be sure, these charges against the film are certainly warranted. However, it is important to remember that similar notions about Brazilian sexuality—and black hypersexuality in particular—have also been promoted and encouraged within the national context of Brazil.

The depictions of women of African descent in this film are like a loop that continuously repeats itself in the past, present, and future. Afro-Brazilian women's bodies have long been featured as an integral part of the lure of Brazil—they are the exotic and erotic resources necessary to ensure a successful and fulfilling trip to Brazil. The tourism industry in Brazil relies on the sexualized bodies of black women to market Brazilian tourist destinations as sites of pleasure and sexual possibility for foreign visitors. Notions of black hypersexuality have come to characterize foreign tourists' imaginaries of Brazil as a racial-sexual paradise. Even the 2014 World Cup was not immune to the tendency to sexualize black women's bodies.

Figure 5.1: The *FIFA Weekly* article "Brazil for Beginners" references a transnational fantasy of black women's hypersexuality and the racialized economy of sex tourism in Brazil. Photo courtesy "Brazil for Beginners," *FIFA Weekly*, March 21, 2014, 19.

Consider the March 21, 2014, issue of *FIFA Weekly* magazine. An article called "Brazil for Beginners" consists of tips to help first-time foreign tourists navigate cultural differences in Brazil.[23] The tips, while probably intended to be humorous, actually reproduce stereotypes of Brazilians, portraying them as perpetually late, drawn to chaos, always waiting until the last minute (for example, when building stadiums for the World Cup), and not respecting the lives of pedestrians, among other things. One tip refers to bodily contact, explaining that Brazilians talk with their hands and touch a lot. Another tip, interestingly, corrects misunderstandings about nudity at the beach: "Going topless: Bared skin and female body art may be familiar at Carnival, but they are not what you will see in everyday Brazil. Indeed, although Brazilian bikinis contain less fabric than comparable products in Europe, they are still worn at all times. Tanning on the beach without wearing them is strictly forbidden and may even result in a fine."[24] What is fascinating is that the expectation of nudity on Brazilian beaches made it on a list of ten tips, even though it is culturally inaccurate. This speaks to how hypersexualized representations of Brazilian women that pervade the transnational tourist imaginary fuel foreign tourists' ideas of what they can expect to encounter in Brazil. Moreover, the image accompanying the article features two brown-skinned Afro-Brazilian women lying face down on the beach donned in the well-known Brazilian bikini bottoms. The women watch a diverse group of men play an exuberant game of *futebol*. While this image is set in Rio de Janeiro, it is consistent with many of the tourism advertisements that I found in my research on sex tourism in Bahia over the years.[25]

Two further examples of the national imaginations of black women's hypersexuality in Brazil can be seen in a 1970 Pan Am poster and the Globeleza commercials.[26] The poster for Pan Am airlines was being auctioned online by Swann Galleries. The description of the image on the website reads: "Oba-Oba dancers from Oswaldo Sargentelli's night-club in Rio de Janeiro, Brazil" wearing ten-inch heels and not much else. Sargentelli, the famed *sambista*, brought mulatto dancers to the world's attention in the late 1960s. Here Pan Am forgoes traditional travel images in favor of a more prurient advertising strategy.[27] The Globeleza commercials announce the beginning of Carnival season on Brazil's most popular television network, Globo. These commercials feature samba-dancing mulatas who are completely nude except for sparkles, body paint, and accessories. *Mulata* is a term that is thought to imply "a certain voluptuousness of the body and the feeling of 'abandonment.'"[28] As Kia Lilly Caldwell writes, the "term mulata has become synonymous with prostitute for many European men who travel to Brazil for the purposes of sexual tourism."[29]

Black Brazilian women—whether or not they are sex workers—are marked as outside the bounds of sexual respectability simply because of assumptions about their hypersexuality. A perfect example of this can be seen in the case of Sirlei Carvalho, a black domestic worker in Rio de Janeiro who was assaulted by five upper-middle-class white youth while she was waiting at a bus stop in the wee hours of the morning.[30] Their excuse was that they thought she was a prostitute, as if that were a justification for beating up a woman on the street. In describing this incident, Christen Smith argues that "society perceives black women's bodies as violable because black femaleness is always already marked in the popular imagination as outside of the moral social order."[31] Similar to Cathy Cohen's argument that some heterosexuals exist on the margins of heterosexual privilege because their sexual choices are seen as abnormal or immoral, I would add that sex workers (regardless of their race) and black people (regardless of whether or not they are sex workers) are both situated on the margins of respectability as a consequence of their stigmatized sexual practices.[32]

The concept of black sexual economies helps us make sense of the ways in which black sexualities are characterized by their connections to regulation and labor, thus breaking down classist and moralizing divisions between sex workers and non–sex workers. In her classic essay, "'Don't Let Nobody Bother Yo' Principle': The Sexual Economy of American Slavery," Adrienne Davis contends that the silences around black female sexuality emerge from the "unspeakability of slavery" (see chapter 1). To correct this silencing, Davis names slavery a "sexual political economy." She emphasizes that this naming provides us with the "tools we need to excavate black women's history, document our exploitation, and archive our resistance." Davis calls slavery a sexual political economy because of the "interplay of sex and markets" in which "law and markets of the antebellum South seized enslaved women's intimate lives, converting private relations of sex and reproduction into political and economic relations." Davis also points out racial differences in sexuality. While the white "lady" "was deprived of her sexuality," "the black woman was defined by hers."

Clearly, the racial differences in sexuality that Davis documented from the antebellum US South still persist today. It is interesting to consider what happens when we consider these racial differences within a transnational framework. Are black women in Brazil and other parts of the African diaspora also defined by their sexuality? If so, are they able to use this in any ways that are fruitful, productive, and empowering for them, or does this serve as yet another example of sexual exploitation and commodification? In the *Arnold Goes to Carnival in Rio* videos, we see racial differences in how Brazilian women's sexuality is represented. While Brazilian women as a whole are sexualized, white Brazilian women are allowed to have voices. They are allowed to express themselves, pontificate on their culture, and serve as a cultural broker or translate for the esteemed foreign visitor. Afro-Brazilian women, on the other hand, appear as props—as a collection of eroticized body parts and sensual movements. As Afro-Brazilian feminist historian Luciana Brito pointed out, the image in *FIFA Weekly* reminded her of how, for young black women, "the eroticization of their bodies and the 'sensuality' contained in their butt and thighs, not faces, are seen as all that matters of their identities."[33]

These racial differences in sexualization can be seen more in the extended version of the video, which features a nearly four-minute montage of slim, mostly white Brazilian women. Soft, soothing Brazilian music plays in the background as we see the women who appear to be models shot in various sensual poses. They are in various stages of action: running, sunbathing topless, rubbing suntan oil on their breasts, rinsing themselves off in the water, and so on. Contrary to the scene of the Afro-Brazilian women in the Oba-Oba nightclub, whose bodies can be grabbed, their personal space open and accessible to invasion by this European bodybuilder/tourist, these white Brazilian women are minding their own business while the camera and viewers act as passive voyeurs. One woman who is slightly more brown-skinned than the rest—perhaps an indication of indigenous ancestry—is sunbathing beside a rooftop pool and an expensive-looking building with a scenic mountain backdrop. The camera zooms in on her in a sarong with one bare breast poking out. This is reminiscent of the mulata, Gabriela, in Jorge Amado's classic novel, *Gabriela, cravo e canela* (1962), whose childlike innocence about her exposed breast was used to indicate the inherent sensuality of mulata women.[34]

Clearly, it is not only women of African descent who are sexualized in the video—white Brazilian women are as well. One common refrain that I often hear from white Brazilian women when I talk about my book is that they, too, feel sexualized in Brazilian culture and in the eyes of European and North American tourists. To be sure, one can argue that Brazilian culture in general is sexualized and seen as erotic, particularly in the global tourist imaginary. For instance, in *Transnational Desires: Brazilian Erotic Dancers in New York*, Suzana Maia describes the aura of exoticism in the Queens-based gentlemen's bars, where the mere "presence of Brazilian women evokes a chain of associations that . . . transforms Brazil into a source of fantasy and desire."[35] However, there is also something unique about the particular ways in which this sexualization and eroticization operates for black women. In the video, there are certainly white and light-skinned Brazilian women who are the objects of Schwarzenegger's bumbling flirtations. However, the clear racial difference is that the white/light women's faces are shown, they are speaking, they can express themselves, laugh, smile, and be heard. The black women, on the other hand, are just bundas: gyrating, writhing bodies that can be groped and grabbed at will.

Maia's ethnography offers useful tools to help us understand the racial differences in how Brazilian women were depicted in the film. Maia chooses to focus on middle-class, mostly white or *morena* Brazilian exotic dancers in New York gentleman's clubs.[36] Maia theorizes morena as a racial category that may suggest racial mixture that occurred before colonization, or it may simply indicate a suntan and the luxury of leisure time spent on the beach. She argues that middle-class people tend to be absent from postcards of Brazil because "they are just not exotic enough, not authentic enough for the tourist gaze." As a point of comparison with the Oba-Oba nightclub scene in Schwarzenegger's films, most of the middle-class Brazilian women in the gentleman's bars where she conducted her research could not dance samba. Maia emphasizes that "the mulata, samba, and carnival became the chief symbols of Brazilian racial mixture, epitomizing the festive and sexualized essence of the Brazilian nation."[37] This resembles Adriana telling Schwarzenegger about the Brazilian "triple threat—the bunda, the mulata, and the samba"—at the nightclub. As a white Brazilian woman, where did Adriana fit into this "triple threat"?

Maia also juxtaposes how mulatas are associated with Carnival parades, while middle-class white women are associated with beauty pageants. In other words, the woman of African descent is associated with *sexiness*, while the white woman is associated with *beauty*.[38] Furthermore, she emphasizes how women of all classes and complexions can *become* mulata during carnival. Similar to Natasha Pravaz's conceptualization of mulata as a professional category, Maia highlights that the term implies "moments of abandon and possession by the spirit of the nation through samba."[39] Maia describes the mulata as the race of the nation—a quasi-abstract entity that implies racial mixing. Moreover, the term also denotes the excessive sexualization of black women and represents Brazil as a racial and sexual celebration of mixture associated with the lower class.[40]

Theorizing and Recuperating Black Sexualities

So how do we theorize black sexualities in the context of sex tourism? What are the silences, openings, fissures, and spaces for productive discussions around agency in this context? Here I draw from Jafari S. Allen's conception of sexuality as a more inclusive concept than just sexual orientation or preference. Allen conceptualizes sexuality as the "everyday lived experience of the sexual(ized) body ... [and] also about the imagination, desires and intentions of the sexual(ized) subject."[41] Scholars have long grappled with the question of how to study and write about black women's sexuality without "re-pathologizing an already stigmatized and marginalized population."[42]

Recent scholarship on black sexual economies has introduced and expanded theorizing of important concepts such as sexual rights, "illicit erotic economy," "outlaw sexuality," erotic autonomy, and bodily integrity that are useful in analyzing the meanings of black women's dancing bodies in the Brazilian Carnivalesque touristscape. Mireille Miller-Young's concept of *illicit erotic economy* "theorizes historical representation of black bodies as sites for [a] vast array of forbidden sexual desires, fantasies, and practices, and how black subjects symbolically and strategically labor within the prohibited terrain of sex."[43] Allen understands sexual rights as how we "work to solve urgent problems while neither casting those in need as helpless victims nor stigmatizing particular groups." Sexual rights include the right to enjoyable, autonomous sexuality; freedom from coercion, rape, and other forms of violence; the right to sexual health; the right to decide if, when, and how to reproduce; and the right to determine one's own sexual identity.[44]

The notion of bodily integrity has long been central to the project of black women recuperating their dignity. However, as Miller-Young points out, the politics of respectability precludes the existence of sexual subjectivity outside of domestic, heteronormative, and bourgeois family relations. Furthermore, in exploring how black women put their hypersexuality to work for their own interests in survival, success, and erotic autonomy, Miller-Young asserts that black women in pornography "employ an outlaw sexuality to achieve mobility, erotic autonomy, and self-care." In the logic of sexual economy, she argues, "some bodies are worth more than others; yet all are evaluated and commodified through the lens of race, gender, class, and sexuality."[45] We can see this difference in how bodies are valued in the racial differences in the sexualization of Brazilian women in the videos.

What does it mean for black women to recuperate their sexuality, to rescue it from the silencing histories and unwanted incursions and impositions? Miller-Young emphasizes that "defining sexual autonomy has not been an easy task" for black women.[46] Miller-Young goes on to cite Evelynn Hammonds, who points out in her classic article, "The restrictive, repressive and dangerous aspects of black female sexuality [have] been emphasized by black feminist writers while pleasure, exploration, and agency have gone under-analyzed."[47] In the Brazilian context, we can look at the case of Valéria Valenssa, the Globeleza model from 1993 until 2004. Valenssa said that she derived great pleasure and satisfaction from dancing samba before large adoring crowds: "When I see people looking at me, the sound of the *batería* [percussion section], the music, the fireworks, this really touches me deep inside. No matter how tired you are, it's impossible to stand still, to think about your tiredness. You forget yourself."[48] I also found in my ethnographic research that black Bahian sex workers often embraced the racialized and sexualized ways in which they were stereotyped to their advantage in pursuing ambiguous entanglements with gringos. In a sense, then, sex tourism in Brazil is nothing new; it is merely a transnational reiteration of these processes of racialized eroticization that have occurred historically in Brazil.[49]

In recent years, Afro-Brazilian feminists have been struggling and debating over the right strategies. One attempt that resonated for some and fell flat for others was the Marcha das Vadias—the Brazilian version of the SlutWalk. The Marcha das Vadias has taken place since 2011 all over Brazil. The SlutWalk originated on a university campus in Toronto after a police chief warned female students that they could avoid being sexually assaulted by not dressing like sluts.[50] As quickly as the movement spread across the globe, it was also critiqued by black feminists transnationally.[51] In the United States, Black Women's Blueprint posted an open letter to SlutWalk organizers on September 23, 2011, in which they stated:

> As Black women, we do not have the privilege or the space to call ourselves "slut" without validating the already historically entrenched ideology and re-curring messages about what and who the Black woman is. . . . Although we understand the valid impetus behind the use of the word "slut" as language to frame and brand an anti-rape movement, we are gravely concerned. For us the trivialization of rape and the absence of justice are viciously intertwined with narratives of sexual surveillance, legal access and availability to our personhood. It is tied to institutionalized ideology about our bodies as sexualized objects of property, as spectacles of sexuality and deviant sexual desire. It is tied to notions about our clothed or unclothed bodies as unable to be raped whether on the auction block, in the fields or on living room television screens.[52]

This open letter certainly raises valid points of critique about the historical par-ticularities of black women that make embracing the word "slut" a problematic endeavor. In the Brazilian context, Ana Flávia Magalhães Pinto, an Afro-Brazilian doctoral student in history and a journalist with the black feminist Coletivo Pre-tas Candangas, wrote a blog about her thoughts about the Marcha das Vadias.[53] When the first SlutWalks occurred in 2011, Magalhães Pinto was studying abroad in the United States as a part of her doctoral program. She later wrote: "Since the experience of being treated negatively as a slut is something that is part of the experience of black women, the proposal [of the Marcha] didn't sound at all un-reasonable. However, some questions soon arose from black women from both countries. The first of them recalled that such treatment has not been reserved for us when we go into the street with short clothes. The negation of our right to our own bodies is independent of the clothes we wear."[54] Magalhães Pinto also mentioned a statement by Paula Balduino de Melo in which she described a meeting between the Coletivo Pretas Candangas and the Marcha das Vadias organizers in which the black feminist group expressed their concerns: "We talked about how we have to confront the hegemonic society on a daily basis to show that we are not sluts, that we don't have the 'color of sin.' We say that we don't want to demand the right to be sluts, but rather to be doctors, lawyers, or PhDs."[55]

On the other hand, a black women's group from Curitiba wrote a manifesto in which they stated: "We are hypersexualized; we are the 'color of sin'; we are the ones who are just for 'fucking' and for labor. . . . [W]e are the cheapest meat at the market." They go on to say: "[We are] those who demystify the sexual image that is attributed to us; we are the ones who demand policies to promote equality; we are the ones who want to 'blacken' feminism." They end the manifesto with a call for black women who want to "blacken" feminism—or increase the racial diversity of feminism—to join them in the Marcha das Vadias to "deconstruct the idea that feminism is white and elite."[56]

In my blog for *Ms. Magazine*, "Slut-Walk: Bahia Style," I describe my experience witnessing the Marcha das Vadias in Salvador in 2011, part of the annual July 2 Bahian Independence Day Parade. A few of the signs I saw read: "Prostitutes are also victims of rape," "Danger: machismo kills," "We are not sex objects, we are desiring subjects," "We are black lesbians—we are women in the struggle." I also saw marchers carrying a poster of a black woman that read: "We are owners of our voice, of our bodies, of our history. Black women: for a life without violence."[57] I also interviewed Iris Nery do Carmo, a twenty-three-year-old Bahian sociologist and feminist activist who participated in the march. She told me that the march was important for Salvador because of the "representation of the Bahian woman—the black woman in particular—as a sexual object, sold on postcards and tourist packages as part of our landscape. Given this patriarchal mentality, the high index of violence against women is not surprising."[58]

In the summer of 2013, when I returned to Salvador to begin research on black feminist activism in Bahia, I interviewed a woman in the leadership of coordinating the Marcha das Vadias in Salvador. This thirty-nine-year-old woman, whom I will call Tatiana, described herself as an activist feminist since the age of thirteen as a result of witnessing her mother suffer from intimate partner violence at the hands of Tatiana's father. She pointed out that the black movement in Bahia was critical of the Marcha das Vadias, and some black women even refused to participate because of the name. However, as a black woman who identifies as bisexual, Tatiana acknowledges that "it is complicated to be a black woman and say *vadia*," yet she has immersed herself in organizing the Marcha das Vadias because of how it brings together the feminist and LGBT movements. Beyond the march on July 2, she was also involved in organizing events and activities to raise awareness and foster dialogue about the march and the issues it raises both in Salvador and in surrounding municipalities.

Yet another example of how black Brazilian women are recuperating and reimagining their sexualities can be seen in Julho das Pretas (July of Black Women), a proposal for a black feminist agenda for Bahia promoted by Odara Institute of Black Women. The purpose of this month is to raise awareness about black women's struggles and achievements in Latin America and the Caribbean. It culminates in the commemoration of July 25, which has been designated as the International Day of the Afro-Latin American and Caribbean Black Woman. Valdecir Nascimento, executive coordinator of Odara, stated, "It is necessary to strengthen the 25th of July throughout the country. . . . [I]t will guarantee respect and visibility for the struggle of black women. We want to mobilize the maximum number of black women's organizations possible in Bahia. . . . [I]t will reaffirm July as a month of black feminist intervention in Bahia." Julho das Pretas now occurs every year and brings together various black women's organizations and entities to have events and activities such as roundtables, musical celebrations in honor of black women, cultural presentations, and workshops on topics ranging from black beauty, hip hop, and youth theater to Afro-Brazilian religions, social development, and violence against women.

Indeed, black feminists are making an important intervention in Bahia and Brazil as a whole to challenge the kinds of images we see of Afro-Brazilian women in Arnold Schwarzenegger's 1983 video—that of the scantily clad, samba-dancing woman who is all bunda and no face, expressions, or desires. On November 18, 2015, the Marcha das Mulheres Negras contra o Racismo, a Violência, e pelo Bem Viver (March of Black Women against Racism and Violence and for Good Living) brought nearly thirty thousand women to the nation's capital, Brasília. The idea for the march emerged in Salvador in 2011 and soon developed into a national mobilization that reached several states across the country. In a video by the March Committee from Pernambuco, black feminist activists articulated some of the issues and concerns underlying the march. Some of the issues include a concern about violence against women, the objectification of black women, the recognition that racism mistreats and kills people ("racismo maltrata e mata"), the lack of access to legal and safe abortions, and the genocide against black youth.[59] Black Brazilian women of all ages, sexualities, and walks of life were mobilizing for a society without racism, sexism, and *lesbofobia*.[60]

In this chapter, I have utilized black sexual economies as a theoretical framework to analyze Arnold Schwarzenegger's *Carnival in Rio* videos in order to show how cross-cultural perceptions of sexual difference are produced and perpetuated within the tourism industry. Although the video was originally produced for the Playboy Channel, I would argue that it is consistent with how the broader tourism industry propaganda utilizes eroticized images to market Brazil to the rest of the world. This is true of Rio de Janeiro and other cities such as Salvador, and it can be seen in everything from postcards to television commercials, films, literature, and even Adidas T-shirts to commemorate the World Cup.[61] I highlight the recent efforts of black Brazilian feminist activists such as the Marcha das Vadias, Julho das Pretas, and the 2015 national march to showcase the diverse ways in which black Brazilian feminists are making efforts to contest and resist these representations. They are interrupting the "single story" that the world likes to tell about Brazilian women (particularly of African descent) and that even Brazil likes to tell about itself.[62]

Notes

1. Williams, *Sex Tourism in Bahia*.
2. See chapter 1 in this volume by Adrienne Davis, "'Don't Let Nobody Bother Yo' Principle': The Sexual Economy of American Slavery"; see also Alexander, *Pedagogies of the Crossing*; Wilson, *The Intimate Economies of Bangkok*.
3. Davis, "'Don't Let Nobody.'"
4. Wilson, *The Intimate Economies of Bangkok*, 9.
5. Washington University Law Center for the Interdisciplinary Study of Work and Social Capital, Black Sexual Economies Project, 2015, accessed June 28, 2017, law.wustl.edu/centeris/pages.aspx?id=7848.
6. For the five-minute, fifteen-second clip, see Josh Simon, *Arnold Goes to Carnival in Rio*, YouTube, July 10, 2006, accessed June 28, 2017, youtube.com/watch?v=pdIjJ8efftk. The extended version of the film used in this article no longer appears on YouTube as of July 28, 2017: Joe Dimon, "Rare Arnold Schwarzenegger Show in 1983 (Rio Carnival)," YouTube, February 19, 2014.
7. Peter Nicholas, "Tabloid Tried to Suppress Videotape," *Los Angeles Times*, September 12, 2005, accessed July 28, 2017, articles.latimes.com/2005/sep/12/local/me-video12/2.
8. Ibid.
9. Allen, "Blackness, Sexuality, and Transnational Desire"; Grewal and Kaplan, "Global Identities," 666.
10. As of April 2018, Brazil is the ninth largest economy in the world, after the United States, China, Japan, Germany, the United Kingdom, France, India, and Italy (Rob Smith, "The World's Biggest Economies in 2018," World Economic Forum, April 18, 2018, accessed December 12, 2018, https://www.weforum.org/agenda/2018/04/the-worlds-biggest-economies-in-2018/).
11. Edmonds, *Pretty Modern*.
12. Williams, *Sex Tourism in Bahia*.
13. Maia, *Transnational Desires*, 91.
14. Caldwell, *Negras in Brazil*; Pravaz, "Brazilian Mulatice."
15. Chris McGowan, "Governor's Gone Wild! Arnold's Raunchy Road to Rio," *Culture Planet*, September 3, 2002, cultureplanet.com/arnold.htm (link disabled).
16. One year after winning Mr. Universe for the first time in 1967, Arnold moved to the United States from Austria in 1968 with dreams of pursuing an acting career. Schwarzenegger filmed *Carnival in Rio* in 1983, one year after his breakthrough role in *Conan the Barbarian* (dir. John Milius, 1982). In 1982 he also released the *Shape Up with Arnold* videotape, and in 1984 he starred in *The Terminator* (dir. James Cameron), which catapulted him to stardom. Other film credits include *Hercules in New York* (dir. Arthur Allan Seidelman, 1970), *Pump-*

ing Iron (dir. George Butler and Robert Fiore, 1977), and *Conan the Destroyer* (dir. Richard Fleischer, 1984). He also published a book, *Arnold: The Education of a BodyBuilder* (New York: Simon & Schuster, 1977), and posed nude for a gay magazine called *After Dark* in 1977. He was elected governor of California in 2003 and served two terms, which he completed in 2011.

17. Nicholas, "Tabloid."

18. One exception to this is *samba de gafiera*, a style of samba danced with a partner. Influenced by Argentine tango, this dance style developed in the 1940s in Rio de Janeiro.

19. Interestingly, the video was filmed three years before he married Maria Shriver on April 26, 1986.

20. Guy-Sheftall, "The Body Politics," 18.

21. Ibid., 18.

22. McGowan, "Governor's Gone Wild!"

23. I first came across this image in Rafael Reis's article "FIFA's Magazine Says That Brazil Leaves Everything to the Last Minute, 'Even Stadiums.'" However, I looked at back issues of *FIFA Weekly* and was unable to find the original source for the image. I then found Hector Viera's blog entry, which noted that on Friday, March 21, FIFA decided to retract the article from the internet for fear of offending Brazilians. Rafael Reis, "FIFA's Magazine Says That Brazil Leaves Everything to the Last Minute, 'Even Stadiums,'" *Folha de São Paulo*, March 24, 2014, folha.uol.com.br/internacional/en/sports/worldcup/2014/03/1429940-fifas-magazine-says-that-brazil-leaves-everything-to-the-last-minute-even-stadiums.shtml; Hector Viera, "A FIFA e o estereótipo brasileiro / FIFA and the Brazilian Stereotype," *Futeboteco*, March 22, 2014, accessed July 28, 2017, futeboteco.com.br/2014/03/22/a-fifa-e-o-estereotipo-brasileiro/.

24. Reis, "FIFA's Magazine Says."

25. Williams, *Sex Tourism in Bahia*.

26. Globeleza is a term that joins the words Globo, the popular Brazilian television channel, and Beleza, which means "beauty" in Portuguese. Every year, a woman is chosen as the *mulata Globeleza* to dance samba in the vignettes aired on Globo in the months leading up to Carnival.

27. This poster is listed on Swann Auction Galleries website under "Rare and Important Travel Posters." The poster sold for $1,200. Swann Auction Galleries, "Sale 2261 Lot 50," November 11, 2011 (DESIGNER UNKNOWN PAN AM / RIO, Circa 1965), catalogue.swanngalleries.com/asp/fullCatalogue.asp?salelot=2261++++++50+&refno=++651927&saletype=.

28. Maia, *Transnational Desires*, 91.

29. Caldwell, *Negras in Brazil*, 60.

30. Smith, "Putting Prostitutes in Their Place."

31. Ibid., 115.

32. Cohen, "Punks, Bulldaggers, and Welfare Queens."

33. Luciana Brito, "Entre Musas e Hontentotes: Explorações da imagem das mulheres negras e latinas ou sobre como o racismo e o sexismo venceram o copa do mundo," July 25, 2014, geledes.org.br/entre-musas-e-hotentotes-exploracoes-da-imagem-das-mulheres-negras-e-latinas-ou-sobre-como-o-racismo-e-o-sexismo-venceram-o-copa-mundo/.

34. Williams, "*Mucamas* and *Mulatas*."

35. Maia, *Transnational Desires*, 89.

36. The ambiguous color term *morena* is often used to mean brown skinned or dark haired, depending on the region a woman is from in Brazil.

37. Ibid., 31, 47.

38. Erica Williams, "Blonde Beauties and Black Booties: Racial Hierarchies in Brazil," *Ms. Magazine* blog, June 11, 2010, accessed July 28, 2017, msmagazine.com/blog/blog/2010/06/11/blonde-beauties-and-black-booties-racial-hierarchies-in-brazil/.

39. Pravaz, "Brazilian Mulatice"; Maia, *Transnational Desires*, 52.

40. Maia, *Transnational Desires*, 49.

41. Allen, "Blackness, Sexuality, and Transnational Desire," 83.

42. Miller-Young, review of *The Politics of Passion*, 119.

43. Miller-Young, "Putting Hypersexuality to Work," 224.

44. Allen, "Blackness," 92.

45. Miller-Young, "Putting Hypersexuality to Work," 220, 231.

46. Ibid., 222.

47. Ibid., 223, citing Hammonds, "Toward a Genealogy."

48. Pravaz, "Where Is the Carnivalesque," 107.

49. Williams, *Sex Tourism*.

50. Erica Williams, "Slut-Walk: Bahia Style," *Ms. Magazine Blog*, August 5, 2007, http://msmagazine.com/blog/blog/2011/08/05/slutwalk-bahia-style/.

51. Black Women's Blueprint, "An Open Letter from Black Women to the SlutWalk," September 23, 2011. The post is no longer visible on the Black Women's Blueprint webpage, but the letter in its entirety is reposted with permission by Susan Brison on the *Huffington Post.* Susan Brison, "An Open Letter from Black Women to SlutWalk Organizers," *Huffington Post,* September 27, 2011, accessed July 28, 2017, huffingtonpost.com/susan-brison/slutwalk-black-women_b_980215.html.

52. Ibid.

53. The Coletivo Pretas Candangas is a black women's collective in the Federal District of Brazil. Pretas Candangas, *Pretas Candangas: Irmandade de mujeres negras do DF,* 2012–16, accessed July 28, 2017, pretascandangas.wordpress.com/.

54. Ana Flávia Magalhães Pinto, "Do Trágico ao épico: A Marcha das Vadias e os Desafios Políticos das mulheres negras" [From the tragic to the epic: The SlutWalk and the political challenges of Black Women], Blogueiras Negras, June 27, 2013, accessed July 28, 2017, blogueirasnegras.org/2013/06/27/desafios-politicos-feminismo-negro/.

55. Ibid.

56. "Manifesto de Mulheres Negras de Curitiba," Marcha das Vadidas CWB, 2011–17, accessed July 28, 2017, marchadasvadiascwb.wordpress.com/manifestos/manifesto-mulheres-negras-de-curitiba/.

57. Williams, "Slut-Walk: Bahia Style." This poster was from a campaign of the Project Crossroads of Rights: Race, Gender, and Confronting Violence against Black Women in Bahia, which was launched in March 2011 by black feminist sociologist and activist Vilma Reis and journalist Céres Santos of CEAFRO, an organization that promotes racial and gender

equality through educational programs. CEAFRO, "CEAFRO: Educação para igualdade racial e de género," accessed July 28, 2017, ceafro.ufba.br/web/.

58. Ibid.

59. Marcha Comunicação, "Marcha das Mulheres Negras 2015: Contra o Racismo, a Violência e pelo Bem Viver—Comitê PE," YouTube, October 17, 2015, accessed July 28, 2017, youtube.com/watch?v=qFP6im9-vo4.

60. Interestingly, the Portuguese language has a word for homophobia against lesbians, while this term does not exist in English.

61. Dave Filmer, "'Sexy' Adidas World Cup T-shirts Pulled after Complaints from Brazil," *Metro*, February 26, 2010, accessed July 28, 2017, metro.co.uk/2014/02/26/sexy-adidas-world -cup-t-shirts-pulled-after-complaints-from-brazil-4321016/#ixzz4dtooCLDX.

62. Chimamanda Ngozi Adichie, "The Danger of a Single Story," TED Global, 2009, https:// www.ted.com/talks/chimamanda_adichie_the_danger_of_a_single_story/up-next ?language=en, accessed December 12, 2018.

CHAPTER 6

"Will the Real Men Stand Up?"

Regulating Gender and Policing Sexuality through Black Common Sense

Marlon M. Bailey and Matt Richardson

It is 2006, and Bishop Alfred Owens has just delivered a bombastic sermon in front of an approximately seven-thousand-member, predominantly black congregation at the Greater Mount Calvary Holy Church of America in Washington, DC. The central theme of Owens's sermon is captured by what he posed as a rhetorical question: "Will the real men stand up?" During the first portion of this sermon, Owens intoned a proud proclamation in the microphone: "I love me some women." This proclamation garnered him a rousing and enthusiastically affirmative response from the congregation. Yet during the same portion of the sermon, he articulated a deep hatred of femininity. The bishop continued by not only expressing a fear that he and the other men in the church were already being displaced by an active population of women who outnumbered them "three to one" but also emphasizing the need to eradicate the *feminine* in what he called "deficient men." Deficient men is a term that, he went on to clarify, constitutes "sissies" and "faggot[s]." For Owens, the most frightening configuration of femininity seemed to be the sissy, for the sissy exposes the instability and precariousness of black masculinity. To reassure him of the presence and prominence of a legible and legitimate masculinity, during the climax of the sermon Bishop Owens called for the "real men" to stand up. What was initially a rhetorical question quickly became a directive in which Owens, literally, said that when he called for the "real men," he did not mean sissies and faggots. Many men in the room obliged Owens's call by standing and walking up to the pulpit in a performative display of black masculinity in front of the congregation.

Yet this performative display of black manhood could not quell Owens's anxiety about the fact that black manhood starts from a structural position of destabilization and vulnerability that is negotiated first by blaming black women (evidenced by his recognition of being outnumbered) and then through a required promenade of masculine valuation and overcompensation. This public performance was an attempt to recuperate patriarchal positioning through a demoralization and subordination of the feminine, as well as other non-gender-conforming men and women. Hence, his sermon is not just a story about homophobia; it is also about the fear of and anxiety around an unstable and precarious black masculinity, a masculinity viewed as soiled and tainted by femininity. Bishop Owens's masculinist request, "Will the real men stand up?" stems from the ways in which black people's bodies have been scrutinized through a variety of regulatory regimes. Because black genders have been overdetermined from larger society, this overdetermination creates anxiety and a desire for complicity that also demands a constant reassurance that the flesh-and-blood penis is still acting in its appropriate and proper function.[1]

This example speaks to how some black clergy unabashedly construct and participate in religious and social discourses that police the boundaries of gender and sexuality in black communities. Although there are many examples of alternative, inclusive, and affirming black churches, Bishop Owens espouses a set of beliefs found in a variety of organized religious traditions in the United States, including evangelicalism, which validates heteronormative patriarchy as the model of manhood.[2] But, of course, these religious institutions are not the only sites through which such regulatory discourses of blackness, gender, and sexuality are produced. In 2009 one of the premier historically black colleges/universities (HBCU), the all-male Morehouse College, instituted the "Appropriate Attire Policy," which bans its students from wearing "women's clothes." Even though only a handful of students in recent memory had the audacity to flaunt their femininity on the campus, the college administrators felt that the threat of a feminine encroachment upon the definition of a "Morehouse man" was dire enough to codify its prohibition in the school's code of conduct.[3]

Thus, Owens's sermon, Morehouse College's "Appropriate Attire Policy," and other black clergy who espouse a homophobic and heteropatriarchal common sense of blackness bring into focus important concerns about the intracultural regulation of black gender and sexuality that we seek to theorize. In this essay, we argue that black sociocultural institutions, such as the family, churches, schools, and political organizations, produce a common discourse about black culture, or what cultural theorist Wahneema Lubiano refers to as "Black common sense." In her essay "Black Nationalism and Black Common Sense," Lubiano suggests that common sense is lived ideology that is "articulated in everyday understandings of the world and one's place in it."[4] We extend Lubiano's theoretical concept by adding that a common sense about gender is produced in black cultural—intragroup—institutions. Furthermore, we base our argument on an examination of various intragroup discursive sites and publics in which gender (and sexual) common sense is produced, such as church sermons and student conduct policies at HBCUs.

These previously mentioned examples reflect an intracultural discourse and shed some light on the profound anxiety in black communities about race and gender relative to the contentious relationship between the terms "black" and "manhood." Blackness and manhood are often represented as constitutive of an authentic racialized gender subjectivity.

We argue that this mandatory "authentic" racialized gender performativity is sutured to normative sexuality and is the means through which queer sexualities are policed and denied. The discourses that we highlight are not marginal; instead, in a variety of ways, they contribute to how many black sociocultural institutions coproduce and participate in such discourses of blackness. This in turn may explain the undergirding secrecy, silence, and violence that plague black communities' relationship to gender and sexual variance. This essay addresses this question in relationship to how transgender and queer gender identities and bodies further put the quandary of black manhood into a productive crisis to the extent that they implode the tension that holds blackness, manhood, and heterosexuality together, perhaps freeing us to explore other genderqueer possibilities. We examine documentary films that focus on black queer experiences, identities, and cultural formations to illustrate genderqueer alternatives and possibilities.

Historically, the "black church" has been one of the most influential social and cultural institutions for black people, even though not all black people are Christian or participate in organized religion, and not all black people attend HBCUs, if they attend college/university at all.[5] Yet it is clear that some black churches and black educational institutions are primary sites of the production of gender common sense. This has implications for the too often violent limits placed on black queer lives, as black queer people are embedded in black communities and institutions. In what follows, we propose a theoretical framework to analyze how black sexuality is policed and queerness is denied through a heteronormative gender common sense. We also draw from representations in two black queer documentaries to highlight the ways in which some sectors of black communities challenge heteronormative gender and sexual logics.

Taxonomies of Gender Entanglements or Genderqueer Phobia

A key component of black common sense about gender is a set of phallocentric assumptions about anatomy, sexual practice, and gender performance. From this perspective, gender is supposed to signify sexual identity (either straight or "gay") through the particular ways that gender is performed. Gender performance also signifies sexual practice, whether it is someone who bottoms (one who gets fucked) or tops (one who does the fucking). Thus, gender performance has tremendous material consequences, as it is meticulously scrutinized and assiduously policed, and those who do not follow the logic of heterogender are often subject to violence and death.[6] Even heterosexuals who do not adhere to this normative gender performance are subjected to oppression. Since black gender nonconformity is the site of constant trepidation and fear, it becomes the means through which sexuality is thus policed, especially because it potentially exposes what is already destabilized and uncertain.

To delineate and examine those genders and sexualities that are "outlawed" within and through black gender discourses, we have constructed a "genderqueer-phobic taxonomy"—a theoretical framework—that illustrates the logics that undergird anxieties and fears about black gender nonconformity and how they are expressed and enacted. It is also worth bearing in mind that this taxonomy reflects the logic that feminine cisgender women are passive receivers in the determination of gender categorization. Misogyny either dismisses cis women from discussion or asks them to justify their facility with a phallus by asking the question, "Do you have a 'real' dick or what?"

The genderqueer-phobic taxonomy consists of four categories:

1. Penis pretenders / penis frauds. This category consists of trans men, cisgender bisexuals or lesbians, and female masculine people. Because these are men who were assigned female at birth or cisgender masculine lesbians or women, they are accused of acting as though they have had an anatomical penis from birth when, in actuality, they have not. The prescription for these people is, "If you don't have a penis, *don't* act like you have one."

2. Penis concealers / penis deceivers. This category consists of pre/nonoperative trans women who are assumed to have a penis, but through their gender performance and identification, they supposedly conceal it and reject its role as dominator and subordinator of the feminine. The mandate for these people is: "Since you have a flesh-and-blood penis, act like it, and make sure everyone knows you have one."

3. Penis misusers. These are cisgender masculine men who penetrate and/or who get penetrated by other men. Because they are masculine cisgender men they are also accused of abdicating or renouncing the power of the penis to subordinate women. The moment that a man is not claiming an exclusive heterosexual sexual domain he is considered to be penetrable and therefore socially relegated to the realm of the feminine.[7] The

directive for this category of people is, "You have a penis, so use it in the way you are supposed to use it."

4. Penis rejecters. These are cisgender men who are feminine and viewed as strictly bottoms because of their feminine gender performance. In general, although he has a penis, the feminine man is not assumed to be someone who penetrates. This person is thought to outright reject his penis and the so-called power that it wields. In other words, this person is seen as someone who has a penis but who does not want to have one and does not use it correctly. The demand for this person is, "Since you have a penis, you need to act like you want it, and you better use it correctly."

We derived these theoretical concepts from an analysis of the black gender common sense produced within black social and cultural institutions, such as some churches, HBCUs, and other sites of knowledge production within black communities. These discourses imply deep beliefs that undergird the policing of black sexuality through gender common sense. It is worth noting that these discourses are hegemonic in that they are also reproduced among black queer communities.

"Strap It On and Slap Some Grease on Your Behind": The Psychosocial Drama of Black Masculinity

Reverend Willie Wilson of the Washington, DC, Union Temple had his own gender panic and homophobic dissolve around the same time as Bishop Owens, in July 2005. In a sermon before his very large congregation about the so-called breakdown of the black family, Wilson suggested that black families are under stress because black women are replacing black men both as breadwinners and as sexual partners. Wilson noted that for him, there are two unlivable conditions: that black women make as much as or more money than men and that the black male is no longer the sole wielder of the penis because of lesbians' use of dildos, replacing men in the sexual arena: "Women falling down on another woman, strappin' yourself up with something; it ain't real. That thing ain't got no feeling in it. It ain't natural. Anytime somebody got to slap some grease on your behind to stick something in you, it's something wrong with that. . . . Bible says, 'God made them male and female. . . . ' There is something unique to man and unique to woman."[8]

Like that of Owens, Reverend Wilson's sermon amounted to a call for a policing of sexuality through a form of communal gender regulation and a consolidation around heteropatriarchal gender norms. Furthermore, according to this logic of black patriarchy, women, specifically lesbians, interfere with black men's access to power vis-à-vis the penis because, as theorist Judith Butler notes, the lesbian phallus enacts the vanishing penis. In her analysis, Butler disconnects the sign of the phallus from the penis, allowing her to displace the privilege that Jacques Lacan ascribes to this phallus signifier in order that she seize a place of power for the white lesbian.[9] For black men, however, this decoupling between the phallus and the penis has already happened through white supremacist racial—figurative and real-life—castration. Hypersexualized masculinity is one of the only places where black men feel they have power and reign. As black men are reduced to the penis, they also revel in the fantasy that they are prodigiously endowed and have a majestic prowess. Therefore, black male castration anxiety includes a fear of losing this position. In this case, however, white supremacy is not the primary threat to black men's power position; instead, it is the black lesbian. Both black lesbians and trans men exist under a racist, misogynist, and hypersexual order that is similar to the one in which cisgender black men exist. According to Wilson's logic, if the dildo can replace the penis and render it not the only source of sexual prowess and libidinal gratification, then how is black manhood to be defined? It is an ontological quandary.

Just as Owens and Wilson fear, black people indeed engage in creative gender possibilities, including the option of being a black man without having been born with a penis or being born with a penis and then finding a variety of creative and feminine uses for it, including, but not limited to, surgical removal. Black gender common sense produced in religious, educational, and other social institutions in black communities create quotidian consequences for queers and other non-gender-conforming black people. This happens, in part, because the phobic discourses that we highlight above become the most prominent ones and are both shrill and predictable.

Let us consider the ways in which the categories of black genderqueer phobia function through black gender common sense in HBCUs. The Morehouse College dress code is a salient example of black gender common sense and, in this case, of the "penis rejecter," or people who do not use their penises "properly" and its connections to class. The "Appropriate Attire Policy" is part of the college's rules of "Etiquette and General Behavioral Expectations." Students are expected to comply with its standards at all campus events and at college-sponsored events held off campus or risk being denied access to classes and college functions ("denied" is in bold).[10] Space does not allow us to list and discuss the entire policy, but for our purposes, here are a few examples of the types of clothing that are forbidden:

1. Caps, do-rags, and/or hoods in classrooms, the cafeteria, or other indoor venues. Do-rags should not be worn outside of the residence halls. This

policy item does not apply to headgear considered as a part of religious or cultural dress.

2. Decorative orthodontic appliances (e.g. "grillz"), be they permanent or removable, shall not be worn on the campus or at College-sponsored events.
3. No sagging—[Defined as] the wearing of one's pants or shorts low enough to reveal undergarments or secondary layers of clothing.
4. Pajamas, shall not be worn while in public or in common areas of the College.
5. [No] Wearing of clothing associated with women's garments.

Clearly, Morehouse College is invested in what it views as the "proper representation" of manhood, calling on "each student" to "promote and portray a positive image . . . [of] themselves and the College." According to the dress code, positive and proper black masculinity is middle class, as evidenced by the prohibitions of "do-rags," "decorative orthodontic appliances (e.g. 'grillz')," and "sagging." The college went so far as to juxtapose the vernacular names with the "proper" descriptions, which, among other things, suggests an expectation of a goal of transformation from "niggas" with "grillz" and "do-rags" to men who eschew "decorative orthodontic appliances." Gender common sense in these guidelines suggests that a proper middle-class affect must be accompanied by the rejection of overtly feminine clothing. It could be argued that at this time proper middle-class manhood is already feminized, but perhaps part of the effect of this policy is to rid the campus of the reminder that black middle-class masculinity is read through the feminine by eradicating its opposite—the thug—from plain view.

This commitment to proper gender and class (self) representation and "appropriate conduct and attire" is designed to achieve an important objective of the Morehouse College mission: "to develop men with the values, knowledge, and skills essential to impact the world as leaders." The code of conduct explicitly urges students to police each other by "holding their peers accountable for being good citizens." Morehouse's stated dedication to reproducing the "good" (read: appropriately classed and gendered) black male citizen-subject is so strong that students who do not comply will be "denied admission into class and various functions and services of the college if their manner of attire" is deemed inappropriate. One can also be expelled from the college under certain circumstances (these are not specified).[11] Of course, all of this policing on the part of the administration does not eliminate class differences among the students, staff, and faculty, or sexual intimacy between men, or gender variance from among the Morehouse "community." But we note that these aims are implied.

The rule in the "Appropriate Attire Policy" that has sparked the most controversy has been the final edict, which states that students are prohibited from the "wearing of clothing associated with women's garments." In relation to the gender taxonomy, there is a constant anxiety that the penis rejecter will represent the college and tarnish the image of black middle-class manhood and/or redefine it entirely. In addition, Morehouse's class-based policies were basically forgiven by some black writers and activists who agreed that they were also "offended by men wearing their pants belted at their knees with their underwear showing," as one feminist blog puts it.[12] To its credit, however, this blog also highlights the contradiction of a Morehouse admission policy that tolerates violence against women.[13]

In an opinion piece about the dress code in *theGrio*, an African American news blog associated with MSNBC, reporter David A. Love agrees that the dress code has its merits with regard to class:

> On one hand, I can understand that a school like Morehouse has a legacy to protect and a brand name to maintain. After all, this is the alma mater of Martin Luther King Jr., Julian Bond, Maynard Jackson, Spike Lee, and others. The value of an institution's stock rises or falls on the quality of its graduates and the leaders it produces. . . . So, old school as it may appear to a younger generation, I can see some good intentions in using the dress code as a way to build character and professionalism.[14]

The specter of "proper" black masculinity hovers as "old school" black activists are named as exemplifying the kind of manhood that will bring Morehouse College (and, by extension, the race) "quality" leaders. Love's comments are buttressed by the equally "old school" notion of black male special status of endangerment. He states that black men are "America's endangered species, and need special protection and some guidance to help them navigate the waters of a nation." Ironically, Love goes on to assert that the dress code is at worst "pure homophobia cloaked in official college stationery."[15] Therefore, for Love, sexual variance (i.e., straight, gay, and bi) is acceptable as long as it is accompanied by appropriate class presentation. Gender variance (i.e., feminine men, trans men and women, and other non-gender-conforming people) is neither acceptable nor necessary to "build [the] character" of the nation of black men. In essence, homophobia is unacceptable, but genderqueer phobia is necessary.

At Morehouse College, this has meant that the small cadre of femme-identified, fiercely dressed students were the subject of harassment and a string of humiliating incidents, including being asked to leave campus by security. In a 2010 article entitled "The Mean Girls of Morehouse," some former and then current students told an interviewer from *VIBE* magazine that they pushed the boundaries of manhood. They asked, "Why can't a man of Morehouse wear makeup, heels and a purse or become a woman?" They asserted that the future of a black institution like Morehouse depends on the answers to their questions.[16] Since black gender nonconformity is the site of deep anxiety and fear, it becomes the means through which sexuality is thus policed, because in the Morehouse case the gendered dress code is about policing sexuality as well as gender.

In no way do we suggest that all black people subscribe to the gender and sexual prescriptions that these black sociocultural institutions advocate. Nor do we mean to suggest that genderqueer phobia and homophobia are unique to black communities. Yet there is a dearth of analyses that take into account the role that these discourses play in shaping black common sense about gender and sexuality. According to the schema that we highlight, misogyny and antiblackness coalesce into an endeavor that seeks to render black femininity into a pure absence. To identify as black and feminine equates to annihilation.

Neither Man nor Woman: Toward a Theory of Black Queer Genders, or How Black Queers Forge Livable Lives

In the final section of this essay, we examine queer genders by drawing from two recent documentaries, *The Aggressives* (2006) and *Still Black: A Portrait of Black Transmen* (2008), that provide two examples of black masculine people and communities who embrace the messiness of black queer gender and therefore present an alternative to the exclusively heterosexist and transphobic black common sense about gender. These two films reveal instances when black gender-variant people "explode common sense from the inside," as black queer theorist Kara Keeling postulates, which is in and of itself a messy proposition of oppositional and status quo practices.[17] The subjects from *Still Black* and *The Aggressives* use gender variance as a way to make a community that demonstrates a decoupling of gender from sexual identity in unconventional ways. However, they also simultaneously participate in the same conventions of sexism and misogyny.

The Aggressives features interviews with non-gender-conforming and female-bodied masculine women who are ensconced in the Ballroom scene in New York City. What is referred to as "the gender system" is forged in Ballroom culture, a black and Latino/a queer community mainly throughout North America. In this film, we observe how Ballroom culture is a way that non-gender-conforming communities of color—mostly black—forge discursive and material spaces that neither consolidate hegemonic gender categories nor completely reject them. Black queer members of communities like Ballroom claim and perform gender in ways that are not always legible according to a common sense schema of gender and sexuality. They reveal the need for theorists to, as Judith Butler argues, understand and account for gender bodies that live outside regimes of gender and sexual legibility and recognition.[18]

Although contemporary Ballroom culture has been around for at least five decades, this community of black and Latino/a LGBTQ people remains largely underground. Since its beginnings in Harlem, New York, more than fifty years ago, Ballroom culture has expanded rapidly to every major city in the United States, including Chicago, Atlanta, Baltimore, Charlotte, Detroit, and Philadelphia.[19] Ballroom culture was first captured in popular media in Jennie Livingston's documentary film, *Paris Is Burning* (1991).[20] Livingston's documentary was the first exposé to bring mainstream exposure to Ballroom practices in the late 1980s in New York City, and it continues to be the film most screened and referenced on this community, even by Ballroom members.[21]

The social practices of Ballroom culture consist of a gender system, a kinship structure (houses), and ball events. Here we focus on the gender system, which is the basis of all Ballroom subjectivities, familial roles, and the competitive performance categories at ball events. In this system, sex, gender, and sexuality are three sets of separate but inextricably linked categories (i.e., sex, gender, and sexuality are linked but not always conflated). Most importantly, the gender system reflects Susan Stryker's point that gender is what we do, not who we are.[22]

It is worth noting that some of the categories in the system are strictly gender categories, such as Femme Queens. Hence, Femme Queens can be straight, lesbian, bisexual, queer, and so on. However, other categories in Ballroom conflate gender and sexuality, such as, for example, the Butch Queen, which is a gay man. Yet the Woman category, consisting of cisgender women, with few exceptions, demarcates gender only, while it can imply a range of sexualities. In Ballroom culture, Women are primarily straight, feminine lesbians or queer.[23]

Yet for the gender categories that do not explicitly indicate sexuality, it is always implied. In other words, although some categories do not include particular sexual categories, such as the Butch, for example, sexual meanings are ascribed to his body through his gender identity and performance. Thus, the gender system of Ballroom culture is always about sexuality and at times reflects the pervasive conflation of sex, gender, and sexuality in broader society that we critique above. In Ballroom, as in larger society, sexuality is interpolated, implied, and regulated primarily through gender performance.

The Ballroom gender system also reveals gender and sexual fluidity and the possibilities for various configurations of romantic, sexual, and nonsexual affinities and interactions between members. Again, sex, gender, and sexuality are malleable and mutable. While this may seem somewhat of a banal point to most gender and sexuality theorists, in the quotidian lives of black genderqueers, the notion that sex, gender, and sexuality are not inherent and fixed is a matter of common sense among members of the community but not for those with whom they interact outside of it.

It is important to briefly point out the role that the gender system plays with regard to the competitive categories at ball events and the kinship system. Each member of the Ballroom community identifies with and is interpellated as one of the six categories in the gender system. The gender system plays just as important a role in the kinship system as it does for the competitive categories at balls by determining which genders can and should take on which parental role(s). Houses are led by "mothers" (Butch Queens, Femme Queens, and Women) and "fathers" (Butch Queens and Butches), who, regardless of age, sexual orientation, and social status, provide a labor of care and love with/for numerous black and Latino/a LGBTQ people who have been rejected by their blood families, religious institutions, and society at large.

One of the aggressives featured in *The Aggressives* is Tiffany, a member of the Ballroom scene in New York City. Tiffany uses female pronouns but considers herself to be a faggot. She also eschews lesbian identity and says that she has "heterosexual sex" with transgender women. In so doing, Tiffany, as a "femme aggressive," resists gender and sexual policing because she does not adhere to or identify herself in ways that are consistent with normative categories of womanhood or manhood, heterosexuality or homosexuality. Tiffany forges a different sense of herself by putting into crisis legible gender and sexual identification within the black queer cultural milieu of Ballroom. First, although she describes herself as a cisgender woman, in the film Tiffany is represented as a Butch and as an aggressive, and she identifies as a faggot, a Butch Queen in Ballroom culture. She has heterosexual sex with transgender women or those who are "female appearing." In Ballroom, Butch Queens are typically cisgender men who have sex with other cisgender men. Yet Tiffany is not attracted to cisgender men, male appearing females, or masculine women. This confounds gender and sexual legibility even in Ballroom culture, let alone in larger society, where she could be considered a penis pretender with a twist. Second, the activities in which Tiffany participates in the Ballroom scene are more associated with Butch Queens. She is shown commentating at balls and doing street outreach for HIV/AIDS prevention in the scene. These activities tend to be those undertaken by and associated with Butch Queens in the Ballroom community.[24]

Part of the messiness of Tiffany's representation is her illegibility in certain terms of masculine gender and her legibility in terms of sexist performance. This makes her a figure that cannot be co-opted easily into a discourse of "pure" resistance. Tiffany would come under the category of penis pretender/penis fraud from our black genderqueer-phobic taxonomy in that she is masculine, often read as male, and presumed to fulfill masculine obligations of gender. In other words, Tiffany "acts" like she has a penis, but she does not have one; thus, she is viewed as a penis fraud. She disrupts gender expectation to the extent that she found it difficult to be a young woman and stay in the NYC public school system. She says that her teachers would continuously question her, "What kind of name is Tiffany for a boy?" As previously stated, part of the masculine gender obligation is the subordination and rejection of femininity. Tiffany does not forgo the responsibilities of masculinity to participate in sexism and misogyny. For example, in one scene from the film, she and an aggressive friend engage a typical performance of masculine dominance in a public street using a calendar with a picture of a semi-nude black woman. "That's the kind of woman I'm going to have," the friend says while pretending to lick the picture. Later, Tiffany reveals her own ambivalence toward gender nonconformity. She boldly states, "I want a real woman. I'm tired of dating transgenders."

In general, Tiffany exemplifies the messiness and incoherence of gender and sexuality in black communities. She also seems to deliberately disturb gender and sexual legibility in Ballroom culture, demonstrating the mutability and malleability of gender and sexual categories in the community. Thus, in many ways, Ballroom culture is a means through which one can transgress and resist discursive and material attempts to regulate and stabilize one's gender and sexual identities and expressions.

Kortney Ryan Ziegler's film, *Still Black* (2008), documents the personal histories of black trans men who resist predictability in their own ways. Each of the six interviews in *Still Black* affords the viewer extended opportunities to listen to black trans men in their homes from across the country. The film is shot mostly in close-ups, and the camera relentlessly focuses on the subjects' faces in a defiant intimacy with each interviewee, rarely moving away from the subject. There is no escaping the black trans point of view in the film; it is filmed from a black trans man's perspective both behind and in front of the camera. The fact that the film is centered on black trans men's faces makes the viewer contend with their thoughts and ideas rather than their trans bodies, especially genitalia, which is the most common interaction that the media has with trans subjects.[25]

This repositioning of the camera away from the medical voyeurism of the surgical bed to the space of the living room takes black trans men in a black context from abstract and different beings to being familiar in a black "home" context.[26] Many of the interviewees speak directly about their families of origin and black childhood communities in a loving manner, stressing the continued joy and connection they have with a variety of family members. The content of the work thus expands what we understand to be "black family," and it questions the previously discussed common sense notions that make being cisgendered a prerequisite for finding "home" in black communities and institutions.

This is most poignantly evidenced in the *Still Black* interview with Carl Madgett, a trans man from Chicago with a wife and two kids. He accepts the terms of heterosexual masculinity: "I know I am a positive Black man. I am married, I have kids, I go to work. I am a minister. I go to church." Ironically, *Still Black* brings us back to the black church as a site of gender transformation through the possibility of the rejection of sexist gender norms, the very norms espoused by the black clergy we highlight earlier in this chapter. In the documentary, Carl is a deacon in the small predominantly black queer Pillar of Love Church in Chicago. His interview gives another version of the black church than what is represented by Bishops Owens and Wilson.

Similar to what performance ethnographer E. Patrick Johnson captures in *Sweet Tea*, an oral history of black gay men in the U.S. South, Carl finds an open and welcoming place in the church.[27] He describes it as a place to "feel love" and "feeling alive," stating, "I can be gay, bisexual, transgender and still have a relationship with God." He says that however someone identifies, "We welcome all." Carl's interview happens entirely underneath pictures of his wife, Wanda, and their twin girls, with a couple of pictures of Carl at church. His interview is the only one that includes another person, signaling that an important part of understanding Carl is his relationship with Wanda. Wanda appears with Carl in an oversized living room chair as they describe the circumstances surrounding the birth of their children. During the interview, Wanda and Carl agree that they have perfectly replicated the American familial ideal. She quips, "We don't have a picket fence yet, but that's it." What is also revealed is that Wanda does the majority of the domestic labor. Visually, the interview shifts to Carl alone again. Instead of the previous animated statements into the camera, Carl is more subdued. The camera pulls back, and the audience can see that Carl is alone in the chair; subsequently, he seems much smaller against the overstuffed backing.

A significant part of the remaining segment revolves around Carl's confession of "the chauvinist in [him]," for the terms of masculinity include the requisite sexism to the extent that the black feminists in the church have described him as "oppressing" his partner. According to Carl, he has structured his manhood in relation to the mainstream of gender common sense, which demands the subordination of women. "It's a learning process on how to make my wife my equal, she's not in front of me, behind me, she's beside me. She's my equal." Even though by mainstream standards of common sense Carl is a penis pretender, he is thought to have a gender expression in line with patriarchal masculinity.

In this context, Carl's gender performance is seen as an oppressive force that instead of being celebrated is revealed for its violence. He says, "There are a lot of feminists in my church. They are letting me see things in a different light. And I'm glad that they have done that. . . . They have shown me: You know, Carl, this how you are, you are very oppressive to your partner." Carl's interaction with his church portrays a messy set of circumstances. Carl's participation in patriarchal family is not predicated by birth anatomy. For Carl, there is a match between his understanding of gender common sense and that of dominant society.

Eventually, Carl receives another perspective on the definition of manhood and masculinity from the women of the church. The church is still in the role of setting black gender common sense, but for another set of outcomes. Through this connection, he is able to "see [himself] becoming an activist" and is "called" to do antiviolence work in a similar way to being "called" to his ministry. In this case, the church is a mirror for a different understanding of black manhood.

Conclusion

In her essay "Deviance as Resistance: A New Research Agenda for the Study of Black Politics," political scientist Cathy J. Cohen calls for the development of a research agenda that emphasizes the experiences of those who stand outside or on the margins of state-sanctioned normative identities or those located at the bottom of society. Guided by Cohen's call, in this essay we have sought to theorize the mainly discursive means through which sexuality is policed and regulated through discourses of gender in black cultural institutions such as churches and colleges/universities. If mainstream institutions create shared and contested understandings of black gender common sense, so do black queer communities and institutions. Black queer gender common sense is a messy combination of dominant gender definitions, alternative black revisions of gender norms, and queer innovations. Demeaning and oppressing the black sissy or the trans man is indeed about policing gender, but it is also about regulating sexuality, that is, the "assumed" fag and dyke, respectively. Through *The Aggressives* and *Still Black* we examined representations of quotidian forms of pushing against gender and sexual regulation. It is essential that black scholars, artists, and activists analyze and challenge hegemonic gender and sexual norms in our communities.

Notes

1. James Jones, "More Gay Bashing from the Pulpit," *Washington City Paper,* May 5, 2006, accessed September 10, 2006, washingtoncitypaper.com/blogs/citydesk/2006/05/05/politics-more-gay-bashing-from-the-pulpit/.

2. Chipumuro, "Pastor, Mentor, or Father?"

3. See the interview with Jamal Lewis about being a gender-nonconforming graduate (2014) at Morehouse College. Hannah Giorgis, "What Happens When You Don't Want to Be a Man at an All-Male HBCU," *BuzzFeed News,* November 7, 2015, accessed November 18, 2015, buzzfeed.com/hannahgiorgis/there-is-a-complexity-to-struggle#.xl39Jk2Pb.

4. Lubiano, "Black Nationalism and Common Sense."

5. Harris, *AIDS, Sexuality, and the Black Church,* 4.

6. There are a myriad of cases in which black people have been killed for not being the "right" gender. Sakia Gunn's murder is an important illustration of this point. For more information on the Gunn murder, see Jonathan Ned Katz and John D'Emilio, "The Murder of Sakia Gunn and LGBT Anti-violence Mobilization," edited by Carl Foote, *OutHistory* "Queer Newark," created by Timothy Stuart-Winter and Whitney Strub, accessed July 28, 2017, outhistory.org/exhibits/show/queer-newark/murder-of-sakia-gunn.

7. In many ways, this is part of the anxiety of the "down low" or black male bisexuality, a black man who could be socially feminized but now lurks undetected in the masculine population.

8. Willie Wilson, "Willie Wilson Sermon" (MP3 audio file, 3:07), Internet Archive, *Our Media*, May 4, 2007, accessed July 27, 2014, archive.org/details/WillieWilsonWillieWilson-Sermon.

9. Judith Butler, "The Lesbian Phallus and the Morphological Imaginary," in Butler, *Bodies That Matter*, 57–92. Butler is in conversation with Jacques Lacan's "The Signification of the Phallus," in *Écrits* (New York: W. W. Norton, 2007).

10. Office of Student Services, "Morehouse College Appropriate Attire Policy," in *Morehouse College Student Handbook 2013–2014*, 38–39, accessed July 11, 2013, morehouse.edu/campus_life/student_conduct/pdf/Student_Handbook_2013–2014.pdf.

11. Ibid.

12. The Blogmother, "Morehouse President Throws 'Hissy Fit,' but NOT over Genarlow Wilson," *What About Our Daughters*, October 18, 2010, accessed July 29, 2013, whataboutourdaughters.com/waod/tag/mean-girls-of-morehouse.

13. See alleged rape accusations against Morehouse students. Holly Pennebaker, "Morehouse Students Face Rape, Other Charges," *11 Alive*, last modified May 2, 2013, accessed July 29, 2013, 11alive.com/news/article/290941/40/Morehouse-athletes-face-rape-other-charges.

14. David A. Love, "Morehouse Dress Code Is More about Homophobia Than Decorum," *theGrio* October 19, 2009, accessed July 29, 2013, thegrio.com/2009/10/19/morehouse-college-that-legendary-institution/.

15. Ibid.

16. "The Mean Girls of Morehouse," *Vibe*, October 11, 2010, accessed July 28, 2017, vibe.com/article/mean-girls-morehouse.

17. Keeling, *The Witches Flight*, 21.

18. Butler, *Undoing Gender*, 242.

19. For a more comprehensive description and examination of Ballroom culture, see Bailey, *Butch Queens Up in Pumps*.

20. *Paris Is Burning*, directed by Jennie Livingston (1990; Burbank, CA: Off White Productions, Inc., Miramax Home Entertainment, Buena Vista Home Entertainment, 2005), DVD.

21. *How Do I Look* (dir. Wolfgang Busch, 2006) and *The Aggressives* (dir. Daniel Peddle, 2005).

22. Stryker, "(De)Subjugated Knowledges," 10.

23. Bailey, "Performance as Intervention," 260; Bailey, "Gender/Racial Realness."

24. Bailey, *Butch Queens Up in Pumps*, 49.

25. One salient example of the insatiable desire in mainstream media for the sensational-ism of the trans body and the trans body in transformation is the show *Sex Change Hospital* (WE TV, 2007–10, and Discovery Fit and Health, 2011). According to its own publicity, it "follows patients—from retired grandfathers to construction workers, businessmen and office managers—as they undergo surgery to transition from one gender to another." "Sex Change Hospital," Top Documentary Films, accessed July 26, 2014, http://topdocumentary films.com/sex-change-hospital/.

26. This is a similar strategy employed by Barbara Smith in her introduction to *Homegirls: A Black Feminist Anthology* and in her short story "Home" in the same volume, as well as the work of Essex Hemphill in *Ceremonies*. Both of these black queer authors stress the estrangement and connection black queer people have with their families of origin and the desire to "go home" to black communities.

27. Johnson, *Sweet Tea*.

CHAPTER 7

"Happy at Last"

Carving the White "Closet" Past,
Creating an "Out" Future

Jeffrey Q. McCune Jr.

> For whom is outness a historically available and affordable option?
> Is there an unmarked class character to the demand for universal
> "outness"? Who is represented by which use of the term, and who is
> excluded?
>
> —Judith Butler, *Bodies That Matter: On the Discursive Limits of Sex*

When my book *Sexual Discretion: Black Masculinity and the Politics of Passing* was published in 2014, I would always give book talks where it was inevitable that someone would ask, "Why don't black men come out?" This question was posed as if outness was an easy move, the only narrative of progress, and the sole way to articulate one's comfort with queer sex and sexuality. This question bothered me most because it was confounding, considering most black men I knew had expressed resistance to outness as a necessary positionality. In fact, during the time of such remarks, there was a frequency of white men being dragged out of the so-called closet, as they occupied positions of power within politics, the church, and other institutional locations where queerness was deemed threatening. As public attention heightened around such acts, I was reminded that white men also practiced "sexual discretion," as they quieted their sexual lives as a response to ideological forces that surveilled them and marked queer sex deviant and dissonant. Most significant was the realization that differences in expressions of sexuality had too often gone unrecognized or unmarked: outness was deemed the ideal positionality for *all* queer subjects. This framing—largely offered from within a white homonormative regime—prompted my realization that while much of this public celebration centered on the work of sexuality, it was as much a commentary on race.

This idea that "white closets" were a done deal can be attributed to a certain public imagining of white LGBT progress narratives (e.g., marriage equality) as marking a changing cultural front. Indeed, LGBT homelessness, racial inequalities within queer communities, and continued sexual stigma suggest otherwise. Nonetheless, popular media and culture conceal these narratives in lieu of more romanticized notions of progress. Literally, LGBT romance narratives took front and center in the American public.

This chapter explores Ang Lee's *Brokeback Mountain* (2005) as a "cowboy love story" that signaled a seismic shift in the public imaginary, becoming a pedagogical film that distilled a queer closet past to secure a narrative of a queer present without sexual discretion or constraint. This film, about two white men constrained by cowboy culture and larger cultural expectations, offered sexual discretion as a psychical-emotional trauma, with little to no room for other interpretations. I argue that white men who practice sexual discretion—especially the closeted "gay cowboys" in *Brokeback Mountain*—are deployed in public discourse as anomalies and outliers. The film, in its containment to a dusty, aged aesthetic, projects nondominant sexuality as a pain of the past. This essay is most interested in how such narratives of once-closeted white men seemingly center the closet narrative in order to celebrate coming out, forging a space where discreet ways of being in the world appear anachronistic, backward, or rare.

More than a decade after the *Brokeback Mountain* explosion, this essay reopens the case of "white men on the DL" to demonstrate how this moment has been instructive for a problematic imagining of "LGBT progress" that now dominates public discourse. Here, I elucidate how the larger discourse of the queer triumphant or queer progress activated an erasure of white queers who do not fit the mold of the out and proud gay subject. This elision constructs a cultural amnesia around other ways of knowing sexuality outside of coming out, enabling a misremembering of a white queer past and present devoid of discretion. These constructions of a white queer past sanitize white queerness and enable a discourse that impacts how white queers not only perpetually privilege progress narratives but potentially demonize or distort queers of color who perform often more illegible enactments of queerness. In essence, many films and other resonant texts have performed a popular queer historiography that misreads or underreads the broader histories and social realities of queer people within and outside of the United States. Rather than reading *Brokeback Mountain* as simply a filmic chronicle of history, it may be more apt to read it as a gesture toward a cross-historical current of discretion within and across queer communities. In this way, the black DL subject, who has largely been demonized as a deviant anomaly, may be a figure who offers a lens through which to understand what whiteness has concealed in the process of monopolizing the modes of doing sexuality. The tyranny of outness enacts (in)advertent violence to subjects of color while also limiting the possibilities for white subjects. In other words, the prevalence and privileging of dominant epistemologies not only deform black sex and sexuality but marginalize white forms of sexual doing outside the accepted or popular paradigm. In this way, the deemed triumphant progress narrative may be a tragic undoing of complex realities in history and the present.

Troubled "Past" Turned Triumphant: McGreevey and the McDonaldization of Outness

In October 2006 I was perusing magazines at the University of Rochester bookstore when I encountered what was then the cover of the *Advocate*'s "Coming Out" issue. On the front page was a picture of former New Jersey governor Jim McGreevey and a man I later learned was his partner engaged in what seemed a jovial tickling moment. Indeed, it was warm and fuzzy. However, what was striking and most jarring for me was the caption: "Jim McGreevey: New Jersey's ex-governor confesses his past and gets on with his life, HAPPY AT LAST!" This caption signaled two somewhat disturbing assertions for me. First, as he "confesses his past and gets on with his life," we are left to assume that this move is actually possible—this act of divorcing one's present from the past through the act of confession. Here, Michel Foucault's notion of "confession" as "all those procedures by which the subject is incited to produce a discourse of truth about his sexuality" is situated in a way that actually uses a fallacy to produce a truth.[1] This fallacious idea—that McGreevey can confess his past and simply move past it, attempts to connect him to a new narrative, a new truth, in service of a specific normalizing homonarrative that has too often been marketed as a queer ideal, hence the fairy-tale conclusive "Happy at Last" juxtaposed to the tickling image, establishing "out" as the quintessential queer position of happiness. This imaging affirms a claim made by Mark Blasius: "The contemporary lesbian and gay movement since Stonewall has made living one's life as an openly gay or lesbian person a criterion of 'liberation.'"[2] While the actualization of Blasius's thesis and the propositions made by the *Advocate*'s imaging here are dissonant with my thinking on how sexuality works and what it entails, they illuminate the ways in which the queer experience, and understandings of that experience, may differ along racial lines. Moreover, they also illuminate how personal narratives are often used to affirm a universal politic that often elides those Zora Neale Hurston might call "the furthest down below," or down low, in this case.

126

The assertions made about the disconnection of past and present, as well as the happiness found out of the closet, are somewhat foreign to how I as a black man who has been a member of the black queer community for seemingly ages understand "quare" performances of sexuality.[3] The glossy, coherent narrative presented by the *Advocate*—though it may express McGreevey's present excitement over his embraced queer identity—unveiled for me a trope within the tradition of white narrations of (queer) history. Particularly, in the *Advocate*'s focus on moving from the past, I was reminded of all the moments when I had witnessed white narrators of history move fast to the finished product rather than explore the historical process that preceded the finale. This tendency greatly differed from the historical narratives of minority subjects, which seem to take the process and recognize the "doing" as much as the "thing done." What situates McGreevey on the front cover is his choice to be "out and proud"—as this is the "Coming Out" issue of the *Advocate*. This, indeed, was a celebration of gay liberation and what, for some, marks another chronicle of queer bravery in light of McGreevey's political sacrifice. In no way do I wish to devalue the bravery involved in outing experiences, but I do not want to permit or endorse a hierarchy for how one should or should not come to understand oneself as a sexual subject.

When we mark that this narrative follows a year of *Brokeback Mountain* craze, the celebration for McGreevey feels like more of a relief than a recognition of his personal ascendancy into liberation. The relief here is that he chose the "national coming-out narrative" rather than succumbing to the closet reality made palpable in the film. Through its consumption as a pastoral scene played before largely urban audiences, we can see how such a filmic rendering may advance the idea of the backward rural where closets run amok, producing a larger compulsory coming-out narrative, offering it up as the progressive alternative within a liberatory queer construct.

While the narrative set forth by the *Advocate* was an extension of the post-Stonewall politics of visibility that has seemingly taken over the queer public agenda, this demonstrates what I had established almost ten years ago in another research project: the *Advocate* magazine and many other gay press outlets are committed to a specific shaping of white queer history.[4] More importantly and consequently, dominant queer media and participants sanitize history by being unconcerned with black queer politics. Here, as the *Advocate* insists upon disconnecting the past and the present and commends and commands compulsory outing, we can predict the dissonance caused by racial presences that almost always evoke history and question the politics of visibility as the most viable politics for queer subjects. For the racialized queer subject, such disconnections—the separation of past from present—mean forgetting multiple identity narratives. To move beyond the closet, or hidden sexual behavior, is not only to deny the closet as differently constructed via culture but also to deny the way in which multiple cultural realities configure our closets and dictate when and where their doors can be left ajar.

This is most apparent when we situate the McGreevey moment within its historical frame. Ironically, ex-governor McGreevey's confession followed a media event in which black men who have sex with other men, but maintain relationships with wives and girlfriends, were subject to public scrutiny. These men, who are often referred to or refer to themselves as "men on the down low," or DL, were discursively demonized and framed as the dangerous vectors of contagion for HIV/AIDS among heterosexual black women. In April 2004, prior to McGreevey's August announcement, DL men (a term that has become a race way of constructing this narrative) were all over newspapers and magazines and took center stage on *The Oprah Winfrey Show*. Nonetheless, this term and its demonizing baggage never followed McGreevey. Yet this descriptor did make its way into written follow-up inside the *Advocate*. After McGreevey discussed his newfound happiness and relationship at length, and directly after he discussed the "risks," he was then asked by the interviewer, "Is there a message in the [forthcoming] book for adults who are on the 'down low' like you were?" Never employing the DL term, which was somewhat imposed by the interviewer, McGreevey then addressed the message for those who engage in "duplicitous" behavior. Nonetheless, the DL was evoked in relationship to disease and duplicitousness, situating McGreevey (a white man) outside this performance of discreet sexual identity (representationally black). Interestingly, McGreevey fits the dominant DL narrative more than any black figure we have seen who has been inscribed with this term in a media context. Yet his rhetoric of guilt, regret, and apologia (read: whiteness) marks him as immune, or at least immunized, from demonizing constructions of his queer performance.

While the *Advocate* article demonstrates awareness of the parallels between McGreevey and media constructions of the "DL man," this article constructs McGreevey outside of this "group," as, in his words, he has moved past this "dark place." In a moment of DL media frenzy—that is, the discourse that frames (black) men who sleep with men while they are also assumed to have girlfriends or wives—such inscriptions escape the bodies of white men like McGreevey (Congressman Foley, evangelist Haggard). Indeed, the absence of these largely blackfaced fictions from white men's performances of actual sexual "deviance" illustrates the unjust treatment of minoritized bodies within media and society more generally. I argue that the *Advocate* engages in what can now be called the construction of a usable white queer history in which images are often sanitized and dehistoricized for the advancement of "queer liberation." The history that has been narrated by contemporary gay/lesbian political frameworks understands the DL as outside of homonormative discourse, as well as white queer "doings." In essence, whiteness is once again the pure substance that is only tainted when in contact with the colored "others." The choice to divorce ex-governor McGreevey from DL discourse, then, is not only a rhetorical move but also a racial one.

Movin' on Up: *Brokeback* Ain't Black

The escape of white men such as ex-governor McGreevey from the pathologizing DL frame to which black men seem a natural subject is even more apparent in the public framing of the film *Brokeback Mountain*. One of the most telling observations is how this film is almost always referred to as a "gay cowboy movie"—the love story of ranch hand Ennis Del Mar and rodeo cowboy Jack Twist—playing up, and playing on, all the romantic possibilities and discursive power available within this construction. On the one hand, such descriptions situate the film within a historic frame of westerns, in which love and action (not simply lust) are central to the narrative. On the other hand, the coupling of gay cowboy undoes the paradox that is inherent in a time when Jack of *Will and Grace* is deemed distant and distinct from Jack the gay cowboy in the film. With this possibility, queer men can be understood within a normative gender structure without having to sacrifice expressions of queer desire. While this may be a transgressive or even a utopian thought, it obfuscates and misconstrues the lived experiences that tell us that this moment has not arrived, only illustrating a temporal moment for which the public can digest a romanticized, ready-made package via Hollywood. Through filmic representation, the cowboys are outed, made into emblems of queer affection, though they do not fit the pretty picture of a politics of visibility.

Brokeback Mountain was for many a filmic triumph as it pressed queer romance into popular cinematic view and celebrated queer affection among the queerest community, cowboys. However, I would like to suggest here that the success of *Brokeback* as feature film rested on its absences, or the things in the shadows. First, there is the film's primary manipulation of the rural as a place that "was" rather than is, as well as its excision of racialized bodies that would potentially call attention to the ways in which *Brokeback* calls forth a usable tragic queer past while denying what for some is their present (within both rural and urban communities). What is the social significance of the film when one is a black queer subject or a Mexican queer subject who engages the film from within Mexico? How might the white queer subject who lives in the rural plains or urban poverty differently understand this film? What does it mean that the triumph of the narrative of *Brokeback Mountain* happens outside the discourses present within the film? So much of what we are cinematically told to read is rendered with an eye toward other discursive currents within dominant Western understandings of sexuality and sexual progress.

Here, I wish to suggest that the rural frame for this film—in our sociocultural imaginary—allows us to read the film not only outside this DL moment but also within a different queer time. Both queer time and DL presence in popular discourse require an urban context to be coherent or consistent with the linear narratives that are used to envelop queerness. In rural Wyoming we are witnesses to a world that exists outside of Stonewall, outside of urban gay ghettos, but inside the farm, on top of Brokeback Mountain—an embodied reality that challenges what Jack Halberstam might call "metronormative ideals."[5] Within this system of thought, the logical way out of the rural closet is urban outness. This "open" location is proffered as the solution to the DL and a way out of the "repressive rural closet." But most significant here is that the rural is always already a closet; it is framed as a location where the old stuff happens while the new politics is formed elsewhere in urban America. It is this mythology that created a certain sentiment around *Brokeback Mountain*'s central narrative, the love affair between Ennis and Jack. What UK reporter Gary Younge notes is instructive: "It is the only movie I have ever heard of where women cry, in sympathy rather than anger, at the sight of two men routinely betraying their wives, set in a place that embraces rather than stigmatizes human frailty—where people cheat because the rules are stacked against them. On the Down-Low up high in the hills."[6]

I wish to draw on Younge's spatial recognition here by examining a very memorable scene in the film. In this scene, Ennis and Jack have left Brokeback Mountain, the space where their relationship developed, and have returned to their different lives—Jack in Texas and Ennis in Wyoming. Ennis has just gotten word via postcard that after four years of absence, Jack is coming to visit him, and Ennis awaits Jack's return. As Ennis relays to his wife the content of the postcard, he tells her it's from his "fishin' buddy." After this exchange, we watch the distance between Ennis and his wife, as every day that Jack could potentially arrive creates a clear and visible internal tension—Ennis is quite immobile and unengaged in the happenings of his domestic family life. After a set of tense scenes, we hear the engine of what we can assume is a pickup truck, and out the door flies Ennis to greet "Jack Fuckin' Twist." First, he runs down the stairs in excitement. He gives Jack an abrasive hug. Then he plants a deep, intense kiss, which causes them both to collide into Ennis's home wall, right below the stairs. As they continue in their wrestle-like erotic exchange, Ennis's wife, Alma, appears at the top of the stairs to silently watch and witness the "love that dare not speak its name." After a long, heavy gaze, she closes the door and returns to what becomes her closet space.

Indeed, there is directorial juxtaposition established here to distinguish one sociosexual location from another. The romantic moment happens down the stairs, down low, if you will. Up the stairs at the door we are reminded of Ennis's present—his wife, Alma, stands in the space where he engaged in reprofuturity and heteronormative desires. Symbolically, the ideal relationship is placed on top, while the queer relationship is relegated to the bottom. Ennis's wife's gaze from up high down low draws our attention away from the erotic to the punitive. This moment of confirmed infidelity now speaks not only to her limited agency as she simply steps away but also to her disempowered gaze, which is deemed not strong enough to interrupt this moment.

However, I would argue that much of the weight of the infidelity piece of the film is removed by the roughneck beauty of Jack and Ennis and the artistic mastery of godly cinematography and glorious music, in addition to the audience's recognition that this erotic performance seemed foreign from these two bodies in 2005. In other words, working against this scene is the sentiment that we have indeed "been there, done that." And though not formal, the overt erotic relations between these men when framed in film become a sort of outing, rather politically or just representationally. In a moment framed as 1967 or even later, these performances, when represented on the 2005 screen, seem distant from what is often understood as contemporary queer experiences, even though as this film is popularized there is a population of minoritized men who are as DL in the city as Ennis and Jack in the rural plains.

Much of the excitement stemmed from the fact that this was the first major motion picture to explicitly take male-male relationships as its nucleus. Still, the film, set mostly in 1963, happens in the rural plains prior to Stonewall; it positions angst-ridden sex between men as an act of the past. Indeed, as many scholars have suggested, the urban space (where most viewed this film) also gives way to the idea that the times of the closet and hidden sex between men are not only unnecessary but an oddity. In essence, it inadvertently celebrates the "progress" made by white gay men to now be able to articulate an openly queer identity without the guise of marriage or heterosexual masking. While this may be part of a more utopian understanding of queer life, the film, which is set in Wyoming and was filmed almost ten years after the brutal killing of Matthew Shepard, cannot escape this tragedy. Indeed, the film captures this tension in the scene when Ennis and Jack return to Brokeback and engage in a dialogue about what we might now call their potential "gay future."

Here, the film interrupts our longing for our queer present in this tale of the "past." More importantly, it reiterates how queers are, as Nella Larsen wrote almost a century ago, "always on the edge of danger."[7] This is a danger, I might add, that reconfigures time and space, as well as one's relationship to the politics of visibility. In this scene and in the film's entirety, *Brokeback Mountain* engages the dialectic of love and violence, which surfaces as almost bookends to the elastic masculine presentations of self evident in both Ennis and Jack. As Ennis recaptures this violent moment when he came to know "partnership"—a psychologically impactful moment I would love to engage psychoanalytically but will not here—the common default to "these men are just simply 'closeted' or 'cheaters'" is incomplete when narrating their life story in its historical context or even outside of it. Thus, Jack and Ennis's retreat back to Brokeback may be understood as a utopic performative in the way that Jill Dolan has masterfully constructed it: "small but profound moments . . . that lift everyone slightly above the present, into a hopeful feeling of what the world might be like if every moment were as emotionally voluminous, generous, aesthetically striking, and intersubjectively intense."[8] Utopia, in this sense, was Brokeback Mountain. Hence, Jack's gesture—"it could be like this . . . just like this . . . *always*"—is indicative of this feeling. Yet Ennis's corrective—"two guys living together . . . *no way!*"—is all about life outside of the utopic Brokeback, a snap from the temporal location into the tense present, a clear recognition of the constraints of space and time, their lives off the mountain and in the range of homophobia, violence, and aggressive masculinity. Jack is engaged in a fantasy of queerness that is isolated from these realities, while Ennis implicitly reminds him of the integral role they play not only in his understanding of their relationship but also in his anxiety around "two guys living together," or, more aptly, a politics of queer visibility.

In later scenes, Ennis makes it clear that the rhythm of their meeting has to halt, creating a dystopia in Jack's world. As Jack is unable to commune with Ennis, he flees to Mexico, confirming Ennis's sentiment when he says, "I know what people do in Mexico." This scene, our first explicit engagement with bodies other than white men and women, situates Mexican men as "others," sexual agents for white male pleasure. In the film, the representation of Mexico is a generic fiesta-like Mexico with storefront liquor distributors, hardy laughs, kids running wild in the streets, and sex workers lurking in the dark shadows of this Mexican parade. Mexico becomes a location of disorder. Most significant here, however, is Mexico's stark contrast to the bright, beautiful, and artistic landscape that is Brokeback Mountain, where white men perform hidden sexual acts—down low, up in the hills. Instead, in the Mexican context—as with contemporary DL narratives—"down low" is flipped to "low down." For Jack, Mexican men act as exotic slaves, deemed only as alternative options for Ennis's whiteness. The portrayal of Mexican men in the shadows makes more visible the whiteness of the film. Indeed, in this framing Mexico is a site that is "not only racialized as brown, it is chaotic, dirty, dim, narrow, and claustrophobic."[9] However, there is another reading possible here. The slip of the filmmaker's pen, which seems to suggests that Latino men and men of color more generally are not the only ones who reside "down low," challenges the idea that tacit and down low subjects are now contained to specific racial and ethnic groups. The dimly lit setting that is Mexico also assists with an imagining of this "dark continent" as otherworldly, the darker side of queerness.

132

While the idea of *Brokeback* as throwback refines the history of white men, it inadvertently situates the "doings" of DL men, or arguably a large contingency of black gay men who choose discretion over the politics of visibility, to appear underdeveloped or simply backward. But more than this, it dishonestly represents a sterilized white queer history by suggesting that these are times of yesterday. Indeed, the embodied performances of those famous white faces mentioned above deny that all white men have the opportunity or desire for outness. These performances replay Judith Butler's inquiry in *Bodies That Matter*: "For whom is outness a historically available and affordable option? Is there an unmarked class character to the demand for universal 'outness'? Who is represented by which use of the term, and who is excluded? For whom does the term present an impossible conflict between racial, ethnic, or religious affiliation and sexual politics? What kinds of policies are enabled by what kinds of usages and which are backgrounded or erased from view?"[10] While the first part of Butler's inquiry is oft-cited and somewhat self-explanatory, as it speaks to some of the more obvious ways that expectations of outness may be complicated for all human subjects, the latter portion speaks directly to what this chapter attempts to deconstruct: the ways that whiteness is enabled through the historicization of queerness. *Brokeback Mountain* facilitates a belief that contemporary white queer communities, as post-Stonewall and post-Reagan, have departed from the rural (here, a metonym for repressive) representation that seems central to the film. Whereas now Jack and Ennis seem distant from later contemporary models of queerness like Jack and Will (of *Will and Grace*), I assert that this cowboy representation may be found even in present-day urban landscapes as an unspoken presence within American culture that may, indeed, be a product of the hypervisibility of queerness. In other words, as white queer politics have embraced the personal equals political equals public mantra, the availability of queer codes and language encourages a retreat back to the so-called closet, maybe even "down low." Thus, when Judith Butler evokes the notion of policies that are "erased from view," I would like to suggest that the regulatory aspects of homonormative demands of confession and disclosure are overshadowed by the excitement of being "out." As visibility becomes the more privileged positionality for queer subjects, there are both gains and losses.

I want to propose that the universal outness as the formula for a coherent, collective queer public may be a regulating apparatus within the lives of politicians, evangelists, and priests because they, like many black queer men, have high stakes in remaining nonvisible to those who seek to police their possibilities. As black men are hypersurveillanced due to the surplus value given to blackness, the hypervisibility that is the norm in the lives of such political-religious figures may serve to deem public queerness as a nonviable option. Thus, to excise the

DL from the white queer equation is to be dishonest about the pressures, forces, and ideological demands that are active in the lives of men such as McGreevey, Foley, and Haggard. While it is easy to engage in queer uplift through the revelry for McGreevey's outness, it is as important to understand the dynamics of his being situated "down low." Here, I employ the term "down low" not to evoke all the media baggage but to signify the truth of the matter: McGreevey, Foley, and Haggard did not come out of the closet, they were brought out, illustrating, as with DL men, that the closet has unnamed agency. It is not until after the "finding out" that outness becomes the celebratory domain, upon which McGreevey in particular appears on the front cover of the *Advocate*. Indeed, many men do find the closet repressive, painful, and desolate; however, it seems to me a dishonest telling of queer history to place value judgments on individual positionality without reading the larger macrocultural influences on decision making and identity construction.

Nonetheless, white queer men—no matter how accurate their DL performances—escape the racialized associations with the DL. I argue that this is due in part to the desire to construct a "usable queer past"—a telling of history that always already includes the accessible, visible subject. Thus, it necessitates those bodies that do not subscribe to the politics of visibility or forces them to attempt to perform within the legitimating discourse in order to be understood or celebrated. The latter can be seen most in the outings of such famed celebrities as NBA basketball player Jason Collins, though African American, who answered the call of coherence, embracing the modicum of coming out even as his disclosure included no other confession other than "I am a black gay man." While this performative utterance has power, I would suggest that he still operates under a stronger politics of discretion: he submits to the surveilling culture of sport and never makes available the actual sex of his sexuality. This move, which was strategically crafted between Collins and *Sports Illustrated*, illuminates how such celebratory discourse has now normalized one particular way of coming into one's sexuality. Rather than allowing for the ways in which Collins's sexuality is complicated by issues of race, gender, and sport, public discourse has instead added him to a queer historical chain of folks who choose outness over the presumably decadent closet. This cultural move, I argue, is about creating a certain type of history in this our postcloset America, one that attempts to undo the narratives of *Brokeback* and McGreevey to present an identity that is more stable, more likeable, dare I say more marriageable. The DL, as understood via media, is the antithesis of these ideals, though the DL in practice is as dynamic and uncovers as much, if not more, about the unfair play between race and sexuality, secrets and society, and the production of fiction for the sake of complexity. In the present dominant cultural frame, it would seem that *Brokeback* could never be black. That is not to say that unapologetic, self-loving, and complicated rural male-male relations between men do not happen for queers of color. Instead, it suggests that the *Black Brokeback* seems impossible in our contemporary queer political moment, where there are clear attempts to sanitize and save a certain brand of queerness that often requires the removal of queer of color consciousness, as these black stories too often speak back and against the dominant experience.

For this reason, the advent of the film *Moonlight* into the spotlight may be said to pose a significant challenge here. This 2016 film, which was written and directed by black men and follows the developmental trajectory of a young man named Chiron, presents what may be understood as the black *Brokeback Mountain*. However, this film uniquely was not shaped out of a white queer imaginary. The black queer aesthetic, in which Barry Jenkins (director) and Tarrell Alvin McCraney (writer) unapologetically place black bodies and things front and center, relegates whiteness to a bare minimum, saving room for a spectrum of black representations of masculinity and sexuality. Nonetheless, it still centers on an attraction between Chiron and Kevin that is made to feel like a rugged intimacy akin to the cowboys in the mountain. While there is a marked similarity in the constrained and contained intimacy, *Moonlight* offers black queerness as a site of more than sexuality and its complexities. It is clear that the film intends to remark upon the queerness that is always blackness both in the reality of its everyday displacements and disparities and in how it must be presented onscreen as a layered presence that can never be instrumentalized just for "gay purposes." Thus, the saturation of black materiality, we might say, refuses the generic "gay thug" paradigm available in urban impoverished DL narratives, speaking back against *Brokeback*'s acceptance of "gay cowboy" motifs.

Moonlight has been celebrated similarly to *Brokeback Mountain*—though it actually won the 2017 Best Motion Picture Academy Award—as a "gay film." The very frequency of extracting out the blackness that is so salient in *Moonlight*'s filmic work, in its rare description as *black* gay film or simply a *black* film, is a tendency that I have noticed and marked as the popular flattening of complexity driven by a sexual-social economy that always desires a universal narrative of sexuality ("gay film" or "coming-of-age story"). The embrace of *Moonlight*, the most comparative film to *Brokeback Mountain* since 2005, does not exhibit a turn to recognize blackness within queerness; instead, it is an extension of the American fascination with creative and powerful black aesthetics. While I admit that *Moonlight* did some important cultural work, introducing a narrative around complex blackness and black sexuality, it was produced within a cultural frame that still preserves a *Brokeback* memory. In this genealogical framework, folks still anticipate the "happily ever after," reaching for what comes after Kevin and Chiron's closing embrace. In a sense, the public imagination is still preoccupied with a coupling, coming-out narrative that transforms the discrete and discreet practices of Chiron and Kevin into a legible queer relationality that satisfies the progress narrative. This desire for a narrative of progress imposes white queer norms into black queer aesthetics and filmic representation, which interrupts the move to see this as strictly a triumphant, transgressive moment. The specter of *Brokeback*—and its accompanying carving of the age-old closet for the sake of coming out as the compulsory contemporary—is alive and well. Nonetheless, *Moonlight* offers us a world in which, even if such a specter is imposed, it is impossible to purely witness this black film narrowly through such rigid and regimented cultural frames.

Notes

1. Foucault, "The Confession of the Flesh," 215–16.
2. Blasius, "An Ethos of Lesbian and Gay Existence."
3. Here I borrow from Johnson, "Quare Studies."
4. When I was at the University of Nebraska in Lincoln, I engaged in an extensive project examining visual representations within the *Advocate*. I concluded that the magazine historically has privileged white male bodies while also re-presenting the aesthetic trends of each era.
5. Halberstam, *In a Queer Time and Place*, 36–37.
6. Gary Younge, "Why There Will Never Be a Black *Brokeback Mountain*," *Guardian*, January 23, 2006, accessed July 28, 2017, guardian.co.uk/comment/story/0,1692548,00.html.
7. Larsen, *Quicksand and Passing*, 143.
8. Dolan, *Utopia in Performance*, 5.
9. Manalasan, "Colonizing Time and Space," 99.
10. Butler, *Bodies That Matter*, 227.

PART III

The Drag of Cultural Dissemblance

CHAPTER 8

Gospel Drag

Intimate Labor and the Blues Stage

Shana L. Redmond

Above all there is the matter of pleasure: intellectual, sensuous, aesthetic.

—Dorinne Kondo, *About Face: Performing Race in Fashion and Theater*

Dressmaker Nettie Dorsey was keenly aware of the negotiations she was making as she sewed and hemmed the dresses for her husband Thomas's most famous protégée, singer Gertrude "Ma" Rainey. Nettie's religious faith was undoubtedly held in tension with the secular and sexual world in which her husband and clients worked, causing no uncertain number of provocations and compromises. The life of this object—the dress—and its relation to sound motivate this chapter. Labor, race, and sexuality are bound up in this object and its production by the little-known Nettie, revealing how these modes of being inevitably animate and innovate the blues idiom and its performance. The economies produced therefrom are then more dynamic and intertextual than the literature announces. I am interested in the close proximities that exist through the costumes sewn by Mrs. Dorsey and worn by Rainey—the relationship between pious respectability and working-class nonheteronormativity, laboring femininity, and sonorous vocalities. Black women's treasured intimacies, especially those that develop and mature in spaces belonging to the domestic sphere, are political projects veiled, in the first decades of the twentieth century, by the politics and economies of respectability. This veil, of course, was porous, allowing glimpses of the happenings behind it, but the genius of these exchanges is also materialized sonically and staged extravagantly. The music made by these women is woven into their dresses, those robes the women lovingly and painstakingly nurtured. The dresses carry with them the types of quiet (and not so quiet) protests that are indicative of both the black church and blues circuits.

Synthesizing the pulpit and the stage was no minor task. It became a coalitional project requiring the talents of large cohorts of musicians, artists, and laborers. The sonic intersections generated on the stages commanded by Rainey and cocurated by Mrs. Dorsey made the music alive through the particular experiential genius of women of color. As Deborah Gray White and other black feminist scholars have documented, black women's location at "the crossroads" of race and gender uniquely positions them within global political landscapes, as well as within the black popular cultures that often represent and mobilize them.[1] Of course, the crossroads is itself a blues idiom and archetype, signaling the epic relations between good and evil, as well as the daily choice between right and wrong. White's language reveals the blues tradition as always gendered in complicated ways through the relationship between identity and sound. Mrs. Dorsey, though not a performer or composer herself, was a formative player within the dynamics that birthed the classic blues form and distinguished its songs as feminine forums of desire and dissent. Rainey's sexuality, class, and voice were magnified by Dorsey's ensembles and were intended to draw attention to the performing body. While Rainey's gender identity was displayed in normative (though lavish) gowns and heels, it nonetheless displayed a type of bending and fluidity between the relatively artificial binaries of the blues tradition that she and her cohort revolutionized and the sacred traditions that brought Nettie into the Dorsey clan. Genre underwrote this drag performance, developing, like the drag scenes observed by Jeffrey McCune, its significance as "more than a cursory exercise, but [rather] an essential observation."[2] Dorsey's dresses destabilized the sonic divisions produced by the church and the nascent popular music industry by materially mediating the voices of the dresses' maker and wearer.

The dress/body are the texts mediating this relation and a number of others within the wider world of sociality and its organizing constructions of race, gender, and sexuality. According to anthropologist Terence Turner, "The surface of the body seems everywhere to be treated, not only as the boundary of the individual as a biological and psychological entity but as the frontier of the social self as well." He names this the "social skin": "The surface of the body, as the common frontier of society, the social self, and the psycho-biological individual; becomes the symbolic stage upon which the drama of socialization is enacted, and bodily adornment (in all its culturally multifarious forms, from body-painting to clothing and from feather head-dresses to cosmetics) becomes the language through which it is expressed."[3] These margins between the skin and the world are not hard-and-fast boundaries; instead, they are porous and permeable, allowing de-lightful trespasses and foreboding transactions that provoke sometimes impulsive, sometimes studied, reactions. As Joanne Entwistle argues:

> Dress lies at the margins of the body and marks the boundary between self and other, individual and society. This boundary is *intimate and personal*, since our dress forms the visible envelope of the self and, as Davis puts it, comes "to serve as a kind of visual metaphor for identity"; it is also social, since our dress is structured by social forces and subject to social and moral pressures. If, as Mary Douglas (1973, 1984) has so forcefully demonstrated, the boundaries of the body are dangerous, it is therefore no surprise that clothing and other forms of adornment, which operate at these "leaky" margins, are subject to social regulation and moral pronouncements. It is no surprise either to find individuals concerned with what to hang at these margins.[4]

Women of color are possessed of the most dangerous boundaries, making our choice of accessory all the more significant, as we are especially vulnerable to the codes that structure social and political imposition and violence. Indeed, "women are more likely to be identified with the body than men, and this may generate different experiences of embodiment. It could be argued that women are more likely to develop greater body consciousness and greater awareness of themselves as embodied than men, whose identity is less situated in the body."[5] This is a re-sult and constituent element of power, the structures of which daily enforce the material significance of textile, cut, and style. As cultural anthropologist Dorinne Kondo provocatively and powerfully asks, "Who can afford to be unconcerned about his/her appearance? Who is *allowed* to ignore it with impunity?"[6] Certainly not women of color, whose proximity to rape and sexual assault, joblessness, po-lice violence, character assassination, and death have overdetermined equations of association and self-presentation for centuries.

In order to be "conscious of the ways we perform ourselves in everyday life, of the ways fashion and theater perform *us*," Kondo argues that we must provide critiques of the capitalist modes of production, as well as "reclaim pleasure as a site of potential contestation that might engage, and at times be coextensive with, the critical impulse."[7] It is with her urging in mind that I pursue the pleasures of affective care that might be seen and heard in Ma Rainey's dresses. Knowing as we do that there were hands on her dress, we must acknowledge the proximity of those hands to her body as they assisted in animating that array. According to Entwistle, "We 'normally' experience dress as alive and 'fleshy': once removed from the body, dress lacks fullness and seems strange, almost alien, and all the more poignant to us if we can remember the person who once breathed life into the fabric." There are at least two bodies to consider as we witness Rainey's dresses:

hers and Dorsey's, both of whom "breathed life" into these creations and made possible the dialectic of body and dress: "Dress works on the body, imbuing it with social meaning, while the body is a dynamic field that gives life and fullness to dress."[8] And since this black, female, laboring, costumed body was also an instrument, we need not only see but also listen.

It is rare to be confronted with the sounds of inanimate objects. Material culture is not often conceived of as a vocal form, but as Fred Moten argued of the enslaved black men and women once considered commodities, "objects can and do resist" through speech/sound.[9] Rather than equate a dress or any other consumable with black people, I instead follow material culture scholars who argue that items/things have agency through their relationship to systems of value. Agency and value are subjective calculations and methods that I briefly investigate here in order to document how those items that black men and women make and use are part of a sonic praxis—they carry the sounds of their makers, their environments, and their wearers, especially when those wearers are themselves materialized by sound. There is an accumulation of vocalities within the material object; the curses and laughter of its making, the sounds of its shop environment, the glee or frustration of its recipient are trapped in the fabric of its composition. In addition to these noises, the dresses made by Nettie Dorsey were part of an ongoing classic blues soundtrack. Her labors during the 1920s accompanied those of her husband, Thomas Dorsey, who is often credited as the "Father of the Gospel Blues," a genre itself at the crossroads of black music making. This sonic formation had not yet developed as a way to manage the sometimes-distinct secular-sacred spheres of black life, but its building was evident in this earlier period, which was dominated by the sounds of the blues women who wore the costumes painstakingly designed and sewn by Nettie Dorsey. Married only one day prior to embarking on tour with Rainey, Nettie and Thomas made for a dynamic pair within the performance traditions of early black vaudeville. What he couldn't produce for the ear, she made for the eye. Their sensory collaborations, which paired his fantastic ears with her able hands, made possible the stage show that launched Rainey into the center of a robust black public sphere of intellectualism, arts making, and industry.

The public sphere of which the blues women were part was a contested and combustible one. Unity, while often fantastically performed through concerts, parades, and congresses, was nonetheless precarious; icons like Marcus Garvey, W. E. B. Du Bois, and A. Philip Randolph circulated in tension with one another in this moment of competing nationalisms and split allegiances. Black women, who continued to struggle both within and from outside of established black protest organizations, and their blues were black popular culture in the 1920s, thereby launching the "fantastic" play and power of culture within developing black internationalisms.[10] The sounds of blues women mapped journeys and travel, in the process creating new worlds for their audiences. The moving black bodies that took flight from the rural U.S. South to urban cities changed the regional demographics of the nation while accompanied by blues men and women who also negotiated relationships to space and declared those negotiations by slowly electrifying their instruments and centralizing black women's voices in popular blues performance. Their articulations comforted the unruly ears of black America, becoming a soundtrack to a diverse and mobile blackness.

Popular culture was a terrain of struggle within intraracial community formations, and the classic blues tradition, of which black women were central, was often a flashpoint for incredible solidarities, as well as spectacular fissures. Blues performances in the 1910s and 1920s celebrated a newly expanded spectrum of black identifications inclusive of the New Negro, asserted through struggles over social and political convention, and post–World War I Pan-African subjects who were multilingual, muscular, and mobile.[11] That these identities also were first considered male made women's interventions within and challenges to these political ideologies all the more significant. Music was an important text and strategy in the overlapping and sometimes-competing formations of blackness in this period, facilitating diverse conversations between communities, cultures, and nations.[12] The blues tradition, which had for so long sustained intimate community spaces in homes, jook joints, and prisons, was by the 1920s a potentially divisive element in the social life of black women and men because it carried with it black women's passions, leadership, and innovation. Rainey's voice, presence, and style set a standard for blues performance, growing an entire industry of music making and giving voice to a contested and regularly isolated segment of the black community. The "politics of respectability" theorized by historian Evelyn Brooks Higginbotham, which included "reform of individual behavior as a goal in itself and as a strategy for [political] reform," was the sociopolitical architecture of the New Negro.[13] Cultural practices were especially susceptible to scrutiny by friends, family, and neighbors for the telltale signs of "deviance," including inebriation, extravagance, explicit discussion and/or display of sex and sexuality, loudness, public confessional, and a lack of nonnormative religious practices. Blues women disrupted these demands for respectability, regularly discussing their independence, drunkenness, same-sex desire, domestic abuse, and laboring conditions to and for working-class communities. As Kevin Gaines argues, uplift ideology was as much about class as it was about race, making economic considerations a deciding factor in equations of acceptable blackness.[14] The collaborations between Mrs. Dorsey and Rainey demonstrate the economies of respectability that organized black artistry and sociality. Within this economy, the exchange of money and other goods was a semipublic affair, as individual advancement and achievement often were promoted as race progress. The ascent of Mrs. Dorsey's work from private homes to the popular stages afforded her prominence of status, yet those stages, which sang of demons and lovers, were blues stages and belonged to the working-class patrons who were pathologized by black and white communities alike for their condition. In this way, the Dorsey-Rainey economy both epitomized and troubled the uplift ideals that organized this revival period.

Changing class dynamics within black communities often pitted migrants against established black working- and middle-class formations. The latter group raised criticisms of the blues women, whom they described as morally corrupt due to their working-class and working-poor roots, practices of independence from men, and rebellious sexualities. Black intellectuals, uplift activists, and religious leaders regularly demeaned and bemoaned Rainey and her blues crew. As Angela Davis wrote of these classic blues women and their relation to the Harlem Renaissance, "Because women like [singers] Bessie Smith and Ida Cox presented and embodied sexualities associated with working-class black life—which, fatally, was seen by some Renaissance strategists as antithetical to the aims of their cultural movement—their music was designated as 'low' culture. . . . Consequently, few writers . . . were willing to consider seriously the contributions blues performers made to black cultural politics."[15] The historical and movement absence described by Davis here is one with implications beyond our understanding of the Harlem Renaissance or even the 1920s. The experiences and narratives of blues women document black displacement and migration, contests over class and respectability, the interiority of black women's lives, and the changes in black musics over a twenty-year period. In that way, their songs are a metalanguage—to borrow again from Higginbotham—that carefully and expertly documents and displays a changing world.[16]

The density of blues women's displays, while lost on some of their peers, is heard and seen throughout their repertoires, which hold in tension reality and ambition, individualism and collectivism, sacred and secular. The relationship between the blues style that epitomized Rainey's career and the gospel style that beckoned her mentor, Thomas Dorsey, was negotiated by both Rainey's sonic practices and her aesthetics. Her voice elicited the resonant emotion and ecstasy that characterizes black musical performance regardless of genre. The sacred-secular division so often applied to popular musics is, performatively and compositionally, a limiting criterion when investigating black musics. There are few hard-and-fast divisions between these two worlds, which, for the African descended, have been combined in fantastic ways on both sides of emancipation. As Pearl Williams-Jones argued, "Many of the practices which we commonly associate with the gospel church, such as dance, the emotional and musical delivery style of sermons, and the spontaneous verbal and non-verbal responses by preachers and congregations, have been appropriated ... by secular performers who seek to recreate what is essentially a genuine spiritual element in an authentic gospel performance." While I would trouble the language of appropriation and authenticity, what Williams-Jones articulates here as "a genuine spiritual element" is present across time and performance practice in black musics. Indeed, "while this spirituality may be one of the most emotionally potent forces in the arsenal of the black aesthetic, it has not necessarily remained the exclusive property of the black church. In the 'world' it is known colloquially as 'soul.'"[17] Rainey's "soul" was composed in part by Thomas's popular blues and Nettie's faith, thereby producing a sound that offered new challenges to and methods within the murky in-between of the sacred/secular.

The merger of a sonic secularity and sacred materiality was spoken to in Rainey's music. In "Gone Daddy Blues," she links her possessions to journeys beyond her immediate sight and knowledge, singing:

> I've got my ticket, *clothes in my hand*
> Trying to find that South bound land
> I'm gonna ride 'til I find that South bound land[18]

The "South" that she situates here is accessible only through a "ride" that, as the tuba bass line suggests, may be on one of the trains that propelled so many of the spirituals and gospel songs. This blues combination of her body (clothing) and deliverance (train) is the synergy of the sonic and the aesthetic, spirituality and soul. This dimensionality within blues women's performances make those performances central texts within what Clyde Woods brilliantly theorized as the "blues epistemology," a uniquely black working-class "ethic of survival, subsistence, resistance, and affirmation" for living in a world organized by regional white supremacies and plantation enclosures.[19] Their music, which spoke of trains and travel, sexual and economic freedom, was an escape materialized by deep and principled connections to the vernacular cultures and ambitions of their audiences.

Although major players in the development of the black cosmopolitan city, which was defined by changing gender roles, alternative geographies and ways of belonging, and a marketable black popular culture, the blues women of the 1910s and 1920s are underrepresented in the literature detailing the growth of modern black social movements. The rise of the inimitable Marcus Garvey and the Universal Negro Improvement Association (UNIA), the largest mobilization of the African descended the world had ever seen, set the tone for black social movements *as performance* and used the knowledge and ambitions of the black working class as their inspiration (fig. 8.1). The blues women so often maligned by black respectability advocates and other movement actors were, in many ways, the voices of this massive working class, especially the women who were still overrepresented in the trades that defined much of their labor under slavery, including domestic work, laundry, and sewing. As Tera Hunter has meticulously documented, these laboring and organized women developed deep solidarities through work and play, making for three-dimensional displays of resistance to the violences of white supremacy, classism, and patriarchy.[20] Nettie Dorsey's role as "wardrobe mistress" for Ma Rainey bridges the labors of antebellum black women with the newer leisure cultures that grew exponentially in black communities after emancipation. Her legacy work in the crafts of black women was only possible through the compositions of her husband and the performances by Rainey—in that way, her dresses were made for, from, and of music.

The performative politics of beauty created by the blues women united the necessities of survival and subsistence with the daily choices made by black people to *live* through enactments of resistance *and* affirmation. The drag within this essay's title is inspired by the clothing worn by Rainey that made her contrary body and performance articulate in the gaps between genres, social classes, and politics; it is the drag that allowed her to hold Thomas Dorsey's blues compositions in productive tension with what would be his greatest musical achievement of the gospel blues; it is the blues dress made by the church's handmaiden, Nettie Dorsey. Well before the boycotts and direct organizing that epitomized the civil rights movement of midcentury, Rainey displayed what Tanisha Ford theorizes as the "politics of adornment," which locates black women's aesthetic choices inside their political thought/work.[21] Like the slow, rich drag of Rainey's voice, this dress was intentional, chosen, performed, and uniquely positioned within the cultures that blues women brought to life; it reflected "the area in which fashion operates," which is described by sociologist Herbert Blumer as "one that is involved in a movement of change, with people ready to revise or discard old practices, beliefs, and attachments, and poised to adopt new social forms; there must be this thrust into the future. If the area is securely established, as in the domain of the sacred, there will be no fashion."[22] Her dress was the container for a blues politics of beauty that refused Western and European American standards, instead privileging the differently hued and built black women of the popular blues stage, whose resilience and popularity was the counterpoint to the caricature and violence that also left black women's bodies "swinging in the southern breeze."[23]

Shared moments between the two women with measuring tape, needle and thread, draping layers of fabric and beads, were a type of queer private space but not one completely beyond the public—they were in fact intended to become spectacularly public, even if Mrs. Dorsey remained behind the scenes. These are blues moments; as Davis argues, "Sexuality is not privatized in the blues: rather, it is represented as a shared experience that is socially produced."[24] As a part of an entertainment economy, both women understood how their collaboration was both reflective and in advance of social mores and conditions, especially those of their migrant and working-class audiences. Their strategy of engagement was grown through the body, which does not exist in the public sphere separate from its flexible accoutrements, which are designed for stunning impact within the context of performance. Like the shiny lures intended to draw the hungry of the ocean, the dangling beads and glossy sequins drew eager listeners' attention to the fleshy, electric inside that, within the blues, is not silenced but announced as the main attraction. The experience of this event relies on the vibrating, shimmying, cursing, and visionary bodies whose sounds echo and represent hopes and desires beyond those of the performer. There is no fourth wall in these blues shows—the only barrier between the audience and the performer is the stitched shell of (non)respectability that holds their bodies within the codes of class and gender.

Reading the dresses worn by Rainey develops a sound and demonstrates the care shared between the two women. Short-sleeved and sleeveless, deep Vs and scoop necks, and shimmering materials draw our attention to the breasts, hips, and flesh of these worldly women. We also hear the swing of the beads, the skin touching skin of her arms, and recognize that though a star, she is one of us—perhaps a better us, a free, loving, sexual us. Rainey's bare neck, arms, and upper back evidence some of the material ways in which the blues women, who were otherwise outside of the dominant frame, "manipulate and control their construction as sexual objects," as Hazel Carby argues.[25] The slight tilt of her head and smile on her face display the confidence also heard in her voice as she told her audiences and lovers to take her or leave her. As she sung in "Leavin' This Morning":

> See me reelin' and rockin', drunk as I can be
> Man I love tryin' to make a fool of me
> I'm leavin' this mornin', I'm leavin' this mornin'
> I'm leavin', tryin' to find a man of my own.[26]

Even in her drunken state Rainey has the clarity, energy, and agency to leave the lover who demeans her. Though she is precarious as a single woman, her flight and its rationale ("to find a man of my own") indicate the self-respect for which the blues women were iconized, especially by other black women.

The queer socialities shared between Rainey and Mrs. Dorsey as they toured the United States together, mediated by an industry three-way with Thomas, are evident in the intimacies of measuring, adjusting, and tailoring each dress to Rainey's body—those moments shared just off-stage, behind the curtains that, when opened, announced each woman's brilliance. Mrs. Dorsey's faith was negotiated through

Figure 8.1: Ma Rainey. Photo courtesy Wikipedia Commons.

these material objects, these dresses that then allowed the blues women like Rainey
to perform the rebellious sexualities that marked their work in and revolution of
popular culture. The exposure of Rainey's skin, however, did more than project
sexuality. It also announced alternative conceptions of beauty—shades darker and
sizes larger than those prized by the mainstream. The beading, fringe, overlay, and
tassels drew attention to those bodies in a way similar to those spectacular male
members of the UNIA who were mobilizing at this very moment in the streets of
Harlem and elsewhere. Their pride was, in part, *worn*, manifesting the self-determination for which they daily struggled (see fig. 8.2). That blues women and the
members of the UNIA costumed themselves as a part of their defiance was not a
coincidence—their protests had grown from similar matrices of black dispossession and migration, therefore signaling their dress as a shared strategy developed in
order to make blackness visible in different ways. Through this, black women's and
men's bodies became a different type of amplifier for modern identity and protest.

The flow, movement, depth, and texture of these blues dresses spoke, making
flashy, genre-bending sounds. Low necklines and forgiving, ungirdled waistlines
allowed Rainey's body to expand, the beading sparkling as her body shifted and
drew breath to relay her songs. The adjectives used to describe her clothing—
beautiful, rich—also were used to describe Rainey's voice; her dresses, then, are
evidence of her sound and were, along with migration, sexuality, racial difference,
gender subordination, black protest movements, and the unique sounds of a
mobile delta, the structure that made black women's voices the representation of
their generation and the histories of a classic blues genre. A dressmaker assisted

Figure 8.2: Marcus Garvey.

in making this music, this history, possible; informed by both her manual and her creative skills, her faith and the love she had for her husband, Nettie Dorsey labored for the blues. The effort to hear Nettie's dresses gets us closer to an understanding of the bonds shared by women, their pleasures, and the alternative sonic, social, and epistemological strategies of resistance built by them.

Notes

1. White, *Ar'n't I a Woman?*, 27.
2. McCune, "Transformance," 156.
3. Turner, "The Social Skin," 486.
4. Entwistle, "Fashion and the Fleshy Body," 327, emphasis added.
5. Ibid., 336.
6. Kondo, *About Face*, 15, emphasis in original.
7. Ibid., 16, 13.
8. Entwistle, "Fashion and the Fleshy Body," 326–27.
9. Moten, *In the Break*, 1.
10. For histories of the role of black culture in global political circuits, see Edwards, *The Practice of Diaspora*; Iton, *In Search of the Black Fantastic*; Iton, *Solidarity Blues*; Kelley, *Africa Speaks, America Answers*; Kelley, *Freedom Dreams*; and Redmond, *Anthem*.

11. See Edwards, *Practice of Diaspora*.

12. See Redmond, *Anthem*.

13. Higginbotham, *Righteous Discontent*, 187.

14. Gaines, *Uplifting the Race*.

15. Davis, *Blues Legacies and Black Feminism*, xiii.

16. Higginbotham, "African-American Women's History."

17. Williams-Jones, "Afro-American Gospel Music."

18. Davis, Blues Legacies and Black Feminism, 219.

19. Woods, *Development Arrested*, 27.

20. Hunter, *To 'Joy My Freedom*.

21. Ford, *Liberated Threads*.

22. Blumer, "Fashion," 286.

23. This reference to Billie Holiday's iconic song, "Strange Fruit" (1939), signals a history of lynching enacted against black women as well as black men. See Feimster, *Southern Horrors*.

24. Davis, *Blues Legacies and Black Feminism*, 91.

25. Carby, "It Jus' Be's Dat Way Sometime," *Radical America*, 913.

26. Davis, *Blues Legacies and Black Feminism*, 226.

CHAPTER 9

Branded Beautiful

Brand Rihanna Meets Brand Barbados

Lia T. Bascomb

"It's not the music industry anymore," says manager Jay Brown, "It's the entertainment industry. The goal is not just to be an artist, it's to be a brand."

—Josh Eells, "Queen of Pain"

The process of branding impacts the way we understand who we are, how we organize ourselves in the world, [and] what stories we tell ourselves about ourselves.

—Sarah Banet-Weiser, *Authentic™: The Politics of Ambivalence in a Brand Culture*

The sky meets the water with a deep bright blue reflecting calm in the morning distance. The air is hot and thick and sweet. There is a heaviness to the hot sun that lands on one's shoulders. Everyone walks covered in a faint sweat, easily mistaken for a magical glow, caressed by a sea breeze whispering age-old secrets that only stillness can decipher. This is Barbados. It is a place where the locals are friendly, the women are beautiful, and everyone is welcome. It is an island that easily fulfills fantasies of the Caribbean, and although its idyllic, timeless qualities are heralded in myriad songs and shouted from windows, on street corners, and in tourism advertisements, the picturesque image is a carefully crafted construction within a much more complex reality.

Because the Caribbean region has always been a site of world markets, identity formation within the region has had to contend with images of the Caribbean as saleable. Part of the pride of being Barbadian lies in the island's reputation as a beautiful, relaxing, desirable place to be. In recent years that reputation has been furthered through one of the island's most recognizable daughters, international pop star Rihanna. Such a reputation, coupled with a tourist economy, presents a struggle for control over the national identity as it becomes tied to an image easily owned by others. The relationship between the classed, gendered, racial, and sexual fissures of Barbadian citizens and the "official" nation-state ideal is one instance in which the complexity of identity politics and representation rears its head. One way in which the state (and private actors) has dealt with this complexity is to shy away from the language of identity politics and use the language of branding.[1]

The 1960s political push toward independence in Barbados occurred simultaneously with an economic shift away from monocrop agriculture toward service industries, mainly tourism. Since then, cultural identity has played an increasingly important role within national discourse, which shifted discussions of culture to structures of cultural industry.[2] Over the past fifty years conversations of promoting and preserving Barbadian culture became inebriated with an elixiric term: brand Barbados. This was one way for the state to circumnavigate the question of "who are we as a nation?" by framing it as "what are we selling?" The term names the conscious branding of all things Barbadian (food, luxury, work ethic, music, history, language, and bodies) for a growing global tourist market that the local economy depends on. In the twenty-first century, the Barbadian nation-state is heavily invested in an ideal for the island that marries the respectability and modernity of its history as "Little England" with the pride and self-determination of independence and the exotic tropical fantasies of the Caribbean that many paying visitors expect. Hoping to exploit such consumption in the service of the nation, the "brand Barbados" discourse navigates any tensions between its colonial past and recent independence by relying on the two concepts that compose the national motto: pride and industry. But what does that mean for the cultural identity of the people who live there? How is such consumption and desire read in and through the bodies of Barbadians? Examining the career of one of Barbados's biggest music stars, Rihanna, provides a starting point from which answers to such questions can be offered.

Robyn Rihanna Fenty entered the music business as a determined sixteen-year-old and quickly came of age in the public eye. Her career rests on the two foundations of desire and consumption. The November 2011 issue of *Esquire* magazine named her the "sexiest woman alive," with a small tag line on the contents page that reads, "Thank you, Barbados." The accompanying images were nudes that focused on her green eyes, her curves, and her skin, covered in dirt and wet seaweed. Visually, she was presented as a dark mermaid with all of the sexual connotations of desire, and textually her connections to Barbados were firmly entrenched in the interview.[3] Readers could buy / buy into the images while choosing whether or not to digest the interview, during which Rihanna and the interviewer tussled over the role of sexuality within her performance.

In other media, Rihanna's tourism commercials for Barbados promote the mythical image of the Caribbean as desirable and consumable, while her image as a pop star branching into fashion, film, and entrepreneurship relies largely on a commodified sexuality. Her entry into pop stardom relied both on standardized models of pop/R&B female sexuality and her background as a Caribbean woman and all of the connotations that raises in a global imagination. Robyn Fenty embodies the brand of Rihanna, but does she also embody brand Barbados? How can a nation benefit from the international celebrity of one of its citizens? What are the risks to the national identity and the nation's tourist economy when they are linked to the global celebrity market? In 2011, as part of a deal with the Barbados Tourism Authority, Rihanna returned to Barbados to perform. Brand Rihanna met brand Barbados. Through an examination of Rihanna's August 2011 LOUD tour concert in Barbados, this chapter argues that the events surrounding the show shed light on the differing sexual economies of pop stardom and national tourism, that such divergences highlight the insecurities of nation-states seeking to make a name for themselves within a global market, and that despite the distinctions it is quite hard for a nation-state to divorce celebrity-focused attention from an ideal national image.

Rihanna has incurred the responsibility of representing the nation that birthed her: first through sheer coincidence of her celebrity and the fact that she was raised on an island whose national identity requires representation, and second through her 2008 acceptance of a cultural ambassadorship. To be Barbadian is to represent Barbados. To say the pledge of allegiance is to declare that one will represent or "do credit to the nation wherever [one] go[es]."[4] And to accept a position as the island's cultural ambassador to youth is to acknowledge and embrace that representational responsibility. In taking on this responsibility, Rihanna has become a living embodiment of Barbadian culture; thus, many view her body and all that she does with it as a national asset to be promoted, protected, and critiqued. Rihanna's image as a pop music star has become very important to the Barbadian nation-state, as "the music industry is probably one of the best examples of an instance where 'culture' is understood primarily in terms of market demands."[5]

Representation within a global economy involves creating a saleable image, usually an ideal. On an island where over 90 percent of the population is of African descent, this negotiation between the real and the ideal is a search to define a sense of modern blackness. Deborah Thomas defines modern blackness in the Jamaican context as "urban, migratory, based in youth-oriented popular culture and influenced by African American popular style, individualistic, radically consumerist, and ghetto feminist."[6] Her definition is based on a Jamaican model whereby a creole middle class proffered a national ideal at independence, but black urban youth offered their own ideal, which by the 1990s had come to symbolize Jamaican particularity within a global context.

Barbados has a similar history with a few key variations. The independent ideal always included working-class culture. It was a means to distinguish an independent Barbados from the cultural hegemony of its English colonizer. But the independent ideal was still very much concerned with a sense of middle-class respectability, one that has never clearly been defined. As Barbados entered onto the global stage as an independent nation the relationship between working-class culture and middle-class respectability became ambiguously intertwined in representations of the nation that often relied on images of bodies and narratives of controlled abandon. The relationship between Barbados and its Caribbean neighbors has wavered between regional cooperation and cultural and economic competition. Could Barbados compete with the growing saleability of Jamaican culture? If it meant imitating Jamaican "rudeness" and all of its assumed violence and overt sexuality, did the Barbadian state want to? How could Barbados create its own sense of modern blackness? In asserting an independent identity and building a national brand within a global economy, Barbados is wrestling to maintain the particularities of Barbadian culture amid Jamaican influences and historical myths of the Caribbean. The sale and consumption within cultural industries shape various understandings of Caribbean cultures as they are branded for international markets. Barbados's heavy reliance on service industries to attract foreign investment in the economy has meant that one of the main projects of the independent nation has been to set and maintain its own cultural standards, in part, to protect its tourism brand. Brand Barbados, then, not only serves as a representation of pride and industry, but also articulates the tensions between working-class sexual ethos, middle-class respectability, and the construction of a modern black culture that can embody each.

Beautiful-Ugly

Shortly after inking the three-year deal with the Barbados Tourism Authority (BTA) to promote Barbados exclusively, Rihanna shocked many with a surprise appearance at one of Barbados's most visible performances of national culture, Kadooment, only days before her 2011 LOUD tour performance on the island. Kadooment is a Carnival road march that occurs as one of the last events of Barbados's Crop Over Festival. It was the first time Rihanna had participated in Kadooment since she left the island to become a star. International celebrity media

Figure 9.1: Rihanna is pictured during Barbados's Kadooment Day Parade. ©Splash.

featured photos of Rihanna dancing with friends, dancing on a truck, and dancing throughout the streets. One online magazine reported, "Rihanna goes back to her rude girl ways getting raunchy as a scantily-clad carnival queen."[7] While Rihanna's presence was duly noted at the festival, she was one of thousands of participants, not the Carnival queen.[8] The same article went on to note her "raunchy moves" as she danced "with a willing fan." The "raunchy moves" are a common part of the national dance, wukking up, and the "willing fan" happened to be one of her closest friends, Negus Sealy.[9]

Many online articles framed Rihanna's behavior as part of her "growing wildness," comparing her Kadooment costume to those she wears onstage and marking her dancing as shocking and disgusting. These reports by and large stemmed from celebrity news sites that focused narrowly on Rihanna, but their reports extended her behavior (and their critiques of it) to the nation of Barbados. While comments on Rihanna's "skimpy" attire floated in cyberspace, fans (and nonfans) sought to correct misinformed media reports in an effort to protect both Rihanna and the festival where she was photographed. The images of a national festival entered into the sexual economy of celebrity through Rihanna's body. Critiques of Rihanna caused the indignation of Barbadians, who were furious that the complex performances of their culture could be grossly misread through uninformed readings of one young woman's body.

Figure 9.2: Rihanna performing during her LOUD tour. Photo courtesy of author.

One report in particular sparked the ire of many. Before the sun had set on Kadooment Day in Barbados, E Online posted a short article titled "Which Singer Is Rocking a Teeny Bikini and Feathers?" The article cautions readers that "[i]t's not surprising to see her in such a getup, because one thing she's definitely famous for is her sense of edgy fashion." Here a costume common to Carnival celebrations worldwide is attributed to the fashion sense of one individual among the many who wore the same thing but were often cropped out of photos. The article states that Rihanna had "returned to her native land of Barbados for the colorful street bash celebrating the annual Kadooement [*sic*] Day parade, where she was the Carnival Queen."[10] Besides misspelling the name of the event and (again) wrongfully giving Rihanna the title of Carnival queen, the language of the statement has overtones of exoticism and eroticized primitivism that continue in the remarks found most offensive to commenters:

> So what the heck is Kadooement [*sic*] Day?
>   It's an ancient tradition and public holiday in Barbados, which involves people masquerading in costumes that consist of natural materials and takes place during the Crop Over Festival. The event rejoices the end of the sugar cane crop harvest and acknowledges the crop sacrifices made to the gods for good luck.

156

Ri-Ri was spotted shaking her booty (Get it, girl!) with friends and (we can assume) wowing those around her with a barely there costume.[11]

Arguably, the "ancientness" of the tradition is another editorial invention, as Kadooment Day began as part of the contemporary Crop Over Festival in the 1970s.[12] Next to photos of Rihanna wearing a bikini made of synthetic materials and decorated with fake feathers and plastic beads, the idea that Kadooment costumes are supposed to consist of "natural materials" comes off as an attempt to "primitivize" the festival by inventing a connection between the participants' bodies and "nature." The assumption that the author, Bruna Nessif, makes—that Rihanna's costume stands out in the crowd—erases the rest of the Baje International band wearing the same costume and the thousands of other participants wearing similar attire. Many Barbadians reading the article wondered why they had never heard of the "crop sacrifices made to the gods for good luck,"[13] but most recognized that they had never heard of such a tradition because it did not exist in the contemporary form of Crop Over. Unlike the *Esquire* cover, these images of Rihanna are also an overt representation of Barbadian culture. Kadooment Day celebrations are a revised reenactment of Barbadian cultural practices and a saleable experience within brand Barbados. Barbadians participating in Kadooment are accustomed to the cultural meanings of bared skin, dance, drinks, and the ways that these practices have been promoted both to Barbadians and a larger tourist market. But celebrity readings of the road march divorced it from both the cultural context and the economic market it usually exists within. These images of Rihanna raise questions of sexual morality and modernity that impose themselves on brand Barbados as well.

About an hour after the article was posted online the comments began to pour in, including statements on the beauty of Rihanna's body, disgust at the public display of her body, support of Carnival celebrations around the world, and, most notably, corrections of the article and others' comments on it. Throughout the 125 comments posted to the article within the week, one of the clearest stances was that of self-identified Barbadians feeling misrepresented, defending the modernity of their culture, defending Rihanna, and declaring their pride. At least a third of the commenters identified themselves as Barbadian either in their comments or in pseudonyms such as IAMABARBADIAN, Barbadian and Proud, 246Bajan, and Offended Barbadian. At least thirty-three of the comments spoke against the article's mention of sacrifices to gods, and many asserted that Barbados is a Christian nation. One comment in particular tried to clear it up for everyone:

Ok to all Bajans getting offended, the part about the festival being about a celebration of the end of the sugar harvest is true (that's why it's called crop over). The part about it being related to the gods is also true, not so much for good luck, but more a way of giving thanks to the gods (... go to the Barbados Museum and check the African Gallery). It was also a way to celebrate African culture which was suppressed year round. Originally the parade was held on various plantations, not one big festival as is the case today with Kadooment. This is of course the original crop over, the one today was brought back by the government in the 70s and still celebrates the end of harvest but emancipation as well. EOnline, get your facts straight, Bajans you too.[14]

Here "facts" are used to dispel both the misinterpretations of celebrity media and the idealistic representations of other Barbadians. Many of these comments not only looked for journalistic accuracy, but vehemently defended the modernity of Barbadian culture. Even in a postindependence Barbados that is proud of its "blackness" and African heritage, the idea of practicing "primitive" sacrifices to various gods was offensive. Barbadian blackness is supposed to be a modern blackness, and commenters bristled at the idea that they would be subsumed under discourses of a "primitive" Africa or Third World.

Such discourses of the modernity of Barbadian culture and cultural representations highlight the main dilemma within both national identity construction and the construction of a national brand within Barbados: how to build an attractive global product that is based on a modern identity but whose attraction is also directly linked to historical myths of the exotically "primitive," images of the tropics as erotically available, and contemporary countercultures of modernity.[15] The commenters here seem to want to offer the kind of "modern blackness" that increases their cultural capital and social capital, but the nation's economy is tied to a tourist practice that relies heavily on eroticized imagery. Kadooment, a celebration that is particular to Barbados but has strong similarities with other cultural practices the world over, offers a specifically Barbadian reference within brand Barbados. However, without control over the representations of the Kadooment celebration, Barbadians are at the mercy of outside interpreters who may not understand the relationship between counterculture and modernity or between Barbadian modernity and the sexual economies of tourism. In this instance, the cultural value of Kadooment got lost in the market value of Rihanna's celebrity image.[16]

Underlying these concerns is the role that Rihanna's body, or, more accurately, the display of her body, plays in representing the nation. As a Barbadian, her attire during Kadooment is perfectly acceptable. In Barbadian culture there is a time and place for everything, and Kadooment is the time for wearing revealing costumes, drinking, and dancing. The level of bared skin for a pop star has different meanings—meanings that change across audiences, contexts, and markets. In this instance, Rihanna's body is read through the lens of celebrity media, and

Barbadian commentators see such a reading as inaccurate because it does not take into account the context of Kadooment Day and Barbadian culture. These sites present a national culture through the lens of the sexual economies of pop stardom. In these few images the focus on Rihanna's individual body promotes a sexuality that is at once a part of an idyllic "primitive" tropical brand and a "modern" global pop brand.

The conversations surrounding Rihanna's presence at Kadooment expose some of the dilemmas facing Barbadians who wish to promote themselves as a modern nation-state in the shadow of myths of exoticism and primitivism, which include a sense of sexual availability that at times serves the tourism product. Barbadian culture is both rigidly conservative and conspicuously laid back. Promotions of the island's culture rely on a carefully constructed image of controlled abandon, one that is easily misread in celebrity news outlets that focus on individuals rather than collective identities. All of these misreadings, their corrections, and the corrections of corrections stemmed from a few photos of one woman circulated out of context. Rihanna's commodified celebrity image threatened to overshadow that of brand Barbados. Rihanna's participation in Kadooment, coupled with her celebrity status, has real effects on how the rest of the world views the nation, and the conversations that ensued exposed some of Barbados's national insecurities. While Rihanna's participation in the festival gave it more publicity than most advertisers could afford, many Barbadians wondered if such publicity was worthwhile if it meant that the festival and the nation could (and would) be grossly misrepresented by celebrity-oriented media. Would the attention she brought to Barbados reach the "correct" market?

Pretty LOUD

As the 2011 LOUD tour made its way across the United States, praise and criticism swirled around it. Most of the criticism surrounded the idea that Rihanna should be a better role model and that the crotch-grabbing, expletive-laced ad-libs, drinking onstage, and "simulated sex" with audience members were perhaps not the most wholesome antics of a young woman in the public eye. While international critiques focused on the intersection of pop star and role model status, Barbadians were reminded that Rihanna is also cultural ambassador to youth on the island. In 2008 then Prime Minister David Thompson proposed the ambassadorship as a way to capitalize on Rihanna's publicity and to show support for her at a time when she was heavily criticized in the Barbadian and international press. While her level of success was to be applauded, her onstage behavior fed an ongoing fear of "rude" culture subsuming "respectable" Barbadian ideals on the island. The social capital of her pop celebrity risked tarnishing the cultural and economic capital brand Barbados sought on a global market. The comments that circulated in the Barbadian press were no different from earlier discussions of her stardom—praising her, criticizing her, and as a child of Barbadian soil protectively doing both—but when it was announced that she would be bringing the show home to the island in August 2011 the conversations changed.

While a few in the business sector voiced concern over the timing of the concert, fearing it might draw the limited funds of Barbadians away from the Crop Over festivities, by and large most Barbadians (Rihanna included) thought it was long overdue.[17] Very few of the concerns voiced included any wariness about the content of the show itself. The BTA reported that the concert "attracted more than 10,000 regional tourists, who pumped $8.6 million into the Barbadian economy."[18] While the BTA emphasized that the show would be the same as every other performance on the tour, others noted that much of the sexuality prominent in Rihanna's ad-libbing and spontaneous performance acts had been noticeably toned down.

Barbados stands at a complicated crossroads, being one of the more conservative cultures in the Caribbean, sustaining relationships with more indulgent cultural influences, and in the twenty-first century facilitating strong conversations surrounding what appropriate sexuality looks like for its youth.[19] On the one hand, it was an important statement of Barbadian modernity for a Bajan artist to bring such a technical show to the island. On the other hand, with the differing cultural contexts, there remained ambiguity around the sexual content of the cultural ambassador for youth's performance. Such ambiguity has become a signature aspect of Rihanna's brand and was evident within the LOUD show itself.

One segment of the show began with a montage of images of Rihanna dressed in menswear in some shots and wearing a dress in others. Not quite androgynous, she flirted with herself onscreen before being revealed seated in a suit onstage. When she began to sing a cover of Prince's hit "Darling Nikki" she played with a cane while her female dancers used the poles to either side of her.[20] During this part of the performance, Rihanna often stopped singing in order to dance with or just touch the dancers' bodies, performing an ambiguous and fluid sexuality. During the song she remained in control of them, but the tables turned as her dancers stripped her down to a black body suit and chained her for the performance of "S&M." The choice to cover a Prince song is telling of the ways in which Rihanna has used her sexuality. One of Prince's largest assets as a star was his in-your-face yet ambiguous sexuality and gender. The ambiguity of his performances extended to his image as he sat squarely between "godliness and promiscuity, machismo and effeminacy, spirituality and material ostentation, futurism and nostalgia, black rhythm and white rock."[21] Prince's endurance in the music industry relied on his musical talent, but also on the power he exerted through an alluring and ambiguous sexuality.

The performance of a Prince cover is not the first instance when Rihanna has used an ambiguous sexuality, one that falls rather squarely outside of a brand Barbados ideal but squarely within Rihanna's brand of pop stardom. In 2009 she released "Te Amo," whose lyrics and accompanying video more than hinted at (bi)sexual curiosity, and in response to questions about her relationship with Matt Kemp she told one reporter, "I hate to burst your bubble . . . but no. I'm dating girls!"[22] Rihanna's displays of fluid sexuality could be read as a transgressive exercise of power; a youthful attempt to exert the kind of control performed through Barbadian and/or queer femininity; a ploy of stardom to remain ambiguous, ambivalent, and thus enigmatic à la Prince; merely a camp performance; or (as she suggested in response to her controversial S&M video) a metaphor for her relationship with stardom.[23] What these performances do is create the possibility of something more in her public image. They tell her audience that no matter how much of her they see or how often they may see her, there's always the possibility of something else. Even in her most revealing costumes her allure is solidified, since "the most charismatic celebrities are the ones we can only imagine, even if we see them naked everywhere."[24] It raises the question: if ambiguity is a constitutive/definitive part of pop stardom, what happens when a pop star is given the task of representing a nation, one that, however ambiguous its national identity may be, has a fairly clear ideal of the image it would like to proffer to the rest of the world?

In the written reports that came out after the show, there were few to no critiques of raunchiness or questions of appropriate or inappropriate behavior, only an overwhelming pride in a young woman who had worked the stage for Barbados. The critiques surrounding the show hardly mentioned Rihanna at all, focusing instead on the BTA's role in the show.[25] One commenter summed it up: "All take a bow. That said, while the Rihanna/RocNation delivery was flawlessly world class, the same cannot be said for the local hospitality and logistic elements of the show," suggesting that in the eyes of the audience at Kensington Oval, brand Barbados needs to catch up to brand Rihanna. One of the complaints was that unlike other performances at Kensington Oval, the national anthem was not played at the outset of the show.[26] In this moment brand Rihanna stood in for brand Barbados. Regardless of her genre, Rihanna performing on Barbadian soil may have been symbolic enough that the customary expression of nationalism through the playing of the national anthem could be momentarily discarded, but not without the notice of her Barbadian audience. Her role as a widely successful pop star who grew up only blocks from the stage she was performing on stood for both the modernity of Barbadian culture and its attractiveness to a global audience.

The praise of Rihanna was slightly stained only months after her performance in Barbados when an interview she gave to *British Vogue* magazine reached stands. Rihanna commented that she owns a small chain that says "cunt" and that the "word is so offensive to everyone in the world *except* for Bajans. You know African-Americans use the n-word to their brothers? Well, that's the way we use the c-word. When I first came here, I was saying it like it was nothing, like, 'Hey, cunt,' until my make-up artist finally had to tell me stop. I just never knew."[27] These comments fueled a variety of criticism over the way that Rihanna was representing the nation, especially after having just signed a three-year deal with the Barbados Tourism Authority. Her casual use of a Barbadian curse word that both invokes and derides the power of feminine genitalia may have been acceptable within shock-and-awe pop standards, but didn't fit the ideal of respectable release within brand Barbados. Some Barbadians questioned where exactly in Barbados Rihanna grew up that she would hear the word used so casually.[28] Others admitted that the word was used often, but with obvious offense.[29] Still others were baffled as to how a young woman who had gone to one of the top secondary schools on the island, who had been said to be so articulate, "never knew" how offensive the word was.[30] Even some of her supporters chimed in, writing articles with titles like "Rihanna, shut up and sing."[31]

The initial celebration of Rihanna as official spokesperson had gone sour as some realized that her pretty face did not mean that she would always have pretty things to say about her culture. The beauty proffered within brand Barbados was much different from and perhaps more fragile than the beauty of Rihanna's pop star image. In relying on Rihanna as a spokeswoman, Barbados has to negotiate images of modernity with Rihanna's reliance on countercultural practices and overt sexuality. Both brand Barbados and brand Rihanna appeal to global audiences, but the markets they appeal to and the stakes are very different. Whereas Caribbean islands have historically been promoted through sexual imagery and notions of availability, such sexuality is often (if even slightly) more covert than the "rude" sexuality of popular culture. As a national brand, hundreds of thousands of people are culturally, socially, and economically invested in the success or failure of brand Barbados, making it much more delicate than the celebrity brand of Rihanna, which is promoted by and directly supports a team of people.

The Barbados government's deals with Rihanna to become a spokesperson for the nation and its youth are an attempt to capitalize on her embodied cultural capital as a young Barbadian woman who has successfully entered into the US music industry and built a global brand name for herself. Their contracts, however, fall short of ownership over brand Rihanna; as a result, Rihanna can afford to dismiss nationalistic critiques as she continues to promote her brand. In a 2012 interview with *Elle* magazine, Rihanna's interviewer explains that Rihanna "refuses to conform to anyone else's ideas about how she should behave."[32] However dependent or entangled brand Barbados is becoming on brand Rihanna, neither the Barbadian government nor Barbadian citizens—whether fans or critics—own the means of production of brand Rihanna.[33] They can only hope to reap the material and symbolic benefits of Rihanna's capital while continuing to build the ideal of brand Barbados into a reality.

Brand Rihanna and brand Barbados rely on different forms of marketable sexuality that meet in the body of Rihanna. While Rihanna uses ambiguity in order to navigate the sexual economy of pop stardom, the Barbadian nation-state seeks to be clearer even if representations of the nation that marry modern black respectability with mythic tropes of the exotic Caribbean are perhaps just as ambiguous in their use of sexuality. Examples such as this one show how young nations use whatever assets they have to promote themselves and the anxieties that arise when issues of commodity meet definitions of identity and images of sexuality within the process of creating a brand.

Notes

1. My use of the term "brand" mirrors that of Sarah Banet-Weiser, who suggests that in the twenty-first century, brands are as much if not more about culture than they are about economics. See Banet-Weiser, *Authentic*™.

2. Harewood, "Policy and Performance."

3. Ross McCammon, "The Sexiest Woman Alive: Thank You Barbados," *Esquire*, November 2011, 110–22.

4. These are the last lines of Barbados's pledge of allegiance.

5. Saunders, "Is Not Everything," 99.

6. Thomas, *Modern Blackness*, 241.

7. "Well That Didn't Last Long . . . Rihanna Goes Back to Her Rude Girl Ways Getting Raunchy as a Scantily Clad Carnival Queen," *Daily Mail*, August 1, 2011, dailymail.co.uk/tvshowbiz/article-2020977/Rihanna-goes-rude-girl-ways-getting-raunchy-scantily-clad-carnival-queen.html#ixzz1e2TkQwVf.

8. While the title of queen has many usages within Caribbean culture and within Carnival culture worldwide, in the context of Barbados's Crop Over, the title of Carnival queen is reserved for the most productive female cane cutter of the season. She is crowned at the opening of the festival, known as the ceremonial cutting of the canes. The 2011 queen of the crop was Judy Cumberbatch.

9. "No Tying Ri-Ri Down," *NationNews*, November 5, 2011, nationnews.com/index.php/articles/view/no-tying-ri-ri-down/.

10. Bruna Nessif, "Which Singer Is Rocking a Teeny Bikini and Feathers?," *E! News*, August 1, 2011, eonline.com/news/which_singer_rocking_teeny_bikini/255643#ixzz1e2csUBgz.

11. Ibid.

12. I say "arguably" because the Crop Over festival (and Kadooment) has roots on seventeenth- and eighteenth-century Barbadian plantations, though in drastically different form, and it is part of a worldwide Carnival tradition also drawing on European, New World, and West and Central African celebratory practices.

13. Nessif, "Which Singer."

14. Enam, August 3, 2011 (10:13 a.m.), comment on Nessif, "Which Singer."

15. See Gilroy, *The Black Atlantic*.

16. See Saunders, "Is Not Everything."

17. There were similar concerns over the cost of the tickets and whether or not they would be affordable to the average Barbadian or target the upper classes on the island and wealthy visitors. "Rihanna Local Concert Long Overdue," *NationNews*, April 15, 2011, nationnews .com/index.php/articles/view/rihanna-local-concert-long-overdue/.

18. Barry Alleyne, "Tourism Minister Pushing Culture," *NationNews*, November 16, 2012, nationnews.com/index.php/articles/view/tourism-minister-pushing-culture/. The amount $8.6 million Barbadian converts to roughly US$4.3 million. The BTA had expected to attract four thousand visitors and spent $4 million Barbadian on the concert. "Barbados Gets Loud!," *Barbados Advocate*, August 5, 2011, barbadosadvocate.com/newsitem.asp ?more=local&NewsID=19123.

19. Debates around whether teens should be able to access medical care without parental consent are framed by opponents around reproductive health care. HIV/AIDS awareness campaigns have affected conversations of responsibility and sexuality.

20. "Darling Nikki" (Prince, *Purple Rain*, 1984) is the song of a woman who is a "sex fiend" and chronicles the singer's encounter with her, beginning with masturbation in a hotel lobby, continuing with a night at a castle, and ending with a good-bye note.

21. Pauline Kael in the *New Yorker* quoted in Taylor, "'Baby I'm a Star,'" 162.

22. Rihanna's 2011 song "Te Amo" explores a budding relationship between two women, one of whom is wary of the sexual overtones. On her relationship with Matt Kemp, see Josh Eells, "Queen of Pain," *Rolling Stone*, April 14 2011, 42.

23. "The song can be taken very literally, but it's actually a very metaphorical song. It's about the love-hate relationship with the media and how sometimes the pain is pleasurable. . . . [P]eople went crazy. They just saw sex. And when I see that video, I don't see that at all. I wanted it to be cheeky. There's no other way to take it" (Jonathan VanMeter, "Living Out Loud," *Vogue*, April 2011, 265).

24. Roach, *It*, 22.

25. She was, however, widely criticized for leaving the after-party after only minutes of attendance, as many who paid for VIP tickets were expecting her presence throughout the night.

26. Carol Martindale, "LOUD Concerns about Rihanna Show," *NationNews*, August 9, 2011, nationnews.com/index.php/articles/view/loud-concerns-about-rihanna-show/.

27. Christa D'Souza, "Rihanna," *British Vogue*, November 2011, 254.

28. See comments on Carol Martindale, "Rihanna, Shut Up and Sing," *NationNews*, October 6, 2011, nationnews.com/index.php/articles/view/rihanna-shut-up-and-sing/.

29. Kay, comment on Rodrigo, "Rihanna Covers British Vogue," *Rihanna Daily,* October 2, 2011, rihannadaily.com/2011/10/02/rihanna-covers-british-vogue/; Gina Spencer, "C-Word for the Publicity?," *NationNews,* October 10, 2011, nationnews.com/index.php/letters/view/c-word-for-the-publicity/; comments on "Rihanna's Love for the 'C-Word,'" *NationNews,* October 4, 2011, nationnews.com/index.php/articles/view/rihannas-love-for-the-c-word/.

30. Spencer, "C-Word for the Publicity?"

31. Martindale, "Rihanna, Shut Up and Sing."

32. Ibid.

33. Rihanna's image was central to the BTA's 2012 campaign.

CHAPTER 10

Framing the Video Vixen

Intraracial Readings of Unruly Desire

Felice Blake

> Oprah [Winfrey] was promiscuous. Maya Angelou was a prostitute. A woman's sexual organs, their functions or reputation will never define or stop her.
>
> —Karrine Steffans, Twitter post, March 6, 2016, http://twitter.com/karrineandco

> Before my "video girl" career, I was known in some circles as a stripper. Others knew me as "Superhead," the insatiable lover of many Hollywood stars, sports figures, and some of music's most influential performers and executives. None of that is who I really am, nor does it tell the whole story.
>
> —Karrine Steffans, *Confessions of a Video Vixen*

Karrine Steffans's 2005 *Confessions of a Video Vixen* is one of the most controversial memoirs written by a Black woman to date. An instant best seller, *Confessions* produced an uproar about Steffans's sexual exploits with the rich and famous from some of the most regarded Black men in the US entertainment and sports industries, including Shaquille O'Neal, Jay Z, Usher, and Dr. Dre. The book delves into the often misogynist world of the Black cultural industries and charts Steffans's life from her experiences of poverty and familial fragmentation on the island of St. Thomas, to her migration to Miami, Florida, to her entry into the world of adult entertainment, and finally to her rise and fall as an actress and model primarily in hip-hop music videos in the late 1990s and early 2000s. Throughout, Steffans narrates her tell-all from her observations as a performer, wife, mistress, girlfriend, model, and lover of multiple Black male celebrities. Exposing the ways that both sexual labor and exploitation are central to the notion of Black men's success in the business of entertainment, Steffans describes in explicit detail not only the erotic trysts she enjoyed with rich and famous men but also the quality of their sexual ability and their ethics of care toward the women who populate their world.

The focus of this chapter is to illuminate what Steffans's *Confessions* presents to its readers: the irresistible identification with the multivalent text of Black female sexuality. Can Black people look at the image of a Black woman as sexual object and not see themselves? Hasn't the constant circulation of hypersexual representations of Black women infiltrated White *and* Black people's consciousness? How, then, could a Black spectator, reader, or critic resist identification with the narrative and images the video vixen reproduces? This chapter seeks to neither champion nor demonize Steffans specifically or the video model generally. Instead, my analysis employs an intraracial lens in order to contemplate Black people's rich negotiation of sexuality between and perhaps beyond the frames of respectability or hypersexuality. I consider intraracial interactions with the representation of Black sexuality through what Mireille Miller-Young calls "illicit eroticism" and what Arlene Keizer terms "unruly desire."[1] Illicit eroticism "symbolically and strategically produces gender identities through the commodification and manipulation of private (sex) acts."[2] Miller-Young's conception of illicit eroticism accounts for Steffans's self-conscious writing of her confessions for circulation and profit in a popular cultural marketplace that continues to trade in Black people's flesh. Keizer discusses "unruly desire" as a feature of Black women's narratives driven by scenes that reimagine the dynamics of pleasure in the context of subjugation.[3] Thus, these theories allow us to consider how Steffans's tactical and pleasurable uses of sex and desire are part of Black women's critical negotiations of illicit and unruly sexual politics and the politics of representation within the Black community. Finally, this chapter recalibrates Adrienne Davis's notion of the Black sexual economy to examine the circulation of sexual and erotic images among Black people specifically.[4] *Confessions* and Black people's responses to it offer new insights about the pleasures and frustrations embedded in the encounter with Black women's erotic representations.

For many critics of the book, the unabashed representation of Black promiscuity seemed to confirm the worst stereotypes about Black life—that Black women not simply are portrayed as oversexed in masculinist hip-hop culture but also actually *embrace* hypersexuality and debasement in what are mostly unhealthy relationships between Black women and men. Murali Balaji argues that Steffans's book glorifies "the notion of Black women compromising their identities and being defined by their sexual prowess."[5] While recognizing the video vixen as a representative site of tensions and affirming the need to include video models' stories in the analysis of their participation in mainstream popular culture, Gwendolyn Pough describes Steffans as buying into the sexism and misogyny that limit the roles women occupy in hip-hop culture.[6] T. Denean Sharpley-Whiting also emphasizes Steffans's seeming complicity in her objectification and connects the publication of *Confessions* with the public disparagement of Black women's lives and accomplishments.[7] Given the existing critiques of misogyny in hip-hop, as well as its relationship to pornography, Steffans's memoir circulates in a critical context saturated by highly sexualized visual representations of Black women that seemingly override any potential value in *Confessions'* written memoir.[8]

Intraracial critiques of Steffans's book force us to confront how Black women's hypersexual narratives are also shaped by Black people's perceptions of the acceptable terms for public representations of sexuality. The critical tension between seeing Steffans either as a person with sexual agency and freedom or as someone trapped by hypersexuality illuminates an analytical crossroads with regard to how we interrogate Black people's negotiations of sexuality and desire. Despite Black feminism's investment in the critical engagement with texts of Black female sexuality, a "Goldilocks" effect still remains at play in the confrontation with contemporary representations of Black women's erotic bodies. The ongoing struggle to navigate critically between hypersexuality and respectability frames the reading of Steffans's book as not quite the right narrative eruption of Black female sexuality. Rather than presenting an important point of view from within the economies of contemporary Black labor and sexual economy, *Confessions* is routinely read and dismissed outright as the articulations of a "snitch" at best and a "ho" at worst seeking to trade on her encounters with famous Black men for a quick profit.

The fascination and disgust with *Confessions* reveals, initially, the "always-present judgmental gaze of White detractors who expect the worst from black people" and thus perpetuate a continuous assault on the Black community collectively.[9] The White gaze on Black sexual life leaves respectability, or the alignment with bourgeois propriety and normative values regarding heterosexual domesticity, as the most promising avenues for protecting Black women and uplifting the community. Although the critics of Steffans's *Confessions* seem to reinforce a politics of respectability, their inability to simply ignore the video vixen indicates that the White supremacist framing of good/bad images of Black female sexuality still compels the analysis of Black erotic representations. As commentators on the book seek to distinguish themselves and protect Black females from Steffans's portrayal of Black sexuality, they are unable to look away from her visual and written texts. This desire for both proximity and distance signals that the representation of the video vixen comes too close for comfort.

Saving Our Daughters? Anxieties of Influence and Irresistible Identifications with the Text of Black Promiscuity

> Our own complicity in our objectification demands scrutiny as
> well. . . . The range of our successes and the diversity of our
> lives and career paths have been congealed in the mainstream
> media into video vixens, thanks to Karrine Steffans's best-
> selling *Confessions of a Video Vixen*.
>
> —T. Denean Sharpley-Whiting, "The Irony of Achievement for
> Black Women"

Confessions of a Video Vixen is a promiscuous text in both content and form. It crosses the genres of autobiography, history, fiction, how-to guidebooks, and cautionary tales. It also transgresses multiple media, including video, film, writing, and photography, bringing together the issues of spectatorship and readership. The book jacket's art presents the author and subject in highly stylized sets and poses that draw the viewer's attention to her breasts and crotch. In each image her eyes lock their gaze on the camera's lens and thus on the viewer/reader who holds her and her *Confessions*. The book's center pages include a mishmash of photographs that feature Steffans variously as a tomboyish teenage student, a traditional mother, a sexy single woman, a model, and the close companion of men like DMX, Irv Gotti, and Bobby Brown in candid photos. The book's formal indeterminacy reflects the nontraditional construction of identity explored throughout the narrative.

In *Confessions'* introduction, "No Shame in My Game," Steffans claims that she wrote her book to reach out to young Black females "aspiring to the kind of life I have led, and there are plenty of young people trying to do just that." Her narrative therefore begins by producing Black women and girls as the targeted audience for hip-hop culture and the implied readers of her text. She also casts herself as being like so many young girls who "watch television and dream about the Beverly Hills lifestyle" of designer labels and exclusive circles. Becoming a video model presents young females with an opportunity to make those dreams a reality. "The days of MC Lyte, Yo-Yo, Sister Souljah, and Salt-n-Pepa have faded away," she asserts. The music industry's drive for profits now destroys, according to Steffans, "the most beautiful thing about us as a culture—our girls and young women." Although her initial comments seem to situate the book within the framework of respectability by offering a cautionary tale about the perils of material ambition and sexual promiscuity, Steffans positions her narrative as the site of sage counsel for a new generation of Black females. "Parents are often either absent or uneducated or both, rendering them largely unaware of what's going on right in their own living rooms," she claims.[10] Instead, *Confessions* imagines itself as a proxy for that parental role, situating Steffans within the history of women in hip-hop and as a champion of young Black women.

The video model's potential influence on a younger generation of Black females is a major cause for intraracial anxiety about hip-hop's visual culture and Steffans's narrative. *Confessions*, however, incorporates that intergenerational conflict over who should have the greatest impact on young people and why. The narrative production of this intragroup conflict is what I call "intimate antagonism," or the representation of tension and disunity in the realm of intimate and interpersonal relations. Racial subordination has long targeted Black intimate life for confinement and control. As Candace Jenkins describes, perceiving Black people as aberrant in their sexual and domestic lives impedes their full participation in the US polity, which bestows "membership in America's 'civilized' sociopolitical world, with all the respectability and assumed normalcy such membership would entail." The realm of the intimate represents a key arena within which Black people struggle both to be full citizens and "to be understood as such."[11] Choosing to depict Black people engaged in illicit eroticism and driven by unruly desires, texts like *Confessions* refuse to limit their portrayals of Black life to representations of intraracial unity in the face of racist oppression. Instead, the depictions of intraracial intimate antagonisms represent critical sites where the realities of racist subordination are negotiated, arbitrated, inculcated, and sometimes resisted.

Intergenerational conflict over the direction of young Black female desires is one instantiation of intimate antagonism that *Confessions* re-creates. Like the parental generation the narrative attempts to supplant, Steffans also has designs on young Black women's bodies. To continue her narrative relationship to these readers, *Confessions* depicts the intimate antagonism between Steffans and her mother. The origins of the video vixen's narrative are situated within the contemporary processes of globalization and its particular racial and gendered effects. These effects are thinly veiled by intragender and intrafamilial conflict. Such intraracial battles point to the struggles over the shifting meaning and representations of Black women in a global context.

Karrine Steffans was born in 1978 on St. Thomas, an island of the US Virgin Islands unincorporated territory. In the chapter entitled "The Sins of the Mother," her depiction of her birth and childhood on the island is figured through the intense hatred she feels toward her physically and emotionally abusive mother, Josephine. Steffans describes her mother as "a one-woman melting pot of Puerto Rican, Jamaican, and Danish heritage" with a penchant for fine clothes and men. Steffans's animosity toward her mother stems from the perception of Josephine's desperation for and debasement by men. Steffans recalls waking to the sounds of men making their escape through the back door. On one occasion, Steffans remembers her pregnant mother losing a tug-of-war battle as the man "wriggled free and charged out the door." Despite her mother's suffering in yet another scene of abandonment, Steffans "can remember not feeling at all sorry for her. In fact, I was a little happy. . . . I was so embarrassed to be my mother's daughter."[12]

Steffans's hatred and embarrassment are also fueled by the belief that her mother's choices and behavior foreclosed her ability to have a childhood relationship with a father figure. "We were all bastards, each of us the product of a different man," Steffans claims, "men who would never stay, men who would never come back. Men who I was forced to call 'uncle,' something for which I resented my mother." Steffans's biological father is an African American from New York who resided in St. Thomas for eight years before returning to the US mainland. An absent figure during much of her childhood, her father is idealized as a witty, handsome, and successful American businessman on the island. While the absence of a male patriarch in the home is portrayed as depriving Steffans of validation and social legitimacy, the female-headed household also rendered the family economically disadvantaged. Only eighteen years old when she gave birth to Karrine, Josephine moved in with her own mother after her child's father returned to New York. Ten family members resided in a four-bedroom house: "Along with me, my mother, and grandmother were also my aunt, two cousins, and two uncles. Later came my two younger sisters."[13] In Steffans's recollection, her family's poverty resulted from her mother's promiscuity and undignified sexual behavior. What Steffans and other adult female members of her community presumed to be socially reprehensible relations with men seemingly became the burden to the family, contributing to their nonnormativity and to their poverty.

Impetuous choices in men, frequent unplanned pregnancies, and bitter mother-daughter conflict are familiar criticisms of poor women of color especially.[14] Women's emotional and economic vulnerabilities in romantic relationships are generally perceived as solely women's responsibility. Whether we recognize or not the uneven playing field in which men and women seek meaningful partnerships (however long they last), women still bear the burden of knowing better or at least choosing better. The tendency to disregard or disavow how heteropatriarchy (the interlock between heteronormativity and patriarchy) affects intimate relations emerges from and protects that system of power. In *Confessions* Steffans contradictorily reveals and endorses that power. Although she depicts the abandonment and poverty that her female-headed family endures, she interprets their suffering as the harsh reckoning for her mother's "sins." Controlling discourses about the pathological Black mother and the hypersexual Black woman determine how Josephine is depicted and contribute to intragender and intrafamilial fragmentation.[15]

The controlling image and discourse of Black female hypersexuality can obscure the issues of labor exploitation and the gendered division of labor in transnational capitalism.[16] Shifts in the exercise of economic, political, and racial power also disrupt intimate relations, limit life opportunities, and disparage those who suffer under these conditions of inequality. Black women's mobility and social lives are shaped by global designs on their bodies as well. In an economy that depends upon tourism and the service-based occupations that support it, Black women find themselves recruited into servile labor and the symbols of its benevolence.[17] The seduction of foreign visitors and capital to St. Thomas capitalizes on erotic fantasies of Black women as sexually available. Normative expectations about how women should conduct their private and public lives also seek to discipline their bodies in the pursuit of transnational profits. Expectations of Black women's bodies correlate to neoliberal discourses of self-regulation. The authoritative logic behind this discourse is based on market-controlled definitions of time and space. Controlling bodies, behavior, leisure, and relations train Black women in the service of global profiteering.

As Kamala Kempadoo describes, conflating "sex with the highest form of intimacy presupposes a universal meaning of sex, and ignores changing perceptions and values as well as the variety of meanings that women and men hold about their sexual lives."[18] Although her analysis centers on sex work, Kempadoo's analysis identifies the proximity between Caribbean women's racial and economic vulnerability and their involvement in stigmatized sexual labors as part of the shifting realities and meanings behind how Black women negotiate their complex sexual lives.[19] Indeed, if the dominant discourses about and regulation of sex work structure the lives of the most vulnerable women in the global marketplace, then they also identify the points of entry into the illicit sexual economy *and* the terms for stigmatization and control.

The disciplining of Black women's bodies makes race, sex, and gender central not only to global interests but also to state initiatives. M. Jacqui Alexander sees these state-sponsored desires as a form of recolonization, or "the attempts by the state, and the global economic interests it represents, to achieve a psychic, sexual, and material usurpation of the self-determination" of a people.[20] The state itself fulfills a patriarchal role, actively engaged in an agenda that defends masculinist economic and political power at the expense of women's individual and erotic autonomy.[21] According to Alexander, instead of supporting Black women's efforts toward self-possession, the state, in collaboration with global capital, revamps "the narrative of colonization as a celebratory one of mutual consent." Alexander also analyzes mother-daughter and other forms of intragender conflict within heteropatriarchy. Traditionally, such dominant power "positions women as their own worst erotic enemies and rivals." For Alexander, challenging these conflicts is inseparable from the efforts toward a form of decolonization that doesn't shy away from the political, economic, discursive, psychic, and sexual.[22] The interconnected systems of patriarchy and global capitalism create the conditions of possibility for Black women's exploitation, as well as their intimate antagonisms.

Although Steffans does not narrate her *Confessions* with such explicit understanding, the episodes she recounts situate her life experiences within the context of racial and gendered exploitation. The fact that she does not articulate her family's poverty and her mother's ostracization in relation to these broader social and economic forces indicates her internalization of dominant perceptions of Black motherhood and sexuality. Steffans's depiction of her mother echoes dominant criticisms of poor Black women and seems to validate the discourse of Black cultural pathology. The conclusion that there are serious defects within Black culture, not within racial, gendered, and economic stratification, locates the burden for challenges that Black people face squarely on Black people alone. *Can* the video vixen speak?

The opening portion of Steffans's narrative positions her as a victim subject to masculine power and abandonment and trapped by women's behavior and competition. Under such terms, she also reproduces the desire for normativity, for a traditional mother, and for economic security. Believing that these desires are related, she distances herself from her mother and again demonstrates the threat of proximity to the sexualized image of Black women that this article examines. Still, a key contradiction of *Confessions* appears in Steffans's attempt to write a cautionary tale to young Black women that is distinct from parental wisdom (or lack thereof) and her narrative of disdain toward her own mother for her sexual choices. This disparagement can only be understood as hypocritical; we, her readers, know that her childhood memories form part of the video vixen's confessions. Steffans's attempt to produce her life's narrative cannot disentangle itself from identification with her mother and the stain of her mother's sins ("we were all bastards"). Steffans's story requires her mother to be a part of the narrative. Characterizing Josephine within the confining terms of the bad Black mother would also restrict Steffans's own experiences to the narrative of hypersexuality. Her inability to articulate a more complex representation of Josephine potentially imperils Steffans's effort to utter her confessions as more than the reproduction of dominant discourses about Black sexuality.

The term "confession," however, also comes under scrutiny in this analysis of Steffans's narrative. Within a Foucauldian framework, confessions about sexuality seek to produce the "truth" *discursively* as a means to transform and control desire from a private experience into a public good.[23] The pleasure-in-looking at the pornographic scene promises the spectator the revelation of something unknown, of the truth about a difference hidden within the performances of bodies on-screen. Although *Confessions* is not a pornographic text, its title and its attempts to discursively reveal the truth of the video vixen's sexuality bring the theoretical concerns about difference, race, and gender into my analysis. As Jennifer Nash argues, "The reliance on a Foucauldian paradigm which presumes that difference—both gender and racial—structures the relationship between spectator and protagonist" erases the Black spectator of Black sexual performance.[24] Sameness rather than difference is the spectacle of representation that Black people negotiate. From the lynched Black male body to the Hottentot Venus, the threat of sameness that these representations provoke within the Black viewer produces an irresistible identification with the Black body marked by violence and desire. The scopic and discursive pleasures of anti-Black racism mean that the video vixen and her confessions always arrive too late. Isn't the entrenched image of Jezebel already written into the image of the video vixen and thus into *Confessions* and the book's value as a commodity? Doesn't the image then reproduce the division of racist culture?

The threat of looking at Steffans, of reading her narrative and gazing at her image, is that young Black females might see themselves and their sexuality within the Black sexual economy *Confessions* describes. Finding oneself in the narrative thus requires Black women (and men, as I discuss later) to negotiate pleasure and desire within the context of racial and sexual inequities. Steffans's anxiety about her own mother's influence ("I was so embarrassed to be my mother's daughter") contradicts her motivation for telling her story to Black girls. Her reactions to her mother's sexual behavior parallel the criticisms of the book and its potential influence on a younger generation. These fretful responses about the representation of Black women's nonnormative sexuality within and regarding *Confessions* are also productive of knowledge. In this instance, knowing *not* to conform to the White supremacist fantasy construction of Black hypersexuality is the knowledge that Steffans and critiques of her reproduce. In other words, Black consciousness about Black female sexuality is also shaped by the infiltration of dominant fantasies into Black people's lives and in conflict with their pleasures—even if such pleasures are made available through the exploration of unruly desires.[25]

Intraracially, this means grappling with images and texts that are at once ours and not ours. While dominant fantasies produce familiar scripts of Black sexual debasement, they also make Black people strangers to themselves and to each other. In essence, such fantasies rob Black people of their own images and replace them with a distorted mirror of Black sexual pathology. Intraracially, however, the dismissal of the video vixen or other representations of Black women's eroticism constrains what can be said about Black women's complex lives and imaginaries beyond the distorted framework of hypersexuality and/or respectability. How do Black women locate the object of their desire when they are so often positioned "as a projection of the desires (and fears) of others"?[26] The video model therefore elicits an irresistible identification precisely because her narrative performance muddles the boundaries between looking at, or in this case reading, and *being* the Black woman eroticized.

As David Marriott carefully describes in another context, such identification can run riot through Black psychic and cultural life.[27] One does not need to be the object of hypersexual representation to understand the dangers associated with Black women being thusly portrayed or to be reminded of the power structures in place that produce the vulnerabilities affixed to Black women's sexual lives. Still, those dominant associations can never fully capture the text of Black women's erotic imaginaries or totally impede Black people's desires to experience themselves and each other differently. The difference intraracially is not found in the perennial struggle for recognition and integration into dominant structures but in a new narrative and analysis of deviation.[28] The critical analysis of deviance, as scholars like Cathy Cohen and L. H. Stallings describe, brings attention to the behaviors and indeterminate identities of those with limited agency in their pursuit of autonomy and pleasure.[29] These and other scholars' insistence on challenging dominant frameworks that ultimately seek to regulate, reform, and recruit these nonnormative bodies into existing power structures looks at the everyday deviant practices that thwart increased surveillance on their lives and evade the demands of heteronormative protocols for behavior.[30] Deviance also provides an analytical point of entry into examining the complex circulation and meaning of nonnormative behaviors intraracially *without* presuming that so-called deviant bodies always share the same tactics and motivations for producing autonomy and experiencing pleasure. As we have seen, the irresistible identification with Black deviance can also produce intimate antagonisms that reproduce aggression and frustration intraracially. Playing with language and representation in order to defamiliarize even the most stereotypical depictions of Black people from Black people themselves is one necessary and perhaps deviant strategy that the video vixen's narrative exposes.

"Hit 'Em Up Style": Do Snitches Get Stitches or Lucrative Entertainment Contracts?

> For if just half of the allegations contained in this spellbinding confession are true, I feel totally vindicated for all of my diatribes against rap as misogynistic.
>
> —Kam Williams, "Book Review: *Confessions of a Video Vixen*"

Critics like Kam Williams read Karrine Steffans's *Confessions* as an affirmation of the now-standard critique of hip-hop culture as hopelessly sexist. Hip-hop head and documentarian Byron Hurt also condemns Black men's investment in the hegemonic masculinity that mainstream rap music seems to promote at the expense of women of color and to the benefit of wealthy White men.[31] Despite her required labor in mainstream hip-hop music videos, the video model is mostly a silent figure. The video model, in particular Karrine Steffans, has been both an object of pleasure and a source of infuriation for many Black men in the entertainment industry and for Black men who consume hip-hop cultural products. Steffans exploits the reader's desire for her confessions and transforms that desire into a profitable commodity of which she will be the beneficiary and master over the Black men who have otherwise profited from her image and her body.[32] The popularity of the video vixen's *Confessions* and her refusal to remain silent expose Black masculine anxieties produced at the encounter with the text of Black female sexual promiscuity.

The documentary *Kiss and Tail: The Hollywood Jump-Off* (dir. Thomas Gibson, 2009) provides a platform to the stars that Steffans allegedly bedded. Steffans's rumored former lovers have curious and seemingly paradoxical responses to her memoir. Rap artist Ja Rule responds to the allegations of his sexual relationship with Steffans by confirming the sanctity of his marriage. "She's not going to mess up a happy home," he asserts as a way to dismiss the rumors of his infidelity and to appease his wife. Although Ja Rule seeks safety in monogamous, heterosexual marriage as protection from the scrutiny and ridicule *Confessions* unleashes, he happily accepts responsibility for giving Steffans the moniker "Superhead" to describe her skills in performing fellatio.[33] R&B singer Norwood Young aligns himself with hegemonic masculinity through his relationship to Steffans as well. Through her, he is able to deny rumors that he is gay, although he claims to have never engaged in sexual relations with Steffans. "I now wish I had," Young taunts, resorting to the most basic form of heteromasculinist affirmation.[34] Actor Darius McCrary is best known for his role as Eddie Winslow on *Family Matters* (ABC, 1989–96; CBS, 1997–98), a television sitcom about a middle-class Black family. McCrary describes how his relationship with Steffans allowed him to get in touch with his "b-boy side," a mode of Black masculine self-presentation he felt was lost through his mainstream sitcom role. Porn actors and producers acknowledge that Steffans was able to "get paid" from selling her memoir, but Suave XXX (aka the "Gangster of Porn") considers her monetary compensation for *Confessions* to be "a foul way of going about getting your money."[35] In fact, Black men perceive Steffans's economic compensation for revealing her sexual exploits and naming her partners as such destructive behaviors that not even the archbishop Don Magic Juan is willing to endorse them. Self-described as a pimp, spiritual advisor, and professional ladies' man, Don Magic Juan complains that the motivation behind her writing *Confessions* was "all about the almighty dollar." Rather than selfish economic gain, he calls for reciprocity between the sexes, arguing that "what's good for her is good for you" and that "fair exchange ain't no robbery."[36]

These responses to Steffans's memoir indicate Black men's perception that she exploits them sexually and monetarily. Their discomfort stems in part from her participation in illicit eroticism for her own autonomy. Steffans's exposure and narration of their less than mythic sexual abilities threaten to expose the fetishization of Black masculinity that they otherwise benefit from economically. Video models convert an otherwise homosocial scene among men into an affirmation of hegemonic masculine desire. Despite their investments in hegemonic masculinity through the personas (as gangstas, thugs, or pimps) that they perform in the cultural marketplace, the video vixen's written narrative does not affirm their attachments to masculine bravado, especially as such masculine portrayals depend upon Black women's silent complicity. Instead, Steffans deviates from the position of silence marked out for the video model in order to siphon from Black male celebrities power and prestige for her professional advancement. In the process, her text recasts Black men into a position where they experience sexual exploitation intraracially. Exchanging positions with men, Steffans as the author of the sexual scripts with these men becomes a competitor with them for both money and power in the global marketplace.

The men featured in *Kiss and Tail* thus articulate their fury against Steffans from the position as victim to such a degree that they too seem to retreat into alignment with sexual respectability in order to protect themselves from being unfairly thrust into objecthood. Frantz Fanon describes crushing objecthood as a result of a Black man's encounter with the image White people have of him and the knowledge that he must be "black in relation to the white man."[37] This experience of objecthood is ego shattering, but it reassembles the Black man in the encounter with and in accordance with White desires for his inferiority as "an imitative perversion of human kind; a being incapable of inhibition, morals or ideas; a being whose supernatural indulgence of pleasure and continued satisfaction cannot deal with the contrary denial or pain; a being whose violent, sexual criminality is incapable of any lasting, or real relationships, only counterfeit."[38] Ostensibly, it is *Steffans's* narrative portrayal of Black male sexuality that provokes Black men's anxiety about being undone. Her public and commercialized confessions about these Black men's sexual lives conjure the long-standing images of Black men as hypermasculine and sexually pathological.[39] In other words, through their representation in Steffans's text, these men affectively experience their sexuality as exploited. This experience is almost inseparable from the images of Black sexual debasement overrepresented in dominant cultural representations of Blackness. As discussed above in relation to Black women, Black men also undergo an irresistible identification in their encounter with Steffans's text of illicit eroticism and unruly desire.

It seems, then, that a Black man cannot look at (or in this case read) the video vixen's *Confessions* and not see himself as well. Under Steffans's authorial control, his otherwise empowered position as spectator of the video model is rearticulated into his simultaneous position as victim vis-à-vis the text of Black female eroticism that conjures his own sexual vulnerability. Black scholars have long understood the entanglement between debased representations of Black men and women since Ida B. Wells articulated the connection between White men's rape of Black women and White men's lynching of Black men for the alleged rape of White women.[40] Again, the video vixen's confessions cannot be told without including the text of Black masculinity and Black men's relationship to desire in the context of subjugation as well.

The historical weight of the representation of debased Black sexuality can and often does reproduce respectability as a compulsory mode of heteronormative self-defense. The undoing that the irresistible identification with the text of Black female promiscuity elicits illuminates the complex process of negotiating the text of Black sexuality intraracially. This undoing proposes a way for Black people to be reflected to themselves and to each other that is distinct from the distorted and phantasmatic image of White desire even as they grapple with the imposition of racial capitalism.[41]

The Video Vixen Rewrites Hip-Hop History

According to Steffans's *Confessions*, Mark "Brother Marquis" Ross of 2 Live Crew and Ice T were among the first people she met upon moving to Los Angeles. Ice T—now espousing "pimpology"—and Brother Marquis ushered Steffans into LA's entertainment scene.[42] She came to the West Coast in a desperate attempt to flee her alleged abusive relationship with Kool G Rap, the father of her son and the putative first successful gangsta rapper on the East Coast. While Kool G toiled to remain visible in the mainstream rap scene, Steffans rose to prominence as a dancer in the strip clubs and private parties of Scottsdale's athletic and business elites.

After a lengthy telephone call with Marquis, a conversation in which Steffans recounted her turbulent experiences with Kool G and her fears about her uncertain future, Marquis devised a strategy. He introduced her to Ice T, believing that the LA-based rapper could help her and her son. Steffans and Ice T began a sexual relationship in which he also functioned as a mentor: "Ice taught me a lot about how to make it in Los Angeles—where to eat, where to shop, how to negotiate, and to know my worth professionally." With this newfound sense of agency, Steffans entered the scene of celebrity life, drug abuse, and sex. After meeting the music-video director Hype Williams on the set of an LL Cool J video, she started working as a video model, beginning with her appearance in Jay-Z's video for the song "Hey Papi."[43]

Steffans's memoir situates her rise in the hip-hop scene in relation to three crucial events: the 1990 trial against the rap group 2 Live Crew, the 1992 trial against Ice T and his rock band, Body Count, and the 1990s conglomeration of multiple media corporations. It is significant that Steffans narrates her entrance into the hip-hop music scene via artists like legendary rapper Kool G, controversial rappers Mark "Brother Marquis" Ross of 2 Live Crew and Ice T, and the artist/mogul Jay Z. She positions herself, via these men, as an invaluable part of hip-hop's history, development, and global popularity. 2 Live Crew, for example, is the group most popularly associated with the expansion and promotion of the unique sound and style associated with "Miami bass" (also known as "booty music" or "booty bass"), which can include "dirty rap," in the late 1980s and early 1990s. Along with the rhythmic lyrics and driving beats, the group also incorporated dancehall's carnivalesque atmosphere of "slackness" or the expression of explicit sexuality.[44] Such unambiguous erotic expressions appear in the music's lyrics and in women's dance moves and fashion. 2 Live Crew's version of slackness in their 1989 album *As Nasty as They Wanna Be* and the group's performance of songs from that album in Hollywood, Florida, were deemed criminally obscene by a federal district judge in Florida in 1990, a ruling that was later overturned.[45]

On the West Coast, rapper Ice T and the punk group Body Count came under national fire because of their song "Cop Killer." Although the group had been performing the song, which was recorded in 1991 and released in 1992, the state of emergency following Los Angeles Police Department officers' beating of Rodney King in March 1991; the acquittal of officers Stacey Koon, Theodore Briseño, and Timothy Wind in 1992; the shooting of African American teenager Latasha Harlins; and the LA uprising of 1992 produced a national rhetoric intended to stop the violence associated with gang activity in impoverished inner cities. Succumbing to pressure from Time Warner, police officers, and police activist organizations like the Los Angeles Police Protective League, Ice T and Body Count decided to pull the song from the album.[46] Although 2 Live Crew was eventually acquitted of obscenity—with the support and expert testimony of African American cultural scholars—Ice T and Body Count were pressured to retract their critique of state-sponsored violence and to censor their articulation of rage.[47]

By the time Ice T was persuaded to withdraw "Cop Killer" from commercial circulation, major record labels had already begun devising strategies to capitalize on so-called gangsta rap. Media-based developments in technology not only changed the formats in which music is stored and replayed, they also facilitated the record industry's ability to gauge the popularity and profitability of diverse artists and genres. As Tricia Rose describes, such market intelligence exploited young people's interests in gangsta rap "swiftly into a multitude of markets and related products." The market aestheticization of hip-hop (its adaptation to mainstream market desires) occurs alongside the consolidation of multiple media corporations into five major media conglomerates, among them Time Warner.[48] Recording labels, radio stations, and video programming are steered by a small, powerful group that shares control over the majority of the US media industry. Despite such transformations in the technologies, production, and promotion of popular commercial music, corporate controls were still impacted by the widely publicized trials occurring on both sides of the country during the early 1990s. The explicit critique of state-sponsored violence against Blacks in the forms of police brutality, mass incarceration, and ongoing ghettoization was out; the explicit portrayal of Black hypersexuality, pimping, and thug life was in. The related images portray Black social and intimate relations as commercially bound and exploitative. It is within this representational and political field that the video vixen, as a cultural figure with staying power, rises in prominence.

I stated above that Black men's furious responses to Steffans's *Confessions* emerged *partially* as a result of her revelation of and profiting from the text of their less than mythic sexual capabilities. Steffans's articulation of explicit sexuality even in the pursuit of power, prestige, and profit uncovers Black men's retreat from the overt critique of state violence into the performance of heteromasculinist dominance. As a Black woman, Steffans's wage potential rivals that of Black men. Economist Sandy Darity writes that forces like the prison industrial complex, permanent unemployment, the service economy, and intergenerational poverty challenge Black men's presence and viability in the economic marketplace.[49] The so-called informal economy of drug dealing and pimping has been generally understood as the bastion of working-class Black male deviance and control.[50] Steffans portrays herself as entrepreneurial and thus a competitor with Black men in the context of collective Black economic marginalization. The condemnation Black men level against Steffans for her *Confessions* reinforces heteropatriarchy rather than illuminating the effects of a repressive police state, corporate conglomeration, and judiciary racism and sexism. The exposure of these convergences in the video vixen's narrative unveils Black men's vulnerability as a result of Black women's testimony about men's failure to fulfill the demands of heteronormativity.

The exercise of racism positions Black men and women as both witnesses to and symbols of each other's degradation. This dynamic produces a displeasing mirroring effect distorted by dominant fantasies of Black hypersexuality. As these intraracial conflicts show, the entrenched images of Black bodies are incompatible in their simplicity with the complexity of Black people's dreams, their penchant for play, their transgressive sensualities, and their unruly desires. The intimate antagonism between Steffans and the Black male celebrities who reproach her has the potential to lock them into the frames of hypersexuality and hypermasculinity. However, the depictions of their "private relations" create sites for public discussions about Black social realities. If the gangsta, pimp, and ho have formed the "unholy trinity" dominating hip-hop's storytelling worldview, then Black men's responses to *Confessions* reveal how hip-hop artists also have to negotiate that imposition.[51] Intraracial intimacy becomes its own site of struggle.

Beyond Beats and Binaries: Black Sexual Economies and the Text of Intraracial Intimacy and Desire

Throughout this chapter I have argued that the issues of illicit eroticism and unruly desire take on unique significance from the vantage point of intraracial interactions. Even as Black people grapple with racial capitalism under globalization and state violence, the meaning of these dynamics for the text of Black sexuality develops in intraracial intimate relations. As we have seen, economic exploitation, a shrinking labor market, and decreased or limited opportunities pressure the ways Black people negotiate relationships, define intimacy, and perceive representations of Black sexuality. Writing and authorship have been central to these determinations.

As Stallings argues, the fluidity and boundlessness of Black culture require us to examine the relationship between hip-hop's visual and written culture. Forgoing concern with "what whites will think," these "hip-hop narratives" provide a key site for examining intraracial intimate antagonisms.[52] *Confessions* engages questions about race, gender, and writing. In terms of plot, the book loosely strings together a series of hyperbolic sexual scenarios and incoherent narrative episodes. Yet it is precisely the hyperbolic tenor of her *Confessions* that helps to reveal the struggle encompassing the contemporary representation of Black women's eroticism. If pleasure is to be located in *Confessions*, it is precisely through the potentially subversive play of language and meanings that has otherwise limited the examination of Black sexuality to demonstrating their victimization or denying their presumed pathology.[53]

But who is the author of these confessions? Throughout her narrative, Steffans states that she is known by the stage name Yisette Santiago, the "alter ego" born after her debut as an exotic dancer.[54] Although *Confessions* is attributed to Karrine Steffans, the author's given name is Karen Antonia Stevens. The narrative is thus the compilation of indeterminate and tentative identities. Fragmentation functions as a narrative strategy both to reveal the author to her readers and to protect her private self from total exposure. Steffans's strategy of narrative fragmentation in her confessions about sexual encounters with other media and mediated figures like DMX, Xzibit, and Jay-Z creates a complicated relation to the "real." Are these the experiences of private people or public figures? Are the representations in her book the extension of their performances in rap songs and videos or the commodification of private sexual encounters for public consumption? Similarly, are these tales of performers living out their public personas in private? Steffans's text is not even a memoir per se but a "confession." Roderick Ferguson argues that for Black people, "the incitement to discourse confirmed and ensured the repetition of stereotype. In other words, it assisted the production of racial knowledge about African Americans."[55] The proliferation and indeterminacy of both identities and narrative fragmentation play with the very notion of confession and its role in reproducing racial stereotypes.

Instead, Steffans's *Confessions* erodes binary frames. She presents her self to be looked at *and* read. She occupies the roles of speaker (as the video vixen) and audience (through her experience as a young girl longing to be a video model).

She fondly recalls her encounters with sex, drugs, and hip-hop even as she cautions against her excesses. *Confessions* as a text is irresolvable and necessarily so. Part of this irresolvability is related to Steffans's two-book contract and thus her legal and economic commitments to produce more narrative.[56] In the aftermath of *Confessions,* however, music and entertainment channels like VH-1 have begun to feature reality programming based on women whose claims to fame are based on their sexual partners. *Basketball Wives, Love and Hip Hop,* and *Hollywood Exes,* to name a few, are both popular and hated for their representations of Black women as promiscuous, materialistic, and cunning. The staying power of such representations, as well as the critiques against them, still captures our attention and still forces us to look. Looking and reading intraracially, especially at the conflicts that emerge through or in response to representations of Black sexuality, provide ways to hone our critical lenses, figuratively, in the break. An intraracial analysis refuses to prioritize White recognition as the primary (even if unspoken) goal of our inquiries. The meanings of Black eroticism and resistance take on new definitions when they are thought beyond the hegemony of the color line. Breaking away from dominant presumptions about Black sexuality also enables an orientation focused on and driven by the complexity of Black people's experiences, pleasures, and desires without presuming intraracial collectivity and unity. Such complexity brings us to the text of unruly desire with anticipation, imagination, and sometimes even pleasure.

Notes

1. Miller-Young, "Hip Hop Honeys"; Keizer, "Gone Astray."
2. Miller-Young, "Hip Hop Honeys," 264.
3. Keizer, "Gone Astray," 1668.
4. See Adrienne Davis's chapter, "'Don't Let Nobody Bother Yo' Principle': The Sexual Economy of American Slavery," in this volume.
5. Balaji, "Vixen Resistin'," 14.
6. Pough, "What It Do, Shorty?," 83.
7. Sharpley-Whiting, "The Irony of Achievement."
8. For critiques of misogyny in hip-hop, see Emerson, "'Where My Girls At?'"; Fitts, "'Drop It Like It's Hot'"; Hunter and Soto, "Women of Color in Hip Hop." For hip-hop's relationship to pornography, see Levande, "Women, Pop Music, and Pornography"; Miller-Young, "Hip Hop Honeys."
9. Jenkins, *Private Lives, Proper Relations,* 4. In addition to Jenkins, see Evelyn Brooks Higginbotham's definitive text on the politics of respectability, *Righteous Discontent.*
10. Steffans, *Confessions,* xiv, xiii, xvi.
11. Jenkins, *Private Lives,* 3, 4.
12. Steffans, *Confessions,* 10, 11.
13. Ibid., 10, 13.

14. For a discussion about the scrutiny of working-class Black women, see Carby, "Policing the Black Woman's Body."

15. Daniel Patrick Moynihan's now infamous 1965 essay, "The Negro Family: The Case for National Action" (Office of Policy Planning and Research, United States Department of Labor, March 1965), cited Black people's inferior economic and social position as a result of female-headed households. See also Roberts's excellent book, *Killing the Black Body*.

16. On the controlling or entrenched images of Black womanhood, see Collins, *Black Sexual Politics*; and Deborah Gray White's classic analysis of the Jezebel and Mammy figures in *Ar'n't I a Woman?*

17. For an invaluable discussion on the relationship between the eroticization of Blackness and sex tourism, see Williams, *Sex Tourism in Bahia*.

18. Kempadoo and Doezema, *Global Sex Workers*, 5.

19. See Kempadoo, *Sun, Sex, and Gold*.

20. Alexander, "Erotic Autonomy," 66.

21. For a discussion of the patriarchal state and a critique of globalization, see Fregoso, "Toward a Planetary Civil Society."

22. Alexander, "Erotic Autonomy," 90, 99, 100.

23. Foucault, *The History of Sexuality*, 21.

24. Nash, *The Black Body in Ecstasy*, 19.

25. Frantz Fanon describes the imposition from without in *Black Skins, White Masks*. See also Marriott, *On Black Men*, viii.

26. Keizer, "Gone Astray," 1670.

27. Marriott, *On Black Men*.

28. For further discussion about the reproduction of normativity, see also Cohen, "Punks, Bulldaggers, and Welfare Queens."

29. Cohen, "Deviance as Resistance," 30; Stallings, *Mutha' Is Half a Word*.

30. See Kelley, *Yo' Mama's Disfunktional!*; Kelley, *Race Rebels*; and Scott, *Domination*.

31. Hurt, "Pornography and Pop Culture," 53.

32. See also Bryan, *It's No Secret*. Jay Z profited from the song "Is That Yo Bitch?" he wrote about Bryan and in opposition to Nas.

33. In a later interview, Steffans stated that the term comes from a song by the rap artist Jadakiss that appeared before the two ever met. Mereb Gebremariam, "Karrine Steffans Explains 'Super Head' Nickname, Lil Wayne's D*ck Size & Men's Obsession with the YMCMB's Manhood," *MStars News*, April 1, 2015, mstarz.com/articles/60882/20150401/karrine-steffans-explains-super-head-nickname-lil-waynes-dick-size-ymcmb.htm.

34. Norwood Young later authored his own memoir, *Getting Back to Me*, in which he comments on his feud with Steffans over her misrepresentation of his sexuality in her subsequent book, *The Vixen Diaries* (New York: Grand Central Publishing, 2007).

35. In *Kiss and Tail* Suave XXX claimed to be the person who introduced Steffans to the majority of the celebrities she writes about in *Confessions*. He also stated that he booked her for her first pornographic role. Pleased by her performance, he contacted the porn actor and producer Mr. Marcus, who booked Steffans for the *Cool Spot* videos he created with Vivid Entertainment, a leader in adult media products. Scenes including Steffans from *Cool*

Spot (2000) were rereleased in the video *Honey* (2006) in order to capitalize on *Confessions'* popularity.

36. Don Magic Juan quoted in *Kiss and Tail.*

37. Fanon, *Black Skin, White Masks,* 110.

38. Marriott, *On Black Men,* x.

39. On dominant images of Black masculinity, see Baldwin, *Notes of a Native Son;* Marriott, *On Black Men;* and Fanon, *Black Skin, White Masks.*

40. See Wells, "To Tell the Truth Freely."

41. On White desire, see Marriott, *On Black Men,* 12.

42. Ice T's notion of pimpology compares the economic relationship between pimps and sex workers to that of a record label and its artists. See tci398, *Ice T's Pimpology,* YouTube, December 28, 2007, youtube.com/watch?v=T5qcoPocRPI.

43. Steffans, *Confessions,* 88, 123.

44. Lipsitz, *Footsteps in the Dark,* 147.

45. Lipsitz discusses how "slackness" and other assertions of masculine privilege in popular music enable men who "experience a global economy increasingly organized around the low-wage labor of women" a way to allay their frustrations by disparaging women's independence (ibid., 152). Racism, xenophobia, and discrimination erode transmigrant men's status and dignity in the United States. Existing structures of patriarchy offer up women's bodies as a repository for these frustrations and anxieties.

46. See Lipsitz's chapter "The Hip Hop Hearings" in ibid.

47. For a discussion of African American scholars' defense of 2 Live Crew, see Crenshaw, "Beyond Racism and Misogyny"; and Jones, "The Signifying Monkees," in *Bulletproof Diva.*

48. Rose, *Black Noise,* 17.

49. See Darity and Myers, "Does Welfare Dependency Cause Female Headship?"; Darity, "Antipoverty Policy"; and Darity, "A New (Incorrect) Harvard/Washington Consensus."

50. See Kelley, *Yo' Mama's Disfunktional!*

51. On the unholy trinity, see Rose, *Black Noise.*

52. Stallings, *Mutha' Is Half a Word,* 179, 182.

53. See ibid. on the use of the "trickster" figure to reconceptualize Black women's texts and articulations of desire.

54. Steffans, *Confessions,* 49.

55. Ferguson, *Aberrations in Black,* 73.

56. Since the release of *Confessions,* Steffans has published eight additional books. The follow-up text to *Confessions* is *The Vixen Diaries* (2007). Other titles include *The Vixen Manual* (2009), *How to Make Love to a Martian* (about her relationship to the rap artist Lil Wayne) (2013), and *Vindicated* (2015). She established Steffans Publishing Enterprises, LLC, in 2005.

PART IV

Beyond Black Social Life as Death

The Erotics of Black Lives

CHAPTER 11

In the Life

Queering Violence in the Stories of G. Winston James

Darius Bost

In an epigraph to *In the Life: A Black Gay Anthology* (1986), Joseph Beam notes that the phrase "in the life," used to describe "'street life' (the lifestyle of pimps, prostitutes, hustlers, and drug dealers), is also a phrase used to describe the 'gay life' (the lives of black homosexual men and women). Street life and gay life, at times, embrace and entwine, yet at other times, are precise opposites."[1] This racialized and spatialized term signals the commingling of pleasure and danger that has continually marked black/gay existence. For Beam, the illicit economies of the street and the illicit sexual labor of black gay men in search of erotic fulfillment commingle "in the life." Though these two illicit economies overlap, "street life" can become oppositional to "gay life" due to the threat that homophobia poses to those who "openly" express same-sex desire. Because of this simultaneous overlap and opposition, the production of black gay subjectivity is often a source of ambivalently experienced pleasure. Essex Hemphill's poem, also titled "In the Life," captures this ambivalence when the speaker describes how he "roams alone at night" looking "for men willing / to come back / to candlelight." In the second stanza, the speaker emphasizes the fatal risk involved when engaging in public sex: "I'm not scared of these men / though some are killers / of sons like me."[2] Though acknowledging the risk involved, the speaker does not seem to fear the threat of death. Seemingly being "in the life" has produced a form of consciousness for the speaker in which the risk of death does not outweigh his quest for desire.

Beam's definition and Hemphill's poem open up a line of inquiry about how the distinct sexual economy of sex publics shapes black queer subjectivity. The sexual economy of sex publics is distinct because of the commingling of pleasure and danger that inheres in these spaces. The anonymity of sex publics enables modes of intimacy not sanctioned by hetero- and homonormative economies of marriage and family. The illicit sexual labor of those engaged in public sex coextends with other illicit street economies to create opportunities for the transgression of class boundaries that often limit the possibilities for social and sexual relations.

This essay explores the entanglements of death and desire that occur in queer sex publics. These entanglements are best illuminated in narratives of black same-sex-desiring men who might be described as "in the life," whose subjectivities emerge in the spaces and times when "street life" and "gay life" intertwine. I will closely read Jamaican American gay male writer G. Winston James's short stories to examine the relationship between the threat of death and public expressions of same-sex desire. Contesting dominant understandings that equate risky sexual practices with self-destructive desire or that blame victims for the consequences that ensue from their engagements in such sexual practices, I argue that black queer subjectivity emerges precisely within the spatiotemporal entanglements of death and desire.

Indeterminacy and Risk

Karla F. C. Holloway discusses how the African American experience has unevenly subjected black bodies in the United States to untimely deaths: "African Americans' particular vulnerability to an untimely death in the United States intimately affects how black culture both represents itself and is represented."[3] Holloway's study of the relationship between death and black cultural representation raises questions about how blacks' "vulnerability to an untimely death" shapes black subjectivities and everyday black life. She presents the African American experience of death and dying as paradoxical in that it is at once anticipated due to its omnipresence and at the same time a persistent interruption to the cycles of everyday black life. Holloway suggests that death not only operates in black life as a site of indeterminacy and risk, as it does for all human subjects and kinship relations, but also shapes black culture itself as a site of indeterminacy and risk.[4] Black culture is shaped not so much by a disavowal of death but by embracing its proximity and interruptions.

Phillip Brian Harper further remarks upon the indeterminacy and risk that pervade minority existence. Harper's published remarks to the "Black Queer Studies in the Millennium" conference are geared toward scholars who are writing about black sexualities, those who must conjecture in the face of cultural silence, historical ruptures, and ephemerality. He argues that minority consciousness is in part constituted by the uncertainty of "even the most routine instances of social activity and personal interaction as possible cases of invidious social distinction or discriminatory treatment." Harper gives the example of a white man who engaged Harper in a conversation while riding the train; the white man misperceived Harper to be Sri Lankan. Harper believes that the man's misperception of Harper's African American identity may have been because he could not fathom being sexually attracted to a black man. Harper is not sure of the man's motives and is left to speculate about the reasons for the man's engagement—and the consequences of such an engagement—had Harper obliged him. Harper jokingly conjectures that the man could have been an "ax murderer" or a "run-of-the-mill homophobe, out to victimize gay men by queer-baiting them first." He ends the speech not by emphasizing the possibility of his own demise but by illustrating how speculation and risk are such mundane experiences for minorities: "Not to proceed speculatively is, to speak plainly, not to live."[5]

I place Harper's comments in conversation with those of Holloway to demonstrate how the untimeliness and omnipresence of death for black subjects continue to structure black experience across axes of difference. Though Holloway discusses the history of spectacular racial violence directed toward African Americans, Harper's discussion extends this legacy of racialized violence to contemporary minority experience. Harper points to both the quotidian nature of such violence and the threat of death that emanates from everyday minority experience. If, as Holloway describes, death's effects on African Americans are paradoxical, "omnipresent" but "untimely," then Harper's description of the proximity of death and desire might provide an explanation for this tension. In other words, I argue that the paradoxical relationship of death to black subjectivity signals the presence of desire. That death is untimely for the black subject evidences a desire to live, even if the threat of death is omnipresent.

By using the example of an impromptu experience of a man "cruising" for a potential sexual encounter, Harper demonstrates how race and sexuality are mutually constitutive categories of minority experience.[6] Reading G. Winston James's collection of short stories, *Shaming the Devil* (2009), this essay examines literary representations of black men's engagement in "risky" public sex to elaborate upon this claim.[7] In James's short stories about public sex, whether the setting is late at night in subway stations or parks or midday in the adult video store, the risk of fatality is central to his representations of black male same-sex desire. James's aptly titled short story collection draws on the black vernacular phrase "tell the truth and shame the devil." Such an imperative indicates that it is the narrative of the characters themselves that disrupts dominant understandings about the boundaries of black queer desire. What is haunting about these particular short stories is not the ghosts of the dead black queers but the brutal honesty with which these characters describe death as a site of pleasure.

The short story genre is critical to James's project in that the transitional space of the short story promotes further speculation, and the structure of the narrative itself is marked by indeterminacy and risk. Four consecutive stories in the collection center black gay men cruising for sex, but "John" and "Somewhere Nearby" are unique in that the narrators' cruising culminates in an encounter with death at the hands of other cruisers. As they do in many other black gay male literary texts, dead and dying black queers propel these narratives.[8] Whereas the reader might associate black queerness solely with trauma and loss, James's characters narrate their own near-death experiences in ways that disrupt these normative affective registers.

These narratives demonstrate that the threat of death or knowledge of impending death does not mark black queer subjectivity as solely "death-bound," nor does queer desire ignore the omnipresence of death as constitutive of black gay subjectivity.[9] These stories foreground the subjective possibilities that emerge from being in the life—spaces and times when queer bodily desire throws into flux dominant understandings of black gay male subjects as always already dead or dying. This chapter looks at two distinct but interrelated stories that further represent the dangers and pleasures of being in the life. Whether fantasizing about death as a space of desire or searching for pleasure in the moments of dying, queer bodily desire figures in these narratives as a site of "speculation" that exceeds the spatial and temporal limits of an everyday black queer existence marked by the threat of death.

Desiring Death

The story "John" opens with the eponymous character, a middle-class black gay man, talking to his therapist. John has been in therapy for six months dealing with multiple experiences of childhood trauma. Through multiple flashbacks in the story, the reader learns that John has been physically and emotionally abused by his mother, sexually abused by his uncle, and arrested as a child for public sex, alongside multiple other traumatic experiences. Remembering the night his mother forced him into a closet, John reveals: "I wasn't even sixteen yet and had been arrested, fucked, raped, spat on and ejaculated into by lots of men, and even her brothers" (99). Flashbacks of these experiences interrupt the narrative, because as John mentions: "During and after therapy, it was always terribly difficult to keep my worst and most insidious memories at bay" (85).

John leaves the therapist's office, supposedly on his way to a friend's piano recital. Because leaving the therapist means that John is walking "back toward the shadowy places of [his] life," he "head[s] directly to that venue where the patient in [him] knew [he] should not go" (84, 85). John ends up at the Show Palace, an adult video store that he frequents. John acknowledges in the juxtaposition between the "patient in him" and his desire to go to the Show Palace how medicalized discourse—particularly psychological discourse—aids in disciplining his body and subjectivity. John walks through the store to the back room, where he can view the peep shows in "buddy booths." In the booths, a mutual agreement is reached between men to lower the windows between each cubicle so that they can view the other masturbating while watching the pornography on-screen. John describes the process of waiting for someone "attractive" and "free": "Worse still, there was no one attractive there who was free. Of charge, that is. Most of the six or seven patrons were hustlers—homeboy rentals dressed in the roughness they knew would sell—to someone—even if sex-appeal failed them" (87). "Street life" and "gay life" have intertwined in the back room of the Show Palace, which is primarily occupied by hustlers and queer men seeking their company.

John's middle-class status differentiates him from that of the hustler, who has caught John's eye, despite his usual shirking of transactional sex. The "street hustler," described as a "muscular black teenager," solicits John to watch a movie in the booth (88). John first ignores him, trying to convince the boy to walk away: "I ignored him, and looked around conspicuously as if to remind him that this was not a Loews theater, and that had it been, someone like him could never have invited someone like me on a date quite so easily" (88). John is well aware of how his class location, coupled with the particularity of the venue, produces a distinct sexual economy. The space is queer in that it exceeds the boundaries of hetero- and homonormativity, where socioeconomic status often constructs the limits of desire. Samuel Delany argues in *Times Square Red, Times Square Blue* that the restructuring of Times Square as a sex district to a family-oriented tourist district is undergirded by a "violent suppression of urban social structures, economic, social, and sexual" and rooted in "a wholly provincial and absolutely small-town terror of cross-class contact."[10] The distinct sexual economy of the Show Palace— with its commingling of pleasure and danger—provides the conditions for such contact.

After the hustler asks John again to watch a movie, John obliges and steps into the "three-by-three-by-seven cubicle" and begins to perform fellatio on him for ten dollars as the film plays in the background (90). John then asks the hustler to "fuck [him]" (93). When the hustler is about to ejaculate, John is surprised to learn that the hustler is not wearing a condom. As they continue to have sex in the tiny booth, an audience of onlookers gathers around the booth, having heard them tussling. The hustler threatens John, proclaiming that he owes him more money because he did not use a condom and because John gave him a "shitty deal" (95). Right before the attendant yanks the booth door open, John says of the hustler: "My heart raced with orgasm and fear. I thought I saw violence in his eyes. As he withdrew, I heard the click-click of a utility knife" (96). The confined space of this occurrence evokes the close proximity of pleasure and danger. Whereas the venue intertwines "street life" and "gay life," the act of penetrative sex in the tiny booth between the hustler and John further blurs the boundaries between two categories. John feels "orgasm and fear" simultaneously; the hustler threatens him right at the point of orgasm. The cramped space of the cubicle speaks to the ways that queer pleasures and transgressive sexual desires are constrained by the "narrow limits of institutionalized sexuality," as well as by the increasingly limited spaces for queer publics in a neoliberal social environment.[11]

Not only is John shamed before the onlookers as he falls out of the booth "with his cum-wet pants bunched at his ankles" and "shit-smeared ass up" (96), he must also face the hustler, who continues to hurl threats at him when he steps outside. After John pleases the hustler with his payment, John gives him his card to call him again. John rationalizes his decision to extend the hustler a standing invitation: "Somehow the hustler had known exactly what I wanted. He'd read me and known I didn't much want to live, and preferred to act oblivious to my dying. He knew that I wanted his dick just as much as anything else he might be carrying" (98). Contrary to dominant understandings that claim risky sexual actions as evidence of a mission of self-destruction, Harper proposes that the danger of public sex "is not the consequence of the search for sexual pleasure itself, but of the constraining circumstances under which [gay men] must conduct such a search in our society."[12] Though Harper rightly argues against the pathologization of queer desire, what might it mean to foreground the notion that fantasies of death can also be erotic? What does it mean for black gay men to desire death?

Sigmund Freud theorizes Eros as a creative force that makes existence possible and postpones the return to the inorganic state. Freud believes that Eros is a life-preserving and life-creating desire counterbalanced by Thanatos, or the death instinct.[13] Georges Bataille extends Freud's theories by defining eroticism as "assenting to life up until the point of death." Divorced from the reproductive drive, eroticism in Bataille's formulation breaks with the social order of work, reason, and calculation.[14] Freud's and Bataille's theories of eroticism provide an entry point for theorizing black queer subjectivity, for which death is constitutive. Eurocentric psychoanalytic and philosophical treatments of eroticism, however, fail to imagine death outside of its Westernized association with negation, fear, and finality. Bataille's theory, even though it links eroticism more closely to death, still imagines death through its Westernized constructions. Conversely, James's short story "John" imagines death as a space of possibility outside of current spatial and temporal limitations placed on the black queer subject within a heteronormative, neoliberal, capitalist society.

During a flashback, it is revealed that during one of John's many suicide attempts as a child, John's mother threatened that God would keep John alive to punish him for being a "sissy." When John imagines what the hustler might do "with that dick, those hands, and even his concealed box-cutter in [his] house" (99), it is because it registers a fantasy of death that might relieve him from what he feels to be his own suffering and punishment. Discussing the construction of "queer space" in the novels of Samuel Delany and Darieck Scott, Gershun Avilez argues that "the disruptive 'logic of fantasy' becomes an extension of the spatial work that desire accomplishes in these novels."[15] Similarly, John's erotic fantasies of the "queer space" of death disrupt the limited spatial logics that relegate black queer desire to the spaces where it meets up with risk. Such logic depends upon risk being an external social phenomenon solely rooted in heteropatriarchal social conditions, as Harper describes. John's fantasies of death register the subjective dimensions of risk and danger internal to the subject. The subjective dimension of risk and danger should not confine black queer subjectivity to the site of the body, however, only locating it in the moments where it meets up with other bodies for pleasure, dangerously risking its finite end. John's fantasies of death signal his refusal to be contained by these normative spatial and temporal logics.

John's "psycho-social distress" shapes his desire for death, but his desire stems from self-preservation rather than self-destruction. As Sharon Holland opines, "Perhaps some people are ready to die because the space imagined—the place of death—is not a dead space but a living space."[16] Drawing on anthropologist Michael Taussig's notion of the "space of death," Holland imagines death not as a finite end but as a liminal space occupied by those who are not considered to have a valuable social existence.[17] If everyday life operates as a space of punishment and a site for reliving his traumatic past, then John's continuous engagement with risk operates as a space of desire, a yearning for psychic self-possession and social freedom. John's desire to remain close to the threat of death can be read as his desire to be in a "living space." Only through an understanding of the heteropatriarchal social conditions through which John must exercise his desire, as well as his desire to be relieved from psychological stress, can we view his speculations about death as erotic longing that transcends the strictures of and boundaries between the psychic and the social.

Letting the Dead Speak

In "Somewhere Nearby," the story that follows "John" in James's collection, an unnamed victim narrates his own torture and death by two black men who lured him to his demise under the premise that they, too, were cruising for sex in Brooklyn's Prospect Park. Sexual desire drives the unnamed victim to follow his assailants despite knowing the invisible parameters of safety: "I'd followed him South and West far past the well, if invisibly demarcated lands of my people. I'd left the safety of the other cruising black men who have sex with men in order to be more alone with him" (102). He positions the "invisibly demarcated lands" of "cruising black men" as fixed in relation to the unbounded "South and West," the directions to which he is lured by his attacker. Even though the scene of the crime is within walking distance from the site marked for cruising, the victim perceives that he has gone "far past" this site. The unbounded spatial terrain implied in "South and West" imagines a space of unbounded desire unregulated by laws, capital, and risk. The perception of going "far past" the safe space of the cruisers implies that moving toward this imagined site of unbounded desire also brings one closer to the space of death. It is the proximity between the spaces of desire and death that the narrator allows us to see.

In his meditation on antiqueer violence, Eric Stanley uses numerous cold cases of mutilated and decomposing queer bodies to ask, "What then becomes of the possibility of queer life, if queerness is produced always and only through the negativity of forced death and at the threshold of obliteration?"[18] Such a question is timely and necessary given the frequency and grotesque nature of violence against queer and trans people in the United States, especially people of color. An emphasis on nonidentity and negation as the primary signifier of queerness, however, silences other stories that these mutilated and decomposing bodies might tell. Following Sharon Holland's inquiry to "unleash the potential of black subjectivity to speak from the dead," I take an alternative approach to the study of violence directed toward black queer bodies by letting the dead speak.[19]

"Somewhere Nearby" begins with the victim identifying himself as a corpse prior to the actual moment of death: "I am a corpse being dragged to shallow burial. My heart is hammering in my chest. My eyes are open. I smell trees above me" (101). Though he is still living, the victim's anticipation of his own death propels the narrative. Interestingly, the reader does not actually see the victim's end. The narrative ends with the line, "I am seeping out" (114). The "I" of this line troubles the conception of death as finality, as it implies that the "I" exceeds the body's undoing. The narrative "I" surpasses the actual time of the body's death. The speculative narrative form gives the reader access to the brutal act of antiqueer violence, which so often occurs without a witness. The black queer subject denoted by the "I" becomes an onlooker and thereby narrates his own demise. The reader learns that speculation as a mobilizing force of black queer subjectivity is a powerful source for reimagining the relations between death and desire.

Sensing his impending death, the narrator speculates about how he will be remembered. The narrator frets over the discovery of his profile on an online sex community, his extensive porn collection, and his antiretroviral medications when family and police enter his home. Recalling how he forgot to log off the online gay cruising site, he thinks: "I don't want to be referred to as 'Hngbttm4Hng' in the media" (104). The heteronormativity often embedded in public and private memorial practices can diminish the value of queer life by blaming victims for their engagement in anonymous sex. The "evidence" found in his room can also operate to shame and "out" queer subjects, demonstrating that the devaluation of queer life is witnessed not only in the numerous cold cases that Stanley uses as archive but also in the cases that are publicized and the lives that are remembered. The narrator desires a more holistic memorialization, such that the fullness of his life is not foreclosed by the circumstances of his death: "I am more than what some passing bird watcher and his binoculars will find in Prospect Park. I am more than this" (113). This line reimagines black queer subjectivity beyond the archives of corporeal remains or other "evidence" found posthumously. Naming himself as a corpse reveals how death aids in the constitution of black queer subject. That the "I" proclaims he is "more than this" reminds the reader that death is not wholly constitutive of black queer subjectivity.

This relationship is further imagined through the narrative landscape. The narrator describes the location of his death as a gothic landscape: "Dank. I can almost hear the leaves, damp and rotting on the ground. Worms, millipedes, beetles and all manner of crawling, slithering, undulating things wending their way among the sheets of detritus" (103). The dark rendering of this location suggests a supernatural haunting where the process of decay is both aural and hypervisible. The "crawling," "slithering," and "undulating" connote constant movement rather than stasis. This description insinuates that the site is marked by death even prior to the murder that is about to take place. As the two men drag the victim by his ankles to the location in which they will torture and kill him, the fatigues that he wears become filthy with "dead leaves, twigs, cigarette butts and dirt" (103). By dragging his body through this terrain, smearing his clothing and body in its filth, the two men enmesh the black queer body in this haunted landscape. If, as Avery Gordon argues, "to be haunted is to be tied to historical and social effects," then figuring the black queer body as a part of this haunted landscape emphasizes the historical traumas that mark all black queer bodies and spaces.[20] We can read the space of death not as a singular space but as existing at the edges of all black queer life, a space that haunts all black queer narratives.

Even though the victim seems to be permanently enmeshed in the space of death, the "I" detaches black queerness from the haunted landscape: "I recall the bats I'd seen darting, angling under the lamps like tiny fighter jets. . . . I thought, as I traversed the field, how bat-like I was there in the park, hunting invisible men. Wondered how I must seem to the occasional nighttime jogger. Did they stop to think of me? Consider me a natural part of the park's nocturnal ecosystem? . . . Another of a precious few wild lives that encroaching development had made increasingly worthy of preservation?" (103–4). Through imagining himself as a bat, also a gothic figure, the narrator seemingly places himself back within the dark landscape. Yet by speculating about his own self-worth, whether or not he, as "another of a precious few wild lives," is "worthy of preservation," the narrator acknowledges the value of black queer life within a culture of capital. It is precisely the "encroaching development" of neoliberal capitalism and its privileging of hetero- and homonormativity that make queer publics "increasingly worthy of preservation." Contrasting American cultural values of endless opportunity with the neoliberal cultural logics that have fostered the shrinking of sex publics, Delany argues that "in a society that prides itself on the widespread existence of opportunity, interclass contacts are the site and origin of what can later be seen as life opportunities."[21] Delany believes that the distinct sexual economy of queer sex publics, particularly the interclass contacts they instantiate, generates opportunities for social mobility. Given Delany's claims, the value of queer publics does not depend upon the gaze of the jogger, whose physical exercise and daily routine stress the longevity and functionality associated with heteronormative time. The jogger's gaze might position queer cruisers as unworthy because their social practices center momentary pleasures and nonreproductive sex. It is the narrator's speculative gaze that constructs queer life as "worthy of preservation," seeing the potential for "life opportunities" in queer publics constructed within the narrow constraints of neoliberal capitalism.

As one attacker holds the narrator, the other assailant violently beats him. The narrator notices that the one holding him has an erection: "He is erect there behind me now. I feel it. A protrusion pressing at the back of my head as he lets me fall slightly to reset his grip" (156). The protagonist's body seems to be caught up in an erotic exchange between the two men violating him. He thinks the one beating him looks like Tupac Shakur: "While I am being beaten by Tupac Shakur without music, the one behind me just keeps saying 'Yeah. Yeah.' Then silence between punches. Then 'Damn. Yeah. Yeah'" (109). These exclamations alongside his erection signal erotic ecstasy in which the protagonist's violated body becomes the conduit. James counters racial logics that construct so-called black-on-black crime as normative and occurring "elsewhere" and heteropatriarchy, which sees black queer subjects as worthless, by restaging the scene of intraracial homophobic violence outside of these logics. The author centralizes pleasure for both the bashers and the victim to illuminate how the assailant's desire is often concealed within dominant narratives of violence against black queer bodies. His erotic rendering of homophobic violence calls attention to the false binary opposition between the violence of black male homophobia and the threatening black queer desire that supposedly produces such violence.

The narrator also summons his own sexual history in an attempt to make sense of his assailant's pleasure. He recalls sexual role play with a Czech dentist who placed a dental spatula in his rectum. The narrator compares his experience of interracial BDSM to his current assailant holding a gun to his head: "I wonder then, shamelessly, if the gun against my temple would feel less threatening if it, too, like the dental spatula, were pressed into my ass" (105–6). Comparing his experiences of interracial BDSM to his current violation by a black assailant reminds us of how whiteness and blackness are intimately constructed through often invisible relations of dominance and subordination. Though black men murder the protagonist, they operate in collusion with white supremacy when they violently discipline black queer male bodies for not meeting up to heteropatriarchal norms of masculinity. By situating his current torture and violation along a historical continuum with his interracial sadomasochistic sexual practices, the narrator's bodily knowledge makes whiteness visible even while his violation by black men is rendered intelligible through the hypervisibility of blackness.

Though the narrator imagines interracial bondage and role play as a training ground for his own murder, he believes that he had been "making [him]self worthy" long before. He recalls stepping in front of the punch of an older boy when he was nine years old as "tearing the hymen of [his] sexuality," as the boy began "apologizing, touching [his] shoulders and face" (110). This serves as a primal scene for his sexual identification, in which he imagines his homosexuality as a desire to be wounded. The wounding not only alleviates the internal pain of dominant male figures but also brings that figure into a relation of forced intimacy: "Punching me, though—slamming his fist into soft flesh and yielding bone—stopped him from crushing and tearing himself against an unfeeling wall. In that moment I knew somehow that I'd helped him" (110). This scene restages the Hegelian struggle for recognition between master and bondsman between two black male subjects. José Muñoz argues that when we insert the fact of blackness into the Hegelian narrative, "then vulnerability is fleshed out." To Muñoz, "recognition, across antagonisms within the social, like sex, race, and still other modalities of difference, is often more than simply a tacit moment of vulnerability. Indeed it is often a moment of being wounded."[22] The protagonist and the men attacking him are black, but the cross-class and cross-sexual identifications position black queer subjectivity as caught up in a violent struggle for recognition that occurs in the moment of its wounding by and intimacy with a hegemonic black masculinity.

This is further supported by the narrator's racial comparison of sex practices. Sex with black men is "good" but "still extracts of pure vanilla." He compares this to the kinky sex he practiced with Eastern Europeans: "Racist though several of my former communists were, they had allowed me to explore sex and my existence in wet, dry and agonizingly pleasurable ways I could not have imagined. . . . Protracted sessions hidden away from the black men and society I knew would have judged and in some way condemned me. As their emissaries are doing now" (110). By categorizing all black men who sleep with men as engaging in vanilla sex practices, he positions these black men alongside society in general as enacting judgment and condemnation. By naming his assailants "emissaries" of "black men and society," he indicts black men, gay and straight, in constructing black queer subjectivity as a wound necessary for their own intelligibility as rights-seeking subjects. In other words, the narrator simultaneously lodges a critique of black gay men's subscription to "homonormativity," in which entrance into the cultural mainstream depends upon maintaining as constitutive those bodies and desires that are still rendered "deviant" (poor, feminine, fat, trans, kinky, disabled, interracial, HIV positive).[23] For the protagonist, the judgment and condemnation of these "deviant" bodies and desires further maintain the social conditions for violence directed toward all black bodies.

In the final moments before death, the victim still searches for pleasure: "Like Audre Lorde, I'm 'going to go out like a fucking meteor.' Fucking. Literally. If I can make it happen" (111). He attempts to make it happen by pulling out the penis of the man who is holding him, whom he calls Jesus. The victim scrambles to open the man's zipper and expose his penis. Only after Tupac lands what seems to be a death blow to the victim's right jaw does Jesus relent and let him hold his penis. Jesus whispers in his ear, "You betta not say nothing," and he cautions Tupac not to kill him too fast (111). Tupac then slows down the punches that mark the tempo of impending death. Provoked by the victim's desperate attempt at anal penetration, however, Jesus beckons Tupac to kill the victim faster, and Tupac becomes a "Whirling Dervish of punches" (113). Seeking further erotic redress, the victim attempts to penetrate himself anally with Jesus's penis: "I know that holding it in my hands is not enough to adequately mitigate this suffering, though. . . . I try to press the head of his dick into my ass, but in so doing, become progressively less innocent a victim" (112). Acknowledging that his incessant desire will position him outside of innocent victimhood, the corpse still demands the pleasure promised from these men as potential sexual partners, even now, as his murderers. The victim refuses to sanitize the messiness of black queerness produced in these tangles of death and desire.

Being in the life collapses spatiotemporalities that mark bodies first as cruisers in the space of safety and then as murderers and victims in the space of death. James's stories demonstrate that black queer subjectivity cannot be confined to the space of death, nor can scholars ignore its proximity to this space. Rather, it is the blurred boundaries between death and desire through which black queerness materializes as a "structure of longing" in the moments of and even beyond death.[24] Black queer narratives, always marked by historical and contemporary trauma, demand a reading practice that acknowledges how this trauma shapes black queer subjectivity but does not define it. A critical black queer studies must hold trauma in critical tension with queer bodily desire, as such speculation is vital to everyday black (queer) life. As I have demonstrated, the narratives of subjects who are "in the life" not only produce a critical knowledge framework for reading black queer narratives but also, more broadly, can open up more nuanced readings of African American literature.

Notes

1. Beam, *In the Life*, 12.
2. Essex Hemphill, "In the Life," in *Ceremonies*, lines 7–9, 10–13.
3. Holloway, *Passed On*, 2.
4. Christopher Peterson argues against the assertion that blackness has a special relationship with death; instead, death and mourning structure all kinship relationships (*Kindred Specters*, 10).
5. Harper, "The Evidence of Felt Intuition," 643, 651, 652.
6. For an in-depth discussion of the mutual construction of race and sexuality in the United States, see Somerville, *Queering the Color Line*.
7. James, *Shaming the Devil*. Hereafter cited parenthetically in the text.
8. Many black queer novels feature dead black queer bodies, and their deaths structure their narratives. See, for example, Baldwin, *Another Country*; Kenan, *A Visitation of Spirits*; James, *John Crow's Devil*.
9. Using the novels of Richard Wright as an example, Abdul R. JanMohamed defines the "death-bound-subject" as a "subject who is formed, from infancy on, by the infinite and ubiquitous threat of death" (*The Death-Bound-Subject*, 2).
10. Delany, *Times Square Red*, 153.
11. Crimp, "How to Have Promiscuity," 253.
12. Harper, *Private Affairs*, 67–68.
13. Freud, "Beyond the Pleasure Principle."
14. Bataille, *Death and Sensuality*, 11.
15. Avilez, "Cartographies of Desire," 137.
16. Holland, *Raising the Dead*, 26.
17. Michael Taussig argues that the space of death "is crucial to the creation of meaning and consciousness nowhere more so than in societies where torture is endemic and where the culture of terror flourishes." He defines the space of death as "a threshold, yet it is a wide space whose breadth offers positions of advance as well as of extinction" (Taussig, "Culture of Terror," 467).
18. Stanley, "Near Life, Queer Death," 1.
19. Holland, "Bill T. Jones," 385.
20. Gordon, *Ghostly Matters*, 190.
21. Delany, *Times Square Red*, 156.
22. Muñoz, "Cruising the Toilet," 362–63.
23. Lisa Duggan defines "the new homonormativity" as a "politics that does not contest dominant heteronormative assumptions and institutions, but upholds and sustains them, while promising the possibility of a demobilized gay constituency and a privatized, depoliticized gay culture anchored in domesticity and consumption" (*The Twilight of Equality?*, 50).
24. José Muñoz defines queerness as a structure of longing to suggest that "this world is not enough, that indeed something is missing" (*Cruising Utopia*, 90).

CHAPTER 12

The Dramedy in Queer of Color

Noah's Arc *and the Seriously "Trashy" Pleasure of Critique*

Pier Dominguez

Much of the work around queer of color cultural production has been based on explorations of the way noncommercial texts—avant-garde performance art, high literary writing, and independent video—might critique racialized heteronormative structures of signification, sociality, and society.[1] When queer of color critique turned to culture industry forms, it found subjects marginalized within these representations. For example, E. Patrick Johnson critiques the homophobia and misogyny of commercial black stand-up comedians such as Eddie Murphy and work like the "Men on . . ." sketches in the Fox network's *In Living Color* program (1990–94). Those skits, featuring David Allan Grier and Damon Wayans performing effeminate affective excess—exclaiming their catch phrase "Hated it!"—in their assessments of movies and other cultural matters, often homophobically conflated black gay effeminacy with misogyny.

In this chapter I am interested in moving away from explicitly "transgressive" avant-garde texts and from programs with caricatured or tokenized queer of color presences to understand how a culture industry televisual genre imagines and interpellates queer of color subjects through serialized storylines. Specifically, I examine *Noah's Arc* (Logo, 2005–6), a "dramedy" featuring four gay men of color that aired for two seasons on the gay cable channel Logo. We might read this program as one in which the kind of affective and performance labor that the "Men on . . ." skits took on as the *object* of their humor is redeployed in a different manner as such objects become humorous subjects that "talk back." Indeed, as I will demonstrate, "Men on . . ." is critiqued within the program itself. I examine

how *Noah's Arc* works within the popular cultural genre of the dramedy to engage with—while also contradicting and disrupting—new normativities of race,
gender, sexuality, and its intersections that characterize black sexual economies
in contemporary media cultures.

First, I contextualize intraracial and interracial anxieties around black middle-
class (hetero)normativity and outline some of the ways in which these anxieties
have been negotiated through aesthetic and affective problems of black televisuality. Then I read *Noah's Arc* from a queer of color perspective to understand
its problematic framing of race, gender, sexuality, and their intersections as an
intraracial problem of gay black masculinities and femininities. While I explore
some of the limitations of this framing, I also seek to understand the program's
campy exploration of queer black socialities on its own terms. *Noah's Arc* has been
criticized for foregrounding its characters' negotiations of gender and sexuality
at the "expense" of their race by ignoring white gay racism and racism in general. Consequently, it is important to understand its campy uses of media self-
reflexivity—in other words, its own representations of the television and film
industry—to critique the normativities of black sexual economies and open up
a space for thinking outside these limitations.

Intraracial Difference and the Black "Struggle for Drama"

Cathy Cohen and Roderick Ferguson have both noted how the 1980s rise of a
precarious black middle class pitted this middle class as an agent of surveillance
against queer, HIV-positive, and poor people of color.[2] This is a dialectic more
recently captured by the title of Michael Eric Dyson's best-selling polemic, *Is Bill
Cosby Right? Or Has the Black Middle Lost Its Mind?* Dyson's work critiques the
punitive ways in which what he terms the African American "afristocracy" views
marginalized black subjects (the "ghettocracy").[3] I invoke Dyson's popular polemic because of the way he turns to US television's most iconic black patriarch
(before he became a nonrespectable symbol of sexual violence) to contest the
assimilationist class politics of the "afristocracy." As a technology of intimacy and
family, television is also deeply implicated in producing ideas about blackness, so
it makes sense that Cosby's celebrity, which circulates through these intersecting
logics of blackness, intimacy, and family, would become a symbolic lightning rod
for these issues.[4]

Philip Brian Harper and Kristal Brent Zook have argued that post-1980s black
televisuality had to deal with the anxieties of locating black authenticity amid
the new middle-class normativity enabled by affirmative action in the 1960s and
1970s.[5] As Harper in particular notes, these anxieties about class and black authenticity most often become articulated as anxieties about black masculinity and its

proper place in US and black culture.[6] Both Zook and Harper argue that, given this concern with "proper" placement, post-1980s black television has often been unable fully to engage questions of intraracial difference such as class. This lack of engagement is partly understood as a problem of form or genre. Zook chronicles the inability of television produced by black creators, featuring black actors or even just representing black subjects, to get industry support for framing intraracial issues through drama. Indeed, television historically has largely maintained traditions of limiting African Americans to such genres as sport, variety, and comedy. Thus, both Zook and Harper note the importance of the dramedy—a television genre that combines melodrama and comedy—as a form that enables the exploration of intraracial issues.

The dramedy is a televisual form that adheres to the half-hour format of the sitcom while eschewing the laugh track, and it is mostly shot with single camera perspective.[7] Its history is often traced to programs with white feminine or black masculine lead characters in the 1980s, such as *The Days and Nights of Molly Dodd* and *Frank's Place*.[8] In his essay on the way that "dramedy" became a contested industry term that indexed not just aesthetic or content questions but also the shifting terrain over definitions of "quality television," Philip Sewell notes how dramedies were seen as "smarter" television, owing to their "special relationship with their audience; their literacy, realism, and sophistication; their testament to authorship; and their marked difference from regular television."[9]

While Harper discusses the dramedy *Room 222* (ABC, 1969–74) for the way it dealt with intraracial class difference, Zook highlights *Frank's Place* (CBS, 1987–88) for dealing with issues of class and colorism. Regarding the dramedy's role in black televisuality and representation, she argues:

> Whereas traditional black sitcom formats demanded a "joke per page," many black productions of the 1980s and 90s resisted such norms by consciously and unconsciously crafting dramatic episodes. With less explicit storylines, unresolved endings, and increasingly complex characters, these "dramedies" allowed for exploration of painful in-group memories and experiences. While dramedies were often praised on white sitcoms (for example, in *Home Improvement*'s treatment of leukemia), such moves on black shows were rarely welcomed by networks, as was made clear with the cancellation of *Frank's Place*, a hard-hitting dramedy that looked at intra-racial class and color differences among other issues.[10]

Zook notes that this "struggle for drama" is one of the main characteristics of black televisuality. I argue that this struggle can also be understood through the way that aesthetic and affective televisual issues intersect with identitarian concerns because it opens the genre to multiple readings. As Sewell explains, because of the absence of a laugh track in dramedies (which is part of their "sophistication"), viewers are allowed to decide what is funny on their own.[11] Sianne Ngai has argued that establishing the tone or "affective disposition" of a text is a complicated matter for both critics and audiences of such texts.[12] Consequently, it is partly this ambiguity of the affective economy of the dramedy that both marks it as a complicated genre to theorize and creates not only difficulties but also particular possibilities for using it to stage complex intraracial issues.

Examining the success of the sitcom *Fresh Prince of Bel Air* (NBC, 1990–96), Zook notes the numerous disputes between the white producers (the Borowitzes) with writers Benny Medina and Will Smith occasioned by the producers' constant requests for more jokes.[13] Given the (largely) white corporate structure and producers in the television industry, these disputes suggest that white affect helps create the "struggle for drama." In other words, it is white anxiety about the possibility that representations of race could be anything other than funny—that the programs, if not outright comedies with affect directed and controlled through a laugh track, would be "too heavy" for white audiences—that partly structures the dramedy's genre mixing and multiplicity.

Such multiplicity is signaled by the very title of *Noah's Arc*: a pun, of course, on Noah's Ark that suggests not only themes of coupling, coexisting, and survival but also a narrative structure involving the use of dramatic arcs in addition to sitcom humor. Further, this "struggle for drama" takes on a particular form through *Noah's Arc*'s queer of color staging of this affective and performance labor of the dramedy. In examining the program's reception, I found viewers who wrote of their discomfort with the program's "tone" in presenting Noah's queerly racialized femme gender presentation. In other words, viewers were discomfited by their lack of understanding whether it was "intended" as a joke or not. This gap between affect and epistemology (the instability created by viewers' inability to interpret or "know" a televisual text's affective intentions), mediated by racialized gender, provides one context for understanding the dramedy's vexed relationship to complex intersecting representations of race, class, gender, and or/sexuality, as in *Noah's Arc*.

Affective Economies of Black Gay Masculinities: Between Black Feminine Drama and White Feminine Dramedy

Patrik-Ian Polk, the black queer creator and writer of *Arc*, started his career as an independent writer and filmmaker. While *Noah's Arc* was not directly based on Polk's debut film, *Punks* (dir. Patrik-Ian Polk, 2000), it was created after that film's critical success. In contrast to the conflation of black gay masculinity and misogyny often joked about in the kind of comedy that takes queers of color as the object of its humor, Polk has described how *Punks* was influenced by the whimsy of the famous Diana Ross vehicle *Mahogany* (dir. Berry Gordy, 1975), gesturing to the aesthetically generative intersections between black femininity and black queer masculinities. *Noah's Arc* is structured by thematic trajectories similar to those of *Punks*. These themes include black men desiring other black men; the gendered politics of black gay masculinities and femininities; and black queer affective investment in divas, relationships, and professional problems, all set within a backdrop of gay clubs. Polk has explained the genesis of *Noah's Arc* in these terms: "I went to a club, Boytrade at the El Rey theater, and it was really packed with Black men from all over the country who come for that weekend every year. And I was suddenly struck by the notion that this was a group with money to spend, travel, rent hotel rooms, rental cars, and attend events like this. It's a viable consumer base but nobody's marketing anything to them. So I left that club vowing that by that time next year the show would be a reality."[14]

Polk's understanding of black gayness in terms of a "consumer base" demonstrates a comfort with the culture industry logics structuring black sexual economies and hints at the way Polk will turn these very consumer logics into the content of his work. The program was initially going to be a straight-to-DVD release, but it got picked up by Logo because the network was looking for "original programming" for its initial launch. Logo promoted *Noah's Arc* as a "comedy about drama" and a "cross between *Sex and the City* (HBO, 1998–2004) and *Soul Food* (Showtime, 2000–2004)—but gay."[15] The publicity's emphasis on the show's status as a dramedy ("a comedy about drama") signals the importance of the genre as a mode for negotiating black televisuality in the culture industry. Given that the show actually focused on gay men of color, it is important to understand the use of a white dramedy (*Sex and the City*) and a black women's drama (*Soul Food*) as frames for making sense of the program. While this was partly a marketing move to reference commercially successful programs, the location of black gayness between white and black femininity and between dramedy and drama raises questions about how this program departs from and adheres to the conventions of these programs.

Soul Food: The Series focuses on three sisters as they negotiate the gendered expectations of middle-class black family dynamics. Given that one sister is a divorced lawyer, one is a married housewife, and one is a married hairstylist, they provide an interesting array of takes on black femininity. An array of gendered positions is evidenced on *Noah's Arc* too, but the biological family of *Soul Food* is replaced with a network of friendships as kinship. In addition, while the married hairstylist sister on *Soul Food* is often in crisis through her unemployed, formerly imprisoned husband, all of *Arc*'s characters are comfortably middle-class professionals, nonprofit workers, and creative culture industry types: their racial nonnormativity is not class based.

Following the white feminine dramedy model of *Sex and the City*, *Arc* is a half-hour show (rather than *Soul Food*'s one-hour episodes, the usual length of television dramas), and it focuses on the life of mostly middle-class urban dwellers (in West Hollywood) navigating professional and personal issues.[16] As in *Sex and the City*, the program focuses on four friends: Noah, a film writer and filmmaker with a Carrie Bradshaw–like flair for fashion, and his "ARC," made up of Alex, a flamboyant, high-camp diva who serves as a kind of "mama bear" of the group (and is married to a hypermasculine nurse); Ricky, a Samantha Jones–style antiromantic sexual pursuer who critiques monogamy; and Chance, a Charlotte York–like university professor married to a lawyer and committed to monogamy. These friends all offer different readings of Noah's personal and professional crises, demonstrating a spectrum of perspectives on desire and the relationships of gay men of color, much in the way that the different friends and sisters in the drama and dramedies mentioned have varying perspectives on domesticity, marriage, and sexuality.

There are important racialized and gendered implications to adopting the white dramedy model for a program featuring gay men of color. In his essay on *Six Feet Under* (HBO, 2001–5), Guy Mark Foster explains how that cable drama's white racial imaginary structures the representation of its interracial gay couple, composed of David Fisher (who is white) and Keith Charles (who is black).[17] Foster argues that Charles's race is mostly elided in order to keep the focus on the characters' gayness and not disrupt the (mostly) white viewership's sense of racial complacency. Thus, despite their visualization as an interracial couple, they are discursively marked only as a gay couple. Part of the way this is accomplished is through Charles's complete disconnection from the larger black community. Yet Foster notes that most queer of color subjects maintain that connection, choosing to endure homophobia from black family members or black institutions as an alternative to possibly facing both racism and homophobia from the larger white community.

Noah's Arc has a particular way of reworking this issue—of the need for turning to the heteronormative black community as a respite from white racism—because the characters are never represented interacting with their (biological) black families, the white gay community, or the larger white community. They are only shown among either their own queer black kinship structures (including at queer black spaces) or the black community. When they do engage with the larger black community—for example, when Eddie and Chance want to get married through their black church and are rebuffed—they often encounter homophobia. In fact,

Eddie and Chance are married by the deacon in a commercial space rather than in the "homophobic" black church, pointing to the way the program often falls into neoliberal logics that find homonormative "commercial" solutions for queer of color conundrums. Presumably paralleling the kind of white mainstream media logics that blamed the passing of Proposition 8 in California on overly religious black churchgoers and the black community, most homophobia in *Noah's Arc* comes from the black community. In the imaginary that structures such logics, gayness is a white phenomenon, blackness is seen as homophobic, and queers of color are erased. In its disruption of such logics, *Noah's Arc* does not imagine gayness as white and offers a way of representing intraracial discussion and community around queer nonnormativities.

The intraracial struggles over these queer nonnormativities are always complex. For example, there is a struggle between the church deacon, who believes in the men's right to marry, and the church elders, who do not. In addition, unlike *Six Feet Under*, in which Charles the cop is represented as existing within a mostly white world, and race is almost never discursively addressed, *Noah's Arc* fully participates in the discursive foregrounding of black queer terminology, slang, and in-group references. During the program's final episode, which takes place at a black gay pride beach party, Chance announces, as he strips to his bathing suit: "Ah, black gay pride! The one day a year a black gay man can feel unproblematically Afrocentric." The program never specifically demonstrates problems with a black gay man feeling Afrocentric; instead, it depicts the problems with Afrocentric men—and women—living out their gayness. Yet the program celebrates the importance of black queer spaces on its own terms. Noah, for example, is shown accidentally stumbling onto a "Blatino Boys Presents 'The Hook Up Party: All the Thugs You Can Hug'"; the poster featuring this nomenclature is prominently featured and an important way in which the program signals intra–queer of color understandings and relationalities. Here, "thug" is no longer a coded white slur stigmatizing the potential violence or fear inspired by black men; instead, it is reclaimed as an eroticized and desirable form of black masculinity. The discursive attention to Blatinos—and the inclusion of Ricky and his love interest Junito, who seem coded as either Latinos or Afro-Latinos—represents an important move away from black/white binaries to relationalities among different queer minoritarian subjects.

In their essay on the program's racialized masculinities and homonormativity, Gust A. Yep and John P. Elia argue, "*Noah's Arc* is primarily an African American, gay, male world where race is hyper visible and racism is neither seen nor discussed."[18] Yet while the program emphasizes black queerness and queer black spectacle without discursively centering racism, it has many moments of racial coding available for "understanding" from a savvy audience. There is a moment, for instance, in which a white superior of Alex's at the HIV health center yells at him during a disagreement regarding the center's purpose. Alex brings in a Latino youth (presumably a sex worker) to make sure he is getting screened regularly. His supervisor, who is trying to implement the Bush-era abstinence and faith-based strategies, yells at him to stop trying to save "street trash from the inevitable overdose."

While neither the supervisor's whiteness nor the youth's Latino identity is explicitly mentioned, his alignment with Bush-era policies and his racially coded reference to a "street" kid allows for an understanding about the racialized class politics of HIV prevention and infection and the way that such strategies would not work for a Latino youth forced to survive through underground economies of sex. These are some of the methods by which the program negotiates the centering of black gay masculinities on commercial television, in some ways sidelining intraracial meditations on racism but enabling other forms of intra–queer of color dialogues. Indeed, as I will elaborate, it is through its centering of gay black men that *Arc* interrogates, for instance, butch/femme dynamics among black gay masculinities and femininities even as the program participates in such black sexual economies.

Intra–Queer of Color Dialogue;
or, The Limits of Black Gay Masculinities and Femininities

The most transgressive aspect of *Noah's Arc* is the fact that Noah, a femme black bottom, is the titular character at the center of the program's narrative arcs. The uniqueness of this becomes particularly apparent when *Noah's Arc* is compared to a contemporaneous white queer drama such as *Queer as Folk* (Showtime, 2000–2005) or a sitcom such as *Will & Grace* (NBC, 1998–2006). Making a black bottom the object of desire and fascination around whom everything circulates disrupts the kinds of presumptions of *Queer as Folk*, whose "circle of friends" (including the ostensible protagonist couple, Brian Kinney and twink Justin) are all white. Similarly, on *Will & Grace*, white femme Jack is relegated to secondary status vis-à-vis homonormative lawyer Will Truman, at least in terms of the program's title and arguably in terms of story arcs as well.

In order to accommodate placing a black bottom at the center of the dramedy's narrative arcs, *Noah's Arc* pairs Noah with hypermasculine Wade. Wade is Noah's primary love interest, and the crises in their relationship constitute many of the program's most important serialized storylines. This pairing of Noah with Wade arguably functions as a stabilizing dyad for the program's racialized gender balance. All of Noah's romantic partners throughout the series run are masculine tops: Wade, who loves football and Vin Diesel films; Maliq, who meets Noah while "defending" him from an aggressive suitor at a hook-up party; Quincy, the deep-voiced, muscled intellectual who takes on Noah's public voice in the aftermath of Noah's gay bashing; and even British hip hop star Baby Gat, who initially pursues Noah and is unafraid of guns and drugs, while Noah is depicted as scared of them. In addition, the program has the men explicitly demonstrate their "topness" either through romantically—and strategically—lighted bedroom scenes that emphasize silhouettes rather than body parts or through dialogue of campy double entendres. To illustrate, one learns about their erotic economies after one bedroom scene in which Noah tells Wade it's his turn to give him oral sex, and Wade replies, "You know I don't eat meat." Thus, through its campy humor, the program produces an understanding of gay black male sexualities as working through polarized and gendered erotic roles.

This feminine/masculine binary structures almost all of the characters' relationships, arguably demonstrating one way in which *Noah's Arc* adheres to homonormative strictures while inserting queer of color characters into these strictures. All socialities among feminine gay characters of color are presented as working through friendship. For instance, when Noah consults femme fashion designer Romeo about his clothes or when he gets advice from Alex, the flamboyant diva of the "arc," femme-femme connections are generated (and generative) through friendships rather than in erotic relationships. Yet even while the program's characters enact gender polarities through their relationships, they constantly engage in dialogue, critiquing the devaluation of effeminacy in black gay male culture, as well as the overvaluation of particular performances of black masculinity. For example, when Ricky questions why his employee at his clothing store is interested in the femme fashion designer Romeo instead of him, Chance lectures him about his assumptions regarding masculine gender and desirability.

In addition to such discussions of effeminacy, the program explicitly addresses the intraracial valorization of and fascination with black hypermasculinity. There are at least two storylines in which this fascination is explored. In one of the first episodes, Wade is discomfited about being outed to his friends by introducing them to Noah at a sports bar because Noah orders a "feminine" apple martini (like Carrie in *Sex and the City*) rather than beer and wears a flamboyant ghetto-chic outfit. In another storyline, Eddie, Chance's husband, cheats with a "down-low thug" because he's bored with his "desperate house-fag" (Ricky's term, in a joking allusion to the campy program *Desperate Housewives* [ABC, 2004–12]).

These problems are all "solved" through the program's staging of these issues as intraracial, interpersonal questions about desirability. For example, after his husband, Eddie, explains that he cheated because he did not want to make Chance feel "inadequate" about Eddie's politically incorrect desires for a version of black masculinity Chance could not perform, Chance comically "slums" with a "homothug" himself to prove that he can but then returns to Eddie. For his part, Noah refuses to tone down his queerness when he and Wade visit the bar again, and Wade's friends engage Noah as he participates in their homosocial one-upping and their game of pool. Thus, black gay femininity is acceptable as long as Wade's straight friends—representing straight black masculinity—are fine with it, affirming Wade's own comfort with Noah's gender presentation and perhaps assuaging the audience's anxieties about Noah's challenge to black masculinity.

On the one hand, it might be argued that the program seems to imply "embrace yourself and others will embrace you too," suggesting that the (de)valuations of racialized effeminacy in affective economies of black masculinity can be resolved within the couples or in each person's intimate relations. Yet at the same time, the program is always attentive to the way such performances are in fact valued in particular ways in representational and erotic economies. Eddie (and Alex) being pursued by someone with the online screen name "DLThugLover," for instance, points to the way that homonormative performances of gay black masculinities are enmeshed and valued in particular ways within digital media cultures. Thus, in order to fully understand the program's intervention into the representation of queers of color in the culture industry, one must attend to the program's own representations of representation.

"The First Black Gay Mainstream Thriller": Self-Reflexive Staging of the Politics of Representation

Noah's Arc addresses the problem of the culture industry and queer of color representation by making it an explicit part of the storyline, combining crises in Noah and Wade's relationship with the crises in their work as filmmakers and writers. Wade writes black homosocial buddy movies in the style of Will Smith and Vin Diesel films, whereas Noah has an indie "film school"—implicitly queer—sensibility. On their first date, Wade lectures Noah about not letting his sexuality define his art. "You write about black folk," Noah retorts. Thus, in the program's imaginary, the importance of black gay representation is counterposed not to white mainstream media but to the heteronormativity of most black cultural production.

The studio rejects Wade's initial script, and Noah is enlisted to "spice" it up by queering it with that "unique twist." Together Wade and Noah come up with a black buddy art heist film (*Fine Art*) in which one of the characters is gay. As they sit in the room with a black female film executive, Brandy, and a white male executive, Brett, Noah pitches the project as a hip hop version of the comedy skit "Men on Film." That skit, part of the *In Living Color* black variety show on Fox, was a parody of Roger Ebert–style televised film reviews featuring flamboyantly effeminate black gay men as the critics, often providing queer readings of commercial films. As mentioned, E. Patrick Johnson has argued that the skit participates in the devaluation of black gay femininity and stereotypes gay men as phalically obsessed misogynists.[19] At the same time, as one of the few spaces of black queer of color televisuality, "Men on Film" had a strong resonance within the black and black queer community. Thus, here Noah performs a form of dis-identification in which he invokes and uses a toxic but commercially successful televisual form to sell his own media industry creation.

After Noah invokes that skit, the white male executive is initially silent, as if he is not "in the know" about the skit. He then laughs—in a comically frat boy mode, exclaiming, "Those guys were hilarious"—and says he loves the new script idea. This complicated scene therefore requires knowledge about black televisuality (specifically, about In Living Color and "Men on Film") and implies that the white straight executive finds the skits "hilarious" through his homophobic complicity with its figurations of black gay feminine men. In a way, this points to how the straight white corporate structure can only "understand" queer blackness through humor, indexing the black "struggle for drama."

Eventually, the studio—through Brandy—asks Noah to turn the characters straight because they need British hip hop star Baby Gat to play one of the lead roles to get financing for the film. In this way, the program comments on the importance of performances of hip hop and black hypermasculinity for getting anything produced in the film industry. Baby Gat—a closeted British hip hop star—refuses to play gay for fear that it might ruin his career. Thus, the program critiques culture industry logics about the "payoff" for playing gay, and it acknowledges that this is a particular problem for a black hip hop star given mainstream expectations of heteronormative hypermasculinity from black men.

Noah's boyfriend, Quincy, hears about the corporate request made of Noah. Without telling Noah, he goes on the diegetic Darnell Damone Show (a Tavis Smiley Show–style public affairs discussion program with a black set, black chairs, and minimalist lighting) to bemoan the dearth of black gay male representation in Hollywood. "Some would argue that there have been great strides in the visibility of black gay characters everywhere, from Six Feet Under to Will & Grace," the host says. "Taye Diggs on Will & Grace just isn't enough," replies Quincy. This allusion to a successful cable drama and network sitcom featuring white gay characters points to the televisual discursive regime that Noah's Arc sees itself as disrupting. It posits television and public affairs programming as an important site for creating consciousness about black gay representation, much in the way that it understands itself as performing similar work. Quincy, the masculine public intellectual who "represents" femme Noah in the black public sphere, goes on to announce that a "proud, out black gay screenwriter" he knows has been asked to turn gay characters straight.

Upon hearing about Quincy's appearance, Brandy, the black diva studio executive, calls Noah in for a meeting. In an interesting parody of corporate marketing speak, Brandy complains to Noah: "Our profile within the industry will be mud if we're seen as the homophobic studio in this age of gay friendly Hollywood." The program never discursively articulates the way in which a black Hollywood studio executive might be under more intense surveillance for signs of homophobia—given cultural logics about the pathological or "more" deeply entrenched homophobia of African Americans—yet it doesn't discourage such a reading either, particularly since white studio executive Brett disappears, and it is black Brandy who is left to manage the PR disaster.

Noah offers to go on the television show and provide his own brand of neoliberal corporate speak about "the realities of what the action movie's target audience is ready to accept right now." In other words, this is the neoliberal multiculturalist assumption that in a "democratic" market-based art economy, the "general public" should get the kind of art they want, demonstrated through the audience's purchasing power. But Brandy directs him otherwise: "No, what you're going to say is that you're proud to be working for this studio; that you're an out black gay man, working in a supportive environment; and that making the lead characters heterosexual was totally your idea; that you feel it has real artistic integrity, and you're very excited about it. . . . That is, if you ever want to work in Hollywood again."

In asking Noah to take personal responsibility for the script, the program uses Brandy to mock the way that culture industry corporations use representative figures—in this case, Noah as "out black gay man"—to respond to broader institutional critiques of racism and homophobia. While Brandy is cast as the black woman enforcing the corporate structure's heteronormativity, her campy diva-ness—as "angry black woman"—again seems to point to the program parodying the way a minoritarian executive is made to deal with identitarian problems.

Once Noah is on *The Darnell Damone Show*, the black host, Damone, asks Noah whether, "as a gay man," he felt comfortable writing a heterosexual-themed script. Thus, we go from Brandy's labeling of him as an "out black gay man" to, on the set of a black public affairs show, Noah's interpellation solely as a gay man writing a straight script. Because *Noah's Arc* always takes for granted a black public sphere when thinking about black queerness—and only occasionally addresses whiteness—it is the queerness that is rendered a problem from a black masculine perspective. Before Noah is able publicly to blame Baby Gat for refusing to play gay, Baby Gat surprisingly bursts into the studio, performing his exaggerated swagger, and his spectacle of British black masculinity immediately calls attention away from Noah. In the studio, Gat dissects the logics behind "gay don't pay." He names Vin Diesel, Will Smith, and Ving Rhames as black actors who have accrued cultural capital through playing gay and says he has "nuts to spare" and is thus unafraid of repercussions on his career. Importantly, his explanation simply repeats the argument—about the way straight black actors playing gay can accrue cultural capital in a multicultural marketplace through such "transgression"—that Noah first proposes to Wade when he seeks Wade's advice about whether he should take the fall for the "straightening" of the script.

After Gat's "reveal" at the talk show, Wade privately tells Noah that he has spoken to Gat, implying that he had convinced him with Noah's logic. The program thus comments on the way that Wade and Gat "understand" each other through a black masculine homosociality from which femme Noah is excluded. Ultimately, Gat simply repeats Noah's logic—about how black actors can gain cachet through playing gay—but through a spectacle of black masculinity that assuages concerns about black homosexuality and effeminacy, once again theorizing the importance of black masculinity for the production and consumption logics of black sexual economies.

This raises the question of how to interpret Baby Gat's parodically excessive performance of hip hop masculinity, coupled with his actual queerness, and the audience's enthusiastic embrace of this spectacle. I argue that it does not mean *Noah's Arc* agrees that Gat's commentary is a genuine solution. Instead, the program exposes and deconstructs the culture industry logics through which such decisions are made. The audience presumably cheers a straight black masculine spectacle of Baby Gat, who is never pathologized as a "down-low" thug; rather, he seems quite happy negotiating his gender, race, and sexuality on his own terms, given culture industry constraints. Likewise commenting on dynamics of race and class, the program shows his model girlfriend as being content to give him "class" while he gives her "edge." "That's show biz," she cheerily announces to Noah. The model's blasé tone conveys something about *Noah's Arc*. Rather than melodramatically preaching about positive or negative representations, the program works by parodying cultural industry logics through its camp approach to the "excess" of racialized gender performances and their valuations in the culture industry. Thus, the program is precisely a critique of the way black masculinities—whether gay or not—become a technology for neoliberal multicultural management. In this way, *Arc* both comments on the gendered and sexual hierarchies structuring black sexual economies and helps open up a space for thinking outside these hierarchies.

Conclusion: *Noah's Arc*'s Fantasy

In closing, I would like to reflect on some of the logics surrounding the reception of *Noah's Arc* because I think they enable us to understand some of the affective and aesthetic work of the program. While fulsomely praising *Noah's Arc* in a review in the *New York Press*, black gay film critic Armond White disapprovingly meditates on the program's reception: "Almost 20 years ago when Marlon Rigg's poetry-doc *Tongues Untied* aired on PBS, its scandalous theme ('Black men loving black men is the revolutionary act of the 21st century') sparked a National Endowment for the Arts funding controversy. Now, Polk's fulfillment of Riggs' proposal gets less attention than the spectacle of ghetto miseries in the TV series *The Wire*—stereotypes our culture is comfortable with."[20] I don't entirely agree with White's implication that *Noah's Arc* represents a "fulfillment" of Riggs's powerful vision of the radical potential and specificities of gay black love, because there are generic and formal differences aside from the temporal divide.

Nonetheless, I think that White raises an important issue regarding the way mainstream cultural logics insist on foregrounding figurations of black masculinity that circulate through what Kara Keeling has called "ghetto-centric" common sense.[21] Linda Williams has ably demonstrated *The Wire's* melodramatic structure, yet it is still valorized as somehow a form of "realism," in part precisely because it frames melodramatic black masculinity through that "ghettocentric" common sense.[22] Thus, I take seriously White's critique of *Arc's* marginalized circulation—and cancellation—which does index something about the way its representational economy disrupts the usual forms through which black sexual economies function, both intra- and interracially.

Consequently, I disagree with arguments that dismiss *Noah's Arc* as a program that "sells out" or simply functions as a new form of neoliberal black gay homonormativity. *Noah's Arc* provocatively exploits a wide range of dramedy strategies—its unstable tone, deployment of serialized narrative, "smart" relationship to "knowing" audiences—in its centering of black gay characters, even as it slyly meditates on some of its "trashy" tactics. As the campy nonmonogamist Ricky reminds us when he quips, "Life isn't a soap opera!" and as I hope to have demonstrated in this essay, one must attend to the aesthetic and affective particularities of the program to understand its politics. The program's use of some soap strategies allows for its affectivity and its ongoing narrative, which enables its untangling of complex identitarian multiplicities and intersections. In its self-reflexivity, *Noah's Arc* itself attends to these very particularities, thus both enacting and commenting on a politics of representation, unraveling while combining pleasure and critique.

We can further unravel the contradictions of the cultural work of *Noah's Arc* through Philip Brian Harper's generative outline of the way that representations of blackness have always existed through tensions between what he terms "simulacral" versus "mimetic" realism. Simulacral realism refers to a program such as *The Cosby Show* (NBC, 1984–92) that is perceived as representing blackness in a "positive" way, showing life as it "could" or "should" be. In contrast, mimetic realism refers to productions that reflect social reality through "relevance," that posit blackness "as it is," despite the risk that this might "confirm" stereotypes about blackness outside of intraracial community formation.[23] The reception of *Noah's Arc* has been caught up in these poles as well and reveals the gendered and sexual imagination structuring such logics. As one self-described black gay viewer, Olukayode Balogun, writes in his Amazon.com review of the program:

> And while I feel that characters like . . . Omar and his cohorts in "The Wire" (if you discount the criminality) are a lot closer to my reality and experience as a black gay man than any of the characters in this show, I do know we're not all the same. I do recognise that many black gay men will identify with the character in "Noah's Arc." Thus, I think every black gay man should have a copy, even if just for laughs. But even if you're not black or gay but would like to get a handle on one man's perspective, (albeit, I suspect, largely drawn from fantasy), on what it means to be young, black and gay in that soup-plate of superficiality otherwise known as Los Angeles in the 21st century, you should definitely check this one out.[24]

Balogun's allusion to fantasy—which he juxtaposes with the "reality" of the characters of *The Wire*, a "reality" that seems mediated by those characters' conventional black masculine gender presentation—points to the fact that in some ways *Noah's Arc* provides the "uplifting" fantasy of simulacral realism and the "realist" disturbances of mimetic realism at the same time. By centering a femme black bottom, the program says, "Here is a 'reality' of black life," in "mimetic" mode, and by making the black gay bottom a nonabject figure, despite the way racism and misogyny (and its specific formation of femme phobia) intersect in both gay and straight cultures to dismiss him in the "real" world, it provides "uplifting" fantasy in simulacral mode. In this way, it participates in a queer of color tradition of using self-reflexivity to craft new convivialities rather than ironic distancing, fusing together irony and belief.

The program thus engages in what José Esteban Muñoz called "queer utopia," one that is not yet here and might never arrive. Yet why can't such utopian "fantasy" be political? As Muñoz wrote: "Often we can glimpse the worlds proposed and promised by queerness in the realm of the aesthetic. . . . Turning to the aesthetic in the case of queerness is nothing like an escape from the social realm. . . . Queerness is about the rejection of a here and now and an insistence on potentiality or concrete possibility for another world."[25] *Noah's Arc*'s careful attention to and fantastic rejection of our racist, femme-phobic present is one spectacular, fabulous, and politically necessary imagining of this "other world."

Notes

1. See Ferguson, *Aberrations in Black*; Muñoz, *Disidentifications*; Johnson, *Appropriating Blackness*; Melamed, *Represent and Destroy*.

2. Ferguson, *Aberrations in Black*, 145.

3. Dyson, *Is Bill Cosby Right?*

4. Torres, *Black, White and in Color*; Gray, *Watching Race*. Both these works attend to the mutual structuration of blackness and televisuality.

5. Zook, *Color by Fox*, 15–18.

6. Harper, *Are We Not Men?*, 160–65.

7. Sewell, "From Discourse to Discord."

8. Ibid. See also Lotz, *Re-designing Women*.

9. Sewell, "From Discourse to Discord," 245.

10. Zook, *Color by Fox*, 9.

11. Sewell, "From Discourse to Discord," 248.

12. Ngai, *Ugly Feelings*, 38–49.

13. Zook, *Color by Fox*, 17–18.

14. Lawrence Ferber, "Bring in the Queers, Bring in the Funk: Noah's Arc," *Windy City Media Group*, June 1, 2004, accessed August 14, 2015, windycitymediagroup.com/gay/lesbian/news/ARTICLE.php?AID=5129.

15. Barnes & Noble, "Editorial Review: *Noah's Arc*," June 1, 2004, accessed August 14, 2015, barnesandnoble.com/w/dvd-noahs-arc-the-complete-first-season-darryl-stephens/114050 64?ean=97368502543.

16. While the program never explicitly references *Sex and the City* within the diegesis, Polk has often talked about its influence in interviews, and the program does refer to the cultivation of queer of color affect around white feminine-centric dramedies such as *Golden Girls*.

17. Foster, "Desire and the 'Big Black Cop,'" 106.

18. Yep and Elia, "Racialized Masculinities."

19. Johnson, *Appropriating Blackness*, 68.

20. Armond White, "Meet the Black Carrie Bradshaw," *New York Press*, October 22, 2008, accessed August 14, 2014, nypress.com/meet-the-black-carrie-bradshaw/.

21. Keeling, *The Witch's Flight*, 118–37. Keeling defines ghettocentric common sense as the repertoire of images of the postindustrial ghetto through which blackness is now understood and as a specific innovation within what Wahneema Lubiano calls "common sense black nationalism" ("Black Nationalism").

22. Linda Williams, "How *The Wire* Is, and Isn't, 'Dickensian,'" *Huffington Post,* July 2, 2014, accessed August 15, 2014, huffingtonpost.com/linda-williams/the-wire-dickens_b_5549385.html.

23. Harper, *Are We Not Men?*, 160.

24. Olukayode Balogun, "Groundbreaking for sure!," Amazon.com review, January 20, 2007, accessed August 14, 2014, amazon.com/Nothin-Goin-On-But-Rent/product-reviews/B000I1A0GU.

25. Muñoz, *Cruising Utopia*, 5.

CHAPTER 13

Cheryl Clarke's Clit Agency

or, An Erotic Reading of Living as a Lesbian

David B. Green Jr.

Intimacy no luxury here.
Telephones cannot be left off the hook
or lines too long engaged
or conversations censored any longer.
—Cheryl Clarke, *Living as a Lesbian*

I have learned not to fear the body I come from.
—Cheryl Clarke, *Living as a Lesbian*

What are the sexual economies of living as a lesbian, and can its rendering and representation in poetic form reveal the heterosexual political economies established by historical narratives of a monolithic black womanhood? The poetry of Cheryl Clarke provides answers to both questions.

The black lesbian feminist, activist, and poet Cheryl Clarke recently retired as the Livingston Dean of Students at Rutgers University, her alma mater. Prior to this administrative appointment, Clarke—a notable feminist in the black women's liberation movement—devoted a large portion of her life to the liberation of all black people. In the 1980s she committed three years of service to the New York Women Against Rape Committee and served as a member of the editorial collective for the feminist literary journal *Conditions*, and in the past twenty-five years she has published countless critical essays, book reviews, and poetry in numerous black, gay, and women's anthologies, journals, and magazines.[1] Additionally,

Clarke has also authored four books of poetry: *Narrative: Poems in the Tradition of Black Women* (1983), *Living as a Lesbian* (1986), *Humid Pitch: Narrative Poetry* (1989), and *Experimental Love* (1993).[2] As Calvin Hernton summarizes, Clarke's literary oeuvre serves to "expose and condemn sexual repression while providing truth, honesty, and sustenance for the liberation of black women."[3]

In the opening line of her second volume of poetry, *Living as a Lesbian*, Clarke writes: "14th Street was gutted" (11). The poem, which describes the racial tensions of a small town in 1968, records urban blight and its physical impacts on both the narrative persona and the neighborhood residents. It describes an event that began as "fire on one side of the street" and then "spread for several blocks" until it ended with physical dislocation. Homes that the residents had known "all [their] lives" were burned by "gauntlets of flames," leaving the speaker's sense of place "cauterized." After days of "debris smoldered with the stench of buildings," a mass exodus took place. The city became "a buffalo / nearly a dinosaur" and, Clarke has the narrator conclude, "as with everything else white men have wanted for themselves / endangered and extinct" (11). If the poem's message conveys anything beyond the tragedy of racism, then it works as a conceit that allegorically comments upon the violation of blackness as a corporal collective: just as "14th Street was gutted," so were its people. Like their ancestors—enslaved peoples bonded by the familiarity and community of home—the residents of 14th Street experienced separation and, in the end, were forced to vacate their city in the aftermath of racial terror. Clarke's poetic insights prophesize the displacement that urban development and gentrification would have on black communities, and her living as a lesbian served as the foundation of understanding the link between space and sexual political economies. Yet for Clarke, space and place exceed the geographies of land or street. Other arrangements of space and place less dependent on ownership can provide a type of fluid agency that can intervene on sexual economies created as a result of the capitalist use of space and its forced relocation of marginalized bodies.

Compare Clarke's opening poem to the volume's last poem, "Kittatinny." Framed by Bob Marley's "I wanna love and treat you, love and treat you right," the first and last stanzas read:

> Kittatinny Tunnel in that holy place you let me hit
> I push on toward your darker part.
> I'll take you there and mean it.
> *
> Tribad, dildo, lick your clit—oris. Come, pee, shit, or fart
> I'll take you there and mean it,
> Kittatinny Tunnel of that holy place you let me hit. (94)

Like "14th Street Was Gutted," "Kittatinny" is a poem of place. The rhetoric in "Kittatinny," however, shifts place from the literal familiarity of home to a less discussed aspect of black subjectivity: "that holy place," the poem's metaphor for a woman's vagina—especially her "darker part." The disruption in the first poem—specifically, the physical and mental damages engendered by racism—leads the living lesbian to a different place, the "Kittatinny tunnel." This "tunnel" facilitates eroticism between women, as well as a freedom to explore their lesbian desires, where they can "practice a funkier art" (94).

On "14th Street," the lesbian persona's agency gets lost among "flames that licked a trail of gasoline" along the road (11). In the "Kittatinny Tunnel," however, she does all the licking. Specifically, "licking your clitoris." The lesbian persona in "Kittatinny" assumes complete control of her personal agency and physical desires by embracing the lesbian intimacy and, ultimately, penetrating Kittatinny. To daringly augment the words of Clarke's contemporary June Jordan, the lesbian persona is—in spite of the tragedy of 14th Street—black, alive, looking back at you, and licking on you all at once.[4]

How are we to make sense of these poems in *Living as a Lesbian,* a text that begins with a discussion of unrest, violence, and urban decay, urban blight, and moves to the clitoris as the holy place? How are we to understand the relationship between the black body's decaying existence, and what does the erotic, that "darker place," offer to such decay? What does it mean to live as a lesbian whose historical context is constituted by blight yet whose living subjectivity manifests through erotic sexual politics? Clarke's *Living as a Lesbian* presents us with these very complicated questions. In this chapter, I argue that Clarke's erotic aesthetic—her interest in explicit lesbian sex and sexuality—works to critique the historic erasure of the black lesbian body in discourses of African American life. Additionally, Clarke pushes toward and away from theories of sexuality that limit and reduce black women's linguistic economies to metaphors of (and for) sexual desire.

Generally speaking, Clarke's literary corpus argues for more robust language practices that firmly imagine and assert black lesbians within larger histories of social life, political resistance, and linguistic decolonization—or what she calls speaking in "pigs latin" (12). Consider, for example, the opening stanza of her famous poem "Of Althea and Flaxie," which she published in her first book of poetry, *Narratives: Poems in the Tradition of Black Women* (1983):

In 1943 Althea was a welder
very dark
very butch
and very proud

love to cook, sew, and drive a car
and did not care who knew she kept company with a woman
who met her every day after work
in a tight dress and high heels
light-skinned and high-cheekboned
who love to shoot, fish, play poker
and did not give a damn who knew her "man" was a woman.[5]

Althea and Flaxie, the poem's two heroines, are bold women. In the decades be-tween the 1940s and 1970s, the two affectionately pronounce their love for one another. What's more, they do so without the fear of public retribution. During these decades, Althea and Flaxie do not fear McCarthyism and its insidious "witch hunts"; they are not victims of pathology or inversion. For contextual humor, we can imagine that Althea and Flaxie are the bona fide lesbian prototypes of Toni Morrison's Nel and Sula; that they represent the dreamy relationship Alice Walker's Celie and Shug nearly accomplished; and that perhaps they knew of Clare Kendry and Irene Redfield's torturous friendship in Nella Larsen's *Passing*.[6] Despite similarities with their imaginative sisters, however, Althea and Flaxie dis-tinguish themselves by a willingness to buck social mores: "In 1950 Althea wore suits and ties."[7] The two women relish their performance of butch-femme gender roles even as "people openly challenged their flamboyance." Their "practice of love," or what Teresa De Lauretis calls the "embodied component of desire," is evident in how they publicly flaunt their relationship.[8]

When the girls bragged over break of their sundry loves
Flaxie blithely told them her old lady Althea took her dancing
Every weekend
And didn't give a damn who knew she clung to a woman.

When the boys on her shift complained of their wives,
Althea boasted of how smart her "stuff" Flaxie was
And did not care who knew she loved the mind of a woman.[9]

In the introduction to her semiautobiographical *The Days of Good Looks*, Clarke writes that "Of Althea and Flaxie" "established a mythology/genealogy of black lesbian love and solidified my reputation as a black lesbian poet."[10] Over the years, Clarke's reputation as a "sexual outlaw" would distinguish her among her con-temporaries. Her writing, seen in exemplary poems such as "Vicki and Daphne," was unapologetically erotic. At a time when many black women poets coded their sexual desires through strident metaphors in exchange for cultural visibil-ity, capital gains, and acceptance within the social economies of expressive arts, Clarke boldly rejected such compromises. Take, for example, her description in

"Vicki and Daphne" of Vicki's anticipation of her lover's arrival home: "Where is Daphne? Surely she'd be home soon so Vicki could / take off her clothes and complain about her aching pussy" (48).

Clarke's *Living as a Lesbian* attends to what I theorize as the agency of the clitoris, or "clit agency." This agency acts as a redemptive life practice for lesbian feminist activists within social economies entrenched by the crippling realities of corporal and bodily decay. In my formulations of Clarke's clit agency, I build upon the work of Jennifer Nash, who, in *The Black Body in Ecstasy*, "lovingly" critiques black feminist articulations of black female pleasure and its representation. Nash shifts the critical lens of black female sexuality from one of "jouissance" to "ecstasy," or what she describes as "pleasures that exceed or transcend the self and [capture] the bliss that exceeds language."[11] Clarke captures this bliss not by "selling hot pussy," to reference bell hooks, but by proclaiming it as a source of willful redemption against a history that denies her the right to proudly enjoy her and other women's bodies.[12] Clarke's clit agency performs a cultural politics in ecstasy that gives shape to her Black Arts aesthetics while simultaneously politicizing blackness—"beyond the self"—in the name of black lesbian sexual freedom. Indeed, as the poems move throughout black experiences in America, Clarke frames erotic sexuality as critical to any present and future possibilities of black freedom. In what follows, I situate Clarke's life and her text *Living as a Lesbian* within a black cultural context. In doing so, I illustrate how her racial and erotic experiences must be understood as inseparable from her creative life and dedication to activism.

Living as Lesbian on the Make

Coming of age in the civil rights and Black Arts movements, Cheryl Clarke struggled to articulate and affirm herself as a black lesbian. Despite a culture of empowerment, there were few positive and visible black lesbians at the forefront of the movement. "My everyday life as a black lesbian writer," she writes, "is marked by the struggle to be a black lesbian, the struggle for the language of sexuality, and the struggle to not be"—in the words of black feminist critic Hortense Spillers—"the beached whale of the sexual universe." It was not until her later years as a doctoral student at Rutgers University during the melee of gay liberation that she found a contingent of affirming, self-identified, and soul-saving political lesbians who enabled her to step out of the proverbial closet and into her life. Barbara Smith, Audre Lorde, Judy Grahn, and Pat Parker were her "foresisters" in an "insurgent multi-cultural feminism"; they made it possible for Clarke to self-assuredly articulate links between lesbian love and black liberation in the 1980s: "I was among a sisterhood of lesbian poets who interpreted the love that had finally begun to shout its name and its complexity in tongues of images and viscerally writing a new cultural history."[13]

The new cultural history that Clarke articulates pivots around theories of black women's representations. Black feminist scholars have pointed to the various ways that black women have been forced to protect their bodies from sexual violence under the regime of slavery and throughout the Jim Crow era; and, as early as the Harlem Renaissance, black women writers sought to construct black women's bodies against racist stereotypes that vilified their sexualities. On the one hand, slavery's legacy led to "a culture of dissemblance" in which black women chose not to confront their experiences with sexual violence in order to survive in domestic and otherwise prejudicial public spaces. On the other hand, the politics of respectability regulated how black women expressed their erotic desires in the early part of the twentieth century.[14]

These theories, which continue to be lorded over black women's sexuality, refuse to consider the multiple ways that black women chose (and choose) to both embrace and express their sexualities against tropes of silence and respectability. As LaMonda Horton-Stallings argues in *Mutha' Is Half a Word: Intersections of Folklore, Vernacular, Myth, and Queerness in Black Female Culture*, critical and theoretical approaches to black women's sexuality in the twenty-first century celebrate only limited expressions of that sexuality. Stallings posits that despite the dearth of recent critical work on black female sexuality—she notes the work of Evelyn Hammonds, Evelyn Higginbotham, Darlene Clarke Hine, and Tricia Rose—there still remain gaps in an exploration of black women's sexuality theorized against and beyond silence and dissemblance. Toward this end, she writes:

> What remains clear is that century after century Black women's discussions about sexuality in critical and creative efforts, as well as in real life and fiction, have been marred by the notion of silence, secrecy, and whispers. Some Black women may have been longing to tell, but there were those Black women who have been telling, and in the telling, they have been bawdy, explicitly, and downright shameless in their expressions of sexual desires, despite reprimands they have received. It is those voices that we still have trouble celebrating.[15]

In spite of Clarke's commitments to black women's liberation and her career as a prolific writer, scholars have not celebrated her voice. Clarke's radical black female sexuality constitutes what June Jordan theorized in the early 1990s as "a new politics of sexuality." Placing emphasis on "new," Jordan directly contests the silence that characterizes sexuality in America. Public discussion of sexuality can, Jordan argues, move folks "out of the shadows of our collective subjugation."[16] Coming years later, Stallings describes this movement in her own work as "wildness." Wildness does not perpetuate the "stereotypes of wild women" associated with the jezebel, wench, tragic mulatto, or trollop caricatures. Instead, this embodiment and performance of sexuality is "a radical Black female subjectivity that consciously celebrates autonomy and self-assertion in the invention process of self."[17]

Clarke's "jouissance," her "ecstasy," and indeed her "wild" "new politics of sexuality" manifest throughout her work as she names herself, her art, and her community as lesbian. In her essay "New Notes on Lesbianism," Clarke describes this self-identifying philosophy as a political act of resistance that in turn subverts narrative regimes of invisibility:

> I name myself "lesbian" because this culture oppresses, silences, and destroys lesbians, even lesbians who don't call themselves "lesbians." I name myself "lesbian" because I want to be visible to other Black lesbians. I name myself "lesbian" because I do not subscribe to predatory/institutionalized heterosexuality. I name myself "lesbian" because I want to be with other women (and they don't have to call themselves "lesbians"). I name myself "lesbian" because it is a part of my vision. I name myself "lesbian" because being woman identified has kept me sane. I call myself "Black," too, because Black is my perspective, my aesthetic, my politics, my vision, my sanity.[18]

Naming herself as a lesbian represents both an "act of resistance" to the sexist, homophobic, and patriarchal culture of her early years as an emerging lesbian feminist and a conscious act that recognizes black women's historical struggles to claim and own their sexuality. Although Clarke mentions her blackness in a few lines, it too governs her political resistance. Thus blackness and sexuality are immutable historical and cultural contexts that shape both her life and the production of *Living as a Lesbian*.

Throughout her work, Clarke dedicates her poetry "to all the women hidden from history whose suffering and triumph have made it possible for me to call my name out loud." Although black lesbian poet Angelina Weld Grimke does not occupy a critical center in any of her poetry, Clarke gestures toward Grimke as a pioneering poet whose "explicitly woman-identified poems" has made Clarke's work possible.[19] Grimke's silence and secrecy, instilled in her during the Harlem Renaissance, further inspires Clarke to "live the text out" very loudly. A brief turn to the life and work of Grimke helps to situate Clarke's radical black female subjectivity as a significant contribution to the history of black women's poetry in the United States.

Writing about Grimke's "buried life," Gloria Hull posits that Grimke "lived her life in virtual isolation."[20] Curious about what it meant to be "a Black Lesbian/poet in America at the beginning of the twentieth century," Hull asserts:

> First it meant that you wrote (or half wrote)—in isolation—a lot which you did not show and knew you could not publish. It meant that when you did write to

be printed, you did so in shackles—chained between the real experience you wanted to say and the conventions that would not give you voice. It meant that you fashioned a few race and nature poems, transliterated lyrics, and double-tongued verses which—sometimes (racism being what it is)—got published. It meant finally that you stopped writing altogether, dying, no doubt, "with your real gifts stifled within"—and leaving behind (in a precious few cases) the little that managed to survive of your true self in fugitive pieces.[21]

During Grimke's life, black artists deployed African American expressivity as propaganda meant to "uplift the race" and contest stereotypical depictions of blackness. The criteria and blueprint for black art were often, however, determined by men. Chief among these taste makers were W. E. B. Du Bois, Alain Locke, and Richard Wright. Unfortunately, the logics undergirding these criteria disavowed an expression of gender and sexuality, placing black women in complicated binds; as a result, black women writers like Grimke were "triply disfranchised." As black, woman, lesbian, there was, Hull argues, "no space in which [Grimke] could move."[22] The literary convention of the day imprisoned Grimke and her contemporaries Georgia Douglas Johnson and Alice Dunbar Nelson.[23] She wrote in hushed and muted tones that favored double entendres, as opposed to a more explicit, honest rhetoric. In this way, Grimke subsequently eschewed the very subject matter that inspired her craft and stimulated her imagination. In her final analysis, Hull writes that "Grimke lived a buried life.... [She] was defeated. Flattened. Crushed. She is a lesson whose meaning each person will interpret as they see fit and are able. What she says to me is that we must work, write, [and] live, so that who and what she was never has to mean the same again."[24] Hull encourages black women writers to use more explicit language that honestly gives voice to their desires and sexuality.

Despite the emergence of black women's liberation and the sexual revolution—in which Grimke did not participate—there was, Clarke explains, evidence of what Deborah McDowell also saw as "the changing same."[25] Although the times were different, black women's sexuality often continued in silence and shame. In her essay " ... She Still Wrote Out the Word Kotex on a Torn Piece of Paper Wrapped Up in a Dollar Bill," Clarke provides "an overview of various linguistic expressions of sexuality, sexual identity, and the erotic" in black women's poetry written after 1969—the year of the Stonewall rebellion, which public historian David Carter believes "sparked the gay revolution." Although this period signifies "a variety of expressions speaking to sexual experience, desire, identity, and gratification," Clarke found that during this time, black women poets began "to evince an explicit consciousness of ourselves as sexual beings."[26] Despite this new movement toward sexual liberation, Clarke contends that her contemporaries—whom she names as Toni Cade Bambara, Mari Evans, Nikki Giovanni,

Alice Walker, Sonia Sanchez, Gayl Jones, Silla Bouce, Toi Derricotte, and Ntozake Shange—often express black women as "heterosexual sexual beings," with notably few exceptions. Indeed, Clarke argues that in spite of the proliferation of erotic discourse that attends to black women's sexuality, black women's sexuality and lesbianism remain fraught with danger, fear, and loss and often rely on coded language to produce their affect.

Critiquing Mari Evans's "I Am a Black Woman" and Nikki Giovanni's "Ego Tripping" for a reliance on hyperbole in their "references to ancient African Kingdoms," Clarke disparages both poets' rhetorical choices: "While we as poets have linguistic options aplenty to feel so deeply about so many things, our metaphors of sexuality, sexual desire, sexual need, and sexual gratification are often not adventurous. We are usually tied to the values of heterosexual sex and sexual monogamy." In her critique of Ntozake Shange's *nappy edges* (1978) and *A Daughter's Geography* (1983), Clarke indicts Shange for continuing the style of "love poetry" that characterized the black poetry of the 1960s as "replete with allusions to Africa, the South, black music, and musicians, black historical figures, and metaphors of love and sex as natural wonders and ancient monuments and latter-day revolutionary movements and third world landscapes. Shange is consistently male-identified in terms of her muses and sexual references in poetry, despite her flirtation with the theme of lesbianism in *Sassafrass, Cypress,* and *Indigo*." As a political lesbian and black poet, Clarke contends that poets—especially black women poets—are "obligated to liberate our sexual discourse, as well as our sexuality from flowers, collard greens, and okra, from nights in Tamaris, from fierce animals, and some black male musician's tenor solo."[27] Clarke turns to the "erotic" as her method of choice to imagine a more liberated and explicit black female sexuality.

In a reflective essay on the life and legacy of Audre Lorde, Clarke asks: "Who else has taught us that sex energy is life energy?"[28] Lorde's essay "Uses of the Erotic: The Erotic as Power" profoundly impacted Clarke's sexual politics as a black lesbian.[29] The erotic provided Clarke the necessary language to politicize her sexuality; most importantly, it enabled her to discuss every aspect of her body without shame or fear. Like Lorde, Clarke viewed the erotic as a power that existed deeply and spiritually within the female body. Unlike Lorde, Clarke advocated for the value of the "pornographic," directly opposing a black feminist stance that Jennifer Nash argues—as I noted earlier—underestimates the ecstatic pleasure women derive from scenes of sexual engagement. Lorde's theory of the erotic, which opposes pornographic material, does not account for the ways in which black lesbian women create their own economies of desire by reclaiming the male gaze. Like Alethia and Flaxie, Clarke doesn't give a damn who is gazing: the power ultimately resides in the electric charges between women. In Clarke's poetry, these electric charges manifest in explicit imagery and language.

Furthermore, Clarke believes that Lorde often relies on sexual metaphors to discuss female eroticism in her poetry, a reliance that Clark critiques for their "hermetic inaccessibility." Consider, for example, Lorde's brief poem "Woman," published in *The Black Unicorn* (1978). According to her biographer Alexis De Veaux, *The Black Unicorn* represents a "literary transformation" in which Lorde discusses "bonds with women as intersections of the political, personal, and erotic."[30] The poem reads:

> I dream of a place between your breasts
> to build my house like a heaven
> where I plant crops
> in your body
> an endless harvest
> where the commonest rock
> is moonstone and ebony opal
> giving milk to all of my hungers
> and your night comes down upon me
> like nurturing rain.[31]

In "Woman" Lorde imagines perpetual, orgasmic ecstasy between women. Clarke would contend that Lorde's rocky metaphors, such as "moonstone and ebony opal," along with phrases like "your night comes down upon me," may obscure the poem's intentions. Because the poem starts with explicit language, the reader can surmise that Lorde intends her metaphors to enhance the poem's eroticism; readers know that somewhere between "breasts" and "milk" the speaker and her object of desire will meet in physical ecstasy, where "night comes down upon me / like nurturing rain." This concluding metaphor belies a general sense of "wetness" and, in particular, the female orgasm.

In contrast, Clarke's poetic language appears much more direct. Take, for comparison, two poems in which Clarke and Lorde turn their attention toward religion. Lorde's poem "About Religion"—also published in *The Black Unicorn*— recalls

> Black shiny women
> spicy as rocking pumpkins
> encased in stiff white covers
> long sleeved
> silk against brick.[32]

Clarke's "palm leaf for Mary Magdalene," on the other hand, sensuously envisions a lesbian nun masturbating to a leaf she believes once belonged to Mary herself. The nun

stroked her unfrocked breasts
and shoulders with it
tied my wrists to hers
with it and took my forgiveness. (28)

The erotic enables Clarke to subvert the tradition of the day, where black femi-nists do not "use language that depicts sex graphically for fear of being judged as 'politically incorrect,' or irresponsible." "I think," Clarke asserts, "[that] black women writers—poets and fiction writers—could stand to lose some primness, some fatalism, and one dimensional sexual perspective: one man (or woman), one body, one way, and fade out to flowers." She then concludes: "I say throw away the Kotex, forget the tampon, and BLEED!" Clarke's *Living as a Lesbian* achieves such bleeding. In the process, she punctures the erotic and shifts it "away from [its] traditional moorings."[33]

Leave Signs of Struggle, Leave Signs of Triumph

In her own words, Clarke asserts that *Living as a Lesbian* "served to advance a lesbian aesthetic and perspective—politically, lyrically, and unequivocally." In fact, she "plainly wanted to advance Audre Lorde's thesis in her piece 'Uses of the Erotic,' by promoting representations of lesbian sex."[34] The connotation of lesbian sex, however, goes far beyond shared eroticism between women. Clarke's text makes the central claim that lesbian sex becomes a source of survival for black lesbians in spite of so much racial and urban disorder. Indeed, *Living as a Lesbian* searches for eros as a life practice in the spirit of crippling decay, social disruption, and psychic despair.

As I referenced earlier in this essay, Clarke's poem "14th Street Was Gutted" reflects such crippling disrepair, disruption, and despair. These themes of violence and urban decay define many of the poems in *Living as a Lesbian*. In "how like a man" Clarke describes the intimate annals of sexual violence enacted by the Ku Klux Klan, while in "Urban Gothic" she explores the mass tragedy of police brutality:

Laying cross the street from the projects—concrete camp where 246 people
    of color
spend their confinement contained—the courthouse belches dark folk
like Squibb labs belches the stench of dog
carcasses. (16)

Here, the disruption of home and the eradication of space convey the social plight of the disposed. Indeed, "the stench of the dog" includes

poor people
black, purple, umber, burgundy, yellow
red, olive, and tan people.
In neat pressed vines.
On crutches.
In drag.
With child and children.
Dissidents, misfits, malcontents, and marginals, serving out our sentences
      on the streets of
America
spread-eagled against walls and over car hoods. (16)

Clarke's attentiveness to the social conditions of African Americans situates the black lesbian—as both persona and narrative voice—in what lesbian novelist Jewelle Gomez calls a "believable cultural context." Here, Clarke takes a social and political interest in the "same circumstances that have shaped our Black society over the past 400 years."[35] To live as a lesbian, specifically as a black lesbian, means that she situates her life within these racial and historical contexts. These contexts, in turn, help Clarke elucidate how black history shapes her social and political subjectivity as a black lesbian. Indeed, a closer reading of the opening poems in *Living as a Lesbian*—"14th Street Was Gutted," "Wearing My Cap Backwards," "How Like a Man," "Urban Gothic," and "Auction"—reveals a trivialization of the black female body, particularly the black lesbian body, as a member of the community and as a living subject.

In the first poem, for example, Clarke recalls "the death of Otis Redding," who died just a year before the gutting of 14th Street. In a different poem that appears much later in the volume, though still similarly vexed by urban strife, Clarke asserts that "her lover" left the city "without warning" but "for a less carcinogenic zone" (69). Despite the poem's intimate subject, Clarke does not establish temporal specificity in "since my lover left the city." When did her lover leave? Did she experience the gutting depicted in 14th Street? The lesbian persona in "since my lover left" embodies an *ahistorical* subjectivity; if it were not for Clarke's allusion to a "carcinogenic zone," readers would be left wondering about the poem's temporal placement. In spite of Clarke's allusions, the lesbian persona amounts to an urban myth, imagined outside of time and space. At the very moment that she is created, she voluntarily distances herself from the community and the buildings that "we had known all our lives." The flight of her body as it absconds to a place elsewhere does not, it seems, have the same value as the memory of Redding's dead body. The currency of a black man's dead body has more value—the body is named and socially situated—than a living body that is female, unnamed, and lesbian.

To track the text's multilayered narrative, we must assume that the black lesbian body has also been removed, gentrified, nearly burned, and belched out by the courthouse alluded to in "Urban Gothic." Here, the black lesbian's fate appears intertwined and enmeshed with the urban community described throughout Clarke's poems. In addition to their focus on post-emancipated urban spaces and African American communities, these poems politely whisper into the reader's ear important concerns about the invisible life of the black lesbian, who is, after all, the raconteur of these narratives. It is not until the poem "Acceptance" that Clarke's lesbian persona negotiates with the black past:

> You say to me, "I need you to let me die,"
> and months of denial are transformed into
> acceptance. I begin to see your funeral
> barge carried off the Cape into the primordial
> Atlantic. (20)

As if needing permission to compartmentalize the history of blackness as indexed by slavery—facilitated by the "primordial Atlantic" and further embodied by the "Ashanti pendant" placed in the hand of the dead—the speaker here performs a ritual of respect for the dead: she dresses the "ears and wrists" with "the aboriginal / turquoise and coral" to ensure "healing and protection." The poem's imagery betrays the speaker's passion for this history of blackness by tending to the importance of ritual colors. Rather than simply commemorating the dead, however, the oral tradition and its ceremonial rites seek "perpetuity and regeneration." Clarke—or the persona she has crafted—does not break with the past, as the poem may suggest. This ritual and this poem's quasi-acceptance speech mark a pivotal moment in the volume: Clarke's own "perpetuity and regeneration." Here, Clarke begins to tell her story in earnest, cultivating her personal history from the black past, present, and future.

No More Encomiums

Throughout Clarke's poetry collection, a sense of history informs the underpinnings of her work. Imagining black women's role in this history, in particular, remains a central concern. Concerning a palm reader who is a witch, Clarke writes:

> The old black witch keeps her sources well
> and does not tell me everything at once
> holds back the unwholesome forecast.
> Retells the ravaged past.
> Closes her misty eyes to the lines,
> tightens her fist against her teeth,

draws her breath
gives me back my hand
and does not tell me everything
at once. (33)

Clark's overarching concern is the palm reader's reticence, which in turn shores up both the silent aspects of black women's history and the silencing of lesbians within that history. She, the palm reader, must carve out and, when necessary, invent her own space; she must reclaim her body while remaining attentive to its corporality as a site of ritual. Understanding the necessity of remembering, respecting, expanding, and creating history reasonably justifies why Clarke follows her poem "Acceptance" with "Living as a Lesbian on the Make," which deliberately shifts the text away from singular narratives (of black experience) toward tales complicated by sexuality and lesbian eroticism.

The phrase "living as a lesbian" constitutes the volume's blues refrain, its jazz scat. Blues and jazz artists—notably Charles Mingus, Stevie Wonder, B. B. King, Jimmy Rushing, Billie Holiday, and Bessie Smith—populate the volume. These artists and the direct lines that Clarke cribs from their albums imbue her poetry with fluidity and movement, as well as a lyricism that further substantiates her interest in the Black Arts tradition and significantly writes her as a lesbian blues poet. Indeed, these music icons interanimate the volume just as much as the refrain "living as a lesbian" recurs in this text. Thus, jazz and blues music provide the text with a sultry and seductive soundtrack that then sets the stage for an erotic Black Arts theater embodied by Clarke's living lesbian(s), where, indeed, Clarke scats multiple iterations of her lesbian life: "Living as a Lesbian on the Make," "Living as a Lesbian in the Journal," "Living as a Lesbian Underground: A Futuristic Fantasy," "Living as a Lesbian Rambling," and "Living as a Lesbian at 35." In this way, Clarke tracks the movement and growth of a black lesbian. Like black music, these poems express pain, lust, desire, intimacy, and eroticism in diverse registers with nuanced meanings. In the end, however, "living as a lesbian" functions as a lyrical and rhetorical framework to reimagine African American life and history from the unique perspective of a black lesbian.

In the first iteration, "Living as a Lesbian on the Make," Clarke imagines a closeted black lesbian deeply aware of her surroundings:

Straight bars ain't so bad
though filled with men
cigarette smoke
and juke noises. (21)

The unnamed (though ever-observant) lesbian persona turns to "a martini straight up and jazz" to achieve a little comfort in an environment indelibly changed by urban renewal. Clarke then introduces an enchanting young woman who captures the speaker's attention.

> Alone she came in denim and a
> magenta tee
> hair cut to a duck tail
> ordered Miller's and smoked two
> cigarettes
> sat at a table close but distant
> was pretty and I was lonely
> and knew she was looking for a woman. (21)

Clarke imagines an allusive lesbian. Without name and without voice, Clarke facilitates the construction of this nearly invisible and mythic lesbian (object). She enters the bar alone, without context, appearing like the lover who "escapes the city for less carcinogenic zones," almost from thin air. She radiates the light given off by her "magenta tee." Her nontraditional hairstyle signals a butch aesthetic. The woman sits at a distance, which means that for some reason she wishes to either preserve or protect herself (or both) from the male gaze that populates the bar. Nevertheless, the focus here remains on constructing both the material lesbian body and its perception; Clarke's persona "knew" that the woman wearing the "magenta tee" was "looking for a woman." As Clarke begins to reimagine space she not only queers this space with a lesbian raconteur but also constructs a lesbian body as central to the remaking of place and space. Crafting this lesbian persona represents a reversal of the gentrification process, in which Clarke endows her subject with the agency to reconstruct the otherwise decimated black lesbian body within heteronormative space. Unfortunately, by the poem's conclusion, this woman vanishes, sending the persona into a blues state of mind; our raconteur is left being serenaded by the "saxophone flugelhorn bass and drum / hitting familiar riffs."

To both explore and expand the brevity of such fleeting experiences, Clarke often retreats to the journal-poem to invent and observe lesbian social worlds. In poems such as "Journal Entry: Sisters," "Journal Entry: The Weekend My Lover Is Away," "Journal Entry: The Last Post Card," and "Fall Journal Entry: 1983," Clarke attempts to capture and savor the unspoken desire between women. These desires, in turn, hang in a delicate balance between life and death, literally; distance and separation act as crucial lifelines for these women, where journals provide the safest space for shared female desire to live and survive. Consider Clarke's poem "Journal Entry: Sisters." Despite sharing a "seductive friendliness," the poem's eponymous subjects "talk very little" in an attempt to keep their love hidden and discrete: "'There's your sister. Better go now,' says the pretty one making herself small in the booth.... Her friend slides past her out the booth" (26). Their secrecy shields and protects them. Public knowledge—even exposure—of lesbian life can be deadly, as in the case of Sharon, the tragic heroine of "Fall Journal Entry: 1983," who "fell / jumped / or was pushed / from" either her fourth- or sixth-floor window (52).

The journal-poem genre that Clarke deploys in *Living as a Lesbian* culminates in her poem "Living as a Lesbian in the Journal." Although the journal-poem enables Clarke to archive her feelings and observations of lesbianism, it alienates her own experiences with women. These poems become archival artifacts for a future lesbian past. In "Living as a Lesbian in the Journal," Clarke time-stamps each stanza: "3/18," "3/19," "3/20," "3/21," and "3/21 (late)." Over this five-day period, Clarke records events scattered across her (or the persona's) daily life. Like the jazz-scat artist, each entry/stanza represents a different timbre or musical note that reflects the entry's mood. What's more, each stanza contains "runs" that go from high to low. Take, for example, the opening stanza, "3/18." In just three lines, the speaker's emotional register dramatically pivots from high to low:

And I hate for the party to be over: the anticipation, the long
drives, the coffee, the women who like me, the hard, fast sleep
the food. Truth is I don't want to be by myself. (54)

The first two line breaks—between "long / drives" and "sleep / the food"—reflect excitement. Clarke inflects the last line, however, with blues notes; the persona does not want to be alone and much prefers—even craves—the excitement of shared female company. This pattern of high and low—these scats—continues throughout the journal-poem. In entry "3/19," the speaker shares her excitement about an upcoming "adventure to Africa" with her lover; in the subsequent entry, she then relishes the bliss of praying to "Moms Mabley, Big Maybelle, and other lesser known fat or skinny / black or yella, grinning or toothless madonnas—live or dead" (54–55). Despite her enthusiasm, Clarke's persona disparages Aretha Franklin's decision to sing in South Africa during (what the reader must assume is) the apartheid regime. "How could she sing in South Africa," Clarke queries in "3/21." There is no sense in these journals that Clarke observed any shape or form of female eroticism. Instead, she archives anxiety, struggle, uncertainty, and fleeing practices of desire.

These journal-poems effectively archive both "signs of struggle" and "signs of triumph," thereby providing future readers with the necessary tools to excavate the lesbian persona from its imprisonment "underground." In "Living as a Lesbian Underground: A Futuristic Fantasy," this is precisely Clarke's point. Although lesbians must constantly negotiate space, dodge social dangers, and often conduct their lives shrouded in the secrecy offered by "basements / attics / and tents," this poem encourages women to resist the impulse to hide and to cultivate instead a fierce sense of conscious resistance:

> So . . . don't be taken in your sleep now.
> Call your assailant's name now.
> Leave the building empty
> The doors unlocked
> And raise the windows high
> When they pass by.
> Leave signs of struggle
> Leave signs of triumph
> And leave signs. (76)

Clarke's final sign, her ultimate act of resistance, constitutes her boldest statement of the volume: lesbian sex. In "Living as a Lesbian at 35," Clarke argues for a sexual freedom that is critical to living her life as a lesbian. The poem, although brief, makes a huge impact. The poem is erotic, pornographic, lusty, wild, and necessary to Clarke's mission of black lesbian affirmation. Clarke—as preserver, as storyteller, as archivist, as an observer of black life and (in)humanity—finally strikes out as a lesbian. Here, she snatches back her body as an erotic site. The opening stanza reads:

> In my car I am fishing in my pocketbook
> Eyes on the road
> For my wallet.
> In my mind I am fishing in your drawers
> Eyes on the road
> For your pussy.
> High speeds evoke fucking.
> Depending on your mood you come.
> It goes on:
> I do too from you
> Over the wheel
> Hand between my thighs
> Eyes on the road
> And the end of all: sex. (91)

If the final stop of Clarke's journey—destiny, freedom, life—is sex, it is therefore pivotal that the speaker embrace this aspect of lesbian life. Here, Clarke slyly imbues lesbian sexuality with tangible value, as indexed by the subject's wallet—if in fact we assume that this mundane object contains its usual material: identification card, cash, credit cards, and other meaningful assets. The wallet then becomes the panties, which further imagines an intersection between eroticism and capital. Where the erotic appears as both a mode of travel and a place of destination, it also functions as a sacred entity salvable in spite of so much blight. In her last poem in the volume, "Kittatinny," Clarke imagines that which lies between her thighs as a holy, sacred space.

> In my car, by the road, in a tent, in a pit
> stop, and practice a funkier art,
> Kittatinny Tunnel of that holy place you let me hit. (94)

Clarke brings into focus the lesbian woman's sacred body. In early poems such as "Palm Leaf for Mary Magdalene," where the persona "[tongues] the holy ghost" of Mary Magdalene's "sex," or in "Vicki and Daphne," where Vicki anxiously waits to massage Daphne's "aching pussy," and even in her poem "Sexual Preference," where the "queer lesbian" persona "does not prefer cunnilingus," Clarke imagines the black woman's pussy as a site of "ecstasy" within a lesbian economy; where, in spite of the vestiges of decay that surrounds her, she relishes the pleasure of an unbound erotic life. At age thirty-five, the lesbian persona / Clarke is not restricted by space or place. Indeed, putting behind her the tragedy of "14th Street," she strikes out with her desires and imagination, heading toward her own freedom, less vested in the heterosexual political economies of a monolithic black womanhood.

Notes

1. Among these titles are Smith, *Home Girls*; Moraga and Anzaldúa, *This Bridge Called My Back*; *Conditions* magazine; *Gay Community News*; and even the academically coveted journals *Signs* and *Callaloo*.

2. Clarke, *Narratives*; Clarke, *Living as a Lesbian*, hereafter cited parenthetically in the text; Clarke, *Humid Pitch*; and Clarke, *Experimental Love*.

3. Cheryl Clarke Papers, Schomburg Research Center for Black Culture, New York.

4. Jordan, "Who Look at Me."

5. Clarke, *The Days of Good Looks*, 3.

6. These are, of course, the imaginative female characters of *Sula*, *The Color Purple*, and *Passing*, written by Toni Morrison, Alice Walker, and Nella Larsen, respectively.

7. Clarke, *The Days of Good Looks*, 4.

8. De Lauretis, *The Practice of Love*, xx.

9. Clarke, *The Days of Good Looks*, 4.

10. Ibid., ix.

11. Nash, *The Black Body in Ecstasy*, 2.

12. hooks, *Black Looks*.

13. Clarke, *The Days of Good Looks*, 232, 267.

14. Jenkins, *Private Lives, Proper Relations*.

15. Stallings, *Mutha' Is Half a Word*, 4–5.

16. Jordan, *Some of Us Did Not Die*, 132.

17. Stallings, *Mutha' Is Half a Word*, 3.

18. Clarke, *The Days of Good Looks*, 85–86.

19. Ibid., 27, 160.

20. Akasha Gloria Hull, "'Under the Days': The Buried Life and Poetry of Angelina Weld Grimke," in Smith, *Home Girls*, 80.

21. Ibid., 77.

22. Ibid., 79.

23. Hull, Color, Sex, Poetry.

24. Hull, "'Under the Days,'" 81.

25. McDowell, *The Changing Same*.

26. Clarke, *The Days of Good Looks*, 156, 158. See Carter, *Stonewall*.

27. Clarke, *The Days of Good Looks*, 168, 178, 180. See Evans, "I Am a Black Woman"; Giovanni, "Ego Tripping"; Shange, *nappy edges*; Shange, *A Daughter's Geography*.

28. Clarke, *The Days of Good Looks*, 150.

29. Lorde, *Sister Outsider*, "Uses of the Erotic: The Erotic as Power."

30. De Veaux, *Warrior Poet*, 216.

31. Lorde, *The Collected Poems*, 297.

32. Ibid., 316.

33. Clarke, *The Days of Good Looks*, 185. I am alluding here to the work of Chela Sandoval and her definition of love as "punctum" and "a hermeneutics for social change." See Sandoval, *Methodology of the Oppressed*.

34. Clarke, *The Days of Good Looks*, 141–42.

35. Gomez, "A Cultural Legacy Denied," 114, 117.

PART V

Imagine

Pedagogy, Black Feminist Arts,
and Creative Methodologies

On Being a Black Sexual Intellectual

Thoughts on Caribbean Sexual Politics and Freedom

Angelique V. Nixon

A few years ago, I was asked to write a blurb in support of the rerelease of the documentary *A Place of Rage* (dir. Pratibha Parmar, 1991). I felt enormous pressure to write the perfect description of my engagement with the film, since for me *A Place of Rage* was more than simply a tool for my teaching or research. I had a hard time writing the piece because of my "place," or lack of place, in the academy. My subject position as a black, Caribbean, same-sex-loving woman from poor working-class roots constantly affects how I engage with space and navigate feelings of belonging. Reflecting on the film, I thought about the connections between anger and struggle, resistance and survival: "I spent much of my teen years and early twenties trying to figure out what to do with my rage. My anger was rooted in poor working-class struggle and many things I could not name. Through reading and studying the works of black women like Angela Davis, June Jordan, and Alice Walker, I discovered myself and found purpose—my rage had ancestral meaning, my rage gave me hope."[1] I also understood this rage as resistance, as survival, as a genealogy of black women knowledge producers. But how do we come to know ourselves as part of this genealogy or trajectory, that is, the black feminist tradition of sharing our stories of survival and resistance? This essay offers a critical and creative ethnography of becoming and being part of a black intellectual and feminist community.

Resistance for me started with education, and learning about these black women writers and thinkers was a vital part of my higher education experience.

They helped me to make sense of the isolation I felt at times in the academy, but they also offered pathways to community building, creativity, and healing as fundamental to knowledge production. It is through my exposure to the works of black women and other women of color writers and scholars that I found the courage to be a teacher and scholar, yet also pursue other passions (activism, poetry, and art) equally. I also learned that we can prioritize and theorize our own experiences through feminist methodologies and postcolonial analyses that challenge the dominant narratives of history and knowledge. In spite of the colonial structures of higher education, there are many examples of resistance and those of us who are engaged in different ways of being knowledge producers, working against white, male, heteronormative patriarchal, and European American centric ways of teaching and doing research.

In conducting research, I prioritize the local, the political, and the sexual-cultural landscape of the places and subjects I engage in order to uncover knowledge that is too often dismissed or ignored. I do this by focusing cultural criticism and research through interdisciplinary approaches, conducting fieldwork, and holding myself accountable to the communities I write in and about—meaning that I place myself and ethical relationships at the center of my scholarly work. During graduate school, I was incredibly fortunate to be in close community with fellow black students in the same program with similar interests in gender, sexuality, sex, and the body. We supported each other, met regularly, read each other's work, and hosted weekly writing sessions that I believe pushed all of us to finish successfully. One person in the group lovingly and sarcastically called us the "sexual intellectuals" after an afternoon of intense discussions on a wide range of topics, from black sexuality to cultural studies and African diaspora literature. We laughed at first but took up the challenge to define this term and perhaps this way of being in the academy. I look back now at those moments as forging a space for ourselves, people of African descent studying black, Africana, African American, and/or Caribbean studies, focusing on gender and sexuality, and grounded in black feminist, postcolonial, and black queer theorizing and knowledge production. In other words, both blackness and sexuality were and continue to be at the center of our intellectual work.

This is certainly not new or unique but another perspective on what it means to be at the intersections and margins of blackness, queerness, and sexuality both personally and intellectually. What does it mean to be a black sexual intellectual? It is not the same as adding the "ist" to the end of an area or field of study—Caribbeanist, social scientist, feminist theorist, and so on. It is not the same as a professional title such as literary scholar or black studies researcher, though it is similar. The flow of words builds upon each other and makes claim to identity, area of study, and public intellectual tradition. It is multiple spaces of being, and it is unapologetically personal and political—reading one's body at the center of politics. It is beyond research and teaching. It is praxis. It means I work hard to put my body where my politics are, especially in the struggle for justice. Embracing the term "black sexual intellectual" also means looking deeply at the intersections of who I am, what I study, how I see myself, and the work I want to create. And it means reflecting on my light-skinned and mixed-race privilege, knowing that when people see me they make all kinds of assumptions and allowances about and for my body. I also know that once I identify in all the ways I do, it can make some people uncomfortable.

My Caribbean blackness. My bisexual, woman-loving queerness. My polyamorous openness. My poor working-class rootedness. My Afrocentric, earth-loving hippy yet urban-chic aesthetics. My soul-driven, recovering Christian, not religious but respectful of all beliefs (as long as you respect mine), meditating, altar-building, spiritual self. My moon-loving conjuring, trouble-making self. My fierce cosmic warrior self. My radical politics focused on decolonization of our minds, bodies, spirits, and institutions. My sex-positive, antiracist, class-conscious, postcolonial feminist and womanist self. My body may make you feel discomfort. My body represents the product of complicated colonial no-other-choice sexual relations. This body has experienced too much violence through flesh and memory. This body will not reproduce flesh. This body produces other things—like praxis, art, poetry, and knowledge.

Caribbean Sexual Politics and Embodied Theories

I spent eighteen years living outside the Caribbean, but during that time I stayed connected to home and the region broadly through frequent travels for research, teaching, and spending time with family. In 2014 I returned to the region to work at the Institute for Gender and Development Studies, University of the West Indies, Trinidad and Tobago. Before that, since 2009 I worked closely on community building and research related to Caribbean sexual minority (LGBTI+) activism and movements through a project called the Caribbean IRN (International Resource Network), which connects researchers, teachers, artists, and activists who do work on diverse genders and sexualities. This project reconnected me to the region in integral ways, contributing directly to my scholarly, creative, and community work on Caribbean sexual politics. It also gave me the courage to be more public about my sexuality in the region.

Through editing and curating two multidisciplinary collections with fellow Caribbean activists and writers, we have worked to disrupt the divide between academic and community theory and knowledge while privileging local voices in Caribbean sexuality studies research.[2] One of the ways we can do this is by being accountable to the communities we write about and research: "The acknowledgement of one's own location is a fundamental aspect of embodied theories, an approach that is particularly relevant in sexuality studies, which are necessarily preoccupied with bodies. An embodied theory is a theory that does not ignore the reality of bodies—either of the people being studied or of those doing the analysis."[3] Theorizing about embodiment falls in line with what Caribbean LGBT activists have argued while also complicating the positioning of Caribbean sexuality studies researchers and activists, particularly those located in the diaspora and Global North activism. Trinidadian LGBTI activist Colin Robinson argues that we cannot place too much emphasis on law and litigation as a means of advancing sexual autonomy in the Global South of the Commonwealth: "If Global North advocates wish to be part of the movement to end 'sexual apartheid,' they must resist the temptation to take the reins. They must engage in genuine North-South dialogue and international solidarity. They need to get behind Global South initiatives and push in the directions carved out by southern activists."[4] Local and regional activists working on LGBTI rights and advocacy are caught in a web of controlling discourses and funding opportunities coming from the Global North that tend to dictate the ways the Global South ought to do human rights work. In moving back to the region, I see these tensions much more clearly than I did when I lived in the diaspora. It has helped me to understand Caribbean sexual politics in very nuanced ways as I work through my writing, research, and activism in the movements for gender and sexual justice. Living full time in the region also gave me the courage to write and theorize about sexuality in my own family, particularly focusing on and embracing the diversity of sexual experiences and nonnormative relationships I was raised around in spite of religious and culturally conservative norms.

In my book, *Resisting Paradise: Tourism, Diaspora, and Sexuality in Caribbean Culture* (2015), I examine how tourism and diaspora affect sexual and cultural identities. I include an autoethnography of my family's sexual outlaw stories: my grandmother's and mother's nonnormative sexual relationships, my mother's transactional sex work, and my own teen experiences of working in the tourism industry and coming to terms with my mother's sexual outlaw behavior and then her passing away from AIDS in 1996. I also theorize my same-sex-loving experiences alongside my family's stories in order to get at the nuances of and silences around Caribbean sexual practices, desires, and identities. Further, exploring embodied theories also means working through the hard and at times uncomfortable issues of language—what Faith Smith describes as the Caribbean being a region languaged by sex and the taboo of homosexuality.[5] She reminds us of the complexities of local discourses about sexuality (Creole terms that describe homosexual activities, sex acts, and transgressive gender performance) and how they are used and produced in ways that are violent and controlling, as well as affirming and liberatory. In other words, the "local" and local terms should not be idealized as a space of liberation or de-colonization in opposition to the imperial Global North terms or language. Yet we cannot deny the at times positive impact of Global LGBTIQ movements on the Caribbean and Caribbean sexual politics. The recent use of the term "queer" across the region in ways that it had not been used before can be seen as an impe-rial use of language, yet "queer" has been embraced by LGBTI and sexual minority organizations and activists across the region because of its global use and appeal. Nevertheless, there is much to critique in terms of power relations and the ways that international funding can adversely affect grassroots and community building in the Global South. Thus, I argue that the work of theorizing and privileging the local/regional is still vital even as we maintain a critical view of how "the local" can be deployed or romanticized.

The term "queer" offers an intriguing example of the regional versus global uses of language inasmuch as it is expansive as a theoretical device and an iden-tifying tool for global LGBTQI+ movement building. However, it also doesn't quite register for many across the region. While I identify with the term "queer" (particularly because of the ways it resonates with fluid notions of sex, sexuality, and gender identity), I must also acknowledge the discomfort and the ways it doesn't work. Yet I have noticed during the past few years of living and working in Trinidad, teaching gender and sexuality studies, mentoring graduate students, and working with local organizations that "queer" has an increasing popularity with young people who are gender nonconforming and identify differently with their sexual experiences and practices. It seems that "queer" can at times be more empowering than local terms that do not offer the same kind of nonbinary or not-so-gendered identity in relation to one's sexuality/sexualities. Therefore, we can understand the seemingly contradictory rejection and embrace of the term "queer" as a reflection of the changing and complex sexual landscape of the re-gion, especially in relation to diverse genders. This is why it is so important to take different kinds of theories and discourses seriously (as I assert elsewhere with Rosamond S. King, defining embodied theories). Omise'eke Natasha Tinsley argues in *Thiefing Sugar* that we must listen to "other kinds of theorists," which includes writers, artists, and activists, among others; further, she insists that the work of theorizing must happen on multiple levels:

> In establishing space for Caribbean woman-loving theory in particular and global queer theories in gender, we must search for foundations not only in the work of theorists like the *creolistes* or Sedgwick but also in the subversive and silenced ways of knowing gender and sexuality embedded in colonial subjects' texts. It is by dialoguing with the concepts of decolonization, queerness, and theory in this way that queer and postcolonial theory will not only come in different colors and

genders but will also come to be decolonized; that we will see not only different flora planted here but also a different organization to the field.[6]

Her provocation encourages us to push the boundaries of our work and theorizing around gender and sexuality. While she grounds her readings with local terms, Tinsley also uses "queer" and "queerness" alongside the key term she uses throughout to describe love and loving among Caribbean women—woman-loving woman. It is important to note that she engages the category of "woman" as a problematic yet necessary term to define the group of people she focuses on in her readings of Caribbean texts. The use of "women-loving women" privileges the local and regional terms and words for same-sex- and same-gender-loving people.

In building on this work, I explore what it would mean for us to theorize "queerness" in the Caribbean through the local,[7] particularly because the Caribbean norm is often located differently from in the Global North or even in the dominant narratives of the Caribbean itself. We must be open to the ways that sex and gender in the local frame are constantly in flux, and this awareness keenly shapes my theorizing, praxis, and organizing. Caribbean normativity is strikingly different from Global North norms, as King demonstrates in her theorizing of what she calls the Caribglobal focusing on sexualities, particularly among women and sexual minorities. She quite deliberately and thoughtfully privileges the local as she contextualizes the region through the global. In her investigation of the breadth and persistence of Caribbean heteropatriarchy and binary gender, she also analyzes "the persistence of transgressive Caribbean sexualities that present other ways of living and loving." King offers an intervention into theorizing the Caribbean and sexuality by connecting "transgressive sexual desires and experiences including promiscuity, homosexuality, and unconventional genders to other themes such as nationalism and diaspora." Her book takes very seriously other kinds of theorists through literature and popular culture to offer an intriguing reflection of the Caribbean sexual imaginary. King focuses not only on the Caribbean imagination but also on desiring Caribbean people in terms of sexual agency and erotic resistance so that "our understanding of both sexual transgressions and the structures being resisted can deepen our understanding of who Caribbean people are and who and how we desire."[8] I see this work as crucially marking the intersections of Caribbean sexuality studies and research, sexual politics and activism—work that inspires and moves us to greater understandings of the region.

Sociopolitical and Sexual-Cultural Landscapes

The Caribbean reflects the complexity of the postcolonial and neocolonial world. It also presents a diverse picture of the African and Asian diasporas (black, Indian, Chinese, European, Amerindian, and all the mixes in between); colonial and neocolonial histories with Britain, France, the Netherlands, Spain, and the United States; and a long history of migration to North America and Europe. As the region celebrates decades of independence, there are many things that remind us of how dependent we are as a region, as well as how the livelihoods of so many depend on the global economy, especially on tourism (especially in the Bahamas, where I was born and raised). As many Caribbean scholars, activists, and artists have argued over the past few decades, the process of decolonization remains incomplete, and we exist in what economists call "dependency capitalism."[9] Some countries remain under some form of colonial/neocolonial rule, namely, Puerto Rico, Turks and Caicos, British Virgin Islands, US Virgin Islands, Saint Martin / Sint Maarten, Guadeloupe, Martinique, Bonaire, and Curaçao. Moreover, through the IMF and World Bank, independent countries are controlled through structural adjustment policies—Jamaica and Haiti being prime examples—that create systemic economic dependency and shift resources from social investment toward austerity regimes that exacerbate the extraction of social wealth for global capital.

Therefore, like that of much of the Global South and formerly colonized countries, the Caribbean's sociopolitical and economic landscape has been racked by the stark realities and challenges of the continued embrace of neoliberal and global capitalist solutions that only exacerbate the post/colonial state's dependency on former colonial powers. As many postcolonial scholars have argued, we must constantly investigate the lingering and long-lasting effects of slavery, indentureship, and colonialism—and we must critique how these institutions impact our current social and political landscape. We remain at a critical juncture because of the insidious and double bind of tourism and foreign investment. I have argued elsewhere and maintain that tourism is a form of neocolonialism, and through an examination of the ways Caribbean cultural workers negotiate and resist the complexities of tourism, I insist that sexual labor in the region is at the center of informal economy and the underbelly of Caribbean paradise. I explore ways of rethinking sexual labor, transactional sex, and sexual agency as potential sites of Caribbean rebellion and freedom. For sexual outlaws in particular, sexual agency and erotic freedom can too easily be controlled through the state, religion, and conservative cultural norms. However, as Kamala Kempadoo argues in her book *Sexing the Caribbean*, we must grapple with the realities of sexual labor being at the center of tourism and the fact that tourism economies directly and indirectly benefit from the often invisible forms of sexual labor.[10] To do this, we would need to acknowledge all forms of sex labor, from transactional sex work to the use of black and brown bodies in the selling, packaging, and imaginings of paradise.

This also means understanding the important role of transactional sex work in Caribbean societies, including consensual sexual relationships, *mati* work, friending, and other sexual agreements that evade the formal capitalist system yet support local economies. Gloria Wekker's groundbreaking research in *The Politics of Passion* remains a testament to the complex ways that Caribbean women (Afro-Surinamese working-class women in particular) have engaged in sexual practice—mati work—outside the bounds of heteropatriarchy and formal economies through rejecting marriage in favor of relationships with women and men.[11] Further, in terms of analyzing (and reimagining) sex work, as L. H. Stallings insightfully asserts (expanding upon Kempadoo's and Wekker's theories) in *Funk the Erotic*, we must consider the role of the imagination in sexual labor and expression: "More than a term of economics, *transactional* alludes to fluid and liminal relationalities that refuse to be narrated by a singular universal narrative. Meanwhile, *mati* rebuffs capitalist understandings of sexual orientation, labor, and expression altogether."[12] Stallings offers a unique way to rethink "transactional" in relation to sex work not only by reminding us of the agency and imagination of people engaged in sex work but also by exploding the very notion of what we define as sex work and sexual labor. For my work in Caribbean sexuality studies, this means that I keep pushing against conservative ideologies and respectability politics, yet I also do more work around open and honest expressions and representations of sex, sexualities, and transactional sex work as vital to our Caribbean futures.

The continued investment in tourism across the Caribbean means more and more sexual labor in both visible and invisible ways. My research shows that *resisting paradise* is a necessary response to the unsustainability of the neocolonial tourism industry, especially for Caribbean working-class people and other people at the margins, namely, sexual outlaws,.sexual minorities, and people who engage in nonnormative sexual relationships. As social and class divides pervade the Caribbean and are exacerbated by globalization, gender and sexual politics can be distorted and used to distract Caribbean publics from current issues such as poverty, debt, economic and ecological challenges, and political corruption. Across the region, fears about same-sex marriage and a so-called gay lobby, which control intersections of respectability and fundamentalist religions, and the perception that there are no gender equality issues in the region have drastically affected movements for gender and sexual justice. Thus, the sociopolitical and sexual-cultural landscape can be very confusing and seemingly at odds yet different across islands. Therefore, we must be ever vigilant in our political advocacy, research, activism, and community building. The questions that continue to drive my Caribbean sexual politics, praxis, and research include the following:

1. How do we represent the realities for sexual and gender minorities and sexual others in the region, especially those of us who are lesbian, bisexual women, trans women, gender-nonconforming persons, and/or

queer? Where are our spaces of resistance? How do we understand our differences across race, ethnicity, class, gender, sexuality, religion, nationality, ability, and so on?

2. How do we strategically address the current struggles around sexual freedom, citizenship, and empowerment for Caribbean people, especially women, as we continue to deal with intense backlash against feminism, women's movements, and the pervasive perception/misconception that women are "taking over" and displacing masculinist power in the Caribbean?

In other words, heterosexist patriarchy, homophobia, and transphobia remain the dominant ideologies at the center of our struggles for gender and sexual justice, for racial and economic justice, for social justice. The challenge, then, for progressive or radical Caribbean teachers, writers, activists, and community workers is to assure exposing these dominant ideologies alongside white supremacy as part of much-needed decolonial work. We must remain vigilant and rebellious in our politics.

Black Queer Politics and Caribbean Rebellion

I aspire to be a revolutionary intellectual—in the spirit and fire of Walter Rodney— because we are at a critical juncture of social, economic, political, and ecological crises across the region and indeed the planet. My work in the academy must not be static or simply in the classroom. Education was my liberation, and now teaching and writing are my magical weapons. I wield them for change and progress inside and outside the university system. Walter Rodney's reflection on the idea that one cannot be both a revolutionary and an intellectual resonates with my own complicated relationship with the academy: "And I felt that somehow being a revolutionary intellectual might be a goal to which one might aspire, for surely there was no real reason why one should remain in the academic world—that is, remain an intellectual—and at the same time not be revolutionary."[13] I hold his words close as I make sense of my years and discomfort in the academy. I think about my travels since I started graduate school. I think about the mobility and access to places and people I may never have had if I hadn't gotten my academic hustle on and funding to present at dozens of conferences around the world, from Brazil to France, all over the United States, and across the Caribbean—my home-spaces, places I have come to know and love because of opportunities afforded me through the academic world. I remember myself as a little girl who dared to dream that I could be something other than poor and troubled and that maybe one day I would leave Nassau and travel. I remember when I found out that there was a thing called university, and I wanted to go, even when I dropped out of high school. I dreamed, worked hard, and took advantage of opportunities as they came my way, knowing that they came with a price and that some of them had something to do with my light skin, being mixed race, and silence about race and class, while others came when I stopped being silent. These are the paradox of difference—of being both invisible and hypervisible.

This body calls attention. This body is not worthy of attention. This mixed black female body is not pure. This body is dirty and poor. This body has light-skinned privilege—yellow skin, big hips, high cheekbones, full lips. This body has been rebuked, raped, and praised, sometimes all at once. This body confuses you, so you walk by and pretend it does not exist. This body draws you into it, so you scream, what are you? This body says, Human, Black, Magic, proudly, and you look away. This body is exotic and seems available for you sexually. This body does not want you. This body fights back and has a hard mouth that likes to cuss and drink rum. This body has been silenced, hands tied and tongue ripped out. This body is silent no more, fire tongue reborn. This body has been hungry. This body is tired. This body wants to be free. This body has desires that have nothing to do with you. This body likes to dance boldly under a full moon and fuck sweetly. This female body, Human Black Magic, loves blackness, dark edges, and the wildness of women-loving women, loving hard against the soul.

I embrace all the in-betweens and contradictions, and I do what I can to create the spaces inside and outside where we can be critically engaged in resistance and revolutionary thinking and rebuild our consciousness, as Sylvia Wynter says we must: "So what our consciousness has been battling against, the regime of 'truth' which has structured our 'consciousness,' is functioning against our best interests. It is negating ourselves; and so there's this constant struggle. You see, it's not just an intellectual struggle. You could call it a psychointellectual struggle."[14] We have been taught to hate ourselves and to negate ourselves. We have worked against our best interests and against our own self-worth—histories, generations, ancestors, spirits. To achieve consciousness, we must work against our own selves—intellectually and psychologically.

Wynter's powerful words remind me of the work we still have to do. She reminds us that teaching, knowledge, and intellectual work remain vital aspects of our freedom. While she focuses on black consciousness and people, her theories on regimes of truth and power resonate at the intersections of marginalization and oppression. I take up her charge as a person of African descent, as a migrant, as a woman, as a woman who loves other women, as a person of color.

I have been womanish a long time, and so I dare to imagine a world where people of color can be human and free. I dream and breathe revolution and freedom on many fronts—sexually, spiritually, economically, socially, and radically. I work actively to put my body where my politics are, which I define as being in the crossroads of black liberation, feminist resistance, and decolonizing transformative politics. This means working against heterosexist patriarchy, white supremacy, and capitalism. It means staying in the struggle for social and environmental justice, for sexual, gender, class, and racial equality, justice, and freedom. It means creating space for resistance and desire and using my voice, my art, my teaching, my writing to be woman centered, class conscious, LGBTI and queer affirming, blackness loving, sex positive, and transgressive in my politics. It also means being in the tradition of all of our ancestors who resisted before/when our revolutions were thought impossible while asserting our right to theorize our own experience, rewrite histories/herstories, imagine and make ourselves whole. Revolution means struggle, but it also means healing and radical self-care and love. It also means taking incredible risks and being a warrior rooted and guided by spirit and the earth.

I am grateful and blessed to have these experiences, as they have made me even more committed to community organizing, creativity, and praxis. In this essay, I share my academic, teacher, writing, and activist self so that you know my investments and commitments, so that you get to know these parts of me, so that you know I am here because of my ancestors, walking with spirit and defiance. My path has brought me back to the region and Caribbean homespaces—to Trinidad, the home of my maternal grandparents, who migrated to Inagua, the southernmost island in the Bahamas, where my grandmother was born. Since living in Trinidad and Tobago for the past few years, I have dedicated much time to various community-building projects across the region: art and reflection projects and workshops on ending gender-based violence; political advocacy work through CAISO: Sex and Gender Justice; cocreating an arts education youth empowerment program using Caribbean models of healing arts; and seven years with Ayiti Resurrect, a grassroots healing collective in Leogane, Haiti, that uses a unique model of African diasporic exchange. My teacher, writer, scholar, activist, and artist selves have emerged fully through these community and artistic projects, which are at their cores about Caribbean decolonial freedom.

I am here in the tradition and boldness of black women-loving women writers and artists like Audre Lorde, Dionne Brand, Cheryl Clarke, Michelle Cliff, June Jordan, and others who consistently through their writing demand space for our bodies, our lives, our politics, our desires, and our sexuality. In thinking about "Black Queer Trouble" in relation to Clarke's work, I offered a proposal for a black queer transformative politics (at the RetroFuturespective symposium honoring her work in 2013 at Rutgers University). I was invited to speak on a panel titled

"Black Queer Trouble" reflecting on Clarke's fierce politics, and I suggested that to be in the poetics and community work of black queer trouble means we must be diligent and confrontational—be outrageous and radical. This means we must question everything—we must critique, challenge, change, transform, and decolonize all these damaged and oppressive institutions that continue to determine our lives. We must be outrageous progressive radical queers in our politics and take back our social movements in order to create new ones. I want to remix that proposal here for the purposes of Caribbean sexual politics centered on lesbian, gay, bisexual, trans, intersex trouble making and for thinking through dimensions of Caribbean sexual freedom and rebellion.

In the struggle for Caribbean sexual justice and freedom, we ought to:

- trouble queer itself but assert our right to use it or not;
- vex (the Caribbean Creole word for "trouble") rigid or essential notions of identity—blackness, Indianness, Chineseness, creoleness, mixed Caribbeanness, and all the in-betweens;
- cultivate and teach a feminist politics that is antiracist, anti-imperial, class and color conscious, and sex and body positive;
- decolonize our minds/bodies/spirits;
- defy gender norms and embrace new ways of seeing and being in our bodies;
- decolonize and dismantle Western and colonial systems of knowledge and institutions, including marriage, the university, K–12 education, archaic colonial laws;
- fight against a politics of respectability that is limiting, controlling, and counter to the decolonization of our minds/bodies/hearts;
- talk openly and frankly about sex and sexual practices and desires, especially among youth and for Caribbean people and communities;
- live and love wildly and boldly—our skin, ourselves, each other, the earth and nature;
- celebrate and embrace all forms of sexual and gender outlaw behavior;
- become sexual and gender outlaws and rebel against any/all social orders that seek to control us.

This could be a manifesto of "Caribbean Sexual Politics and Justice." This is more than research, more than a guide or set of questions, more than another project. This manifesto will be a way of living and loving freely. Reasoning. Decolonial feminist visioning of Black and Caribbean Queer Radical Praxis. Being and Becoming. Fierce Joy. Beyond Human. Being Outrageous. Conjuring Ancestor Rage. Obeah Magic. Saltwater Resistance. Survival. Healing. We be in states of knowing. We take flight.

Notes

1. A Place of Rage Facebook page, 3 December 2009, https://www.facebook.com/pg/APlaceOfRage/notes/.

2. See King and Nixon, *Theorizing Homophobias,* http://www.caribbeanhomophobias.org/; and King and Nixon, *Love | Hope | Community,* http://www.caribbeansexualities.org/.

3. Nixon and King, "Embodied Theories."

4. Colin Robinson, "Decolonising Sexual Citizenship: Who Will Effect Change in the South of the Commonwealth?," UK Commonwealth Advisory Bureau, April 2012, 5–6, https://core.ac.uk/download/pdf/13120179.pdf.

5. Smith, "Introduction: Sexing the Citizen," 2–9.

6. Tinsley, *Thiefing Sugar,* 28.

7. See Nixon, "Troubling Queer Caribbeanness: Embodiment, Gender, and Sexuality in Nadia Huggins's Visual Art," *Small Axe: Visualities* 1 (2017), http://smallaxe.net/cqv/issue-01/.

8. King, *Island Bodies,* 13, 19.

9. See Thomas, *The Power and Powerless*; Barry, Wood, and Preusch, *The Other Side of Paradise*; and Patullo, *Last Resorts.* These scholars all define the structures of dependency capitalism and explain how the Caribbean is controlled through transnational corporations, foreign investment, and tourism.

10. Kempadoo, *Sexing the Caribbean.*

11. Wekker, *The Politics of Passion.*

12. Stallings, *Funk the Erotic,* 15–16.

13. Rodney, *Walter Rodney Speaks,* 19.

14. Greg Thomas, "ProudFlesh Inter/Views: Sylvia Wynter," *ProudFlesh: New Afrikan Journal of Culture, Politics, & Consciousness* 4 (2006), africaknowledgeproject.org/index.php/proudflesh/article/view/202.

CHAPTER 15

The Book of Joy

A Creative Archive of Young Queer Black Women's Pleasures

Anya M. Wallace and Jillian Hernandez

You have to document, you are forced to document.

Same-sex love disorganizes the life of the homophobe.

Why are there no images of black lesbians in space?

I like black and white when it comes to queer lives because it means we were here before color.

—Zanele Muholi speaking at the University of California, San Diego, April 29, 2014

Curatorial Statement

The place is Miami, Florida.

The work is arts based, woman of color feminist, queer, and sex positive.

The work is known as the Vibrator Project, created by Anya, and Women on the Rise! created by Jillian. These projects engage young women of color as always already *knowers* and *creators*.

Women on the Rise! is a space for critical conversations and art making with young women of color inspired by the work of contemporary feminist, queer, and antiracist artists. The Vibrator Project is a creative collective designed with and for young black women and girls to investigate pleasure in their lived experiences.

Taking our cue from the practice and passion of Zanele Muholi, a black queer South African artist and activist based in Johannesburg who generates portraits of queer communities, we have compiled an eclectic collection of images, poems, and interview transcripts culled from our research on queer young black women's sexualities and arts-based community work.

We purposefully stray from our typical essay-writing practice here in order to situate an evocative and more direct accounting of queer young black women's erotics within the larger framework of this anthology. Although the work of our participants is nevertheless mediated through our process of collection, selection, framing, and ordering, we, like Muholi, believe that the creative expression and documentation of queer black lives is a significant politic—with or without the conferral of legitimacy via scholarly and institutional modes of production and dissemination.

The images will give you what the words can't.
The poems will reveal what essays might scramble and miscode.

Feminist legal scholar Adrienne Davis developed the concept of "sexual economy" to examine how black sexualities have been and continue to be intimately linked to wider economic and political structures in the United States.[1] Through researching how black women's sexualities have been framed through the institution of slavery as violable and readily available for consumption and sale through a sexual economy, Davis aims to provide an opening "for black women to reclaim our sexuality, our intimate selves, from all of the people and forces who would seek to expropriate it, regulate it, define it, and confine it."[2] As artist-scholars we are attuned to how black sexual economies are entrenched in the field of the visual by paying particular attention to how black women's bodies and sexualities have been mutually marginalized in dominant visual culture.

The typological images rampant in popular culture that include the Mammy, the Tragic Mulatto, the Sapphire, the Jezebel, and the Black Best Friend or Sidekick frame black women's and girls' sexualities as shameful, spectacular, and/or unremarkable. The need to trouble these tropes stems from our desire to witness and consume representations of black women's sexualities that are diverse, full, and comprehensive. In curating this exhibition, we draw on our participatory action research, which was designed to facilitate collective learning experiences with young black women and girls in regard to visual culture, sex, sexuality, and pleasure.

The visual and narrative artworks produced by our participants do the necessary work of transforming black sexual economies to account for desires, pleasures, and intimacies that are fluid, uncontainable, and perpetually in the process of becoming. These are representations rarely found in popular culture. For example, in a recent interview in which a reporter asked Angela Davis to discuss her thoughts on the film *12 Years a Slave* (dir. Steve McQueen, 2013), she stated, "One thing I missed in that film was some sense of joy, some sense of pleasure, some sense of humanity."[3] When the discussion of queer young black women's lives is either nonexistent or saturated by the overwhelming realities of harassment, trauma, depression, and violence that can also mark them, a focus on joy becomes an urgent project. As students of Davis's *Blues Legacies and Black Feminism*, we center the true producers of our work here—the young women artists whom *we* learn from.[4]

> *We present incitements and provocations—narratives, poems, and possible (mis)*
> *rememberings.*
> *There is truth in here.*
>   *There is also theory in crafted image, word, and flesh.*

*   *   *

My sexual voyage is explicitly mine
I birth pleasure through my fear and curiosity
I fuck gods . . . transparent beings
that create reactions within me
Suck my frustration Bite my fear
Swallow my insecurity . . . My eyes
orgasm my words bleed through
my quivering lips
Fuck the ignorance with me
Lick me as deep as my
beckoning spirit
Cling to me Moan to me on beat
And drive me to the edge of my sexuality
Dare me to jump off
Jump off I'll be your jump off
Die in me and make me resurrect
in your screams
squeal for me hurt me
Love me sexually
And introduce me to myself
inside of me
—Bridget

*   *   *

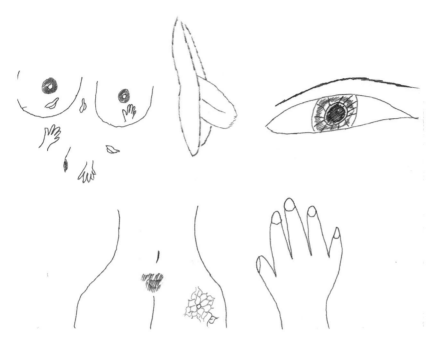

Figure 15.1: Artwork by Women on the Rise! Participant Qualisa Thomas inspired by artist Shoshanna Weinberger. Photo courtesy of Qualisa Thomas.

—Qualisa Thomas

*   *   *

WICKY TO JILLIAN: On a normal day I'm in some nice comfy boxers and some nice low jeans to show the boxer line—and a simple shirt.

JH: What is it that you like about your boxer shorts and your jeans?

WICKY: Oh my god do you know how sexy that is?!

JH: Because you find it sexy in other people?

WICKY: No! Because girls find it sexy in *me*!

JH: What do you think girls like about it?

WICKY: It's cute, it's attractive.

*   *   *

JILLIAN: If you're walking around like "Kevin" [her masculine alter ego], what do you think people will know about you?

Q: That I have an ego. Especially when I used to do it in the past I would always go to the mall and my friends would love it. Because I would have

Figure 15.2: Women on the Rise! / the Vibrator Project participants. All images made during a collaborative project with girls as part of Women on the Rise! and the Vibrator Project in Miami, Florida, 2010–13. Photo courtesy of Aurelia-Anna Florestal and Devontie Edwards.

on my jeans, I don't do the whole baggy thing when I do boyish—I do clean, like, you could tell I'm doing well [financially] type of look. I like to wear the button ups and the vests, so every time I used to do that I would have females walk up to me and be like "You must have a job or somethin.'" They would walk up to me because I have that confidence. I have on my hat and my braids, my braids pulled back, so I would have that swag going on and females would just love it because it seems like I was confident, and I would go up to people more easily and they would just be like "Hey, how are you doing?" It was so much easier. With me it was with ease. Because I'm already tall, I'm broad. It was one of those things where, it came out so naturally. I don't know, it was just confidence, people saw that I was really confident. I exuded that confidence more when I was dressing boyish.

*   *   *

i lay in your bed with my head resting on your stomach and my fingers tracing your thighs. Listening to you breathing as Marsha sings in the background watching your legs tremble as i write how i feel about you on your caramel skin. Kissing the spot that makes you hot but knowing this isn't what you want, you rarely pleased by the tongue that's just a tease. It just makes your skin hot and your body flush it isn't what you crave at the end of the night, but i kiss and lick your pussy and clit anyway wanting to taste you, the greatest flavor I have come to know I just want to taste you on greedy tongue. I dip my tongue deep in your nectar taking in its juices going deeper as your moans get louder letting me know that i getting closer to the sweet spot almost killing me in the process of getting your pleasure. But, I came here to please you in every way you want and i know you loved to be dicked down, pussy throbbing, and be loved. I want to spread your legs and slide inside feel your body connect with mine look you in the eyes and feel like im at home. Your body is my temple and i just want to praise it and love it whatever way possible leaving marks on my back that i will keep as badges having your moans in my ear telling me you're getting closer to heaven and i had you close so that you stay on earth with me as you come down from your heavenly high wrapped in my arms. . . . I wish i could have you that way again.

—Qualisa Thomas

More than the world. . . . More than the world you were. . . . Are
More than a reality . . . a dream come true you were . . . a goal met you were.
   . . . Are
What felt like a dream tragically crashed in too many nights of nightmares
Of issues long left revisited, nightmares of unequal comparisons. . . . of
   skeptical realities
I've never felt so fragile . . . out of all the abuse and misuse I've never felt so
   fragile
Like at the world's glances I would crumble
Given my last hope, I was empty . . . Am
As I watched you walk away I pleaded with myself to save what was not mine
I was in love . . . am
With who I thought you were . . . who you could be
I was blind . . . STILL asking myself if the actuality of this presence is a
   reality
My expectations still get the best of me
I was confused. . . . am with how your words were never equivalent to your
   actions
I am . . . was . . . was confused with how your eyes can still get me to jump
   from a bridge not knowing if there is a safety net there to catch me .
   .I'm confused
Holding on to my hope you still possess I expect you to crush me
Although I pray you won't . . . This time I pray you bury me instead of
   abandoning me to mend what is dead
I'm confused . . . Was I just a piece of ass . . . am
Given you what I had on preserve . . . my first . . . with what I had taken so
   many years to build . . . what I thought I understood
Partly my fault . . . NO solely my fault! that I am unable to come down from
   this painfully blissful trip
Sad . . . honestly that your name is still chiseled into every fabric of my DNA

Figure 15.3: Participant artwork. Photo courtesy of Tamyra Benjamin. Photograph credit: Devaedne Mond.

My soul still cries out to you in the heat of my passion
I'm addicted, rehabbed, and relapsed
possibility blocked out by vision of the perhaps
I'm sad
Please crush me kill me then bury me
I'm tired of being alone in this insanity
It's time for me to get a dose of reality
So that I can pick up the pieces and rebuild this shit correctly
—Tamyra Benjamin

*   *   *

We close with a poem by PhD student P. M. Trotter. We witnessed it being read at the Hip Hop and Punk Feminisms Conference at the University of Illinois, Urbana-Champaign in December 2013.

Blurred Lines of Invisibility:
Queering Black Girlhood, Femininity, and Masculinities

Somewhere between the hoodies and the hoops
Sometimes it's bow ties, wingtips, and 3 piece suits.
Regardless, the Black girl located there we never, or too little, mention

Knowing and remembering hair done in the kitchen: pressed, permed or
    getting extensions
But realizes over time she prefers the hairstyle that requires the blade
Clippers—getting an Usher and maybe next time just a side taper or perhaps
    a bald fade

This Black girl, Black woman some of us know her: sitting in the barber's not
    a beautician's chair
She is beautifully handsome and handsomely beautiful
Black girl. Black woman (Have you seen her?)

Figure 15.4: Photograph of Quailsa Thomas in a workshop exploring Zanele Muholi's work, alter egos, and queer identities by Tamyra Benjamin.

Binaries—man. woman—she can't seem to escape
To be hyper-feminine or -masculine for her is a requisite to be shoddy and fake
So much is at stake when her Black girl Black womanhood is left out of the
    necessary talks Hip hop, Black feminisms and nationalism are the
    aesthetics, the theories that inform her politics, her scholarship and
    swag like walk

Blank
Her Eyes glaze over
She becomes dazed when the only mention is the Black girl with the Afro,
    weaves, and braids
Not Beyoncé enough? Huh—Bitch, she too runs the world
If only you'd recognize, she too could teach you soooo much about being a
    Black girl. Black Woman

Hold up, let's not pretend, none have ever wondered and perhaps even
    discussed:
"Does she like women, men, or both?" [chuckles]
Stereotypes of a Black girl, Black woman misunderstood

But like Biggie said: it's still all good

Figure 15.5: Photo of Jillian (*left*) with Zanele Muholi (*right*) by Anya Wallace.

Hair is often, too often, used as a marker of respectability, gender and even
   sexuality—trappings of a white supremacist society bent on boxes and
   boundaries
Criminally minded, like Carter G. Woodson said: miseducated

You know, Westernly blinded to the Black girl, Black woman just wishing to live
Nothing but light and love that Black girl Black woman has to give

Figure 15.6: Tamyra Benjamin. Photograph by Women on the Rise! and the Vibrator Project participants.

Terrorist attackers. Living in the instinctual.
Focused on her sexual preferences: such a basic level queer sensibility
Here's the question: Where's the analysis that sees her as
The unexpected
The unplanned interruption
The Black girl that's free
Have you seen her? Tell me, have you seen me?

—P. M. Trotter[5]

Dedicated to the memory of black women who have been seen as disposable, although they were some of our greatest teachers of how to challenge fiercely limited portraits of blackness, namely, Black Girl and Black Womanhood. Particularly, I pay tribute to Islan Nettles and the other 237 transgender people, mostly nonwhite women, who were brutally murdered in 2013.

Notes

1. Adrienne Davis, "'Don't Let Nobody Bother Yo' Principle': The Sexual Economy of American Slavery," in this volume.

2. Ibid.

3. Patt Morrison, "Angela Y. Davis on What's Radical in the 21st Century," *Los Angeles Times*, May 6, 2014, accessed August 3, 2017, latimes.com/opinion/op-ed/la-oe-morrison-davis-20140507-column.html#page=1.

4. Davis, *Blues Legacies and Black Feminism*.

5. P. M. Trotter, "Blurred Lines of Invisibility: Queering Black Girlhood, Femininity, and Masculinities" (presentation, "Hip Hop and Punk Feminisms" conference, University of Illinois at Urbana-Champaign, December 5, 2013). Trotter's poem was part of the session, "Hip Hop Feminist Monologues: Kitchen Table."

CHAPTER 16

The Mist and the Rain

A Trickster Tale

L. H. Stallings

In the longs time past, before rabbit and turtle was just two competing animals trying to finish a race, when trees talked and people listened, there was this song and dance that all creatures on earth had to learn how to sing so they could eat and live. If they did it wrong, they stayed animals forever, but if they did it right, they became gods. So one day rabbit and turtle right near the water, and rabbit dares turtle to sing the song. "Sing the song, turtle, sing the song," rabbit say. Turtle ain't no fool, though, so he ain't singing nothing. But he tell rabbit he know the dance and the song. Know what he need to get it just right. Rabbit ain't believing him, though. So turtle go near the water, and he start humming right into the water. Hmmmm UhhhHmmm. Water hum back. Ohwohw! Turtle walk around in a circle counterclockwise and make a circle in the sand. And gets to humming again and start tapping his little green legs in the sand. Drumming and humming. So now rabbit getting scared. Thinking turtle gone beat 'em to the punch and be a god amongst all the animals.

Rabbit jump in the circle and start doing the same thing turtle doing. They both drumming and humming. Not a one singing yet. But the water hear, and the trees hear 'em, and the other animals heard and came to watch turtle and rabbit try to be gods. Before you know it, fishes jumping out of the sea, the sun is coming down to meet the earth, the birds surround the two, and all manner of beast chants around them, drumming, listening to the rhythm of the ocean. And so now neither turtle nor rabbit can back out. They have to keep going, but only one of 'em's listening, listening when they start singing and dancing. And so there they were, rabbit and turtle dancing and singing, and all the animals drumming and moving in a slow turning circle. Rabbit doing good, but not as good as turtle, 'cause turtle listening. Rabbit start singing, but don't nothing happen to rabbit. Rabbit still the same. Turtle singing and starting to change, but turtle don't know turtle change. Turtle too caught up dancing, singing, listening, listening, dancing, and singing, and that's when it happen. Turtle change, first to a man. And rabbit stay that way for a while. And the circle start moving faster, turtle trying to keep up with them that brought 'em the song, with them that were meant to make a god out of a shell being.

Soon turtle changes, and turtle not a man no more but a woman. And everything move quicker than before, turtle still keeping up, know the song now, and won't stop. Soon turtle not a man or woman. Turtle becomes the air and the water, then more than that. But rabbit still there, still the same old rabbit, and mad about it too. So rabbit, knowing how easy it is to throw turtle off balance, throws a stone into the air that is turtle, into the water that is turtle. The stone cuts through the air, and water falls from the sky. The stone finally lands in the water, and from where the stone drops, the ripples of the water flow to the land as mist bringing turtle back as a woman. The dancing stop, the singing stop, the drums stop. The song goes. The song goes. The song goes.

But all the animals are happy for the rain. They know they will eat and live. And life is good for them again. But turtle remembers what man was like, what woman was like, what air and water was like. Even as woman, turtle cannot forget that what she was, that what she was trying to be and almost was. Folks from my day say that when woman touches herself like that, it's turtle trying to transform into the water goddess. And if she do it right, for just a moment the hard shell disappears, and she becomes the air and the water. The mist and the rain all over again.

References

Alexander, M. Jacqui. "Erotic Autonomy as a Politics of Decolonization: An Anatomy of Feminist and State Practice in the Bahamas Tourist Economy." In *Feminist Genealogies, Colonial Legacies, Democratic Futures*, edited by M. Jacqui Alexander and Chandra Talpade Mohanty, 63–100. New York: Routledge, 1997.

———. *Pedagogies of the Crossing: Meditations on Feminism, Sexual Politics, Memory, and the Sacred*. Durham, NC: Duke University Press, 2005.

Allen, Jafari S. "Blackness, Sexuality, and Transnational Desire: Initial Notes toward a New Research Agenda." In *Black Sexualities: Probing Powers, Passions, Practices, Politics*, edited by Juan Battle and Sandra Barnes, 82–96. New Brunswick, NJ: Rutgers University Press, 2009.

Amado, Jorge. *Gabriela, Cravo e Canela*. New York: Alfred A. Knopf, 1962.

America, Richard F. *Paying the Social Debt: What White America Owes Black America*. Westport, CT: Praeger, 1993.

Avilez, Gershun. "Cartographies of Desire: Mapping Queer Space in the Fiction of Samuel Delany and Darieck Scott." *Callaloo* 34, no. 1 (2011): 126–42.

Bailey, Marlon M. *Butch Queens Up in Pumps: Gender, Performance, and Ballroom Culture in Detroit*. Detroit: University of Michigan Press, 2013.

———. "Gender/Racial Realness: Theorizing the Gender System in Ballroom Culture." *Feminist Studies* 37, no. 2 (July 2011): 365–86.

———. "Performance as Intervention: Ballroom Culture and the Politics of HIV/AIDS in Detroit." *Souls: A Critical Journal of Black Politics, Culture and Society* 11, no. 3 (2009): 253–74.

Balaji, Murali. "Vixen Resistin': Redefining Black Womanhood in Hip-Hop Music Videos." *Journal of Black Studies* 42, no. 1 (September 2010): 5–20.

Baldwin, James. *Another Country*. New York: Vintage, 1992.

———. *The Fire Next Time*. New York: Vintage Books, 1993.

———. *Notes of a Native Son*. Boston: Beacon Press, 1955.

Bancroft, Frederic. *Slave Trading in the Old South*. 1931. Reprint, Columbia: University of South Carolina Press, 1996.

Banet-Weiser, Sarah. *Authentic™: The Politics of Ambivalence in a Brand Culture*. New York: New York University Press, 2012.

Baptist, Edward E. "'Cuffy,' 'Fancy Maids,' and 'One-Eyed Men': Rape, Commodification, and the Domestic Slave Trade in the United States." *American Historical Review* 106, no. 5 (December 2001): 1619–50.

Barker, Meg, and Darren Langdridge, eds. *Safe, Sane, and Consensual: Contemporary Perspectives on Sadomasochism*. Hampshire, UK: Palgrave, 2007.

Barry, Tom, Beth Wood, and Deb Preusch. *The Other Side of Paradise: Foreign Control in the Caribbean*. New York: Grove Press, 1984.

Basu, Biman. *The Commerce of Peoples: Sadomasochism and African American Literature*. Lanham, MD: Lexington Books, 2012.

Bataille, Georges. *Death and Sensuality: A Study of Eroticism and the Taboo*. New York: Walker and Company, 1962.

Beam, Joseph, ed. *In the Life: A Black Gay Anthology*. New York: Alyson Books, 1986.

Bean, Joseph W. *Leathersex*. San Francisco: Daedalus, 1994.

Beckmann, Andrea. "'Sexual Rights' and 'Sexual Responsibilities' within Consensual 'S/M' Practice." In *Making Sense of Sexual Consent*, edited by Mark Cowling and Paul Reynolds, 195–208. New York: Ashgate, 2004.

Berlin, Ira. *Many Thousands Gone: The First Two Centuries of Slavery in North America*. Cambridge, MA: Belknap Press of Harvard University Press, 1998.

Bernasconi, Robert. "Crossed Lines in the Racialization Process: Race as a Border Concept." *Research in Phenomenology* 42, no. 2 (2012): 206–28.

Blair, Cynthia M. *I've Got to Make My Livin': Black Women's Sex Work in Turn-of-the-Century Chicago*. Chicago: University of Chicago Press, 2010.

Blasius, Mark. "An Ethos of Lesbian and Gay Existence." In *Sexual Identities, Queer Politics*, edited by Mark Blasius, 143–77. Princeton, NJ: Princeton University Press, 2001.

Blassingame, John. *The Slave Community: Plantation Life in the Antebellum South*. New York: Oxford University Press, 1972.

Blumer, Herbert. "Fashion: From Class Differentiation to Collective Selection." *Sociological Quarterly* 10, no. 3 (Summer 1969): 275–91.

Brooks, Siobhan. *Unequal Desires: Race and Erotic Capital in the Stripping Industry*. Albany, NY: SUNY Press, 2010.

Brown, Elsa Barkley. "Imaging Lynching: African American Women, Communities of Struggle, and Collective Memory." In *African American Women Speak Out on Anita Hill–Clarence Thomas*, edited by Geneva Smitherman, 100–124. Detroit, MI: Wayne State University Press, 1995.

Bryan, Carmen. *It's No Secret: From Nas to Jay Z, from Seduction to Scandal—a Hip-Hop Helen of Troy Tells All*. New York: Pocket Books: 2006.

Burnham, Margaret A. "An Impossible Marriage: Slave Law and Family Law." *Law and Inequality* 5, no. 2 (1987): 187–225.

Butler, Judith. *Bodies That Matter: On the Discursive Limits of Sex.* New York: Routledge, 1993.

———. *Gender Trouble: Feminism and the Subversion of Identity.* New York: Routledge, 1990.

———. *Undoing Gender.* New York: Routledge, 2004.

Caldwell, Kia Lilly. *Negras in Brazil: Re-envisioning Black Women, Citizenship, and the Politics of Identity.* New Brunswick, NJ: Rutgers University Press, 2007.

Carby, Hazel V. "It Jus' Be's Dat Way Sometime: The Sexual Politics of Women's Blues." *Radical America* 20, no. 4 (June–July 1986): 9–22.

———. "'It Jus Be's Dat Way Sometime': The Sexual Politics of Women's Blues." In *Unequal Sisters: A Multicultural Reader in U.S. Women's History*, 2nd ed., edited by Ellen Carole DuBois and Vicki Ruiz, 330–41. New York: Routledge, 1994.

———. "Policing the Black Woman's Body in an Urban Context." *Critical Inquiry* 18, no. 4 (Summer 1992): 738–55.

———. *Reconstructing Womanhood: The Emergence of the Afro-American Woman Novelist.* Oxford: Oxford University Press, 1987.

Carter, David. *Stonewall: The Riots That Sparked the Gay Revolution.* New York: St. Martin's Press, 2004.

Chase-Riboud, Barbara. Excerpt from *Central Park. Callaloo* 32, no. 3 (Summer 2009): 999–1013.

Chipumuro, Todne Thomas. "Pastor, Mentor, or Father? The Contested Intimacies of the Eddie Long Sex Abuse Scandal." *Journal of Africana Religions* 2, no. 1 (2014): 1–30.

Chude-Sokei, Louis, Ariane Cruz, Amber Jamilla Musser, Jennifer C. Nash, L. H. Stallings, and Kirin Wachter-Grene. "Race, Pornography, and Desire: A TBS Roundtable." *Black Scholar* 46, no. 4 (December 2016): 49–64.

Clarke, Cheryl. *The Days of Good Looks: The Prose and Poetry of Cheryl Clarke, 1980 to 2005.* New York: Carroll & Graff, 2006.

———. *Experimental Love.* New York: Firebrand, 1993.

———. *Humid Pitch: Narrative Poetry.* New York: Firebrand, 1989.

———. *Living as a Lesbian.* New York: Firebrand, 1986.

———. *Narrative: Poems in the Tradition of Black Women.* New York: Kitchen Table / Women of Color Press, 1983.

Cobb, Thomas. *An Inquiry into the Law of Negro Slavery in the United States of America.* Philadelphia: T. & J. W. Johnson and Co.; Savannah, GA: W. T. Williams, 1858.

Cody, Cheryl Ann. "Naming, Kinship, and Estate Dispersal: Notes on Slave Family Life on a South Carolina Plantation, 1786 to 1833." In *Black Women in United States History: From Colonial Times through the Present, Volume 1*, edited by Darlene Clark Hine, 241–60. New York: Carlson Publishing, 1990.

Cohen, Cathy J. "Deviance as Resistance: A New Research Agenda for the Study of Black Politics." *Du Bois Review* 1, no. 1 (March 2004): 27–45.

———. "Punks, Bulldaggers, and Welfare Queens: The Radical Potential of Queer Politics?" *GLQ* 3 (1997): 437–65.

Collins, Patricia Hill. *Black Feminist Thought: Knowledge, Consciousness and the Politics of Empowerment.* London: Routledge, 1990.

———. *Black Sexual Politics: African Americans, Gender, and the New Racism.* New York: Routledge, 2004.

———. *Coming to Power: Writings and Graphics on Lesbian S/M*. Edited by Samois. Boston: Alyson Publications, 1981.

Cowling, Mark, and Paul Reynolds, eds. *Making Sense of Sexual Consent*. Aldershot: Ashgate, 2004.

Crenshaw, Kimberle. "Beyond Racism and Misogyny: Black Feminism and 2 Live Crew." *Boston Review* 6 (December 1991): 6–33.

Crimp, Douglas. *Cruising Utopia: The Then and There of Queer Futurity*. New York: NYU Press, 2009.

———. "How to Have Promiscuity in an Epidemic." *October* 43 (1987): 327–71.

Cruz, Ariane. "Beyond Black and Blue: BDSM, Internet Pornography and Black Female Sexuality." *Feminist Studies* 41, no. 2 (2015): 409–36.

———. *The Color of Kink: Black Women, BDSM, and Pornography*. New York: New York University Press, 2016.

Curtin, Philip D. *The Atlantic Slave Trade: A Census*. Madison: University of Wisconsin Press, 1969.

Darity, William A., Jr. "Antipoverty Policy: The Role of Individualist and Structural Perspectives." In *The Oxford Handbook of the Economics of Poverty*, edited by Phillip N. Jefferson, 780–96. New York: Oxford University Press, 2012.

———. "A New (Incorrect) Harvard/Washington Consensus: Review of William Julius Wilson's *More Than Just Race: Being Poor in the Inner City*." *DuBois Review* 8, no. 2 (Fall 2011): 467–76.

Darity, William A., Jr., Mary Lopez, Olubenga Ajilore, and Leslie Wallace. "Antipoverty Policy: The Role of Individualist and Structural Perspectives." In *The Oxford Handbook of the Economics of Poverty*, edited by Phillip N. Jefferson, 780–96. New York: Oxford University Press, 2012.

Darity, William A., Jr. and Samuel L. Myers Jr. "Does Welfare Dependency Cause Female Headship? The Case of the Black Family." *Journal of Marriage and Family* 46, no. 4 (November 1984): 765–79.

Davis, Adrienne D. "'Don't Let Nobody Bother Yo' Principle': The Sexual Economy of American Slavery." In *Sister Circle: Black Women and Work*, edited by Sharon Harley and the Black Women and Work Collective, 103–27. New Brunswick, NJ: Rutgers University Press, 2002.

———. "Identity Notes Part One: Playing in the Light." *American University Law Review* 45 (1996): 695–720.

Davis, Angela Y. "Bad Girls of Art and Law: Abjection, Power, and Sexuality Exceptionalism in (Kara Walker's) Art and (Janet Halley's) Law." *Yale Journal of Law and Feminism* 23, no. 1 (June 2011), digitalcommons.law.yale.edu/yjlf/vol23/iss1/2.

———. *Blues Legacies and Black Feminism: Gertrude "Ma" Rainey, Bessie Smith, and Billie Holiday*. New York: Vintage, 1998.

———. "Reflections on the Black Woman's Role in the Community of Slaves." In *The Angela Y. Davis Reader*, edited by Joy James, 111–28. Malden, MA: Blackwell, 1998.

———. *Women, Race, and Class*. New York: Random House, 1983.

Davis, David Brion. *The Problem of Slavery in Western Culture*. Ithaca, NY: Cornell University Press, 1966.

DeFrantz, Thomas F., and Anita Gonzalez, eds. *Black Performance Theory*. Durham, NC: Duke University Press, 2014.

Delany, Samuel. *Times Square Red, Times Square Blue*. New York: NYU Press, 1999.

De Lauretis, Teresa. *The Practice of Love: Lesbian Sexuality and Perverse Desire*. Bloomington: Indiana University Press, 1994.

De Veaux, Alexis. *Warrior Poet: A Biography of Audre Lorde*. New York: W. W. Norton & Company, 2004.

Dolan, Jill. *Utopia in Performance: Finding Hope in the Theatre*. Ann Arbor: University of Michigan Press, 2005.

DuBois, Ellen Carole, and Vicki Ruiz, eds. *Unequal Sisters: A Multicultural Reader in U.S. Women's History*. 2nd ed. New York: Routledge, 1994.

duCille, Ann. "'Othered' Matters: Reconceptualizing Dominance and Difference in the History of Sexuality in America." *Journal of the History of Sexuality* 1, no. 1 (1990): 102–27.

———. "The Unbearable Darkness of Being: 'Fresh' Thoughts on Race, Sex, and the Simpsons." In *Birth of a Nation'hood: Gaze, Script, and Spectacle in the O. J. Simpson Case*, edited by Toni Morrison and Claudia Brodsky Lacour, 293–338. New York: Pantheon Books, 1997.

Duggan, Lisa. *The Twilight of Equality? Neoliberalism, Cultural Politics, and the Attack on Democracy*. New York: Beacon Press, 2003.

Dyson, Michael Eric. *Is Bill Cosby Right? Or Has the Black Middle Class Lost Its Mind?* New York: Basic Books, 2008.

Edmonds, Alexander. *Pretty Modern: Beauty, Sex, and Plastic Surgery in Brazil*. Durham, NC: Duke University Press, 2010.

Edwards, Brent Hayes. *The Practice of Diaspora: Literature, Translation, and the Rise of Black Internationalism*. Cambridge, MA: Harvard University Press, 2003.

Elliot, E. N., ed. *Cotton Is King and Pro-Slavery Arguments: Comprising the Writings of Hammond, Harper, Christy, Stringfellow, Hodge, Bledsoe, and Cartwright, on This Important Subject*. Augusta, GA: Pritchard, Abbott, & Loomis, 1860.

Ellis, Havelock. *Studies in the Psychology of Sex*, vol. 3, *Analysis of the Sexual Impulse, Love and Pain, the Sexual Impulse in Women*. Philadelphia: F. A. Davis Company, 1917.

Emerson, Rana. "'Where My Girls At?': Negotiating Black Womanhood in Music Videos." *Gender and Society* 16, no. 1 (February 2002): 115–36.

Engerman, Stanley L., and Joseph E. Inikori, eds. *The Atlantic Slave Trade: Effects on Economies, Societies, and Peoples in Africa, the Americas, and Europe*. Durham, NC: Duke University Press, 1992.

Entwistle, Joanne. "Fashion and the Fleshy Body: Dress as Embodied Practice." *Fashion Theory: The Journal of Dress, Body and Culture* 4, no. 3 (2000): 323–47.

Evans, Mari. "I Am a Black Woman." In *I Am a Black Woman: Poems by Mari Evans*. New York: Writers & Readers, 1993.

Fanon, Frantz. *Black Skin, White Masks*. Translated by Richard Philcox. 1967. Reprint, Berkeley, CA: Grove Press, 2008.

Feimster, Crystal N. *Southern Horrors: Women and the Politics of Rape and Lynching*. Cambridge, MA: Harvard University Press, 2009.

Ferguson, Roderick E. *Aberrations in Black: Towards a Queer of Color Critique*. Minneapolis: University of Minnesota Press, 2004.

Fishburn, Katherine. *Women in Popular Culture: A Reference Guide*. Westport, CT: Greenwood Press, 1982.

Fitts, Mako. "'Drop It Like It's Hot': Culture Industry Laborers and Their Perspectives on Rap Music Video Production." *Meridians* 8, no. 1 (2008): 211–35.

Ford, Tanisha C. *Liberated Threads: Black Women, Style, and the Global Politics of Soul*. Chapel Hill: University of North Carolina Press, 2015.

Foster, Frances Smith, Beverly Guy-Sheftall, and Stanlie M. James, eds. *Still Brave: The Evolution of Black Women's Studies*, edited by James Stanlie, Frances Smith Foster, and Beverly Guy-Sheftall, 215–33. New York: Feminist Press, 2009.

Foster, Guy Mark. "Desire and the 'Big Black Cop': Race and the Politics of Sexual Intimacy in HBO's *Six Feet Under*." In *The New Queer Aesthetic on Television: Essays on Recent Programming*, edited by James R. Keller and Leslie Stratyner, 99–112. Jefferson, NC: McFarland Publishing, 2005.

Foucault, Michel. "The Confession of the Flesh." In *Power/Knowledge: Selected Readings 1972–1977*, edited by Colin Gordon and translated by Colin Gordon, Leo Marshall, John Mepham, and Kate Soper, 194–229. New York: Pantheon, 1980.

———. *Ethics: Subjectivity and Truth*. Edited by Paul Rabinow, translated by Robert Hurley and others. New York: New Press, 1994.

———. *The History of Sexuality*, vol. 1, *An Introduction*. Translated by Robert Hurley. New York: Vintage Books, 1990.

Fregoso, Rosalinda. *meXicana encounters: The Making of Social Identities on the Borderlands*. Berkeley: University of California Press, 2003.

Freud, Sigmund. "Beyond the Pleasure Principle." In *The Standard Edition of the Complete Psychological Works of Sigmund Freud*, vol. 18, edited by James Strachey, 1–67. London: Hogarth Press, 1955.

Fung, Richard. "Looking for My Penis: The Eroticized Asian in Gay Porn Video." In *How Do I Look?*, edited by Bad Object Choices, 145–68. Seattle, WA: Bay Press, 1991.

Gaines, Kevin Kelly. *Uplifting the Race: Black Leadership, Politics, and Culture in the Twentieth Century*. Chapel Hill: University of North Carolina Press, 1996.

Genovese, Eugene D. *Roll Jordan, Roll: The World the Slaves Made*. New York: Pantheon Books, 1972.

Getman, Karen A. "Note, Sexual Control in the Slaveholding South: The Implementation and Maintenance of a Racial Caste System." *Harvard Women's Law Journal* 7 (1984): 115, 130–32.

Gilroy, Paul. *The Black Atlantic: Modernity and Double Consciousness*. Cambridge, MA: Harvard University Press, 1993.

Giovanni, Nikki. "Ego Tripping." In *Ego-Tripping and Other Poems for Young People*. Chicago: Chicago Review Press, 1993.

Gomez, Jewelle. "A Cultural Legacy Denied and Discovered: Black Lesbian Fiction by Women." In *Home Girls: A Black Feminist Anthology*, edited by Barbara Smith, 110–23. New Brunswick, NJ: Rutgers University Press, 2000.

Gopsill's Street Guide of Philadelphia, vol. 59 (1902), reel 5. City Archives, Philadelphia.

Gopsill's Street Guide of Philadelphia, vol. 60 (1903), reel 5. City Archives, Philadelphia.

Gordon, Avery. *Ghostly Matters: Haunting and the Sociological Imagination*. Minneapolis: University of Minnesota Press, 1997.

Gray, Herman. *Watching Race: Television and the Struggle for Blackness*. Minneapolis: University of Minnesota Press, 2004.

Grewal, Inderpal, and Caren Kaplan. "Global Identities: Theorizing Transnational Studies of Sexuality." *GLQ* 7 (2001): 663–79.

Griffin, Susan. *Pornography and Silence: Culture's Revenge against Nature*. New York: Harper & Row, 1981.

Gross, Ariela J. "Litigating Whiteness: Trials of Racial Determination in the Nineteenth-Century South." *Yale Law Journal* 108, no. 1 (1998): 109–88.

Gross, Kali N. *Colored Amazons: Crime, Violence, and Black Women in the City of Brotherly Love, 1880–1910*. Durham, NC: Duke University Press, 2006.

———. *Hannah Mary Tabbs and the Disembodied Torso: A Tale of Race, Sex, and Violence in America*. New York: Oxford University Press, 2016.

Gutman, Herbert G. *The Black Family in Slavery and Freedom, 1750–1925*. New York: Pantheon Books, 1976.

Guy-Sheftall, Beverly. "The Body Politics: Black Female Sexuality and the 19th Century Euro-American Imagination." In *Skin Deep, Spirit Strong: The Black Female Body in American Culture*, edited by Kimberly Wallace-Sanders, 13–31. Ann Arbor: University of Michigan Press, 2002.

Halberstam, Jack. *In a Queer Time and Place: Transgender Bodies, Subcultural Lives*. New York: NYU Press, 2005.

Hall, Stuart. *Representation: Cultural Representations and Signifying Practices*. Thousand Oaks, CA: SAGE, 2007.

Hammonds, Evelynn M. "Toward a Genealogy of Black Female Sexuality: The Problematic of Silence." In *Feminist Genealogies, Colonial Legacies, Democratic Futures*, edited by M. Jacqui Alexander and Chandra Talpade Mohanty, 170–82. New York: Routledge, 1995.

Hanna, Cheryl. "Sex Is Not a Sport: Consent and Violence in Criminal Law." *Boston College Law Review* 42, no. 2 (2001): 239–90.

Harewood, Susan. "Policy and Performance in the Caribbean." *Popular Music* 27, no. 2 (2008): 215–18. doi: 10.1017/S0261143008004029.

Harper, Philip Brian. *Are We Not Men? Masculine Anxiety and the Problem of African American Identity*. New York: Oxford University Press, 1998.

———. "The Evidence of Felt Intuition: Minority Experience, Everyday Life, and Critical Speculative Knowledge." *GLQ* 6, no. 4 (2000): 641–57.

———. *Private Affairs: Critical Ventures in the Culture of Social Relations*. New York: NYU Press, 1999.

Harper, Robert Goodloe. *Cotton Is King and Pro-Slavery Arguments.* Edited by E. N. Elliott. New York: Vintage Books, 1976.

Harris, Angelique. *AIDS, Sexuality, and the Black Church: Making the Wounded Whole.* New York: Peter Lang, 2010.

Harris, Cheryl. "Whiteness as Property." *Harvard Law Review* 106, no. 8 (June 1993): 1707–91.

Hartman, Saidiya V. *Scenes of Subjection : Terror, Slavery, and Self-Making in Nineteenth-Century America.* New York: Oxford University Press, 1997.

Hemphill, Essex. *Ceremonies: Prose and Poetry.* New York: Plume Books, 1992.

Hernton, Calvin. *Sex and Racism in America.* New York: Grove Press, 1977.

Higginbotham, A. Leon, Jr., and Barbara K. Kopytoff. "Racial Purity and Interracial Sex in the Law of Colonial and Antebellum Virginia." *Georgetown Law Journal* 77 (1989): 1967–2029.

Higginbotham, Evelyn Brooks. "African-American Women's History and the Metalanguage of Race." *Signs* 17, no. 2 (Winter 1992): 251–74.

———. "Rape and the Inner Lives of Black Women in the Middle West: Preliminary Thoughts on the Culture of Dissemblance." *Signs* 14 (Summer 1989): 912–20.

———. *Righteous Discontent: The Women's Movement in the Black Baptist Church, 1880–1920.* Cambridge, MA: Harvard University Press, 1993.

Hine, Darlene Clark. "Female Slave Resistance: The Economics of Sex." In *Hine Sight: Black Women and the Re-construction of American History,* edited by Darlene Clark Hine, 27–36. New York: Carlson Publishing, 1994.

———. "Rape and the Inner Lives of Black Women: Thoughts on the Culture of Dissemblance." In *Hine Sight: Black Women and the Re-construction of American History,* edited by Darlene Clark Hine, 37–49. New York: Carlson Publishing, 1994.

———. "Rape and the Inner Lives of Black Women in the Middle West: Preliminary Thoughts on the Culture of Dissemblance." *Signs* 14 (Summer 1989): 912–20.

Hirshman, Linda R., and Jane E. Larson. *Hard Bargains: The Politics of Sex.* New York: Oxford University Press, 1998.

Hodes, Martha. *White Women, Black Men: Illicit Sex in the Nineteenth-Century South.* New Haven, CT: Yale University Press, 1997.

Holland, Sharon P. "Bill T. Jones, Tupac Shakur, and the (Queer) Art of Death." *Callaloo* 23, no. 1 (2000): 384–93.

———. *The Erotic Life of Racism.* Durham, NC: Duke University Press, 2012.

———. *Raising the Dead: Readings of Death and (Black) Subjectivity.* Durham, NC: Duke University Press, 2000.

Holloway, Karla. *Passed On: African American Mourning Stories.* Durham, NC: Duke University Press, 2002.

hooks, bell. *Ain't I a Woman: Black Women and Feminism.* Boston: South End Press, 1981.

———. *Black Looks: Race and Representation.* New York: Routledge, 1992.

Hull, Akasha Gloria. *Color, Sex, Poetry: Three Women Writes of the Harlem Renaissance.* Bloomington: Indiana University Press, 1987.

———. "'Under the Days': The Buried Life and Poetry of Angelina Weld Grimke." In *Home Girls: A Black Feminist Anthology,* edited by Barbara Smith, 73–83. New Brunswick, NJ: Rutgers University Press, 2000.

Hunter, Margaret, and Kathleen Soto. "Women of Color in Hip Hop: The Pornographic Gaze." *Race, Gender, and Class* 16, no. 1–2 (2009): 170–91.

Hunter, Tera W. *To 'Joy My Freedom: Southern Black Women's Lives and Labors after the Civil War*. Cambridge, MA: Harvard University Press, 1997.

Hurt, Byron. "Pornography and Pop Culture: Beyond Beats and Rhymes: A Hip-Hop Head Weighs In on Manhood in Hip-Hop Culture." *Off Our Backs* 32, no. 1 (2007): 53.

"Interview with Audre Lorde: Audre Lorde and Susan Leigh Star." In *Against Sadomasochism: A Radical Feminist Analysis*, edited by Robin Ruth Linden, Darlene R. Pagano, Diana E. Russell, and Susan Leigh Star, 66–71. East Palo Alto, CA: A Frog in the Well, 1982.

Iton, Richard. *In Search of the Black Fantastic: Politics and Popular Culture in the Post–Civil Rights Era*. New York: Oxford University Press, 2008.

———. *Solidarity Blues: Race, Culture, and the American Left*. Chapel Hill: University of North Carolina Press, 2000.

Jacobsen, Matthew Frye. *Whiteness of a Different Color: European Immigrants and the Alchemy of Race*. Cambridge, MA: Harvard University Press, 1998.

James, G. Winston. *Shaming the Devil*. New York: Top Open Press, 2009.

James, Marlon. *John Crow's Devil*. New York: Akashic Books, 2005.

JanMohamed, Abdul R. *The Death-Bound-Subject: Richard Wright's Archaeology of Death*. Durham, NC: Duke University Press, 2005.

Jefferson, Thomas. *Thomas Jefferson's Farm Book: With Commentary and Relevant Extracts from Other Writings*. Edited by Edwin Morris Betts. Princeton, NJ: American Philosophical Society, Princeton University Press, 1953.

Jenkins, Candice. *Private Lives, Proper Relations: Regulating Black Intimacy*. Minneapolis: University of Minnesota Press, 2007.

Johnson, E. Patrick. *Appropriating Blackness: Performance and the Politics of Authenticity*. Durham, NC: Duke University Press, 2003.

———. "'Quare' Studies, or (Almost) Everything I Know about Queer Studies I Learned from My Grandmother." In *Black Queer Studies: A Critical Reader*, edited by E. Patrick Johnson and Mae Henderson, 124–58. Durham, NC: Duke University Press, 2005.

———. *Sweet Tea: Black Gay Men of the South*. Chapel Hill: University of North Carolina Press, 2008.

Johnson, V. M. *To Love, to Obey, to Serve: Diary of an Old Guard Slave*. Fairfield, CT: Mystic Rose Books, 1999.

Johnson, Walter. *Soul by Soul: Life inside the Antebellum Slave Market*. Cambridge, MA: Harvard University Press, 1999.

Johnston, James Hugo. *Race Relations in Virginia and Miscegenation in the South: 1776–1860*. Amherst: University of Massachusetts Press, 1970.

Jones, Jacqueline. *Labor of Love, Labor of Sorrow: Black Women, Work, and the Family from Slavery to the Present*. New York: Basic Books, 1985.

Jones, Lisa. *Bulletproof Diva: Tales of Race, Sex, and Hair*. New York: Anchor, 1997.

Jordan, June. *Some of Us Did Not Die*. New York: Basic/Civitas Books, 2002.

———. "Who Look at Me." In *Directed by Desire: The Collected Poems of June Jordan*, edited by Jan Heller Levi and Sara Miles, 7–18. Port Townsend, WA: Copper Canyon Press, 2007.

Kantrowitz, Arnie. "Swastika Toys." In *Leatherfolk: Radical Sex, People, Politics, and Practice*, edited by Mark Thompson, 193–209. Los Angeles: Daedalus Publishing Company, 1991.

Keeling, Kara. *The Witch's Flight: The Cinematic of the Black Femme and the Image of Common Sense*. Durham, NC: Duke University Press, 2007.

Keizer, Arlene. "Gone Astray in the Flesh: Kara Walker, Black Women Writers, and African American Postmemory." *PMLA* 123, no. 5 (October 2008): 1649–72.

Kelley, Robin D. G. *Africa Speaks, America Answers: Modern Jazz in Revolutionary Times*. Cambridge, MA: Harvard University Press, 2012.

———. *Freedom Dreams: The Black Radical Imagination*. Boston: Beacon Press, 2002.

———. *Race Rebels: Culture, Politics, and the Black Working Class*. New York: Free Press, 1994.

———. *Yo' Mama's Disfunktional! Fighting the Culture Wars in Urban America*. Boston: Beacon Press, 1997.

Kempadoo, Kamala. *Sexing the Caribbean: Gender, Race, and Sexual Labour*. New York: Routledge, 2004.

———, ed. *Sun, Sex, and Gold: Tourism and Sex Work in the Caribbean*. New York: Rowman and Littlefield Publishers, 1999.

Kempadoo, Kamala, and Jo Doezema, eds. *Global Sex Workers: Rights, Resistance, and Redefinition*. New York: Routledge, 1998.

Kenan, Randall. *A Visitation of Spirits*. New York: Vintage, 2000.

King, Rosamond S. *Island Bodies: Transgressive Sexualities in the Caribbean Imagination*. Gainesville: University Press of Florida, 2016.

King, Rosamond S., and Angelique V. Nixon, eds. *Love | Hope | Community: Sexualities and Social Justice*. Digital Multimedia Collection (Caribbean International Resource Network, 2017), caribbeansexualities.org.

———. *Theorizing Homophobias in the Caribbean: Complexities of Place, Desire and Belonging*. Digital Multimedia Collection (Caribbean International Resource Network, 2012), caribbeanhomophobias.org.

Klein, Herbert S. *The Middle Passage: Comparative Studies in the Atlantic Slave Trade*. Princeton, NJ: Princeton University Press, 1978.

Kleinplatz, Peggy, and Charles Moser, eds. *Sadomasochism: Powerful Pleasures*. New York: Routledge, 2006.

Kolcbin, Peter. *American Slavery: 1619–1877*. New York: Hill and Wang, 1993.

Kondo, Dorinne. *About Face: Performing Race in Fashion and Theater*. New York: Routledge, 1997.

Larsen, Nella. *Quicksand and Passing*. Edited by Deborah Powell. New Brunswick, NJ: Rutgers University Press, 1986.

Levande, Meredity. "Women, Pop Music, and Pornography." *Meridians* 8, no. 1 (2008): 293–321.

Ley, David. *Insatiable Wives: Women Who Stray and the Men Who Love Them*. New York: Rowman and Littlefield Publishers, 2012.

Lindemann, Danielle. "BDSM as Therapy?" *Sexualities* 14, no. 2 (2011): 151–72.

———. *Dominatrix: Gender, Eroticism, and Control in the Dungeon*. Chicago: University of Chicago Press, 2012.

Lipsitz, George. *Footsteps in the Dark*, Minneapolis: University of Minnesota Press, 2007.

Lorde, Audre. *The Collected Poems of Audre Lorde*. New York: W. W. Norton & Company, 2000.

Lotz, Amanda. *Re-designing Women: Television after the Network Era*. Urbana: University of Illinois Press, 2006.

Lowe, Richard G., and Randolph B. Campbell. "The Slave Breeding Hypothesis: A Demographic Comment on the 'Buying and Selling' States." *Journal of Southern History* 42 (August 1976): 401–12.

Lubiano, Wahneema. "Black Nationalism and the Common Sense: Policing Ourselves and Others." In *The House That Race Built*, edited by Wahneema Lubiano, 232–52. New York: Vintage, 1998.

MacKinnon, Catharine A. *Feminism Unmodified: Discourses on Life and Law*. Cambridge, MA: Harvard University Press, 1987.

———. *Toward a Feminist Theory of the State*. Cambridge, MA: Harvard University Press, 1989.

Maia, Suzana. *Transnational Desires: Brazilian Erotic Dancers in New York*. Nashville, TN: Vanderbilt University Press, 2012.

Manalasan, Martin F. "Colonizing Time and Space: Race and Romance in Brokeback Mountain." *GLQ* 13, no. 1 (2007): 97–100.

Marriott, David. *On Black Men*. New York: Columbia University Press, 2000.

McBride, Dwight A. *Why I Hate Abercrombie & Fitch: Essays on Race and Sexuality*. New York: NYU Press, 2005.

McCune, Jeffrey Q., Jr. "Transformance: Reading the Gospel in Drag." *Journal of Homosexuality* 46, no. 3/4 (2004): 151–67.

McDowell, Deborah. *The Changing Same: Black Women's Literature, Criticism, and Theory*. Bloomington: Indiana University Press, 1995.

McLaren, Angus. *Sexual Blackmail: A Modern History*. Cambridge, MA: Harvard University Press, 2002.

Mercer, Kobena. *Welcome to the Jungle: New Positions in Black Cultural Studies*. New York: Routledge, 1994.

Meier, August, and Elliott Rudwick. *From Plantation to Ghetto*. 3rd ed. New York: Hill and Wang, 1976.

Melamed, Jodi. *Represent and Destroy: Rationalizing Violence in the New Racial Capitalism*. Minneapolis: University of Minnesota Press, 2011.

Miller-Young, Mireille. "Hip-Hop Honeys and Da Hustlaz: Black Sexualities in the New Hip-Hop Pornography." *Meridians: feminism, race, transnationalism* 8, no. 1 (2008): 261–92.

———. "Putting Hypersexuality to Work: Black Women and Illicit Eroticism in Pornography." *Sexualities* 13, no. 2 (2010): 219–35.

———. Review of *The Politics of Passion: Women's Sexual Culture in the Afro-Surinamese Diaspora*, by Gloria Wekker. *Feminist Theory* 9, no. 1 (2008): 119–20.

———. *A Taste for Brown Sugar*. Durham, NC: Duke University Press, 2014.

Mitchell, Michele. "Comments on Her Article 'Silences Broken, Silences Kept: Gender and Sexuality in African-American History.'" *Gender & History* 11, no. 3 (1999): 433–44.

Moore, Wilbert E. "Slave Law and the Social Structure." *Journal of Negro History* 26 (1941): 171–202.

Moraga, Cherríe, and Gloria Anzaldúa, eds. *This Bridge Called My Back: Writings by Radical Women of Color*. New York: Kitchen Table / Women of Color Press, 1983.

Morris, Thomas D. *Southern Slavery and the Law: 1619–1860*. Chapel Hill: University of North Carolina Press, 1996.

Morrison, Toni. *Beloved*. New York: Knopf, 1987.

———. *Sula*. New York: Knopf, 1973.

Morrison, Toni, and Claudia Brodsky Lacour, eds. *Birth of a Nation'hood: Gaze, Script, and Spectacle in the O. J. Simpson Case*. New York: Pantheon Books, 1997.

Moten, Fred. *In the Break: The Aesthetics of the Black Radical Tradition*. Minneapolis: University of Minnesota Press, 2003.

Moynihan, Daniel Patrick. "The Negro Family: The Case for National Action." Office of Policy Planning and Research, United States Department of Labor (March 1965).

Mumford, Kevin. *Interzones: Black/White Sex Districts in Chicago and New York in the Early Twentieth Century*. New York: Columbia University Press, 1997.

Muñoz, José Esteban. "Cruising the Toilet: Leroi Jones / Amiri Baraka, Radical Black Traditions, and Queer Futurity." *GLQ* 13, no. 2–3 (2007): 353–67.

———. *Cruising Utopia: The Then and There of Queer Futurity*. New York: New York University Press, 2009.

———. *Disidentifications: Queers of Color and the Performance of Politics*. Minneapolis: University of Minnesota Press, 1999.

Nash, Jennifer C. *The Black Body in Ecstasy: Reading Race, Reading Pornography*. Durham, NC: Duke University Press, 2014.

———. "Strange Bedfellows: Black Feminism and Antipornography Feminism." *Social Text* 26, no. 4 (Winter 2008): 51–76.

———. "Theorizing Pleasure: New Directions in Black Feminist Studies." *Feminist Studies* 38, no. 2 (Summer 2012): 507–15.

Newmahr, Staci. *Playing on the Edge: Sadomasochism, Risk, and Intimacy*. Bloomington: Indiana University Press, 2011.

Ngai, Sianne. *Ugly Feelings*. Cambridge, MA: Harvard University Press, 2005.

Nixon, Angelique V., and Rosamond S. King. "Embodied Theories: Local Knowledge(s), Community Organizing & Feminist Methodologies in Caribbean Sexuality Studies." *Caribbean Review of Gender Studies* 7 (2013): 6–10.

———. "Troubling Queer Caribbeanness: Embodiment, Gender, and Sexuality in Nadia Huggins' Visual Art." *Small Axe: A Journal of Caribbean Criticism* (forthcoming).

Northrup, Solomon. "Twelve Years a Slave: Narrative of Solomon Northrup." In *Puttin' on Ole Massa*, edited by Gilbert Osofsky, 225–406. New York: Harper and Row, 1969.

Oakes, James. *The Ruling Race: A History of American Slaveholders*. New York: Knopf, 1982.

Oates, Thomas P. "The Erotic Gaze of the NFL Draft." *Communication and Critical/Cultural Studies* 4, no. 1 (March 2007): 74–90.

Ogas, Ogi, and Sai Gaddam. *A Billion Wicked Thoughts: What the Internet Tells Us about Sexual Relationships*. New York: Dutton, 2011.

Olmsted, Frederick. *The Cotton Kingdom*. Edited by David Freeman Hawke. Indianapolis: Bobbs-Merrill, 1971.

Owens, Leslie Howard. *This Species of Property: Slave Life and Culture in the Old South*. New York: Oxford University Press, 1976.

Painter, Nell Irvin. "Of *Lily*, Linda Brent, and Freud: A Non-exceptionalist Approach to Race, Class, and Gender in the Slave South." In *Half Sisters of History: Southern Women and the American Past*, edited by Catherine Clinton, 94–106. Durham, NC: Duke University Press, 1994.

———. "Soul Murder and Slavery: Toward a Fully Loaded Cost Accounting." In *US History as Women's History: Feminist Essays*, edited by Linda K. Kerber, Alice Kessler-Harris, and Kathryn Kish Sklar, 125–46. Chapel Hill: University of North Carolina Press, 1995.

Parish, Peter J. *Slavery: History and Historians*. New York: Harper and Row, 1989.

Patterson, Orlando. *Slavery and Social Death: A Comparative Study*. Cambridge, MA: Harvard University Press, 1982.

Patton, Stacey. "Who's Afraid of Black Sexuality?" *Chronicle of Higher Education* 59, no. 15 (December 7, 2012).

Patullo, Polly. *Last Resorts: The Cost of Tourism in the Caribbean*. New York: Monthly Review Press, 1996.

Peterson, Christopher. *Kindred Specters: Death, Mourning, and American Affinity*. Minneapolis: University of Minnesota Press, 2007.

Portillo, Tina. "I Get Real: Celebrating My Sadomasochistic Soul." In *Leatherfolk: Radical Sex, People, Politics, and Practice*, edited by Mark Thompson, 49–55. Los Angeles: Daedalus Publishing Company, 1991.

Pough, Gwendolyn. "What It Do, Shorty? Women, Hip-Hop, and a Feminist Agenda." *Black Women, Gender, and Families* 1, no. 2 (Fall 2007): 78–89.

Pravaz, Natasha. "Brazilian Mulatice: Performing Race, Gender, and the Nation." *Journal of Latin American Anthropology* 8 (2003): 116–47.

———. "Where Is the Carnivalesque in Rio's Carnaval? Samba, *Mulatas* and Modernity." *Visual Anthropology* 21 (2008): 95–111.

Raboteau, Albert J. *Slave Religion: The "Invisible Institution" in the Antebellum South*. New York: Oxford University Press, 1978.

Redmond, Shana L. *Anthem: Social Movements and the Sound of Solidarity in the African Diaspora*. New York: New York University Press, 2014.

Reid-Pharr, Robert F. *Black Gay Man: Essays*. New York: NYU Press, 1999.

———. "Clean: Death and Desire in Samuel R. Delany's *Stars in My Pocket Like Grains of Sand*." *American Literature* 83, no. 2 (2011): 389–411.

Reti, Irene. "Remember the Fire: Lesbian Sadomasochism in a Post–Nazi Holocaust World." In *Unleashing Feminism: Critiquing Lesbian Sadomasochism in the Gay Nineties*, edited by Irene Reti, 79–99. Santa Cruz, CA: Her Books, 1993.

Richeson, Marques P. "Sex, Drugs, and Race to Castrate: A Black Box Warning of Chemical Castration's Potential Racial Side Effects." *Harvard Black Letter Law Journal* 25 (2009): 95–132.

Roach, Joseph. *It*. Ann Arbor: University of Michigan Press, 2007.

Roberts, Dorothy. *Killing the Black Body: Race, Reproduction, and the Meaning of Liberty.* New York: Vintage, 1998.

Rodgers, J. A. *Sex and Race: A History of White, Negro, and Indian Miscegenation in the Two Americas,* Vol. II. 1942. St. Petersburg, Florida: Helga M. Rogers, 2000.

Rodney, Walter. *Walter Rodney Speaks: The Making of an African Intellectual.* Trenton, NJ: Africa World Press, 1990.

Rose, Tricia. *Black Noise: Rap Music and Black Culture in Contemporary America.* Middletown, CT: Wesleyan University Press, 1994.

Sandoval, Chela. *Methodology of the Oppressed.* Minneapolis: University of Minnesota Press, 2000.

Saunders, Patricia J. "Is Not Everything Good to Eat, Good to Talk: Sexual Economy and Dancehall Music in the Global Marketplace." *Small Axe* 7, no. 1 (2003): 95–115.

Schafer, Judith Kelleher. "Sexual Cruelty to Slaves: The Unreported Case of *Humphreys v. Utz*." *Chicago-Kent Law Review* 68 (1993): 1313–40.

Schwalm, Leslie A. *A Hard Fight for We: Women's Transition from Slavery to Freedom in South Carolina.* Urbana: University of Illinois Press, 1997.

Scott, Darieck. *Extravagant Abjection: Blackness, Power, and Sexuality in the Literary Imagination.* New York: New York University Press, 2010.

Scott, James. *Domination and the Arts of Resistance: Hidden Transcripts.* New Haven, CT: Yale University Press, 1990.

Sewell, Philip W. "From Discourse to Discord: Quality and Dramedy at the End of the Classic Network System." *Television & New Media* 11, no. 4 (2009): 235–59.

Shammas, Carole. "Black Women's Work and the Evolution of Plantation Society in Virginia." *Labor History* 5 (1985): 5–28.

Shange, Ntozake. *A Daughter's Geography.* New York: St. Martin's Press, 1983.

———. *nappy edges.* New York: St. Martin's Press, 1978.

Sharpe, Christina E. "The Costs of Re-membering." In *African American Performance and Theater History: A Critical Reader,* edited by Harry Elam Jr. and David Krasner, 306–28. New York: Oxford University Press, 2001.

———. *Monstrous Intimacies: Making Post-slavery Subjects.* Durham, NC: Duke University Press, 2010.

Sharpley-Whiting, T. Denean. "The Irony of Achievement for Black Women: Notes on Black Women and the Culture of Disrespect." *Ebony,* July 2007, 86–88.

Shimizu, Celine Parreñas. *The Hypersexuality of Race: Performing Asian/American Women on Screen and Scene.* Durham, NC: Duke University Press, 2007.

Smith, Barbara. "Home." In *Home Girls: A Black Feminist Anthology,* edited by Barbara Smith, 64–72. New Brunswick, NJ: Rutgers University Press, 2000.

———, ed. *Home Girls: A Black Feminist Anthology.* New York: Kitchen Table / Women of Color Press, 1983.

———. Introduction to *Home Girls: A Black Feminist Anthology,* edited by Barbara Smith, xxi–lviii. New Brunswick, NJ: Rutgers University Press, 2000.

Smith, Christen. "Putting Prostitutes in Their Place: Black Women, Social Violence, and the Brazilian Case of Sirlei Carvalho." *Latin American Perspectives* 41 (January 2014): 107–23.

Smith, Faith. "Introduction: Sexing the Citizen." In *Sex and the Citizen: Interrogating the Caribbean*, edited by Faith Smith, 1–18. Charlottesville: University of Virginia Press, 2011.

Somerville, Siobhan. *Queering the Color Line: Race and the Invention of Homosexuality in American Culture*. Durham, NC: Duke University Press, 2000.

Sontag, Susan. *Under the Sign of Saturn*. New York: Farrar, Straus and Giroux, 1980.

Spillers, Hortense J. "Mama's Baby, Papa's Maybe: An American Grammar Book." *Diacritics* 17, no. 2 (July 1987): 65–81.

Springer, Kimberly. "Policing Black Women's Sexual Expression: The Cases of Sarah Jones and Renee Cox." *Genders* 54 (Summer 2011). colorado.edu/gendersarchive1998–2013/2011/11/01/policing-black-womens-sexual-expression-cases-sarah-jones-and-renee-cox.

Stallings, L. H. *Funk the Erotic: Transaesthetics and Black Sexual Cultures*. Urbana: University of Illinois Press, 2015.

———. *Mutha' Is Half a Word: Intersections of Folklore, Vernacular, Myth, and Queerness in Black Female Culture*. Columbus: Ohio State University Press, 2007.

Stampp, Kenneth M. *The Peculiar Institution: Slavery in the Antebellum South*. New York: Knopf, 1956.

Stanley, Eric. "Near Life, Queer Death: Overkill and Ontological Capture." *Social Text* 29, no. 2 (2011): 1–19.

Staples, Robert. *The Black Family: Essays and Studies*. Belmont, CA: Wadsworth Publishing, 1999.

Star, Susan Leigh. "Swastikas: The Street and the University." In *Against Sadomasochism: A Radical Feminist Analysis*, edited by Robin Ruth Linden, Darlene R. Pagano, Diana E. Russell, and Susan Leigh Star, 131–36. East Palo Alto, CA: A Frog in the Well, 1982.

Steffans, Karrine. *Confessions of a Video Vixen*. New York: Harper Collins, 2005.

———. *How to Make Love to a Martian*. New York: Steffans Publishing, 2013.

———. *Vindicated*. Dallas, TX: BenBella Books, 2015.

———. *The Vixen Diaries*. New York: Grand Central Publishing, 2007.

———. *The Vixen Manual: How to Find, Seduce, and Keep the Man You Want*. New York: Grand Central Publishing, 2009.

Sterling, Dorothy, ed. *We Are Your Sisters: Black Women in the Nineteenth Century*. New York: W. W. Norton, 1984.

Stevenson, Brenda E. *Life in Black and White: Family and Community in the Slave South*. New York: Oxford University Press, 1996.

Stryker, Susan. "(De)Subjugated Knowledges: An Introduction to Transgender Studies." In *The Transgender Studies Reader*, edited by Susan Stryker and Stephen Whittle, 1–18. New York: Routledge, 2006.

Suggs, Jon-Christian. *Whispered Consolations: Law and Narrative in African American Life*. Ann Arbor: University of Michigan Press, 2000.

Sutch, Richard. "The Breeding of Slaves for Sale and the Westward Expansion of Slavery, 1850–1860." In *Race and Slavery in the Western Hemisphere: Quantitative Studies*, edited by Stanley L. Engerman and Eugene D. Genovese, 175–210. Princeton, NJ: Princeton University Press, 1975.

Tadman, Michael. *Speculators and Slaves: Masters, Traders, and Slaves in the Old South*. Madison: University of Wisconsin Press, 1989.

Taussig, Michael. "Culture of Terror—Space of Death: Roger Casement's Putumayo Report and the Explanation of Torture." *Comparative Studies in Society and History* 26 (1984): 467–88.

Taylor, Lisa. "'Baby I'm a Star': Towards the Political Economy of the Actor Formerly Known as Prince." In *Film Stars: Hollywood and Beyond*, edited by Andy Willis, 158–73. New York: Manchester University Press, 2004.

Thomas, Clive Y. *The Power and Powerless: Economic Policy and Change in the Caribbean.* New York: Monthly Review Press, 1988.

Thomas, Deborah. *Modern Blackness: Nationalism, Globalization, and the Politics of Culture in Jamaica.* Durham, NC: Duke University Press, 2004.

Thomas, Greg. "Proud Flesh Inter/Views: Sylvia Wynter." *Proud Flesh: New Afrikan Journal of Culture, Politics, & Consciousness* 4 (2006): africaknowledgeproject.org/index.php/proudflesh/article/view/202.

Tinsley, Omise'eke Natasha. *Thiefing Sugar: Eroticism between Women in Caribbean Literature.* Durham, NC: Duke University Press, 2010.

Tomlins, Chris. "Why Wait for Industrialism? Work, Legal Culture, and the Example of Early America." *Labor History* 40 (February 1999): 5–52.

Torres, Sasha. *Black, White and in Color: Television and Black Civil Rights.* Princeton, NJ: Princeton University Press, 2003.

Turner, Terence S. "The Social Skin." *HAU: Journal of Ethnographic Theory* 2, no. 2 (2012): 486–504.

Walker, Alice. *The Color Purple.* New York: Harcourt, 1982.

Wayne, Linda. "S/M Symbols, Fascist Icons, and Systems of Empowerment." In *The Second Coming: A Leatherdyke Reader,* edited by Pat Califia and Robin Sweeney, 23–44. Los Angeles: Alyson Publications, 1996.

Weinberg, T. S. "Sadomasochism and the Social Sciences: A Review of the Sociological and Social Psychological Literature." In *Sadomasochism: Powerful Pleasures*, edited by Peggy J. Kleinplatz and Charles Moser, 17–41. New York: Harrington Park Press, 2006.

Weiss, Margot. *Techniques of Pleasure.* Durham, NC: Duke University Press, 2011.

Wekker, Gloria. *The Politics of Passion: Women's Sexual Cultures in the Afro-Surinamese Diaspora.* New York: Columbia University Press, 2006.

Wells, Ida B. "To Tell the Truth Freely." In *Crusade for Justice: The Autobiography of Ida B. Wells,* edited by Alfreda M. Duster, 69–75. Chicago: University of Chicago Press, 1991.

Wells-Barnett, Ida B. *Southern Horrors: Lynch Law in All Its Phases* [1892]. Project Gutenberg, 2005. gutenberg.org/files/14975/14975-h/14975-h.htm.

Williams, Erica Lorraine. "*Mucamas* and *Mulatas*: Black Brazilian Feminisms, Representations, and Ethnography." In *Transatlantic Feminisms: Women and Gender Studies in Africa and the Diaspora,* edited by Cheryl Rodriguez, Dzodzi Tsikata, and Akosua AdomakoAmpofo, 103–22. Lanham, MD: Lexington Books, 2015.

———. *Sex Tourism in Bahia: Ambiguous Entanglements.* Champaign: University of Illinois Press, 2013.

Williams, Linda. "Skin Flicks on the Racial Border: Pornography, Exploitation and Interracial Lust." In *Porn Studies*, edited by Linda Williams, 271–308. Durham, NC: Duke University Press, 2004.

Williams, Mollena. "BDSM and Playing with Race." In *Best Sex Writing 2010*, edited by Rachel Kramer Bussel. San Francisco: Cleis Press, 2010.

Williams-Jones, Pearl. "Afro-American Gospel Music: A Crystalization of the Black Aesthetic." *Ethnomusicology* 19, no. 3 (1975): 373–85.

Wilson, Ara. *The Intimate Economies of Bangkok: Tomboys, Tycoons, and Avon Ladies in the Global City*. Berkeley: University of California Press, 2004.

Wiseman, Jay. *SM 101: A Realistic Introduction*. 2nd ed. San Francisco: Greenery Press, 1996.

Woods, Clyde. *Development Arrested: Race, Power, and the Blues in the Mississippi Delta*. New York: Verso, 1998.

Yep, Gust A., and John P. Elia. "Racialized Masculinities and the New Homonormativity in LOGO's *Noah's Arc*." *Journal of Homosexuality* 59, no. 7 (2012): 890–911.

Young, Norwood. *Getting Back to Me: The Chronicles of Norwood Young*. New York: Norwood Publishing, 2010.

Zook, Kristal Brent. *Color by Fox: The Fox Network and the Revolution in Black Television*. New York: Oxford University Press, 1999.

Contributors

Marlon M. Bailey is an associate professor of women and gender studies in the School of Social Transformation at Arizona State University. Marlon's book *Butch Queens Up in Pumps: Gender, Performance, and Ballroom Culture in Detroit* was published by the University of Michigan Press in 2013. It was awarded the Alan Bray Memorial Book Prize by the GL/Q Caucus of the Modern Language Association. In 2014 it was a finalist for the Lambda Literary Book Award in LGBT studies. Dr. Bailey has published essays in *Feminist Studies, Souls, Gender, Place, and Culture,* the *Journal of Gay and Lesbian Social Services, AIDS Patient Care & STDs, LGBT Health, Signs,* and several book collections. His essay "Black Gay (Raw) Sex" was published in *No Tea, No Shade: New Writings in Black Queer Studies,* edited by E. Patrick Johnson. Marlon is also a theater/performance artist and recently presented his solo performance in progress, "Exploring Black Queer Sex, Love, and Life in the Age of AIDS," at Concordia University in Montréal, Canada.

Lia T. Bascomb is an assistant professor of African American studies and affiliated with the Institute for Women's, Gender, and Sexuality Studies and the Center for Latin American and Latino Studies at Georgia State University. She is trained as an interdisciplinary black studies scholar with emphases in diaspora theory, cultural theory, visual culture, performance studies, gender and sexuality, and literature. Her scholarly interests focus on representations and performances of nation, gender, and sexuality across the African diaspora with an emphasis on the Anglophone Caribbean.

Felice Blake is an associate professor at the University of California, Santa Barbara. She specializes in twentieth-century African American literature and also studies Afro–Latin American literatures, racial communities in the post–civil rights era, and critical analyses of gender and sexuality. Dr. Blake received her PhD from the Literature Department of UC Santa Cruz and was a UC President's Postdoctoral Fellow at UC Berkeley before joining UCSB's English Department. She has published work on contemporary racism in a global context in *Al Jazeera*, *Ethnic and Racial Studies*, and *SOULS: A Critical Journal of Black Politics, Culture, and Society*. Her book *Intimate Antagonisms: Black Love and Black Hate in African American Literature* examines representations of intraracial conflict in twentieth-century fiction.

Darius Bost is an assistant professor of ethnic studies in the School of Cultural and Social Transformation at the University of Utah. He received his PhD in American studies from the University of Maryland–College Park. His research focuses in the areas of African American and African diaspora literary and cultural studies, gender and sexuality studies, queer studies, and trauma studies. His first book, *Evidence of Being: The Black Gay Cultural Renaissance and the Politics of Violence* (University of Chicago Press, 2019), examines black gay male cultural and political movement activity in Washington, DC, and New York City from the late 1970s to the mid-1990s, alongside the (extra)ordinary forms of violence directed toward black gay men during this same period. His research has been published or is forthcoming in *Criticism: A Quarterly Journal of Literature and the Arts*, *Occasion*, and *Journal of West Indian Literature*. His research has been supported by the Center for the Study of Race, Ethnicity, and Gender in the Social Sciences at Duke University, Office of Research and Sponsored Programs at San Francisco State University, Penn Predoctoral Fellowship for Excellence through Diversity at the University of Pennsylvania, and the Martin Duberman Visiting Scholars Program at the New York Public Library, among other sources.

Ariane Cruz is an associate professor in the Department of Women's, Gender, and Sexuality Studies at the Pennsylvania State University. She holds a PhD from the University of California, Berkeley, in African diaspora studies with a designated emphasis in women, gender, and sexuality. Her book, *The Color of Kink: Black Women, BDSM, and Pornography*, was published with New York University Press in 2016. Her publications appear in journals such as *Camera Obscura*, *Feminist Studies*, *Hypatia*, *Women & Performance*, the *Journal of American Studies*, the *Black Scholar*, and *Souls: A Critical Journal of Black Politics, Culture, and Society*. Her writing also appears in books such as *The Feminist Porn Book: The Politics of Producing Pleasure* (Feminist Press at CUNY), *Black Female Sexualities* (Rutgers), and *The Philosophy of Pornography: Contemporary Perspectives* (Rowman & Littlefield).

Pier Dominguez received his PhD in American studies from Brown University. His dissertation, "The Melodramatics of Queer Race," examined "nonrespectable" melodramatic texts deemed trashy, kitschy, and racially inauthentic from *The Bodyguard* to *The Real Housewives of Atlanta*. His essays and reviews have appeared in *Camera Obscura: Feminism, Culture, and Media Studies, GLQ: A Journal of Lesbian and Gay Studies, Racialicious, New York Newsday,* Univision's *Track Record,* and other publications in his native Colombia.

David B. Green Jr., PhD, is director of diversity and inclusion and lecturer in the Department of Interdisciplinary Studies at the Sage Colleges.

Jillian Hernandez is an assistant professor at the Center of Gender, Sexualities, and Women's Studies at the University of Florida. She is a transdisciplinary scholar interested in the stakes of embodiment, aesthetics, and performance for Black and Latinx women and girls, gender nonconformers, trans people, and queers. She is currently completing her first book, tentatively titled *Aesthetics of Excess: The Art and Politics of Black and Latina Embodiment,* which is under contract at Duke University Press, and developing additional book-length projects on the radical politics of femme of color art and performance and Latinx creative erotics, ontologies, and relationalities. Hernandez received her Ph.D. in women's and gender studies at Rutgers University. Her scholarship is based on and inspired by over a decade of community arts work with Black and Latinx girls in Miami, Florida, through the Women on the Rise! program she established at the Museum of Contemporary Art in North Miami in addition to her practice as a curator and creative.

Cheryl D. Hicks is a professor of Africana studies and history at the University of Delaware. Her research addresses the intersections of race, class, gender, sexuality, and the law. She has published in the *University of Pennsylvania Law Review,* the *Journal of the History of Sexuality,* and the *Journal of African American History.* Her first book, *Talk with You Like a Woman: African American Women, Justice, and Reform in New York, 1890–1935,* received the 2011 Letitia Woods Brown Book Award from the Association of Black Women Historians and honorable mentions from both the 2011 John Hope Franklin Prize from the American Studies Association and the 2011 Darlene Clark Hine Prize from the Organization of American Historians. Her new book project, "Black Enchantress: Hannah Elias, Interracial Sex, Murder, and Civil Rights in Jim Crow New York," interrogates the trajectory of a covert, consensual, interracial relationship that ultimately precipitated murder, scandal, and civil rights protest.

Xavier Livermon is associate professor of African and African diaspora studies at the University of Texas at Austin. His research exists at the intersection of popular culture, gender, and sexuality in postapartheid South Africa and the African diaspora. His forthcoming book, *Kwaito Bodies: Remastering Space and Subjectivity in Post-apartheid South Africa* (Duke University Press), examines postapartheid youth culture as a series of performances enacted to test the limits of postapartheid possibility. His second project, tentatively entitled *Queer(y)ing Freedom: Construction Black Queer Belonging in South Africa*, has resulted in a number of published essays in *GLQ*; *Gender, Place, and Culture*; and *Feminist Studies* and examines how black queer South Africans construct forms of cultural and national belonging in a climate where progressive constitutional rights do not always translate in quotidian practice.

Jeffrey Q. McCune Jr. is an associate professor of African and African American studies and women, gender, and sexuality studies at Washington University in St. Louis. He is the director of the Mellon Mays Undergraduate Fellowship Program. Dr. McCune is the author of *Sexual Discretion: Black Masculinity and the Politics of Passing*, awarded the National Communication Association's 2015 GLBTQ Book Award and several other book honors. For his service in scholarship and to the field, Dr. McCune was awarded the 2015 Modern language Association's GL/Q Caucus Michael Lynch Service Award. He is presently working on two book projects, the first, a full-length manuscript, "Read: An Experiment in Seeing Black," and the other titled "On Kanye: A Philosophy of Black Genius." McCune has received international recognition for a course related to the latter. In addition to these works, Dr. McCune is also in the process of collecting ethnographic and archival material to complete a second play, "AFTERLIFE: An Archive of Violence," which explores the day-to-day impact of state-sanctioned violence on individuals within black and brown communities. McCune has been featured on *Left of Black* and *Sirius XM's Joe Madison Show* and has been a guest expert on *Bill Nye Saves the World*.

Mireille Miller-Young, PhD, is an associate professor of feminist studies at the University of California, Santa Barbara. She researches and teaches about race, gender, and sexuality in US history, popular and film cultures, and the sex industries. Her book *A Taste for Brown Sugar: Black Women in Pornography* (Duke University Press, 2014) was awarded the Sara A. Whaley Prize by the National Women's Studies Association and the John Hope Franklin Prize by the American Studies Association. Dr. Miller-Young was a coconvener of the Black Sexual Economies Project, a multiyear research scholar think tank at Washington University School of Law, and is a founder and convener of the New Sexualities Research Initiative at UC Santa Barbara. Dr. Miller-Young has published in numerous anthologies, academic journals, and news outlets, including *Blackness and Sexuality, Porn Archives, Sexualities, Meridians*, the *New York Times, Ms.*, the *Washington Post*, and *$pread*, a sex worker magazine. With Constance Penley, Celine Parreñas Shimizu, and Tristan Taormino, she is an editor of *The Feminist Porn Book: The Politics of Producing Pleasure* (Feminist Press, 2013), which was a finalist for the Lambda Literary Award for Best LGBT Anthology.

Shana L. Redmond is the author of *Anthem: Social Movements and the Sound of Solidarity in the African Diaspora* (NYU Press, 2014) and an associate professor of musicology and African American studies at the University of California, Los Angeles. She is coeditor and contributor to *Critical Ethnic Studies: A Reader* (Duke University Press, 2016) and coeditor of the Music of the African Diaspora series with the University of California Press. Her work has appeared in a variety of print and online venues, and she has received numerous fellowships, including the inaugural Ella Baker Visiting Professor Fellowship at the University of California, Santa Barbara. She is currently pursuing the post–civil rights assemblage and movement science of Paul Robeson.

Matt Richardson is an associate professor in English and in the Department of African and African American Studies and a core faculty member of the Center for Women's and Gender Studies at the University of Texas at Austin. He has published articles in various academic journals such as *GLQ, Sexuality Research and Social Policy: Journal of the NSRC,* the *Journal of Women's History,* and *Black Camera.* He also has published fiction and poetry in publications like *Pharos, Sinister Wisdom,* and *Feminist Studies.* He is a coeditor of the transgender issue of *Feminist Studies* and a coeditor of the issue on blackness for *Transgender Studies Quarterly.* His latest book is entitled *The Queer Limit of Black Memory: Black Lesbian Literature and Irresolution,* published by Ohio State University Press.

L. H. Stallings is professor of African American studies at Georgetown University. She has published essays in *African American Review,* the *Journal of Bisexuality, Black Renaissance / Renaissance Noire, Black Camera, Obsidian III, Revista Canaria de Estudios Ingleses, CR: The New Centennial Review, Western Journal of Black Studies, Feminist Formations, MELUS,* and numerous edited collections. Her first book, *Mutha' Is Half a Word: Intersections of Folklore, Vernacular, Myth, and Queerness in Black Female Culture* (2007), critically engages folklore and vernacular theory, black cultural studies, and queer theory to examine the representation of sexual desire in fiction, poetry, stand-up comedy, neosoul, and hip-hop created by black women. Her second book, *Funk the Erotic: Transaesthetics and Black Sexual Cultures* (University of Illinois Press, 2015), explores how black sexual cultures produce radical ideologies about labor, community, art, and sexuality. It has received the Alan Bray Memorial Award from the MLA GL/Q Caucus and the 2016 Emily Toth Award for Best Single Work by One or More Authors in Women's Studies from the Popular Culture Studies Association/ American Culture Association (PCA/ACA), and it was a 2016 Finalist for the 28th Annual Lambda Literary Awards for LGBT Studies.

Anya M. Wallace, a PhD candidate in art education and women's, gender, and sexuality studies at Penn State University, is a multimedia artist-scholar with skilled concentration in black-and-white craft photography and painting. Her work in photography is shaped by a desire to visually narrate the stories of black girlhood. She has worked in the service of girls through program and curriculum development with the Girl Scouts of the USA and recently as the director of MOCA, North Miami's Women on the Rise! outreach program for girls. She is the founder of the Vibrator Project, a creative space designed to investigate young black women's and girls' self-knowledge of about sex, sexuality, and pleasure. Her artistry extends to the kitchen—a site for her own pleasure—where she re-creates the memories, oral histories, and visual narratives of her ancestral connections in tasty dishes. She coins such an experience "photographic taste."

Erica Lorraine Williams is an associate professor in the Department of Sociology and Anthropology at Spelman College in Atlanta, Georgia. She earned her PhD and MA in cultural anthropology from Stanford University and her BA in anthropology and Africana studies from New York University. Williams's research has focused on the cultural and sexual politics of the transnational tourism industry in Salvador, Bahia, Brazil. Her first book, *Sex Tourism in Bahia: Ambiguous Entanglements* (2013), won the National Women's Studies Association / University of Illinois Press First Book Prize. She has also published articles and book chapters in *Transatlantic Feminisms: Women and Gender Studies in Africa and the Diaspora* (2015), *Gender, Place, and Culture: A Journal of Feminist Geography, Policing Pleasure: Global Reflections on Sex Work and Public Policy* (2011), *Taking Risks: Feminist Stories of Social Justice Research in the Americas* (2014), the *Encyclopedia of Globalization* (2012), and *The Feminist Wire*. She teaches courses on issues of gender, sexuality, globalization, and the African diaspora, and she received the Vulcan Materials Teaching Excellence Award in 2013.

Index

The letter f following a page number denotes a figure.

abjection, 74, 79–81, 82n1, 214
agency, 15, 92, 99–100, 142, 147, 168, 175, 217–18, 230; of black men, 51; and Caribbean sexualities, 242–44; clit, 220; of the closet, 134; and cuckolding, 47, 51, 53, 55; limited, 175; and race play, 80–82; and value, 142
Aggressives, The, 116, 118, 121
Allen, Jafari, 90, 99
Amado, Jorge, 98
ambiguity, 62, 160–61, 163
archive, 3, 16–17, 195, 231, 250–59
art, 10, 140, 142–43, 222–23, 238–39, 247, 250–59; blues (*see* blues); economy of, 211; hip-hop, 176, 178, 180; jazz, 229, 231
assignation house, 63–64

Bahamas, The, 243, 247
Bahia, 90, 100–103
Barbados, 9; class in, 154; cultural ambassador to youth in, 153, 159, 160, 162; and modernity, 157–58; national identity in, 152–54, 158–59, 161; sexuality in, 157
Bataille, George, 192

BBC (Big Black Cock), 7, 43, 45–49
BDSM, 8, 73–88, 196–97; consent and, 79–80; and feminism, 80–81. *See also* domination; humiliation, sexual; race play; sadomasochism; submission
Beam, Joseph, 187
black body, 10, 141, 167–68, 174, 176–77, 239, 246, 247; black lesbian body, 218, 227–28, 230, 232; black male body, 45–46, 48, 174, 227; black queer body, 193–95; and decay, 218. *See also* body/mind
black female sexuality, 61, 97, 100, 148, 167–68, 174, 220–21; and BDSM, 74–75, 82; construction of, 36n56; radical, 221, 224
black femininity, 31, 116, 204
black feminism, 1, 220, 224, 226, 257; scholarship, 4, 8–9, 73, 78, 100, 140, 220–21, 224, 237–38; and sexuality, 4, 168, 100–103, 220–21, 224 (*see also* ecstasy; pleasure)
black gay men, 120, 133, 187, 189–90, 192, 198, 209, 214
black girls, 169, 174, 250–59, 253, 254f; enslaved, 17, 25–26, 28; and respectability, 16
blackmail, 59, 61, 66, 67
black male sexuality, 41–42, 48, 50, 52, 56n4, 177; and religion, 108–10, 112–13

blackness, 9, 69, 148, 220, 222–23, 238–39, 246–48; construction of, 3; and death, 199n4 (*see also* death); discourses of, 109–10; history of, 228; and homophobia, 206; hypervisibility of, 133, 197; legal, 22–24; and manhood, 110; modern, 73, 153–54, 158; and music, 143 (*see also* blues); and possession, 54; and queerness, 135, 210, 238; and television, 201, 213–14, 215n4; violation of, 217

black queer subjectivity, 129, 192, 194–95

black queer trouble, 247–48

black sexuality, study of, 1–6, 10, 99–100, 238–39

black social movements, 145, 248

blues, 252; and dress, 142, 145, 146; epistemology, 145; and gospel, 144–45; in poetry, 229–31; and respectability, 143

body/mind, 75–76, 78, 80–82

Brazil, 8; marketing of, 91, 95, 103; racialization in, 97–100; sexualization of women in, 95–98

breeding fetish, 34n28, 35n36, 37n72, 46, 56n17

Brokeback Mountain, 125, 127, 129–35

bunda, 91–94, 98–99, 103

butch, 117–18, 207, 218–19, 230, 253–54

butch queen, 117–18

Caribbean feminism, 245, 242–44

Caribbean sexualities, 239–44, 248; LGBTQI, 161, 240–41, 248; and neocolonialism, 243; politics of, 153, 240

Carnival, 91–94, 96, 99, 100, 105n26, 154–57, 163n8, 164n12

Carvalho, Sirlei, 97

celebrity, 41, 154–55, 157–60, 201

Clarke, Cheryl, 216–33, 247–48

clit agency, 220

closet, the, 124–36, 175, 210, 220, 229

Cohen, Cathy, 97, 121, 175, 201

common sense, 8, 109–21, 213, 215n21

community work, 245, 248, 251

consent, 36n52, 63–64, 164n19; and cuckolding, 47–48; and race play, 79–80

consumption, 6, 89, 127, 152, 154, 199n23; of sexuality, 32, 91, 181, 212, 251

creativity, 192, 251

Crop Over festival, 154–60, 163n8, 164n12

cruising, 189–90, 193–94

cuckolding, 7, 13, 15, 17, 56n12, 57n18; black women and, 42, 49, 56n13; sociality, 7, 41–42, 44–49, 51–55, 57n18. *See also* mandingo

Davis, Adrienne, 1–2, 8, 42, 89, 97, 167, 251

Davis, Angela, 18, 27, 30, 144, 146, 237, 252

death, 5, 9–10, 199n4, 230; as paradoxical, 188–89; as pleasure, 192–93, 198; space of, 193–95, 198, 199n17

Decker, Damien, 52–53, 55, 58n31

Delany, Samuel, 191, 193, 196

desire, 51, 55, 70, 173, 219, 221–23, 230–33, 242, 247; and BDSM, 74–75, 79, 82, 83n4; of black men's bodies, 41–42, 45; black queer, 189, 193, 196; and blues, 140, 143; and Brazil, 98–101, 103; and consumption, 50, 152; death and, 188–89, 192–94, 198; economies of, 2, 224 (*see also* sexual economy); illicit, 42; interracial, 43, 45–49, 52–53, 64; queer, 49, 55, 129, 187–90, 192–93, 196–97, 218–19, 224–25; and space, 190, 193–94; unruly, 167, 177, 180, 182

deviance, 2, 7–9, 128, 143, 180; as framework, 175

dissemblance, 8–9, 31, 37n72, 73, 87, 221

domination, 8, 46, 54, 55, 74, 76, 79, 81, 82n3. *See also* BDSM

Dorsey, Nettie, 9, 139–40, 142–44, 146–47, 149

Dorsey, Thomas, 9, 139, 142, 144–47

"down low" (DL), 50, 122n7, 125–26, 128, 130–34, 208, 212; and whiteness, 125, 128–29, 134

ecstasy, 54, 144, 196, 220, 222, 225, 233

embodied theories, 239–42

embodiment, 11, 50–51, 53, 92, 130, 133, 141, 144, 153, 162, 219, 222

erotic, 4–5, 131, 172, 174–75, 181–82, 193, 196, 251; aesthetic, 10, 218; Bataille and, 192; and Brazil, 91–92, 95, 97–98, 103; and death, 9, 192–93, 198; economies, 208–9; and exoticism, 156, 158; fantasies, 172, 193 (*see also* desire); Freud on the, 192; labor, 77–78; lesbian, 218, 221, 224–26, 229, 231; and poetry, 218–26, 229, 231–33; and race play, 7, 74, 76–80; resistance, 242–43; value, 40–41. *See also* erotic capital; eroticization; homoeroticism; illicit eroticism

erotic capital, 6, 8, 49, 62, 64, 78, 81

eroticization, 76–77, 91, 103, 156, 158; of the body, 81, 97–98; in pornography, 41, 43; and race, 43, 74, 100

explicit sexuality, 28, 43, 45, 47, 132, 167, 179–80, 218, 223–25

fancy trade, 28–29, 63

feminism, 1, 3–4, 27, 90, 102, 168, 220, 245, 248, 251, 257; activism, 101–4; black, 1, 4, 8–9, 74, 78, 91, 100–103, 120, 140, 168, 221, 224, 226, 238–40; decolonial, 248; lesbian, 80–81, 217, 220, 222; sex wars, 80–81, 85n53; transnational, 90

femme queen, 117–18

fetishism, 7, 54, 62, 76, 80; racial, 42–43, 45–50, 54, 75

FIFA, 95f, 95–96, 98

Freud, Sigmund, 192

Garvey, Marcus, 142, 145, 149f

genderqueer-phobic taxonomy, 111–12, 115, 118

geography, 145, 217

Globeleza, 96, 100, 105n26

gospel drag, 139–49

Green, Andrew H., 65–67

Grewal, Inderpal, 90

Guy-Sheftall, Beverly, 93

Hammer, Art, 50–51, 55, 57n24

Hammonds, Evelyn, 4, 100, 221

Harlem Renaissance, 144, 221–22

Harper, Phillip Brian, 188–93, 201–2, 213

haunting, 32, 82, 189, 195

Hemphill, Essex, 123n26, 187

Holloway, Karla F. C., 188–89

homoeroticism, 46, 53, 55

homonormativity, 128, 133, 188, 191, 196, 198, 199n23, 206–9; and whiteness, 8, 125

Hot Wife (cuckoldress), 43, 46–49, 51, 57n21. *See also* cuckolding

humiliation, sexual, 43, 48, 55, 76, 79, 115

hypersexuality, 9, 89, 167–68, 179–80; black female, 171–74; black male, 41–43, 46, 51, 53, 113 (*see also* mandingo); in Brazil, 95–97, 100, 102

illicit eroticism, 99–100, 167, 170, 176–77, 180

illicit sex, 9, 48–49, 60, 172, 187–88

infidelity, 65, 67, 130–31; performative, 45, 47–48, 51

interracial, 26, 49, 55, 67, 69, 74, 75, 198, 201, 205, 213; labor agreements, 69; sex, 7, 41–42, 45, 47, 49, 50, 55, 60, 63, 74–76, 196–97, 38n73; sexual abuse, 26, 38n73. *See also* cuckolding; mandingo; neomiscegenation drama; race play

"in the life," 187–88, 190, 198; poem by Essex Hemphill, 187

intimate antagonism, 170, 172, 175, 180

James, G. Winston, 9–10, 188, 189

James, LeBron, 39–41, 40f, 55

Jordan, June, 73, 218, 221, 237, 247

Julho das Pretas (July of Black Women), 102–3

Kadooment, 154–59, 155f

Kaplan, Caren, 90

Keeling, Kara, 116, 213, 172, 243

Kempadoo, Kamala, 172, 243

King, Rosamond, 242

kink, 76, 79, 197–98

lesbian, 107n60, 111–13, 216–19, 220; and ballroom culture, 117–18; black, 4, 10, 102, 218–20, 223, 224–29, 232; and the "down low," 128; feminism, 80–81, 217, 220, 222; as label, 222; sexual economy, 233

Living as a Lesbian, 10, 216–33

Lorde, Audre, 81, 224–26

LOUD tour, 9, 153–54, 156f, 159–61

Maia, Suzana, 91, 98–99

mandingo: as archetype, 41–42, 51, 53, 55; parties, 47–50. *See also* cuckolding

Marcha das Vadias, 101–3

marriage, 47, 55, 131, 205, 244, 248; rights of the enslaved, 25

masculinity, 119–21, 131–32, 167, 172–73, 177, 180, 184n45, 197, 253, 256–59; black, 4–5, 43, 54, 108–16, 135, 176, 177, 197, 201–4, 206–14; hegemonic, 175–76; hypermasculinity, 55, 175–77, 180, 207–8, 210; queer, 203–9; white, 27, 44, 51; of women, 116–18, 253, 256–59

masochism. *See* BDSM; sadomasochism

McGowan, Chris, 92, 95

Miller-Young, Mireille, 78, 100, 167
mistress, 28, 60–61, 63–65, 67, 73, 76
Moonlight, 135–36
Morehouse College, 109, 113–16
Muholi, Zanele, 251, 258f
mulata, 91–92, 96, 98, 99
Muñoz, José, 197, 214

neocolonialism, 242–43
neomiscegenation drama, 42, 46, 54, 55, 57n18
New Negro, 143
nonnormativity, 143, 171, 174, 175, 205, 206, 240, 244

Odara Instituto da Mulher Negra (Odara Institute of Black Women), 102–3

Paris is Burning, 117
phallus, 111, 113
Platt, John R., 59–61, 63–70
pleasure, 11, 167, 181, 182; autonomy and, 175; of black men, 50–52, 54, 56, 175; of black women, 8, 60, 74, 78, 80–82, 93, 95, 149, 167, 174, 181, 220, 224, 233, 250–52, 255; in Brazil, 89–91, 93, 95; and cuckolding, 42, 45–56; and danger, 187–88, 190–92; and death, 192–93, 198; in looking, 173–74; and profit, 53; queer, 192; race play and, 74–78, 80–82; and sexual labor, 50–52, 54, 56, 60, 64, 70; and slavery, 28–31; study of, 10, 60, 89–90, 100, 141; white, 7, 16–17, 28, 45, 48, 51, 132. *See also* ecstasy
poetry, 10, 187, 213, 216–19, 222–33
popular culture, 143, 148, 162, 168, 251–52; black, 140–43, 145; black sexuality in, 60, 252; black women in, 8, 60, 148, 251; mandingos in, 53
pornography, 7, 53, 55, 57n21, 75–76; black women and, 78, 100; cuckolding, 41–50, 53; the pornographic, 224, 232
public sex, 187–88, 189, 190, 192
pussy, 254–55; personification of, 78, 80; and pleasure, 220, 233

queer of color critique, 3–4, 200
queerness, 75, 110, 125, 133, 199n24; and aesthetics, 135–36; black, 135, 190, 195, 198, 206, 211 (*see also* black queer subjectivity); in the Caribbean, 241–42 (*see also*

Caribbean sexualities); and politics, 127, 133, 135; potential of, 42; racialization and, 75, 132; and sex publics, 188, 196; and space, 146, 193; and time, 130, 131; visibility and, 129, 131, 133; white, 125, 127, 128, 133–34

race play, 7–8, 73–82; and BDSM community, 75–76; black women and, 73–76, 78–82, 82n11, 83n5, 84n48; definition of, 74; pleasure and, 74–75, 77, 78, 81–82
Rainey, Gertrude "Ma," 9, 139–48, 148f
resisting paradise, 240, 244
respectability, 154, 163, 167, 168–69, 174, 178, 258; and black masculinity, 114–15; and blues performance, 145, 147; politics of, 100, 139, 143, 168, 221, 224, 248; sexual, 9, 96–97, 177
Rodney, Walter, 245
rude culture, 159, 162

sadomasochism (S&M), 46, 53, 55, 77, 79, 81, 82n3, 83n21, 197. *See also* BDSM
samba, 92–93, 99
Sargentelli, Oswaldo, 91, 96
Schwarzenegger, Arnold, 90, 91–95, 104n16
sexual discretion, 50, 124–25, 133, 134. *See also* "down low"
sexual economy, 2, 7–8, 60, 172; and black masculinities, 212; framework of, 7, 17, 30–32, 89, 97, 251; and sex publics, 188
sexual labor, 7–9, 55, 78, 172; of black gay men, 187–88; and black male hypersexuality, 37n66, 42; Caribbean, 243–44; forced, 17, 29–30; of mandingos, 50–53; and pleasure, 50–52, 54, 60–61, 63, 65, 70
sex work, 50, 65, 172, 243–44; in Bahia, 96–97, 100; and mandingos, 50; terminology of, 17
SlutWalk, 101
Smith, Christen, 97
Still Black: A Portrait of Black Transmen, 116, 119–20
submission, 51, 74, 79, 82n3; and cuckolding, 46, 49; and race play, 74, 80, 81. *See also* BDSM

thug, 135, 206; fantasies, 50, 51–52; and queerness, 135, 208–9
Tinsley, Omise'eke Natasha, 241–42

tourism, 103, 153, 243; in Brazil, 91, 95; sex tourism, 95, 99–100

trans, 110, 119–21, 123n25

transactional sex: in the Caribbean, 64, 243–44; and cuckolding, 52–53; as terminology, 244

Trinidad and Tobago, 241, 247

Valenssa, Valeria, 100

Vibrator Project, 11, 250, 254f, 258f

vocality, 139, 142

Walker, Alice, 85n56, 219

White, Deborah Gray, 140

white women, 48, 51–52; labor during slavery of, 18–19, 24–25, 32; in mandingo fantasies, 43–44, 47–48, 55 (*see also* Hot Wife); treatment during slavery of, 27, 35n45

wildness, 155, 221–22, 246

Williams, Cornelius, 65–66

Women on the Rise!, 250, 253f, 254f, 258f

Ziegler, Kortney Ryan, 119

The New Black Studies Series

Beyond Bondage: Free Women of Color in the Americas   *Edited by David Barry Gaspar and Darlene Clark Hine*

The Early Black History Movement, Carter G. Woodson, and Lorenzo Johnston Greene   *Pero Gaglo Dagbovie*

"Baad Bitches" and Sassy Supermamas: Black Power Action Films   *Stephane Dunn*

Black Maverick: T. R. M. Howard's Fight for Civil Rights and Economic Power   *David T. Beito and Linda Royster Beito*

Beyond the Black Lady: Sexuality and the New African American Middle Class   *Lisa B. Thompson*

Extending the Diaspora: New Histories of Black People   *Dawne Y. Curry, Eric D. Duke, and Marshanda A. Smith*

Activist Sentiments: Reading Black Women in the Nineteenth Century   *P. Gabrielle Foreman*

Black Europe and the African Diaspora   *Edited by Darlene Clark Hine, Trica Danielle Keaton, and Stephen Small*

Freeing Charles: The Struggle to Free a Slave on the Eve of the Civil War   *Scott Christianson*

African American History Reconsidered   *Pero Gaglo Dagbovie*

Freud Upside Down: African American Literature and Psychoanalytic Culture   *Badia Sahar Ahad*

A. Philip Randolph and the Struggle for Civil Rights   *Cornelius L. Bynum*

Queer Pollen: White Seduction, Black Male Homosexuality, and the Cinematic   *David A. Gerstner*

The Rise of Chicago's Black Metropolis, 1920—1929   *Christopher Robert Reed*

Living with Lynching: African American Lynching Plays, Performance, and Citizenship, 1890—1930   *Koritha Mitchell*

Africans to Spanish America: Expanding the Diaspora   *Edited by Sherwin K. Bryant, Rachel Sarah O'Toole, and Ben Vinson III*

Rebels and Runaways: Slave Resistance in Nineteenth-Century Florida   *Larry Eugene Rivers*

The Black Chicago Renaissance   *Edited by Darlene Clark Hine and John McCluskey Jr.*

The Negro in Illinois: The WPA Papers   *Edited by Brian Dolinar*

Along the Streets of Bronzeville: Black Chicago's Literary Landscape   *Elizabeth Schlabach*

Gendered Resistance: Women, Slavery, and the Legacy of Margaret Garner   *Edited by Mary E. Fredrickson and Delores M. Walters*

Racial Blackness and the Discontinuity of Western Modernity   *Lindon Barrett, edited by Justin A. Joyce, Dwight A. McBride, and John Carlos Rowe*

Fannie Barrier Williams: Crossing the Borders of Region and Race   *Wanda A. Hendricks*

The Pekin: The Rise and Fall of Chicago's First Black-Owned Theater   *Thomas Bauman*

Grounds of Engagement: Apartheid-Era African American and South African Writing   *Stéphane Robolin*

Humane Insight: Looking at Images of African American Suffering and Death   *Courtney R. Baker*

Word Warrior: Richard Durham, Radio, and Freedom   *Sonja D. Williams*

Funk the Erotic: Transaesthetics and Black Sexual Cultures   *L. H. Stallings*

Spatializing Blackness: Architectures of Confinement and Black Masculinity
   in Chicago   *Rashad Shabazz*
Painting the Gospel: Black Public Art and Religion in Chicago   *Kymberly N. Pinder*
Radical Aesthetics and Modern Black Nationalism   *GerShun Avilez*
Sex Workers, Psychics, and Numbers Runners: Black Women in New York City's
   Underground Economy   *LaShawn Harris*
Slavery at Sea: Terror, Sex, and Sickness in the Middle Passage   *Sowande' M. Mustakeem*
Booker T. Washington in American Memory   *Kenneth M. Hamilton*
Black Post-Blackness: The Black Arts Movement and Twenty-First-Century
   Aesthetics   *Margo Natalie Crawford*
Archibald Motley Jr. and Racial Reinvention: The Old Negro in New Negro Art
   Phoebe Wolfskill
Building the Black Metropolis: African American Entrepreneurship in Chicago
   Edited by Robert E. Weems Jr. and Jason P. Chambers
Jazz Internationalism: Literary Afro-Modernism and the Cultural Politics of Black
   Music   *John Lowney*
Black Public History in Chicago: Civil Rights Activism from World War II to the
   Cold War   *Ian Rocksborough-Smith*
Building the Black Arts Movement: Hoyt Fuller and the Cultural Politics of the
   1960s   *Jonathan Fenderson*
Black Sexual Economies: Race and Sex in a Culture of Capital   *Edited by Adrienne D. Davis
   and the BSE Collective*

The University of Illinois Press
is a founding member of the
Association of American University Presses.

Composed in 10.75/13 Arno Pro
with Trade Gothic LT Std display
by Lisa Connery
at the University of Illinois Press
Cover designed by Jennifer S. Fisher
Cover illustration: Art by Megan Spencer
Manufactured by Sheridan Books, Inc.

University of Illinois Press
1325 South Oak Street
Champaign, IL 61820-6903
www.press.uillinois.edu